Bargaining for Brooklyn

Bargaining for Brooklyn

Community Organizations in the Entrepreneurial City

NICOLE P. MARWELL

The University of Chicago Press
Chicago and London

Nicole P. Marwell is associate professor of sociology and Latina/o studies and director of the Workshop on Nonprofit Organizations in Economy and Society at Columbia University.

The University of Chicago Press, Chicago 60637
The University of Chicago Press, Ltd., London
© 2007 by The University of Chicago
All rights reserved. Published 2007
Printed in the United States of America

16 15 14 13 12 11 10 09 08 07   1 2 3 4 5

ISBN-13: 978-0-226-50906-8 (cloth)
ISBN-13: 978-0-226-50907-5 (paper)
ISBN-10: 0-226-50906-0 (cloth)
ISBN-10: 0-226-50907-9 (paper)

Library of Congress Cataloging-in-Publication Data

Marwell, Nicole P.
    Bargaining for Brooklyn : community organizations in the
entrepreneurial city / Nicole P. Marwell.
        p. cm.
    Includes bibliographical references and index.
    ISBN-13: 978-0-226-50906-8 (cloth : alk. paper)
    ISBN-13: 978-0-226-50907-5 (pbk. : alk. paper)
    ISBN-10: 0-226-50906-0 (cloth : alk. paper)
    ISBN-10: 0-226-50907-9 (pbk. : alk. paper)
    1. Community development—New York (State)—New York.
2. Community organization—New York (State)—New York.   3. Urban
renewal—New York (State)—New York—Citizen participation.
4. Sociology, Urban—New York (State)—New York.   5. Brooklyn
(New York, N.Y.).   I. Title.
HN80.N5M27   2007
30.7.3'4160974723—dc22

                                                2007009522

⊗ The paper used in this publication meets the minimum requirements of the
American National Standard for Information Sciences—Permanence of Paper
for Printed Library Materials, ANSI Z39.48-1992.

To my mother and father

CONTENTS

ILLUSTRATIONS

CHAPTER ONE

Formal Organizations and the Problem of Social Order in the City

The 1970s were bad times for the cities of the northeast and midwest United States. After a century in which these densely populated areas flourished with a manufacturing-dominated economy, the swells of industrial change unleashed a tidal wave of problems onto urban streets. Factories producing consumer goods like cars and clothes, and raw materials like steel and fabric, slammed shut their doors. Tax revenues plummeted, and city governments scrambled to find funds to fill in the potholes, pick up the garbage, put out the fires, and maintain myriad other city services at even minimal levels. Increasing numbers of unemployed residents meant less and less money circulating within local economies, as well as mounting deprivation and despair. Some turned to drugs or crime; heroin addiction soared to unprecedented levels, and robbery, burglary, and assault statistics spiked. The unfortunate coincidence of these economic events with the migration of African Americans and Latinos to urban areas unfairly linked the changing complexion of the cities to their declining fortunes. Faced with fewer jobs, a steadily worsening quality of life, and a pernicious whispering campaign about the dangers of racial change, many white city residents decamped for the suburbs. Whereas the African American and Latino migrations had held city populations stable during the white flight of the 1960s, the 1970s brought a downward spiral. New York City lost 10 percent of its population in that decade. Other cities did even worse: Chicago lost 11 percent, Philadelphia 13 percent, Detroit a staggering 20 percent.

At the start of the twenty-first century, these same cities look positively shiny in comparison. Some, like New York, have more of a gleam than others—Detroit and Cleveland, for example, have logged some improvements but will likely never recapture their glory days. Still, the contrast between 1975 and 2005 is striking. For the urban rich, things have never been better: luxury housing, restaurants, spas, entertainment, and a slew of chances to enrich their children are all readily within reach. Members of the middle class, in contrast, are struggling to sustain the life to which they have become accustomed, an increasingly difficult task as gentrification and the wealthy claim more and more of the available housing and services. The poor mostly continue to be poor. The dot-com boom and company stock options passed them by, and the rapidly rising cost of a college education has placed even this traditional tool of upward mobility beyond the reach of many. Ironically, these lingering and growing inequalities can be harder to spot now, because many of the neighborhoods where the urban poor live look much better than they did in the 1970s: fewer burned-out buildings, vacant lots, splintered sidewalks, empty storefronts, dirty parks. These neighborhoods are also much safer today than they were in the 1970s—or in the 1980s, when the crack epidemic sparked frightening violence. No longer do nightly newscasts track the perverse competition to see which American city will be this year's "murder capital."

Still, the underlying problems of the urban poor remain. As does the way that the rest of the country sees the poor. Though the particular crises may change from year to year, what has persisted is the American conviction that the key to understanding poverty is the nature of the impoverished individual. The welfare mother, the crackhead in the alley, the gangbanger on the corner, the pregnant high school dropout—we have created many archetypes to help us make sense of the poor. Sometimes we damn these individuals, like the welfare mother demonized by Republicans and Democrats alike in order to pass welfare reform legislation in 1996. Occasionally we lionize them, as well-meaning journalists, documentary photographers and filmmakers, and social scientists have long done, showing us how a single mother or hardworking teenager has overcome devastating circumstances to escape poverty and its many pitfalls. In both kinds of stories, we focus on individual people trying to prevail under difficult conditions—praising their triumphs or condemning their failures.

The problem with this focus on the individual, however, is that it loses sight of the bigger worlds in which poor people, like all of us, live. As we go about our daily lives, the opportunities we find, the obstacles we butt up against, and the dangers we confront shape what each of us, as individuals, can accomplish. One common understanding of how our individual capacities are augmented (or diminished) by the workings of a social realm beyond ourselves is captured by the concept of "networking"—the idea that personal relationships give rise to particular possibilities in life and steer us toward certain behavioral choices. These relationships are formed in families, schools, neighborhoods, churches, workplaces, voluntary associations, leisure sites, and many similar kinds of settings. Social scientists have been particularly interested in how the individual behaviors implicated in escaping or remaining mired in poverty are learned within networks, and have presumed that two sites of personal relationships are most likely to influence this kind of social learning: families and neighborhoods. Over the last twenty years, scholars interested in the impacts of these two kinds of social worlds have developed focused and frutiful programs of research from which we have garnered many insights.[1]

In this book, however, I take a different approach. I open up a wider lens on the social processes underlying poverty, opportunity, and inequality in an attempt to understand how elements of social structure that extend beyond interpersonal relationships contribute to poverty and its related social problems. Specifically, I examine how formal organizations working toward a variety of economic and political ends make decisions that collectively produce the conditions that poor people face in everyday life, and under whose constraints the poor make daily choices.

Sociologists who study organizations sometimes use the term "field" to describe a set of organizations linked together as competitors and collaborators within a social space devoted to a particular type of action—such as a market for certain products, the pursuit of urban development, or the realm of electoral politics.[2] Agreements struck among the organizations that compose a field set the bounds on what kinds of organizational and individual action are possible. Because field-level outcomes are the collective product of interorganizational agreements, new outcomes can be produced when

1. See, e.g., Brooks-Gunn, Duncan, and Aber 1997; Chase-Lansdale et al. 2003; Duncan and Chase-Lansdale 2001; Jencks and Mayer 1990; McLanahan and Sandefur 1994; Morenoff, Sampson, and Raudenbush 2001; Rankin and Quane 2000; Saegert, Thompson, and Warren 2001; Sampson and Groves 1989; Sampson, Morenoff, and Earls 1999; Sampson, Morenoff, and Gannon-Rowley 2002; Sampson, Raudenbush, and Earls 1997; Small 2004; Small and Newman 2001; J. R. Smith et al. 2000.

2. The organizational sociology literature contains references to several similar concepts, including "interorganizational field" (Aiken and Alford 1970; R. L. Warren 1967), "institutional field" (J. W. Meyer and Rowan 1977), "organizational field" (e.g., DiMaggio and Powell 1983; Fligstein 2001; Scott and Meyer 1991), and "strategic action field" (Fligstein and McAdam 2005). A related but distinct concept of "field" has been presented by Bourdieu (1984); for an innovative adaptation of Bourdieu's core field components of position and power to processes of urban development, see McQuarrie (2007). See Fligstein and McAdam (2005) for a discussion of the emergence and relations of some of these concepts.

interorganizational agreements change. In the coming chapters, I examine the workings of three different fields whose outcomes have profound implications for the life chances of the poor: housing production, public services spending, and paid work.

My window onto the contentious economic and political organizational systems I refer to as fields is one of their least powerful players: the nonprofit community-based organization (CBO). CBOs are formal organizations tied to particular geographic places (like urban neighborhoods), which work to improve local residents' quality of life and enhance their (or their children's) chances of escaping poverty. CBOs provide a multitude of goods and services to lower-income people: affordable housing, child care, drug treatment, cultural programs, services for the elderly, food, legal advice, foster care, job training, and much more. Over the past forty years, CBOs have become common in U.S. cities, the result of increasing racial and ethnic diversity, political activism by traditionally excluded groups, and changes in the structure of state social provision. CBOs maintain proud identifications with their own neighborhoods, and address themselves to the needs of local residents.[3] But because their work is embedded in wider fields, they must engage regularly with other formal organizations that operate outside of and across neighborhood boundaries. A key argument of this book is that an empirical focus on CBOs and their field-level contexts allows us a more complete perspective on the structural dimensions of poverty.

3. Not all nonprofit organizations are CBOs. The nonprofits I classify as community-based organizations are, first of all, "community based"—that is, they are organized around a particular geographic place ("community"), such as an urban neighborhood. CBOs generally operate programs *only* in that local area; this distinguishes CBOs from larger nonprofits that operate at multiple sites (for example, the Red Cross and the National Urban League), as well as from broad-based movement organizations (e.g., Kriesi et al. 1995; D. S. Meyer and Tarrow 1998). There are exceptions to this rule: some CBOs that have developed successful programs in their home areas have been asked by funders to expand their reach to other neighborhoods. Even so, these organizations remain rooted in particular geographic communities. Second, CBOs have as their mission to attend to the needs of disadvantaged "community members"— residents of their geographic place—who are understood to be receiving insufficient resources and consideration from government and market entities. Their attention takes the form of service provision to, and/or advocacy work on behalf of, "the community." This orientation toward the disenfranchised distinguishes CBOs from other nonprofit organizations located in poverty-stricken areas. The primary mission of nonprofit hospitals, for example, is to provide health care; the fact that an inner-city hospital serves large numbers of residents from its immediate area is simply an operational externality, not central to its organizational identity. Finally, CBOs are characterized by the significant participation of community members in the organizations' daily activities, e.g., as staff, volunteers, or board members. See Marwell (2004b) for further discussion.

The Structure of Poverty: Fields, Organizations, and Individuals

This study uses data from nearly three years of participant-observation in eight CBOs in two neighborhoods in Brooklyn, New York, to detail how these groups construct and maintain relationships with other organizations as part of their efforts to complete specific projects or more generally fulfill their missions. Many of the resources CBOs require for their work are neither located in their neighborhoods nor controlled by neighborhood actors. My research shows how CBOs can mediate and sometimes modify the ways in which the workings of economic and political fields impact the poor—effects that are arguably as important as the family and neighborhood relationships on which studies of the poor often focus. Interactions within families and neighborhoods are of course crucial for communicating the kinds of individual behaviors prohibited, accepted, and rewarded in society. But the social contexts within which poor people make their everyday behavioral decisions are in fact much bigger than these networks of interpersonal interaction suggest.

Poverty is associated with certain family characteristics, such as poor parenting skills, the presence of only one parent, limited supervision of children, and unemployment. When poor children grow up and become poor adults, parents are often fingered as the primary culprits; social processes within their families are said to have contributed to the children's slower cognitive and social development, allegedly lax attitudes toward school and (later) work, and greater propensity to become involved with negative, dangerous, or illegal activities. Similarly, the interpersonal interactions that occur in poor neighborhoods are thought to reinforce individual behaviors that increase the likelihood of becoming (or remaining) poor, such as dropping out of school, disdaining regular work, using drugs, having children while still a teenager, committing crime, and so on. The heavy concentration of these kinds of behaviors in poor neighborhoods argues for a contagious process: the proverbial "bad influence."

Ideas about the contributions of family and neighborhood to poverty rely on linking individual behavior—say, dropping out of school—to social learning: parents not insisting that children attend and do well in school, or peers encouraging each other to disdain school. Accordingly, efforts to prevent poverty frequently focus on teaching different social lessons, with the goal of altering individual behavior. Parents may be urged, for example, to read with their children every day as a way of modeling the importance of education and encouraging school attendance. Individuals' behavioral choices, however, are demarcated not only by direct interpersonal influences but by a range of broader economic and political processes. In some cases, these broader processes open up a world of opportunity for at least some individuals; a town government's decision to allow only single-family, owner-occupied housing within its borders, for example, excludes people with incomes below a certain threshold but ensures that the higher-income residents will enjoy a strong tax base and have access to excellent education through the local public schools (Alba and Logan 1993; Charles 2003; Logan and Stearns 1981; Stearns and Logan 1986). At other times, the operations of economic and political systems impose severe limitations on individuals, as when banks and insurers "redline" certain urban neighborhoods, making it impossible for residents to secure home mortgages or home owners' insurance—thus excluding them from a primary form of wealth accumulation in U.S. society (Nesiba 1996; S. L. Ross and Yinger 2002; Squires 1997; Squires, DeWolfe, and DeWolfe 1979; Squires and Kim 1995; Squires and Kubrin 2005; Yinger 1995).

Although these and many other economic and political processes have profound implications for the choices available to poor individuals, we have more often emphasized the effects of interpersonal interactions within family and neighborhood in trying to explain individual behavior and the possibilities for moving people out of poverty. Social scientists measure a range of individual- and family-level characteristics—income, education, occupation, marital status, family size, and so on—along with neighborhood characteristics—like poverty rate, racial composition, and social cohesion—and then draw conclusions about how family and neighborhood social contexts influence where individuals end up in socioeconomic terms.

Many of the field-level processes that affect poor people's decisions, behaviors, and outcomes, however, take place in settings far from their homes, street corners, and neighborhoods. As a result, these processes are harder to see and to analyze—for casual observers, academic researchers, policy makers, and the poor themselves. This does not mean that the workings of fields are either nebulous or ephemeral. Indeed, they can be traced to the specific actions of real people out there in the world. Often, these people act within formal organizations whose decisions and practices produce field-level outcomes that arrange the complex system of urban stratification and change. These organizations, their actors, and their decisions, become visible if we make them the focus of analysis.

For example, the physical decline of many inner-city neighborhoods that began in the 1950s can be understood as an outcome produced by the field of urban development. Decisions made by home builders, mortgage lenders, and insurers to concentrate investment in the emerging suburbs, and by federal and city policy makers to pursue "urban renewal" programs, left few resources for the original inhabitants of inner-city areas. As mortgages, home-improvement loans, and home owners' insurance became impossible to secure, properties deteriorated and real estate values spiraled downward in a vicious cycle. The dilapidated buildings, vacant lots, and eerie, empty streets that embody poor neighborhoods in the popular imagination thus reveal a story of an urban development field seeking new sources of growth and profit, and have little to do with how poor people attempted to make homes for themselves on inner-city streets sucked dry of capital investment. At the same time, the federal government's decision to make government-insured mortgages available to first-time (usually white) home buyers lowered the risk to lenders, primed the engine for suburban home builders, decreased costs to individual buyers, and gave whites an economic advantage over African Americans (Fishman 1987; Jackson 1985). In other words, organizational practices produced two distinct field-level outcomes: the seeding of an entire generation of suburban home owners, and the abandonment of city residents to fight a rising tide of decay.

An organizational rendering, then, can elucidate ways in which seemingly faraway market forces, as well as political decisions, facilitate or deny poor people access to power and resources. In political fields, both elected officials and line staff at public agencies move the levers of government action, determining, among other things, where and on what government funds will be spent, how stringently particular laws and regulations will be enforced, and who will have the opportunity to voice their concerns about government practices. A wide range of formal organizations—from for-profit firms and corporate lobbyists to nonprofit agencies and citizens' advocacy groups—attempts to influence these and other governmental decisions in their favor. Through agreements struck among the various players in political fields, the resources of government are parceled out: contracts to provide goods and services; investments in such public structures as roads, parks, schools, and firehouses; and regulatory permissions to pursue private gain. Poor neighborhoods and their residents frequently find themselves shortchanged in this process, as political fields yield decisions that give priority to the needs and desires of other places and of groups that are better organized or have greater resources.

When community-based organizations work to improve conditions in poor neighborhoods, they essentially attempt to reshape economic and political fields, recalibrating the extent to which their outcomes advantage some of us while disadvantaging others. When CBOs successfully shift field-level outcomes to direct greater resources and opportunities to the poor residents of their neighborhoods, these organizations can impact individuals' life chances. The CBOs I explore in this book tackle a wide range of issues. In Brooklyn's Williamsburg neighborhood, for example, the South-side United Housing Development Fund Corporation (known colloquially as "Los Sures") began in the late 1960s as an effort to find low-cost methods to improve the neighborhood's dilapidated housing—without displacing residents into a state of prolonged homelessness. The approach stood in stark contrast to the large-scale demolition that was the hallmark of urban renewal, a strategy that had already removed thousands of families from Williamsburg while enriching developers and bankers who used urban decline as a way to drive suburban growth. The Los Sures activists collaborated with a few similar groups in the city's other poor neighborhoods to gradually reshape the contours of New York City's housing production field.[4] After a few years of working with poor residents on self-help housing rehabilitation tactics, Los Sures persuaded city government to contribute public funds to its efforts. This strategy soon leveraged additional resources from the private sector, and gradually reshaped the nation's overall approach to urban redevelopment. Los Sures was an important early player in a movement that today comprises some fifteen thousand community development corporations in cities and rural areas across the nation.

Because of their well-recognized contributions to revitalizing poor urban neighborhoods across the country, community development corporations are perhaps the best-known type of CBO. But other kinds of CBOs engage in a variety of service, development, and organizing activities, all of which have the potential to reshape fields in ways that enhance the opportunities and resources available to poor people. For example, many CBOs assist the often low-skill, badly educated residents of their neighborhoods in finding viable pathways into paid work. These organizations recognize that getting people to work requires more than just matching them to available jobs, and so they have intervened in the field of paid work, creating jobs that take into account the skills and preferences of poor neighborhood residents and making affordable child care available to working parents.

In the Brooklyn neighborhood of Bushwick, one such CBO, the Ridgewood-Bushwick Senior Citizens Council, has grown since its founding in

---

4. New York City's housing production field can be considered a subset of a bigger field of urban development. For a discussion of this "Russian doll" quality of fields, see Fligstein and McAdam (2005). For an empirical examination of this larger urban development field, see McQuarrie (2007).

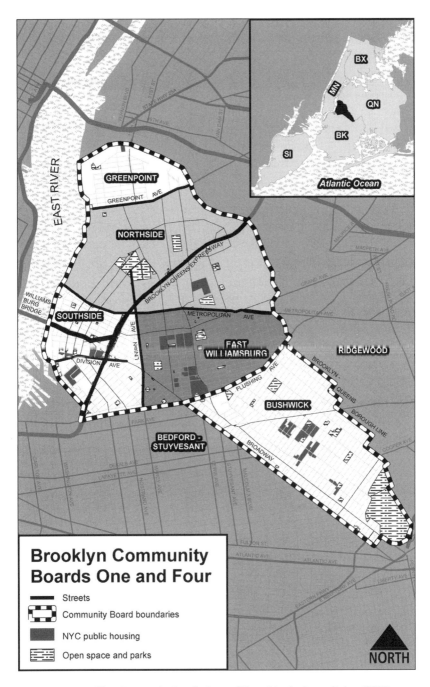

Map 1. Brooklyn Community Boards One and Four. Map by James Quinn, ISERP, Columbia University.

1976 into a vast, multiservice enterprise with some two thousand employees. Many of these employees are local residents whose commitment to community issues has provided a ticket into an entry-level position. Ridgewood-Bushwick is well aware of its role as a major neighborhood employer and continually seeks out new opportunities to expand its stock of jobs. In Williamsburg, the Nuestros Niños Child Development Center similarly provides jobs for local residents, most of them women who migrated to Brooklyn from Puerto Rico or the Dominican Republic. In addition to the jobs it has created directly, Nuestros Niños—which means "our children" in Spanish—facilitates employment for hundreds of other low-income Williamsburg parents by providing a safe, reliable, and affordable place to leave their children during the workday.

Many facets of CBO activity involve harnessing the material resources and regulatory powers of government in order to shift field-level outcomes in ways that benefit poor people. CBOs sometimes advocate for changes in public policy, but more commonly they attempt to influence the everyday decisions of government agencies that directly impact people's lives on the ground. At Saint Barbara's Catholic Church in Bushwick, groups of parishioners form part of the East Brooklyn Churches community organizing federation, which helps local residents learn about the pressure points to which elected officials and government agencies respond in their decision making. Through grassroots outreach and specific "actions" initiated and planned by group members, Saint Barbara's has attempted to influence everything from the placement of traffic lights to the performance of the public schools.

The Ridgewood-Bushwick Senior Citizens Council has pursued a political strategy quite different from that of Saint Barbara's. Working from the premise that the more jobs and assistance it can provide to Bushwick residents, the better off they will be, Ridgewood-Bushwick concentrates its political activity on the government contracting process. In an arrangement that recalls the old-style political machine, it focuses on winning government contracts that provide the financial resources necessary both to employ and to serve local residents in its many neighborhood programs: youth activities, housing development, legal services, adult education, tenant organizing, health care, programs for senior citizens, and more. While this approach produces different results than the Saint Barbara's strategy, both of these CBOs aim fundamentally to influence the operation of the city's political field in ways that benefit the residents of their neighborhoods.

One begins to see that CBOs' importance to their neighborhoods must be understood substantially in terms of their relationships to the field-level processes that structure opportunity, inequality, and poverty in the contemporary city. Most of the resources and bureaucratic controls that CBOs rely on to conduct their work do not lie within poor neighborhoods themselves. Rather, CBOs help poor residents secure a decent place to live, find jobs, nurture and educate their children, and influence government decisions by connecting them into larger organizational systems of economic and political decision making. Individuals' ability to progress socially and economically arguably has just as much to do with the opportunities that are afforded them by these fields as it does with the relationships they have with the people who live near them—just ask any suburban home owner who believes that fences make the best neighbors, or the residents of an upscale twenty-story apartment building who stand silently together as the elevator whooshes them from floor to floor. These individuals got good educations, have well-paying jobs, live in low-crime neighborhoods, have access to health insurance, are confident elected officials will respond to their major concerns, and often have pensions that will contribute to their financial security in retirement. None of these contemporary hallmarks of stability has anything to do with how well these individuals know their neighbors. Rather, they derive substantially from their advantaged access to the distribution of resources and opportunities within particular fields of economic and political action.

To better understand how CBOs' operation within fields yields opportunities and resources that make a difference in the lives of the poor, consider the following real-life experiences of a few residents of Williamsburg and Bushwick. Natalio and Amantina Duran, a husband and wife who hail from two small villages in the Dominican Republic, came to Williamsburg in 1967. A few years later, Amantina helped start a tiny day care cooperative—the precursor to the Nuestros Niños Child Development Center. Cognizant of the vast need for child care among the Puerto Rican and Dominican families of Williamsburg, whose economic necessity usually required both parents to work, Nuestros Niños pursued government funds to underwrite child care for several hundred neighborhood families. In 1974, the organization hired Natalio as a full-time custodian, allowing him to provide steady wages and medical insurance for the family. Each of the Durans' five children received child care at Nuestros Niños, allowing both Natalio and Amantina to work, and laying a foundation for all of the children to attend college. Amantina spent many years doing low-paying factory work, but other CBOs in Williamsburg offered her English classes, a GED program, and a child care certification class. In 1990, on the strength of the education she had received from local CBOs, Amantina was hired by the family day care program at Nuestros Niños, where she worked for over ten years until illness forced her to retire.

Felicita Polo, a Puerto Rican woman now nearing seventy, has lived for years on a block in Bushwick once widely known for its intensive open-air drug market. Some twenty years ago, she began working with tenant organizers at the Ridgewood-Bushwick Senior Citizens Council to improve the conditions in her dilapidated apartment. The building was a mess: no hot water, no heat, no lock on the front door, no functional plumbing. Drug dealers had set up shop inside the building, and the landlord stayed away while almost all the other tenants moved out. Felicita refused to budge, despite the fact that when she wanted to use the toilet or take a shower, she had to walk past the drug dealers to a friend's apartment in the building next door. Where else could she afford to pay rent on her tiny fixed income, she asked? The staff at Ridgewood-Bushwick helped Felicita document the housing code violations in her apartment, took the landlord to court to force repairs, and made sure she maintained her government housing subsidy. The organization also began to work with the police department to get rid of the drug dealers: the police closed down all coming and going to the block and lit it up with floodlights all night long. After a long summer under these conditions, the dealers moved away. Now, with her housing situation stabilized, Felicita continues to find support at Ridgewood-Bushwick through its senior citizen activity programs, as well as the regular meetings the organization sponsors to allow local residents to communicate their concerns and needs directly to city officials. Ridgewood-Bushwick was able to assist Felicita because it worked within the wider fields in which the resolutions to her difficulties could be effected.

Annie Vega first got involved with Los Sures—the Southside United Housing Development Fund—in 1987, when she moved into a building in Williamsburg in which conditions were very bad. She couldn't afford a better place; she was a new mother, and money was tight. Annie and the other tenants began working with a tenant organizer at Los Sures, who helped them navigate the same complex housing bureaucracy that Felicita and thousands of other low-income renters in Brooklyn turn to for redress when their landlords refuse to provide basic services and upkeep in their buildings. Annie also soon enrolled her daughter in the family day care program at Nuestros Niños, which ensured that she could continue working without compromising her child's cognitive, social, and emotional development.

When I met her in 1998, Annie was preparing to become the president of the tenants' association in her new building, where she would continue working with Los Sures to maintain good conditions at affordable rents.

Vincent Hall, Antonia Vazquez, and Alberta Williams are all parishioners at Saint Barbara's Catholic Church in Bushwick, as well as active members in their church's delegation to the East Brooklyn Churches (EBC), an organizing federation affiliated with the Industrial Areas Foundation (Rooney 1995; M. R. Warren 2001). These three long-term residents of Bushwick watched their neighborhood go up in flames during the 1970s and, in the early 1980s, got involved with EBC's efforts to make city officials pay closer attention to Bushwick's economic, educational, safety, and housing needs, along with many other concerns. Over the years, they have worked alongside other residents of East Brooklyn to draw greater government resources into their neighborhoods, and EBC has established itself as an important voice in the city's political field.

These examples begin to show how the activities of CBOs in various fields can make real change possible in poor individuals' lives. In some cases, CBOs have successfully turned status quo procedures on their heads, forging new approaches to social challenges in partnership with other players. At other times, CBOs have run up against their own limits, their impact narrowed or eclipsed by the operation of more powerful actors within their fields. These different outcomes are conditioned by how fields have been structured in the past, as well as by how field players continue to relate to one another, to larger conditions of social and economic change, and to the opening of new opportunities within the field. CBOs like those in Williamsburg and Bushwick have continually kept one eye turned inward, surveying the needs of their neighborhoods' low-income residents, and the other eye focused outward to assess, maneuver through, and attempt to influence the outcomes produced by the fields relevant to their work. These organizations' successes and failures at expanding the opportunities and resources available to the poor thus speak to a classic question in sociology: the production of social integration and social order.

The Challenge of Social Integration and Social Order in the City

For nearly a century, sociologists have argued that the social problems of the modern city, such as poverty, crime, unemployment, and family disruption, arise when a group of people living together lacks "community"—that is, a set of social agreements about how group members should conduct themselves in economic, cultural, political, social, family, and religious life.[5] Community both provides standard pathways by which members of a society become integrated with their fellows and establishes social order by imposing sanctions upon transgressors. This understanding of community derives from an imagined, premodern human settlement, small in size and relatively isolated, where multiple, overlapping, and dense social ties impose and easily maintain social agreements among individual community members. Although industrialization and urbanization long ago consigned this premodern entity to the trash heap of history, the idea and functions of community persist as a fundamental basis for understanding human society. In the United States, with its founding traditions of collective self-governance, community has remained a particularly powerful trope (e.g., Mansbridge 1980; Putnam 1993b; Tocqueville 1835, 1840; M. R. Warren 2001).

In the early twentieth century, when large-scale urbanization had transformed most Western societies, a group of sociologists at the University of Chicago made the search for community in the modern city the focus of its analytic project. How, these scholars asked, could the residents of large, dense, and heterogeneous Chicago agree to live together in a way that yielded both social integration and social order (Abbot 2002; Wirth 1938)? These twin foundations of the community concept—integration and order—took the individual as their ultimate object of concern and relied on a specific set of causal mechanisms and relationships. If individuals were integrated into some form of community, the argument went, they would be well-adjusted and would behave in accordance with collective expectations; this in turn would lead to the enactment of an orderly society. If, on the other hand, individuals found themselves continually wheeling past one another, unable to establish any kind of shared experience and stability, this would not only negatively affect their own psyches but would foster antisocial behavior and give rise to general social disorder. In the Chicago scholars' own terms, "personal disorganization"—individuals' alienation and disconnection from a meaningful social group—and "social disorganization"—a set of social problems including everything from poverty and unemployment to drunkenness and crime—continually reproduced one another in the absence of community (Fischer 1975; Kornhauser 1978; Shaw 1930; Thomas 1923; Thomas and Znaniecki 1918; Wirth 1938).

---

5. See, e.g., Anderson 1923; Bursik 1988; Drake and Cayton 1945; Hawley 1944, 1950; Hunter 1974; Kasarda and Janowitz 1974; Park 1915, 1936; Sampson and Groves 1989; Sampson, Raudenbush, and Earls 1997; Shaw and McKay 1942; Thomas and Znaniecki 1918; Warner and Lunt 1941; Wirth 1928; Zorbaugh 1929.

This narrative emphasizes the authority that community exercises over individual dispositions and behaviors (e.g., Durkheim 1912; Foucault 1977; Janowitz 1975; E. A. Ross 1896). In seeking to determine where the teeming modern city might produce such authority, the Chicago scholars offered up their science of "human ecology." The leading figure in this effort, Robert E. Park, proposed that two distinct but related social processes are at work in the formation of community in the city (Park 1915, 1936). First, a process of differentiation, wherein the operation of what Park called the "biotic order" sorted residents into a series of "natural areas" within the geography of the city. These "natural areas" not only were determined by physical attributes of the city—being bounded, for example, by bodies of water, highways, industrial tracts, parks, and the like—but also drew into themselves residents exhibiting certain historical, cultural, linguistic, ethnic, or racial characteristics. Once residents were so segregated, a second social process began: the development of the "moral order" of each "natural area." Park wrote that as "each separate part of the city is inevitably stained with the peculiar sentiments of its population," the physical space becomes "a locality with sentiments, traditions, and a history of its own"—in other words, the "natural area" becomes a "community."[6]

Park's understanding of community as both a bounded geographic segment of the city and a source of collective authority over individuals guided subsequent generations of sociologists attempting to understand the production of social integration and social order in modern urban life. Park's ecological approach proved particularly influential during the 1980s, when social scientists began trying to understand the unusual and disturbing concentration of social problems becoming entrenched in certain city neighborhoods: extremely high rates of individuals dropping out of school, never being employed in the traditional labor market, getting pregnant at young ages, committing violent and illegal acts, and going to prison. It was abundantly clear that certain areas of the city were becoming chronically poor and problematic, their residents less and less integrated with the larger society, with crime and other threats to social order multiplying.

Efforts to understand these developments led social scientists back to Park's ecological vision: the city as a "mosaic of little worlds which touch but do not interpenetrate" (Park 1915, 608), each characterized by a coherent "moral order" that rendered it a "community." This formulation not only boasted the distinguished theoretical imprimatur of the Chicago

6. For insightful discussions and critiques of the ecological tradition and its deployment in the study of urban poverty, see, among others, O'Connor (2001) and Venkatesh (2003).

School but also possessed a certain intuitive rationale. The idea that groups of proximately located individuals, such as the residents of a particular neighborhood, would interact in ways that mattered for both individual outcomes—such as educational achievement, employment, family formation, and criminal activity—and the characteristics of local places—the extent of social ills like dropping out of school, unemployment, out-of-wedlock childbearing, or crime—is powerful. It makes sense that children would respond to pressure from friends on their block who were also their classmates at school, their playmates in the park, and their pewmates at church. It makes sense that a new single mother would turn to public assistance if the only parents she knew were other single mothers living nearby who relied on welfare payments for their children's subsistence. It makes sense that young men seeking employment would find it, as have many of their peers, in the underground economy: working odd jobs off the books, selling stolen merchandise, or dealing drugs.

Park's fateful linking of the geographic space of the city with the mechanisms of social integration and social order, however, has wrought two important theoretical consequences for later researchers concerned with urban poverty and social problems. First is the idea that integration and order emerge in the city as the result of interpersonal relationships among community members—a premise, it should be noted, that presumes a mechanism of community formation akin to that in the imagined rural village.[7] Both ethnographic and quantitative studies have placed interpersonal relations front and center in attempting to understand how urban residents create social integration and social order. In much ethnographic work, "community" finds tiny form, the product of repeated exchanges of resources, companionship, and understanding among a small group of individuals (e.g., Anderson 1978, 1999; Bourgois 1996; Duneier 1992, 2000; Liebow 1964; Stack 1974; Whyte 1943). Working from a conceptually similar base, and inspired by studies in network analysis (e.g., Burt 1992; Coleman 1988, 1990; Laumann and Knoke 1987; Laumann and Pappi 1976), quantitative researchers have examined how the state of interpersonal relationships within distinct geographic territories of the city relates to the extent and prevalence of poverty and its related social problems—a construct that recent literature terms "neighborhood effects."[8]

7. Studies that conceptualize community in a nongeographic sense nonetheless share this emphasis on interpersonal interaction as the foundation of community (Fischer 1982; Wellman 1979; Wellman et al. 1997).

8. See, e.g., Ainsworth 2002; Hawley 1944, 1950; Jencks and Mayer 1990; Peterson, Krivo, and Harris 2000; Sampson and Groves 1989; Sampson, Morenoff, and Earls 1999; Sampson,

Park's second legacy to urban sociologists is the nearly uncontested notion that the primary locus of integration and order in the modern city is the geographic subdivision we call "community" or "neighborhood."[9] Ethnographic researchers have long conducted "community studies" within bounded geographic areas (e.g., Drake and Cayton 1945; Gans 1964; Hannerz 1969; Kornblum 1974; Molotch 1972; Susser 1982; Venkatesh 2000; Whyte 1943), while quantitative analysts treat variation across neighborhoods as an important phenomenon to explain (e.g., Sampson, Morenoff, and Gannon-Rowley 2002). Although scholars have largely replaced Park's emphasis on morality with the more neutral concept of "differential social organization" (Angell 1942; Gans 1964; Sampson and Groves 1989; Shaw and McKay 1942; Shevky and Williams 1949; Whyte 1943), they still treat geographic communities as the primary source of social integration and social order in the modern city.

Probably the most famous analysis of contemporary urban poverty that relies on these two assumptions is William Julius Wilson's influential book *The Truly Disadvantaged* (1987). In this now-canonical account, Wilson argues that the restructuring of the U.S. economy that began in the 1960s hit segregated African American neighborhoods particularly hard. As unemployment rose, residents with no jobs—and few prospects for jobs— came to disdain certain behaviors considered appropriate in our society: going to school, working regularly, having children only when we can support them, abstaining from illegal activities, and so on. When middle-class residents—those who still had jobs and still hewed to generally accepted standards of behavior—found the barriers of segregation had dropped, they fled their unemployed, badly behaved neighbors. This only reinforced the inclinations of those who remained behind in increasingly impoverished inner-city ghettos to drop out of school, use or sell drugs, refuse to work, have children out of wedlock, and commit crimes. Wilson contended that this combination of unemployment, poverty, and bad behavior had bred a group of people fundamentally different from the rest of us: a "socially

---

Morenoff, and Gannon-Rowley 2002; Sampson, Raudenbush, and Earls 1997; Shaw and McKay 1942; Shevky and Williams 1949; Yen and Kaplan 1999. Note that many studies prior to about 1980 used the terms "neighborhood" and "community" to mean different things, though both were geographically based. "Neighborhood" referred to smaller geographic units where meaningful social bonds might actually be said to exist, while "community" indicated the concatenation of a number of "neighborhoods" into a still-identifiable, yet less socially coherent geographic space (e.g., J. M. Gillette 1926; Hawley 1950).

9. For important exceptions in urban sociology, see Wellman (1979), Wellman et al. (1997), and Fischer (1982).

isolated" "underclass" (Auletta 1982; Jencks and Peterson 1991; Murray 1984; Wilson 1987, 1989).

Wilson's discussion of the negative influences circulating among residents of "underclass" neighborhoods has clear roots in Park's ecological tradition: interpersonal interaction within specific geographic areas of the city attenuates the authority of the community, yielding antisocial behavior and a crisis of social order (cf. Shaw and McKay 1942). Inspired by this part of Wilson's argument, scholars subsequently developed a focused program of research to operationalize the differential social organization of urban neighborhoods and to test its relationship to a range of resident and neighborhood characteristics, such as poverty, income, teenage childbearing, and crime.[10] At the same time, however, researchers neglected the second—indeed, *prior*—piece of Wilson's argument: that by the late twentieth century, *certain key processes of social integration and social order no longer operated at the level of the neighborhood*.[11]

Wilson's particular interest, of course, has been in how urban job markets have shifted dramatically, stimulating the emergence of "underclass" behaviors in inner-city African American neighborhoods (Wilson 1987, 1999). He claims that these neighborhoods deteriorated in a specific causal sequence. First, major shifts in the U.S. economy caused a decline in manufacturing industries, which had long provided low-skilled yet well-paying jobs for city residents. Job growth then shifted largely to service industries, where low-skill workers found mostly low-paying, part-time jobs that lacked important worker benefits such as health insurance, sick leave, and retirement pensions (Danziger and Gottschalk 1994; Levy 1988). African

10. See, e.g., Briggs, Mueller, and Sullivan 1997; Harding 2003; Morenoff, Sampson, and Raudenbush 2001; Peterson, Krivo, and Harris 2000; Rankin and Quane 2000; Sampson, Morenoff, and Earls 1999; Sampson, Morenoff, and Gannon-Rowley 2002; Sampson, Raudenbush, and Earls 1997.

11. Some authors working in the ecological tradition do recognize, on a theoretical level, the nonisolated nature of urban neighborhoods; see especially Sampson (1999). Furthermore, quantitative studies based on the ecological tradition have long displayed tension between the two parts of Park's scheme: a "biotic order" that differentiates neighborhoods with an eye toward interdependence, and a "moral order" that organizes the internal dynamics of neighborhoods. See Kornhauser (1978) and Marwell (2005) for extended theoretical discussions. For interesting recent quantitative work that empirically recognizes that processes external to neighborhoods have significant effects on outcomes within neighborhoods, albeit without strong theoretical explanation for this finding, see Morenoff, Sampson, and Raudenbush (2001). For ethnographic work that implicitly recognizes the impact of external processes on neighborhoods, but also does not fully articulate a theoretical explanation, see Susser (1982), Marwell (2004b), and Gregory (1998). For one attempt at theoretical explanation of this issue, see Hunter (1985); Carr (2003) draws explicitly on Hunter in a more recent attempt to address similar issues.

Americans bore the brunt of these macroeconomic changes, as many held jobs in the declining manufacturing sector and thus were more likely than whites or members of other racial and ethnic groups to become unemployed. It was only as African American neighborhoods had the economic rug pulled out from under them, then, that residents began to behave in ways contrary to mainstream expectations. Wilson's concept of "social isolation" must thus be applied not only to the individual behaviors of the inner-city poor, but also to the social organization of the urban job market that *preceded* the emergence of those behaviors.

As Wilson himself has acknowledged, the connection between the two pieces of his argument was insufficiently developed in *The Truly Disadvantaged*.[12] Accordingly, the bulk of recent urban poverty research has focused on his discussion of how the absence of certain kinds of interpersonal interaction in inner-city neighborhoods—specifically, the lack of middle-class residents modeling appropriate behavior for their poor neighbors—plays a key role in the reproduction of "underclass" behaviors among the poor. This intellectual trajectory has resulted in few attempts by urban poverty researchers to grapple seriously with the myriad elements of economic, political, and social organization that no longer operate on a neighborhood basis, but that remain fundamental to the creation of social integration and social order in the modern city.[13] As I discuss in the next section, many key aspects of integration and order can be empirically located outside both the boundaries of urban neighborhoods and the realm of interpersonal interaction.

An Organizational Perspective on Social Integration

In the transition from rural to urban life, the informal, personalized relationships of the village gave way to formal, standardized rules and proce-

12. Personal communication, August 5, 2005. For a commensurate reading of Wilson's concept of social isolation, see Venkatesh (2003).

13. Strangely, urban poverty researchers since Wilson have largely ignored a long-standing political economy tradition in urban sociology, which begins with an analysis of the city as a unique center of accumulation and consumption in a global capitalist society (e.g., Castells 1977; Harvey 1973; Sassen 1991; Saunders 1986; N. Smith 1984; N. Smith and Williams 1986). The opposite is also true—political economy theorists have largely ignored the work of urban poverty researchers. This mutual indifference is often traced to an allegedly fundamental contradiction between ecological theory and political economy theory; for reviews, see Jaret (1983) and Walton (1993). The works of Harvey Molotch and John Logan have been important exceptions to urban poverty scholars' general disregard of the political economy perspective (Alba and Logan 1993; Logan and Molotch 1987; Logan and Stearns 1981; Molotch 1976; Stearns and Logan 1986).

dures that sought to impose order over the fleeting and often anonymous social contacts of city living (Durkheim 1893; Redfield 1941; Toennies 1887). The German sociologist Max Weber called the rule of formal organizations "bureaucratic domination" and worried that modern urbanites would become imprisoned in an "iron cage" of purely formal social relations (Weber 1905, 1914). Indeed, the sheer size and complexity of the modern city required the construction of a formal organizational infrastructure to manage a wide variety of economic, political, social, legal, and other tasks, none of which could be piloted any longer through informal, interpersonal interaction. Reflecting on this fundamental historical change, the sociologist Charles Perrow has argued that since the turn of the twentieth century, we have been living in "a society of organizations"—that is, in a social order so thoroughly colonized by formal organizations that they absorb the very notion of society (Perrow 1992).

In their quest to understand why certain parts of the city seem to have lost all semblance of social integration and social order, urban sociologists have remained curiously uninterested in moving beyond the Chicago ecological paradigm of community formation. Ironically, this is not true of the man who is widely considered to be the greatest interpreter of the Chicago School: Morris Janowitz, a distinguished and controversial member of the University of Chicago's sociology department from 1946 to 1986. Janowitz first raised the idea of the receding importance of urban neighborhoods for social integration and social order in the early 1950s (Janowitz 1952). Noting that neighborhoods increasingly mattered only for certain aspects of daily life, foremost among them child rearing and schooling, Janowitz argued that the residential neighborhood had become a "community of limited liability"—a place to which individuals and families owed only marginal allegiance, and thus wherein only certain kinds of social integration could take place (Janowitz 1952; cf. Foley 1950, Kasarda and Janowitz 1974, Logan and Molotch 1987). In his later writings, Janowitz further developed his ideas about the challenge of integration and order in contemporary society. He argued that the central problematic of the modern, urban world concerned how to "articulate" entities small enough to operate through interpersonal interaction—such as neighborhoods, workplaces, and interest-based organizations—with larger economic and political processes that spanned the city, the nation, even the world (Janowitz 1978).

Janowitz's particular (and contentious) agenda was to create greater consensus within U.S. society. He imagined the development of a system of organizational communication that simultaneously made powerful economic and political decision makers more aware of the needs and preferences of the smaller groups affected by their decisions, and drew these smaller groups closer to the directions set by decision makers higher up. Janowitz's consensus vision of society owed much to Park's ecological idea that the "biotic order" of the city strives toward equilibrium, and both authors have been similarly critiqued as failing to recognize that society (and the city) may in fact be riven by irreconcilable interests (Castells 1977; Harvey 1973; Jaret 1983; Mollenkopf 1983; Walton 1993). Writing from a late-twentieth-century perspective, however, Janowitz did recognize that the social organization of the city was once again undergoing massive change—and so were its foundations of social integration and social order. Indeed, by the end of his career Janowitz turned decisively toward a search for integration and order within the formal organizational structures of society—structures that cut across the geographic boundaries of neighborhoods in ways unforeseen by the Chicago sociologists half a century before him (Janowitz 1978; Marwell 2005).

In the last few years, students of urban poverty have begun to consider formal organizations as potentially relevant to the tasks of creating social integration and establishing social order. This effort, however, has been dominated by theories that predict benefits to poor individuals as a result of their becoming involved in some kind of neighborhood organizational activity.[14] In contrast to this view of neighborhood organizations as places conducive to individual transformation by way of collective participation, I argue in this book that organizations in poor neighborhoods should be understood in the way that Janowitz implied: as components of the larger systems of economic, political, and social activity that structure contemporary urban life. I consider neighborhood organizations to be agentic actors in their own right, capable of addressing and influencing other organizations in ways that individuals, or even the agglomerations of individuals envisioned by theories of participation, cannot. These empirically observable interorganizational relationships produce field-level outcomes that advantage certain groups in society while disadvantaging others. More often than not, field outcomes leave the poor with minimal resources and correspondingly few opportunities and choices about how to act in the world.

The most forceful argument made to date about the importance of organizational action in structuring the lives and life chances of the poor concerns the linked issues of residential racial segregation and the operation of

---

14. See, e.g., Bartelt and Brown 2000; Briggs, Mueller, and Sullivan 1997; Morenoff, Sampson, and Raudenbush 2001; Perkins, Brown, and Taylor 1996; Peterson, Krivo, and Harris 2000; Saegert, Thompson, and Warren 2001; Silverman 2001, 2002; Stoll 2001; Wood 1997.

dual real estate markets (that is, separate housing markets for whites and African Americans). In their landmark book *American Apartheid* (1993), Douglas Massey and Nancy Denton tell their own version of Wilson's story of "social isolation." Massey and Denton argue that when macroeconomic restructuring occurred, racial residential segregation produced disproportionately negative impacts on African American neighborhoods. The formal organizations that imposed, facilitated, or failed to challenge racial segregation—real estate brokers, home owners' associations, and various government agencies—thus played a key role in the declining fortunes of African Americans and the emergence of "underclass" neighborhoods. Massey and Denton thus clearly understand the "social isolation" of African Americans as a process of economic and political exclusion enacted by organizations—and not as rooted in interpersonal interaction among local residents.

In a similar vein, studies of dual housing markets, "place stratification," and banks' discriminatory lending practices point up the importance of organizational action in setting the conditions within which African Americans and the poor are asked to make individual choices about residential location, financial investment, and related issues. Dual housing markets have consistently forced African Americans to pay more than whites for lower-quality housing (Logan and Molotch 1987; Molotch 1972). African Americans and the poor have been denied access to certain urban neighborhoods and suburban municipalities by zoning and other bureaucratic regulations (Alba and Logan 1993; Logan and Stearns 1981; Stearns and Logan 1986). And the widespread practice of "redlining" by banks and insurers long prevented residents of poor and African American neighborhoods from securing home mortgages and home owners' insurance (Nesiba 1996; Squires 1997; Squires, DeWolfe, and DeWolfe 1979; Squires and Kubrin 2005; Yinger 1995). All of these processes resulted from specific decisions by formal organizations, which in turn created field-level outcomes that fundamentally affected individuals' quality of life and opportunities for improving their own (and their children's) futures.

Sociologists have pointed out repeatedly that people—including the poor—live their daily lives in networked social spaces, which may or may not be shaped by place of residence (Duneier 1992, 2000; Fischer 1982; Hannerz 1969; Oliver 1988; Small 2004; Wellman 1979; Wellman et al. 1997). The material and political conditions poor people confront in everyday life, however, are shaped by formal organizations that take action and make decisions within the contexts of their fields. In other words, the people with whom a young mother directly interacts produce one set of effects on her; an entirely different set of consequences derives from the economic and political fields that determine whether or not she can get a home mortgage, have a park or playground nearby for her children to run around in, or be represented politically by a member of her own ethnic group. Discussions about how individuals behave, and how the behaviors of others in their interactional world affect their behavioral choices, are most pertinent when limited to the small units where people actually interact with one another. Discussions about the material and political conditions that shape individuals' scope of opportunity, however, must address the larger fields where those conditions are produced.

Accordingly, in this book I examine a number of organizational and field-level processes that have profound implications for poor people's ability to enjoy a decent quality of life, find economic and social stability, and improve their (or their children's) life chances. Recent attention by scholars and policy makers to formal organizations in poor neighborhoods, however, has not followed this line of inquiry.[15] Instead, most of the discussion has focused on how neighborhood organizations foster resident participation in local affairs, thereby encouraging a stronger sense of collective ownership and responsibility.[16] The rationale behind this perspective is that as individuals become more attached to their neighborhood and their neighbors, they will behave in more socially appropriate ways, and presumably will end up less poor.[17] Most existing studies that examine the prevalence of organizations in poor neighborhoods thus are interested in how these groups serve as proxies for individual participation and involvement in the local context—and little else (Morenoff, Sampson, and Raudenbush 2001; Peterson, Krivo, and Harris 2000).

I do not deny the potential contributions of resident participation in local organizations to improving neighborhood-level safety and public behavior. Indeed, there are substantial payoffs for residents who reclaim the

15. To date, research that attempts to quantify the effect of "neighborhood organizations" on individual outcomes and neighborhood characteristics has used data on a wide range of formal organizational structures, including religious congregations, ethnic organizations, block associations, local businesses, civic groups, and neighborhood improvement associations (Guest and Oropesa 1984; Peterson, Krivo, and Harris 2000; Sampson, Morenoff, and Earls 1999; Small and McDermott 2005). Many of these groups—with the exception of local businesses and possibly federated civic organizations like the Elks or Masons—function much like CBOs and so can be understood in much the same way.

16. Bartelt and Brown 2000; Briggs, Mueller, and Sullivan 1997; Gittell and Vidal 1998; Putnam 2000; Saegert, Thompson, and Warren 2001; Silverman 2001; Small 2004; Stoll 2001; Wood 1997.

17. For a bracing critique of this perspective, see DeFilippis (2001).

power to act in a climate of intimidation by, for example, calling the parents of a group of truants on the corner, giving police information on drug-dealing locations and strategies, or organizing letter-writing campaigns out of a local church (e.g., Putnam 2000; Sampson, Morenoff, and Earls 1999). I do argue, however, that current research's focus on individual-level interaction interferes, both conceptually and methodologically, with our ability to see the ways in which organizations in poor neighborhoods are themselves actors embedded within broader economic and political fields (e.g., DiMaggio and Powell 1983; Fligstein 2001; Laumann and Knoke 1987; Pfeffer and Salancik 1978; Powell and DiMaggio 1991; Susser 1982; M. R. Warren 2001). Viewed from this perspective, CBOs are not simply undifferentiated shells within which individuals meet to build social networks and interpersonal trust within the neighborhood. Rather, they are contenders within systems of economic and political decision making, and their efforts to strike better bargains within these fields can sometimes lead to improved opportunities for individuals on the ground. It is in this sense that CBOs and other neighborhood organizations can contribute to improved social integration and social order in the city and beyond.

The Rise of Community-Based Organizations in the City

In the 1960s, a new kind of organization emerged in urban neighborhoods hard-hit by both racial segregation and socioeconomic decline. While controversial social change groups like the Black Panthers, the Student Non-Violent Coordinating Committee, and the Weather Underground captured our attention during this turbulent era, a small army of less visible organizations with similar aspirations for social justice was slowly taking shape in the back rooms of churches, in cheap rented office space, and on the streets of poor neighborhoods across the country.

Efforts to help the urban poor, of course, did not originate with these less-visible community-based organizations. By the end of the nineteenth century, most U.S. cities had a Charity Organization Society, which sent middle- and upper-class "friendly visitors" to the homes of the poor to offer advice on how to get out of poverty: work harder, spend more thriftily, stay away from alcohol, and generally become more austere and disciplined as individuals. These mostly Protestant organizations were later joined by similarly oriented Catholic and Jewish social agencies, which catered to the new immigrants who swelled city populations by the early twentieth century. The CBOs that arose in the 1960s, however, were set up and run mostly by residents of poor neighborhoods who sought to substitute their "indigenous" knowledge and skills for the often paternalistic and controlling approach of the charities. CBOs located themselves even closer to the poor than had the settlement houses of the Progressive era. While the latter groups pioneered the idea of outside experts living and providing services from inside poor neighborhoods, CBOs went further, putting organizational leadership into the hands of poor residents themselves.

The African American activism of the civil rights movement opened the doors to the creation of CBOs. Despite mounting legal victories during the civil rights period, African Americans' economic marginalization remained substantial, and became ever more visible as a result of demographic changes in the nation. The large numbers of African Americans who migrated from the rural south to cities in the Northeast and Midwest did not escape the racial segregation confronted by their forebears but instead found an urban version of the same hardship. Poverty-stricken ghettos grew quickly, and municipal and state governments did little to address their deteriorating conditions. As always, urban political machines were slow to incorporate the new arrivals to the cities, preferring instead to rely on labyrinthine election rules to keep voter participation low and minimize the numbers they needed to maintain a voting majority (Erie 1988). With few incentives to reach out to African American voters, local and state politicians continued to cater to the needs and preferences of their long-standing white constituents.

The clear unwillingness of city and state governments to respond to African American—and, increasingly, Puerto Rican and Mexican American—misery sparked activists and private philanthropists to seek out alternative strategies for addressing economic and social conditions in the ghettos. In New York City, a group formed out of discussions at the Henry Street Settlement House sought to test the theories of sociologists Richard Cloward and Lloyd Ohlin, who argued that the alarming rise in juvenile delinquency was the result of blocked opportunities for ghetto youth: low-quality and racist education, few decent jobs, and no apparent path for socioeconomic advancement (Cloward and Ohlin 1960). In 1960, with funding from the National Institute of Mental Health, Cloward and Ohlin helped establish a CBO called Mobilization for Youth on New York's Lower East Side. The group aimed to organize neighborhood residents to pressure the city's welfare, education, housing, and other agencies into responding more effectively to the dismal conditions facing the city's poor (Helfgot 1981; Marris and Rein 1969). Though Cloward and Ohlin called their approach an "opportunity theory," in effect the strategy was based on a vision of improved social integration and social order: if ghetto residents could find pathways into the city's dominant social, economic, and political systems, they would form the same attachments to those systems and their social rules that city residents fortunate enough to be educated, employed, and politically represented already had. Mobilization for Youth envisioned the resources and power of government as the principal tools for accomplishing this goal.

By 1961, the philosophy undergirding Mobilization for Youth also was bubbling up from a small number of similar organizations emerging in other parts of the country, and the approach began gaining recognition and support. President John F. Kennedy formed his Committee on Juvenile Delinquency and Youth Crime, a federal grants program for groups that organized residents of poor communities to collectively press government bureaucracies for change. Simultaneously, the Ford Foundation set up its Grey Areas Program to direct funds toward these types of activities. By 1964, Ford had allocated multiyear grants totaling over twenty million dollars to six community-based organizations across the country, and the President's Committee had sent nearly eleven million dollars to thirteen CBOs (Marris and Rein 1969). In all, the federal government and the Ford Foundation helped establish seventeen new CBOs, the vanguard of what would soon become a widespread and legitimate structure for social action in poor neighborhoods.[18]

As this organizational structure slowly evolved, President Lyndon Johnson led a drive to convince the nation that the conditions faced by the increasingly urbanized African American poor differed significantly from the poverty of other groups (L. Johnson 1965). Echoing the original Mobilization for Youth strategy, Johnson argued that government was not doing nearly enough to guarantee equal opportunity to African Americans in either the public or the private sector. As such, not only were African Americans much more likely to be poor than whites, but their chances of getting out of poverty, via the American Dream's prescription of education and hard work, were drastically less. The federal government's charge, said Johnson, was to realign the exclusionary structures of society in order to afford African Americans the same opportunities as other Americans. This understanding of African American poverty led Johnson to embrace the strategy of improved social integration that underlay Mobilization for Youth, the Grey Areas Program, and the President's Committee on Juvenile Delinquency. The result was Title II of the Economic Opportunity Act of 1964: the Community Action Program of the War on Poverty.

---

18. For alternative interpretations of the motivations underlying the Ford Foundation's and other funders' support for CBOs, see Domhoff (2005) and Taub et al. (1977).

The Community Action Program called for cities and rural counties to address their specific conditions of poverty through locally driven agenda setting and program implementation. These antipoverty efforts would be supported directly by federal funds and coordinated by locally based community action agencies (CAAs). These newly established agencies took different legal forms, including public-private corporations and public agencies, but the majority were established as independent, nonprofit organizations run by volunteer boards of directors (R. F. Clark 2000). Most CAAs concentrated on setting antipoverty policy for their local areas and established lower-level organizations—for example, at the neighborhood level in cities—to implement programs (R. F. Clark 2000; Levitan 1969; Vanecko 1969). Although state and local governments had long-standing traditions of joint public-private social provision via their support of the old-line charities (Hall 1992; Katz 1996; Salamon 1995; S. R. Smith and Lipsky 1993), the War on Poverty marked the federal government's first significant commitment to directly supporting nongovernmental organizations. This new venture had both policy and political purposes, and it introduced unusual financial implications into the relationship between federal, state, and municipal governments.

The federal charge to the CAAs was to attack poverty on two levels: by overseeing the delivery of services that would help poor people improve their socioeconomic circumstances, and by organizing the poor to demand greater attention to their needs from government and the private sector. With respect to service delivery, this entailed channeling public dollars directly to the independent CAAs for distribution to underserved populations—usually African American, Mexican American, and Puerto Rican—rather than sending the money to state and municipal governments to implement their own versions of the federal policy. In political terms, the Community Action Program meant using federal expenditures to leverage political support from ghetto residents for the agenda of the national Democratic Party (Piven and Cloward 1971).

To the consternation of the architects of the War on Poverty, however, the Community Action Program very quickly became a lesson in the difficulties of controlling state and local politics from Washington, D.C. Governors and mayors bristled at the growing organizing successes of neighborhood organizations funded by the CAAs, and feared being thrown out of office by newly mobilized, mostly poor and minority voters (Andrews 2001; M. L. Gillette 1996; Quadagno 1994). After three years of federally sponsored critique and protest of city and state government practices, mayors, governors, and state and municipal legislators had finally had enough. Working with their congressional representatives, the lower levels of the system struck a crippling blow to the federal program. In 1967, Congress passed the Green Amendment to the Economic Opportunity Act of 1964, requiring that community action funds only be released to CAAs that had been approved by the elected heads of local government. This meant that CAAs with radical or critical agendas—especially those that sought to fundamentally reshape the workings of public agencies or private corporations—would not be certified as eligible to receive federal funds (R. F. Clark 2000; Eisinger 1969).

The Green Amendment returned the upper hand to local political establishments, marginalizing the CAAs and undercutting their efforts to push for fundamental changes in the outcomes of economic and political fields. In the delicate relationship of federalism, states and municipalities won an important victory: they would control the allocation of federal social provision dollars coming into their jurisdiction. By the end of the 1960s, with state and local elected officials once again in control of these decisions, the experiment in the social integration of the poor that had been the Community Action Program was dying. After a series of debilitating budget cuts by Congress, the program was ended in 1970. New federal, state, and city funding streams slowly emerged to support some of the services initiated by the Community Action Program, and the many small, local nonprofit organizations that the CAAs had birthed began following their own trajectories of restructuring, expansion, or dissolution.

Community-Based Organizations in Brooklyn

Chicago may have dominated urban sociologists' attention in the early part of the twentieth century, but other large U.S. cities experienced many of the same dynamics of population shift, economic reorganization, political succession, and social change. By midcentury, the cities of the Northeast and Midwest had developed clear patterns and similarities. In Boston, New Haven, New York, Philadelphia, Newark, Baltimore, Cleveland, Chicago, Detroit, Milwaukee, and many other cities, the children of immigrants had come of age, working steady, well-paying jobs in a booming, manufacturing-dominated economy. In 1950, for example, the vast expanse of Brooklyn, New York, was home to the largest number of people in its history—before or since. More than 2.7 million souls lived in New York City's most populous borough. In many ways, Brooklyn stands in the popular imagination as the paradigmatic example of city living during this period, and its trajectory both before and after 1950 serves as a window onto the larger twentieth-century U.S. urban experience.

Many think of the 1950s as the last great decade in Brooklyn's history, before the forces driving subsequent depopulation and decline kicked in. Most any native Brooklynite from those days will reminisce nostalgically about, among other things, stoopball, the local candy store, Coney Island, and the company of endless aunts, uncles, and cousins. In 1954, Brooklyn reached its peak as a manufacturing center rivaling Chicago, with 235,000 workers tending the borough's sugar mills, breweries, shipyards, garment factories, and all manner of other heavy and light industry. But as the end of the decade neared, signs of Brooklyn's impending decline and reorganization were impossible to ignore. The long-running borough newspaper, the *Brooklyn Daily Eagle*, closed in 1955; the beloved Brooklyn Dodgers decamped for Los Angeles in 1957; and the immigrants' grandchildren were steadily heading out to the suburbs to raise their families. When the Brooklyn Navy Yard, which had done the nation proud, producing record numbers of warships and materiel during the World War II years, closed in 1966, an era ended in Brooklyn. Over the next twenty years, the borough's population would dwindle and many of its neighborhoods would become dilapidated and dangerous. At the same time, however, a new cycle would commence in the borough's long history as a port of entry for the immigrant poor and working classes.

Ironically, Brooklyn's decline helped place it on the leading edge of a new approach to urban problems. As Mobilization for Youth was getting under way in Manhattan, Brooklyn's African American neighborhood of Bedford-Stuyvesant gave birth to an organization called Youth-in-Action. Like Mobilization, Youth-in-Action, as well as a similar group in Harlem called HARYOU-ACT, was part of the inspiration for the federal government's Community Action Program. When Community Action began operation in New York City in 1965, the city's CAA began funding program and political work in fifteen neighborhood poverty areas, including six in Brooklyn: Bedford-Stuyvesant, Brownsville, East New York, Fort Greene, South Brooklyn, and Williamsburg (Eisinger 1969, 28).[19] In each of these

19. New York City's Community Action Program has a complicated and unusual history. It was initially run by a federal agency, the Committee on Economic Opportunity, with significant input from the administration of Mayor Robert Wagner. In January 1966, Wagner undertook a major reorganization of the city's overall agency structure, placing the Community Action Program under the Community Development Agency, a subunit of the newly formed Human Resources Agency. Within the Community Development Agency, the Anti-Poverty Operations

neighborhoods, local nonprofit organizations formed to supervise and implement antipoverty efforts.

After the demise of the Community Action Program, Bedford-Stuyvesant's Youth-in-Action transformed itself into the nation's first federally designated community development corporation: the Bedford-Stuyvesant Renewal and Rehabilitation Corporation.[20] New York senators Robert F. Kennedy and Jacob Javits spearheaded this seminal event by introducing federal legislation to establish community development corporations as new partners in the effort to reverse the decline of poor urban neighborhoods. This high-profile sponsorship meant Bedford-Stuyvesant would long garner the lion's share of the attention paid to the economic and social problems of Brooklyn's numerous ghetto areas. Just north and east of Bedford-Stuyvesant, however, the neighboring areas of Williamsburg and Bushwick faced similarly blighted conditions.

Williamsburg lies directly across the East River from the Lower East Side of Manhattan. In the mid-1800s, when Brooklyn and New York were still separate cities, Williamsburg was known as a fashionable suburb populated by German, Austrian, and Irish industrialists and professionals. When the Williamsburg Bridge opened in 1903, factories moved into the area, along with their working-class Jewish, Polish, Italian, Slavic, and Russian employees. The wealthier residents of the area gradually moved out, and their stately brownstone houses gave way to tenements and cold-water flats. By 1917, Williamsburg was home to the most densely populated blocks in New York City. The Great Depression bankrupted many Williamsburg businesses, dispatching the last of the area's early, better-off residents. Williamsburg's working-class character was cemented by its increasingly industrialized landscape and low-quality housing stock, which still attracted white ethnic workers seeking to be close to their factory jobs on the Brooklyn waterfront.

Board (and later the Council against Poverty) was designated as the official community action agency for New York City (Institute of Public Administration 1966). In response to a 1966 federal amendment to the Economic Opportunity Act of 1964, the Council against Poverty revamped its board of directors to consist of twenty-eight members; half were drawn from city government and old-line charities, while half directly represented the neighborhood poverty areas (Kifner 1966). In addition to the citywide CAA, several New York City nonprofit organizations served as their own CAAs, receiving funds directly from the federal government; these organizations mostly predated the Community Action Program, and included Mobilization for Youth and HARYOU-ACT (cf. R. F. Clark 2000).

20. Shortly after its founding, the organization split into two based on differences among its leadership. One maintained the original name, the other became the better-known Bedford-Stuyvesant Restoration Corporation, under the leadership of Franklin Thomas, who went on to become president of the Ford Foundation in 1984.

Just prior to World War II, Hasidic Jews fleeing the Nazis began arriving in Williamsburg; their rapid migration in the postwar period quickly established a dense settlement in the area. In the 1950s, migration from Puerto Rico, a U.S. territory, peaked in response to the plentiful manufacturing jobs available in the northeastern United States. New York was the Puerto Ricans' primary destination, and many of them came to Williamsburg, whose factory jobs were easily accessible, but where urban renewal demolition was wreaking havoc on the physical and social structures of the neighborhood. As the 1960s commenced, earlier generations of white ethnics streamed out of Williamsburg and a trickle of arrivals from the Dominican Republic began; this new migration accelerated rapidly after that country's long-running and bloody political feuding subsided in 1965 and changes in U.S. immigration law opened the doors to larger numbers of Latin American, Caribbean, Asian, and African newcomers. The high levels of poverty and physical dilapidation in Williamsburg led New York City's CAA to designate the neighborhood as one of its original fifteen poverty areas.

The neighborhood of Bushwick is wedged in between Williamsburg (to the northwest), Bedford-Stuyvesant (to the south), and Ridgewood, Queens (across the borough line, to the east). Around 1840, a large influx of German immigrants began arriving in Bushwick, bringing with them one of their specialty industries: brewing beer. By the late 1880s, fourteen breweries were operating in Bushwick, offering jobs not only to Germans but also to later-arriving English, Irish, Russian, and Polish immigrants. Many of the German residents of this era were well-to-do, and they constructed a number of beautiful mansions along several streets in Bushwick. Between Prohibition and the Depression, however, most of the breweries closed down, and the German population in the area started to decline.

In the 1930s and 1940s, Italian Americans began moving into Bushwick, finding jobs in the still-vibrant Brooklyn Navy Yard and other manufacturing concerns in the area. By 1950, Bushwick had become the second-largest Italian American community in New York. But the city's manufacturing economy was now entering its period of decline, which brought significant changes to Bushwick. African Americans and Puerto Ricans, many displaced by nearby urban renewal clearance, began moving into the neighborhood. Some of the Italian Americans, especially those who had lost their local jobs, left. Still, many Bushwick residents—old and new—worked steadily in factories or for the city, and this helped the neighborhood maintain a mostly stable, working-class feel into the 1960s (Musuraca [1991?]). Even so, the die was cast, and in 1966, when the city added ten more poverty neighborhoods to the Community Action Program, Bushwick was among them (Pollinger and Pollinger 1972).

For residents of neighborhoods like Williamsburg and Bushwick, the CAP offered a new strategy for confronting their intensifying poverty. Previously, the poor had primarily relied on public assistance and the old-line charities. These resources aimed to temporarily relieve recipients' suffering with modest material support, while at the same time pointing them toward the middle-class behaviors that would presumably lift them out of poverty—thrift, hard work, education, chastity, and so on. In contrast, the CAP presented a new calculus for the poor, positing that their poverty resulted not from individual shortcomings but from the outcomes of economic and political fields that systematically denied them opportunities while reproducing existing structures of advantage and disadvantage (Cloward and Ohlin 1960). Despite the fact that federal support for the CAP had all but ended by 1970, the program left an important, and lasting, legacy in U.S. cities: a large number of community-based organizations in poor, mostly African American and Latino neighborhoods. Many of these organizations soon benefited from a general trend toward the privatization of public services—including social provision services—that accelerated in the 1970s and 1980s (Marwell 2004b; Salamon 1995; S. R. Smith and Lipsky 1993). Supported by government funds, many of these CBOs continued their efforts to reshape the economic and political fields in which they operated, seeking improved social integration of the poor and improved social order within the city as a whole.

In the following pages, I detail a variety of historical and contemporary achievements and struggles in which the CBOs of Williamsburg and Bushwick have engaged. These stories illuminate the complex organizational environments in which these groups operate and point to the possibilities for both individual advancement and enhanced social integration and social order. CBOs operate within particular fields of action, competing and collaborating with external organizations in an effort to reshape the conditions on the ground in their neighborhoods. Sometimes they succeed in creating new possibilities for the residents they serve. Other times they fight losing battles against more powerful forces. Long and complex maneuvers are often required to bring new efforts to fruition, or simply to maintain existing gains. CBOs' multiplicity of tasks require capacities that go far beyond encouraging local residents to participate in their activities. Instead, the CBOs of Williamsburg and Bushwick seek to produce employment, housing, child care, educational, and political opportunities for thousands of local residents, whose individual stories are far too numerous to recount here.

CHAPTER TWO

A Place to Live

A place to live is one of the most basic human needs. The characteristics of a person's home may reveal much about his economic fortunes: a shanty in a sprawling slum, a single room in a broken-down hotel, a tightly packed two-bedroom apartment, a capacious penthouse with a view—each tells a tale about its occupants and their place in society's hierarchy. For poor people, access to a safe, well maintained, sufficiently large, affordable place to live can make an enormous difference in their everyday lives. Higher rates of criminal victimization in the neighborhoods where poor people are concentrated make home safety a paramount concern. Basic amenities that nonpoor people take for granted—hot water, heat, electricity, a working refrigerator, intact windows, a secure mailbox—are frequently missing from poor people's homes. The poor are more likely than the nonpoor to spend more than the recommended 30 percent of their income on housing costs, leaving less money for food, clothing, transportation, child care, and other necessities. Even so, overcrowded housing is more prevalent among the poor, meaning longer lines for the bathroom, no place for children to sit quietly and do their homework, no room for the family to sit down together at the table for dinner, greater wear and tear on floors, plumbing, electrical wiring, and more. Many poor families live in small spaces because there simply isn't enough money for a bigger place.

Poor-quality housing may seem like a natural condition of a poor neighborhood. But neither housing nor a neighborhood becomes—or remains—poor in a vacuum. Many poor neighborhoods now plagued by ramshackle housing once had streets lined with tidy houses or apartment buildings. These homes fell into disrepair for numerous reasons that had little to do with the actions of their individual residents, and everything to do with how organizations outside the neighborhood made decisions that affected those

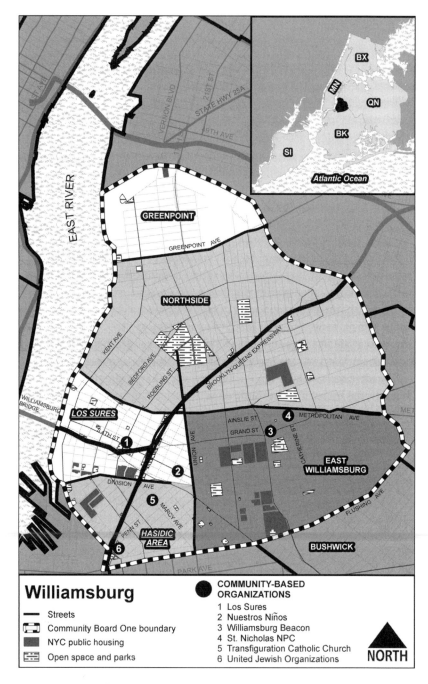

Map 2. Williamsburg. Map by James Quinn, ISERP, Columbia University.

residents. For example, the once-common practice of "redlining"—banks refusing to make home loans and insurers to issue home owner policies in certain neighborhoods—is a well-known cause of the physical deterioration of housing. Similarly, government's lax enforcement of housing code regulations designed to maintain minimum standards of housing quality leads to increased dilapidation, while also placing residents at risk of injury. These and other organizational practices play a key role in housing decline and the downward spiral of once-stable neighborhoods, and contribute to these areas' continued marginality as places only the poor will live.

One of the most important and measurable contributions of community-based organizations to the conditions of poor neighborhoods has been the large-scale improvements these groups have made to the housing stocks of these areas. Community development corporations and other nonprofit housing developers across the nation have rehabilitated and built from scratch hundreds of thousands of units of housing in the places where poor people live. These organizations have also managed and maintained many of these units far better than many private owners—and some public housing authorities—in the same neighborhoods. All of this activity has resulted in far better housing conditions for many poor urban residents, and these once-fringe CBOs have become institutionalized as a major component of the nation's housing policy. But the processes by which these organizations emerged and created new approaches to meeting poor people's housing needs are complex, embedded in broader economic and social changes that have transpired in U.S. cities over the past fifty years.

This ball got rolling with the midcentury decline of cities as residential spaces for the white working and middle classes, a phenomenon fueled by group members' changing housing preferences. No longer content with the aging housing stock, high density, and changing racial complexion of the city, these residents turned toward the promised joys of a new kind of metropolitan living: a house in the suburbs. As several landmark studies of the rise of American suburbs have shown, however, urban residents' new preferences for single-family houses—owned rather than rented, equipped with the latest appliances, set on small private patches of open space, and located a sufficient yet manageable distance from the city—did not arise spontaneously. Each of these components of suburban living was carefully cultivated, financed, produced, and marketed by a consortium of real estate developers, bankers, and product manufacturers—assisted substantially by the federal government (Fishman 1987; Gans 1967; Jackson 1985).

During these years, the suburbs became the prime feeding ground for what sociologist Harvey Molotch famously called the urban "growth machine"

(Molotch 1976; cf. Logan and Molotch 1987). While members of any given city's business community might disagree with each other about certain aspects of managing the local economy, and might also at times have different priorities than local government leaders, Molotch argued that all of these elites could make common cause around one premise: that a general trajectory of *constant growth* was fundamental to the success of the local urban economy. This mandate to pursue growth aggressively at all costs sent (and still sends) business and government elites in search of new opportunities to intensify land use in the city and its environs. As land becomes occupied by additional businesses or housing, it invariably generates new income for landowners, new development opportunities for builders, and new financing opportunities for bankers—these business elites always benefit from growth. Less clear is the benefit to government; although growth machine advocates claim that growth brings government new tax revenues, these are often offset by the infrastructure and other costs it incurs in order to entice private investment. The benefits of growth to local residents—the poor and, increasingly, the middle class—are similarly unclear (Logan and Molotch 1987).

The growth machine saw the new suburbs of the 1950s and 1960s as low-hanging fruit on the urban development tree. Urban residents from the working, lower-middle, and middle classes already had been convinced of the desirability of suburban living, and they formed a ready market for suburban houses. Land in the suburbs was comparatively cheap and plentiful, making large-scale building affordable and relatively hassle-free. And thanks to federally secured mortgages and highway funds, new suburban residents not only could safely make the leap into property ownership but also could commute rapidly to their jobs in the city. At the same time, then, the pattern of suburban growth satisfied the growth machine, the housing preferences of erstwhile (mostly white) urban dwellers, and the needs of employers whose sunk costs in city locales precluded their own migration for another generation. Constitutive of the suburban indulgence of the growth machine, the working and middle classes came to view cities as places in which to work and through which to drive—but not as places to live, and certainly not as places to raise children. Increasingly, the city became the province of the upper classes and the poor: the former rich enough to privately maintain their genteel quality of life—including the high costs of private education and recreation for their children—and the latter able to salvage homes from the cast-offs of the suburban vanguard.

This chapter tells the story of what grew in the void left behind when the growth machine abandoned Williamsburg, Brooklyn—a neighborhood whose pre–World War II working class, immigrant residents decamped for the suburbs during the 1950s—and what happened to its new, poorer denizens when the growth machine returned in the 1990s. It is a story that revolves around the activities of several community-based organizations devoted to seeking, creating, and protecting housing for poor local residents. It is also a story about how these organizations' ability to secure their constituents places to live has been facilitated and constrained by the particular manifestations of larger economic and political forces operating in the city.

The organizations discussed in this chapter made great entrepreneurial strides when the growth machine abandoned Williamsburg—their innovations created housing, shaped housing policy, incorporated new immigrants into the neighborhood, and challenged exclusion from the protections of government. But because housing production is one of the fundamentals of the growth machine, an engine as well as an indicator of its success, this organizational work eventually helped draw the growth machine back to the Williamsburg streets. As it sputtered back to life, finding poor people places to live became much harder. Competition between the neighborhood's dueling poor, ethnic communities for the shrinking pool of low-income housing reached epic proportions, with local housing organizations fighting each other tooth and nail over every last unit of affordable housing. More and more, politically managed solutions proved necessary, as city government sought to tamp down neighborhood tensions and avoid a conflagration. The growth machine's increasingly urgent interest in Williamsburg brought the situation to a head at the end of the 1990s. The organizations on one side of the ethnic divide ultimately proved more adept at maneuvering the political component of the growth machine, engineering a far more secure escape from its designs on their living space in Williamsburg.

By the Hand of Robert Moses: Population Succession in Williamsburg

Between 1925 and 1965, one man nearly single-handedly transformed the entire New York City metropolitan landscape. Robert Moses, the city's immensely powerful development czar, possessed a vision so breathtaking and a drive for power so ruthless as to render him both hero and villain to generations of New Yorkers (Caro 1974). One of Moses's top priorities was the construction of a massive system of highways designed to link the city to the open spaces and fast-growing suburbs of Long Island, Westchester, and New Jersey. He believed the highways circling through and around the city would serve as a technological engine to power the economic development of New York. No longer would trucks carrying goods, or cars ferrying workers, need to crawl through local streets on their way in and out of the Manhattan business districts. Just as the assembly line was speeding up the production of all manner of household and leisure goods, the highways would rev the engine of American consumerism and provision the growing suburban class.

Moses discovered the Williamsburg section of Brooklyn when he identified it as a key link in one of his most cherished projects: an uninterrupted highway chain connecting Manhattan to Brooklyn, Queens, and the Bronx, then onward to the suburbs of Westchester and Long Island. Williamsburg lay just across the East River from lower Manhattan, an easy ride across the Williamsburg Bridge. The neighborhood's location in north Brooklyn, the narrowest section of the borough, minimized the distance from Manhattan to Queens; for Moses, this made Williamsburg an indispensable fulcrum of his planned Brooklyn-Queens Expressway (BQE). Moses's vision for the BQE was realized in sections, built over a nearly twenty-five-year period. He aimed to take advantage of the multiple East River crossings into lower Manhattan—the Williamsburg Bridge, the Manhattan Bridge, the Brooklyn Bridge, and the Brooklyn-Battery Tunnel—by running the BQE past each of them. Commuters would be able to get on the BQE from any of several highways that extended out to the suburbs and get off at whichever bridge or tunnel best served them.

The first section of the BQE opened in eastern Queens in 1939, picking up incoming traffic from the Long Island suburbs, then heading west to the Brooklyn-Queens dividing line. Moses next started building backward from the East River crossings, stretching new sections of the highway to meet up with the segment coming in from the east. The connection to the Brooklyn-Battery Tunnel was to have been built first, starting in 1941, though the onset of World War II delayed construction for a number of years (*New York Times* 1946). After the war, Moses picked up the pace substantially, turning to the routes leading up to the Williamsburg and Brooklyn Bridges. In 1948, Moses began demolishing buildings in Williamsburg to make way for an elevated six-lane highway connecting to the Williamsburg Bridge. The structure slashed through the heart of the neighborhood, destroying the vibrant business district on Broadway and bisecting the cohesive community of Orthodox Jews, Italians, Poles, Slavs, and Russians.

By 1952, commuters from the Long Island suburbs could realize Moses's vision of entering the BQE in eastern Queens, traveling at high speed all the way to the Williamsburg Bridge, and arriving in the Lower East Side of

Manhattan in record time (*New York Times* 1952). The highway's effect on the residents of Williamsburg was rather less salutary. Indeed, as in many other residential neighborhoods throughout the city that were split apart by Moses's highways, the fallout in Williamsburg was massive (e.g., Caro 1974, chaps. 37–38). The working-class white ethnics who had long lived in the tenement houses adjacent to Broadway found themselves suddenly displaced. While some of the Orthodox Jews, loathe to be separated from Williamsburg's thriving Orthodox community, moved south across Broadway into the more middle-class heart of the Jewish area, most of the others were forced to seek housing outside of Williamsburg (Kranzler 1961). Many of the businesses that had stood for years on Broadway never reopened. The population dispersal and business destruction sparked by Moses's highway commenced a prolonged capital drain from Williamsburg, a trend that would proceed ever more rapidly over the next two decades.

In the midst of the displacement wrought by demolition for the BQE in Williamsburg, Congress passed the Housing Act of 1949. Title I of the act provided for "slum clearance and community development and redevelopment," the official description of what came to be known colloquially as "urban renewal." Moses was quick to incorporate the provisions and resources of the urban renewal legislation into his ongoing reshaping of the city and its environs. By 1951, working through one of his many bureaucratic fiefdoms, New York City's Committee on Slum Clearance, Moses proffered plans for a set of seven Title I projects. Only one—Williamsburg— was located outside of Manhattan.[1] The Williamsburg project, slated for the Southside section of the neighborhood (see map 1), was by far the largest of the seven. It involved the condemnation of forty-five acres of land comprising fifteen contiguous city blocks stretching south from Broadway almost to the Brooklyn Navy Yard. Part of this area was reserved for the centerpiece of the renewal project: Williamsburg's second contribution to the BQE, a section of the highway that would connect the Williamsburg Bridge to the artery running north from the Brooklyn-Battery Tunnel. On the cleared land alongside the highway, Moses proposed building fifteen twenty-story residential towers, a junior high school, and a shopping mall (Slum Clearance Committee 1951).

When the city's plans for large-scale demolition in Southside Williamsburg became known in 1951, capital investment in the area virtually halted. Owners of residences in the targeted blocks saw little reason to invest

---

1. The other sites were in the South Village, Washington Square South, Corlears Hook, Delancey Street, North Harlem, and Harlem (Slum Clearance Committee 1951).

in upkeep, given that city officials would soon condemn their property. Banks stopped making loans in the area that would shortly be transformed, though in ways too uncertain to predict what the resulting neighborhood values would be. With the dust barely settled on the first Williamsburg section of the BQE, Moses began demolition of an even bigger slice of the neighborhood. By 1954 the bulldozers had cut such a scar through the area south of Broadway that one contemporary observer remarked that "Williamsburg looks partially as if hit by a few bombs" (Kranzler 1961, 22n18).

As was his style, Moses insisted on running the highway along his planned trajectory, despite the fact that the blocks targeted for demolition were home to the more middle-class segment of the Orthodox Jewish community, including shopkeepers, skilled workers, and professionals. Many of these longtime Southside Williamsburg residents were forced to leave their beloved community behind; the housing that escaped the bulldozer, though relatively cheap, became ever more dilapidated, proving no match for the newer, better quality, less expensive housing in other Brooklyn neighborhoods, Queens, and Long Island (Kranzler 1961). For two groups of new, poorer arrivals, however, the aging, crumbling housing stock in Williamsburg offered an affordable—if somewhat uncomfortable—place to live.

Since 1947, the southern and western fringes of the Southside's now-disrupted Orthodox Jewish area had been filling up with coreligionists of a different stripe: Hasidic Jews from a series of small towns in Hungary. Although the Orthodox followed many prescriptions of Jewish law assiduously, the Hasidic interpretation of Judaism demanded even stricter standards, was infused with an ecstatic mysticism, and followed faithfully the dictates of a charismatic leader (the rebbe). The largest group of Hasidim to arrive in the Southside hailed from the Hungarian village of Satumare, led to this corner of Brooklyn by the Satmar rebbe, Joel Teitelbaum.[2] After a narrow escape from the Nazis—legend has it that Teitelbaum was on a train to Auschwitz when some followers bribed the German guards to let him out—the rebbe committed himself to rebuilding his religious community in Williamsburg.

In the even more broken-down areas of the Southside north and east of Broadway, Puerto Ricans arriving as part of the 1950s' concentrated migration from the island to New York built up their own dense settlement. They began calling their new community "Los Sures" (literally "the souths"),

---

2. Other Hasidic sects that settled in Williamsburg included the Pupa, Bobover, Klausenburg, and Viener, but their numbers came to be dwarfed by those of the Satmar.

after the Spanish denominations of the Southside streets where they made their homes: South First Street (Sur Uno), South Second Street (Sur Dos), and so on (see map 2). Although the Puerto Ricans packed most tightly between South First and South Eleventh Streets, they also filtered throughout the Southside more generally, including the parts of the neighborhood where the Hasidim were concentrated. The relatively dispersed nature of the Puerto Rican settlement in the Southside made for less social cohesion in comparison to the Hasidim.

Both the Hasidim and the Puerto Ricans proved poorer than the older populations they replaced, further contributing to the declining economic conditions in the Southside. By 1960, the highway construction, urban renewal demolition, and population shifts left the neighborhood a very different place from what it had been just a decade earlier. Throughout the 1960s, as cleared land lay fallow and capital investment continued to stay away, the rents commanded by the Southside's remaining housing fell. As in poor neighborhoods around the world, low rents meant less incentive for property owners to maintain their buildings. Tenants waited longer for landlords to repair broken windows, paint peeling walls, replace crumbling stoops, or fix faulty wiring. Each month, when the rent was due, tenants complained about their increasingly dilapidated apartments and buildings. Sometimes, after pocketing tenants' hard-earned cash, the landlords responded, making cheap repairs of the most egregious problems; more often, they simply made empty promises that help would arrive soon. Any desire by the Hasidim to move into better conditions was offset by their need to be close to their rebbe. Members of the Southside's growing Puerto Rican population, while theoretically more mobile than their Hasidic neighbors, often found themselves blocked from moving by a lack of financial resources and the constraints of racial segregation and discrimination. Still, as long as the dilapidated apartment buildings remained more or less habitable, the Southside's poor could make them their homes.

Your Slum Is My Community: Building Organizations in the City

By 1960, it was clear that the growth machine had turned its back on Williamsburg, producing the antithetical outcomes of deintensified land use and reduced population. The new Puerto Rican and Hasidic residents of the Southside, however, were already in the midst of the new cycle of immigrant community formation. Both groups looked very much like the ideal-typical immigrant community first described by the Chicago School sociologists W. I. Thomas and Florian Znaniecki in their classic study of

Polish immigrants to Chicago (Thomas and Znaniecki 1918). Thomas and Znaniecki wrote that as the immigrants grew steadily in number, they gave birth to a succession of formal organizations to provide for their needs: the Polish American boardinghouse (1513); the Polish American "society," which begins as a mutual assistance enterprise, then grows into other functions (1517–22); the Polish American parish, which represents the "great work of the society, through which it assures the permanence of the social cohesion of the [Polish American] colony" (1523); the parish's religious fraternities and associations (p. 1531); the parish school (1531–33); and, finally, the Polish American press (1541–44). As each of these organizations emerged, it further concentrated the Polish American population within a particular territory, until the "Polish American community," with its full complement of formal organizations, became synonymous with a geographic area of the city (1547).

The Hasidic and Puerto Rican communities of the Southside followed a similar line of development, from newly formed abstractions in the late 1940s to, by the mid-1960s, geographically identifiable settlements anchored by inwardly focused organizations that helped community members reestablish some semblance of their homeland's social order (cf. Gans 1967, chaps. 3, 4, 7). One of the first acts of the Satmar rebbe upon arriving in the Southside was to establish the Yetev Lev congregation, the organizational foundation of a post-Hitler Satmar presence. Soon came a host of related religious and commercial enterprises, all necessary to the maintenance of the insular Hasidic life. The Puerto Ricans similarly began their organizational life in the Southside through religious involvement: shortly after their arrival, they began filling the pews at the area's three Catholic churches. Groups of migrants from the same island town often settled near one another throughout the Southside, and they soon founded hometown associations to socialize, talk politics, and remind each other of the places they had left behind. Although many of these nascent Puerto Rican organizations served small, discrete patches of the Southside, the Catholic churches provided an important measure of continuity, bridging some of the organizational divides through the parish system (Price 1979, chaps. 2, 4).

In 1965, the arrival of President Lyndon Johnson's War on Poverty reoriented the organizational infrastructures of the Puerto Rican and Hasidic communities of Southside Williamsburg. Much has been written about the accidental, shortsighted, and naïve inclusion of the Community Action Program (CAP) in the War on Poverty, when the federal government encouraged residents of poor urban neighborhoods to seek new, homegrown solutions to their conditions of blight, exclusion, and despair (M. L. Gillette 1996; Moynihan 1969; Sundquist 1969). The CAP urged poor people to challenge the institutions of local government that kept them on the margins of American society, thereby harnessing government's power and resources to help them do better. In New York City, one of the nation's largest recipients of CAP funds, Williamsburg was one of fifteen neighborhoods targeted by the city's first CAP efforts (Institute of Public Administration 1966). Both the Puerto Rican and Hasidic communities took an interest in this new government approach to poverty, and sent delegates to the 1965 Williamsburg Community Convention to help elect the program's local governing board (Price 1979).

Over the course of the next five or six years, struggles for control over Williamsburg's CAP funds between representatives of the Puerto Rican and Hasidic communities, the few remaining Orthodox Jews, and the small African American population would teach new, hard-nosed strategies for collective action to all concerned. The several Hasidic sects (by now numerically dominated by the Satmar) and the Orthodox Jews threw in their lots together, forming the United Jewish Organizations of Williamsburg. Working through this group, which they soon controlled, the Satmar pressed for and won numerous resources from the CAP. The Southside Puerto Ricans, whose population had always been less territorially concentrated than the Hasidim, formed organizations in this same scattered pattern, ending up with numerous bodies competing for CAP funds. Taking seriously the CAP's call for organizing the poor into a transformative political force, these Puerto Rican groups set out in pursuit of grassroots initiatives among the people of the Southside.

The arrival of the CAP heralded two fundamental changes in the life of the Southside's Puerto Ricans and Hasidic Jews. First, the availability of government funds to address the widespread poverty of both groups via locally controlled organizations meant that community life would no longer be organized mostly on the basis of internal group dynamics. While religious congregations, hometown associations, and similar organizations had served as the primary source of collective assistance to both Puerto Ricans and Hasidim, new resources were being made available through externally managed and often contested policy processes. This in turn led to the CAP's second profound impact on Southside life: the entrenchment of a prolonged and increasingly tense competition over government resources between organizations representing Hasidim on the one side and Puerto Ricans—and, increasingly, other Latinos—on the other.

Growth Machine Lull:
Los Sures and the Neighborhood Housing Movement

By the time the CAP arrived in Williamsburg, the material conditions of the neighborhood, particularly its rapidly declining local housing, had become an increasingly urgent concern. The growth machine's prolonged abandonment of the area meant that many Southside Williamsburg properties were drawing close to—or crossing over—the thin line between (barely) viable residences and unhealthy, dangerous dwelling spaces. Families were often forced to share toilet or bathing facilities with neighbors because the plumbing in their own apartments no longer worked and landlords refused to make repairs. Water leaking through roofs and windows spread stains across ceilings and floorboards, then ate through the plaster and wood to leave gaping holes between floors. Radiators became blocked, providing only the barest of heat—if any at all—in the dead of winter. Most dangerous, electrical wiring slowly disintegrated, sparking fires without warning.

Throughout the 1960s across New York City's poor neighborhoods—Williamsburg, Harlem, the South Bronx, Bedford-Stuyvesant, and others—the rate of residential fires climbed steadily. At the same time, the city's impending fiscal crisis led to major cutbacks in public services, such as police, fire protection, sanitation, and subway maintenance. Beginning in 1972, a number of fire engine and ladder companies were closed, staffing levels at remaining firehouses were reduced, and the number of fire engines sent as a standard response to a fire was cut. Over the next five years, residential fires became epidemic, destroying buildings and sometimes whole blocks as fire response times increased and companies arriving at fires often had insufficient manpower to adequately deploy their equipment (Wallace and Wallace 1998).

Partly as a result of fires, between 1960 and 1970 Brooklyn's Community District One (Williamsburg-Greenpoint) lost nearly 9 percent of its population, dipping from 193,000 to 176,000. Most of this population decline occurred in the poorer Williamsburg section of the district (Susser 1982), home to Hasidim, Puerto Ricans, and, after 1965, a growing population of immigrants from the Dominican Republic.

Nothing about the 1960s, however, prepared local residents for the extent of neighborhood deterioration and depopulation they would experience during the 1970s. As the value of Williamsburg property slid downward, owners of its residential buildings weighed the rapidly rising costs of heating oil, electricity, materials for repairs, and property taxes against the rents that tenants in their deteriorating buildings were willing and able to pay. Many owners calculated a net loss and moved from "milking" their buildings for rents to simply abandoning them, leaving the tenants to fend for themselves without heat, hot water, trash disposal, maintenance, and other necessary services. More and more rapidly, once-vibrant buildings became only partially occupied; a glance up at many façades revealed more broken or boarded-up windows than working ones. Some buildings became so badly neglected that structural walls collapsed, forcing tenants out into the street or—even worse—to remain in dangerous conditions because they had nowhere else to go.

A few optimistic owners sought to recoup their investments by selling their buildings, but this usually proved a losing proposition. No buyers were looking to come into Williamsburg, where conditions afforded few opportunities for the growth machine to operate. The neighborhood sank deeper into population loss, poverty, and crime. More and more, buildings mysteriously went up in flames in the middle of the night, as owners employed arsonists in a last-ditch effort to recover their investments through fire insurance payments. Apartment-by-apartment depopulation was thus repeated at the level of buildings, leaving blocks pockmarked by crumbling structures, burned-out shells, and vacant lots. The refusal of owners to maintain their buildings, and the disturbing frequency with which they took steps to destroy them, marked the nadir of Williamsburg's real estate value. As apartments deteriorated beyond habitability, buildings fell down or burned, and vacant lots increasingly replaced structures, Williamsburg lost housing units at an alarming rate. The resulting population decline was severe: over the course of the 1970s, Williamsburg-Greenpoint lost nearly a quarter of its population (Susser 1982).

For the thousands of Puerto Ricans and Dominicans who remained in Southside Williamsburg during these increasingly difficult times, the urgent need for an affordable place to live won out over the ramshackle conditions of their homes. By the end of the 1960s, several small groups of community activists, including the pastors of the three Southside Catholic churches, were beginning to develop new strategies to recover the disappearing use value of their neighborhood's housing (Southside United Housing Development Fund Corporation 1975). The activists set themselves a modest goal: to work with the Puerto Rican and other Latino residents of the Southside to restore individual apartments to livable conditions—nothing fancy, just safe places to live and raise a family. They began identifying landlord-abandoned buildings, where basic services—heat, hot water, garbage removal, maintenance—were no longer being provided. They then encouraged the tenants to pool the funds they would have spent on rent to purchase these services themselves. In buildings with vacant apartments in need of rehabilitation to make them habitable, organizers found new tenants, moved them into the apartments, and allowed them several months before they were required to start paying into the building services fund. This practice allowed new tenants to spend "rent" money on initial renovations, and then integrated them into the larger structure of the building, making the entire building more viable.

The Latinos of the Southside were not alone in their self-help housing strategies. Similar ad hoc efforts to preserve abandoned apartment buildings were under way in other poor neighborhoods, including the Lower East Side, the South Bronx, Bedford-Stuyvesant, and Harlem (Leavitt and Saegert 1990; Mele 2001; Schur and Sherry 1977; von Hassell 1996). As all these grassroots activists slowly recorded successes, observers of the New York housing scene—planners, lawyers, social service providers, church leaders, city officials, and others—took notice. They began to consider these community-based strategies as an alternative to urban renewal for addressing the housing problems of the city's poor. In 1972, aware that a significant shift in city housing policy was afoot, the Southside activists banded together to formalize their efforts. They incorporated as a 501(c)3 nonprofit organization, which they named the Southside United Housing Development Fund Corporation. Colloquially, the group became known as "Los Sures," thereby neatly cementing the organization's identity with the by-now heavily Latino section of the Southside where it concentrated its activities (see map 2).

That same year, Los Sures, a few of the city's other recently formalized neighborhood housing groups, and Brooklyn Legal Services Corporation A (the Williamsburg division of Brooklyn's civil equivalent of the public defender's office) finally convinced the city's Housing Development Agency to put some support behind their housing organizing strategy (Schur and Sherry 1977). Faced with a growing inventory of residential properties seized from their private owners for nonpayment of real estate taxes, the city was looking for a better way to administer its far-flung collection of buildings. By the end of the 1970s, the city controlled forty thousand such buildings, referred to as being in receivership or "in-rem" (Plunz 1990). Unfortunately, the city often proved no better at providing services to in-rem tenants than their private landlords had been, and miserable housing conditions continued. Pressed by neighborhood housing activists to give their approach a try, the city contracted with Los Sures to manage two in-rem buildings, to see if the organization could bring the buildings up to code and adequately service the tenants (Southside United Housing

Figure 1. Late 1970s organizing efforts by Southside United Housing Development Fund Corporation (Los Sures). Photo courtesy of Los Sures.

Development Fund Corporation 1975). The experiment worked. Slowly, in Southside Williamsburg and other similar neighborhoods, the city's newly christened Community Management Program handed over in-rem properties to community-based housing organizations and paid for the unique services these groups were able to provide.

The Community Management Program represented an unprecedented partnership between neighborhood activists and city government, made possible only by the transformation of ad hoc self-help activism into formal community-based organizations. In the Southside, staff at the newly founded Los Sures brought with them knowledge of the local Latino community, the trust of its members, and a willingness to work long hours alongside tenants in the scruffy business of rehabilitating severely dilapidated properties. The organization also offered jobs and on-the-job training in property rehabilitation and management to local residents—a substantial contribution during a time of high unemployment and inflation. From its end, the city contributed financial resources on a scale that far exceeded what activists and residents could generate on their own. The city also wielded the power to create a stable legal and regulatory environment in which Los Sures and pioneering groups in other poor and devastated areas could pursue their rehabilitation efforts. Together, the city and its neighborhood partners capitalized stable organizations inside poor neighborhoods while also germinating a new approach to housing policy. Within a decade, the approach would become institutionalized as an important piece of the nation's urban redevelopment strategy.

Among New York's community housing organizations, Los Sures soon was carrying one of the heaviest portfolios. Data gathered in 1976 documented 116 units of housing under Los Sures management, and the organization was in discussions with the city to manage an estimated 200 additional units. In both categories, Los Sures outpaced all of the city's other nonprofit housing managers (Schur and Sherry 1977). The work required of Los Sures varied depending upon the state of each building it took over. In some cases, tenanted buildings needed only a conscientious management entity to assess building maintenance, prioritize repairs, arrange for services, collect rents, and pay the bills. More intensive work was required in the many buildings that were only partially inhabited. In those buildings, Los Sures employed its "free rent" strategy to get families to invest their own minimal resources in making decrepit apartments habitable. As further incentive to would-be tenants, Los Sures secured city funds to address major building system needs, such as replacing a roof, boiler, or plumbing system.

Los Sures facilitated this range of investments via its formal position as intermediary between local residents and city government, extracting labor, small capital investments, and collaborative goodwill from residents, and substantial funds and regulatory permissions from the city. This marrying of resources could only happen within the structure of a formal organization such as Los Sures, whose nonprofit status enabled it to fulfill the financial and legal responsibilities involved in real estate management and the disbursal of public monies. For the poor Puerto Rican and Dominican residents of the Southside, the end result of the organization's work was a slow but steady return of decent, affordable housing to the neighborhood's streets. From the city government's perspective, the reintensification of the Southside's land use presaged a potentially bright future for the growth machine. If Los Sures could return abandoned, in-rem buildings to full occupancy and private ownership, the neighborhood might begin to turn around. Beyond the property and other taxes these newly restored buildings would generate, potential for additional development would accrue. This new confluence of formal community-based organizations, public policy directed toward housing rehabilitation, and public financing of policy directives carried out by nongovernmental entities provided poor people with desperately needed housing in the short term—and eventually established a new frontier for the growth machine.

Public Housing and Particularist Politics:
The United Jewish Organizations

In the years since Robert Moses demolished large swaths of Williamsburg for the Brooklyn-Queens Expressway, the wheels of urban renewal had been grinding slowly. By 1976, over twenty years after the highway opened to traffic, Williamsburg's urban renewal area had become home to six large, government-subsidized housing developments. Both the Puerto Rican and the Hasidic communities initially resisted the construction of high-rise, low-income public housing in the neighborhood (Price 1979). The Puerto Ricans feared the high-density towers would create an alienating atmosphere. The Hasidic opposition was more vociferous: they worried that public housing's accessibility to all low-income New Yorkers would bring strangers into their midst, and that having to ride elevators to the upper floors of high-rises on the Sabbath would violate Jewish law. In fact, during the planning stages of the first two developments in the late 1950s, the Hasidim's objections derailed a project slated to rise in the heart of their section of the Southside (Grutzner 1958, 1959).

When the Satmars' plans to relocate their community to rural New Jersey fell through, however (Honig 1963), it became clear that their fast growing population desperately needed additional housing in the Southside. This need serendipitously aligned with the local political establishment's growing unease about the replacement of its traditional Orthodox Jewish and white ethnic constituency by Hasidic and Puerto Rican newcomers. The Southside's Seneca Democratic Club, a major force in Brooklyn politics for most of the last fifty years, feared that the neighborhood's ethnic succession would bring about the rise of new ethnic politicians who would oust them from power. The club's leaders decided to move forcefully to garner the political support of the Hasidim, whom they felt would prove far more predictable and sympathetic constituents than the Puerto Ricans (Price 1979).

The Seneca leadership realized that the policy imperatives of urban renewal made a ready ally of the New York City Housing Authority (NYCHA), the city agency responsible for administering the new public housing developments being built with urban renewal funds in the Southside. City governments were required by federal urban renewal legislation to maintain what was called "racial balance" in areas cleared of slum housing and then rebuilt. Practically, this meant retaining white residents in areas that had been on the point of "tipping" into all-minority populations. The Seneca Democrats saw the new public housing developments as a resource they could use to satisfy both their own political interests—holding off ethnic political succession in Williamsburg by shoring up their white constituency—and the city's racial balance mandate. The Seneca leaders could woo Hasidic support by offering access to the developments' brand-new apartments with their modern amenities, and at the same time help NYCHA maintain the required white population in the Southside urban renewal area.

The Seneca Democrats placed themselves at the fulcrum of this mutually beneficial exchange. As detailed by Price (1979), about a year prior to the 1964 opening of the first Southside public housing development, Jonathan Williams Plaza, the Satmar rebbe began referring Hasidic housing seekers to officials at the Seneca Club, who in turn placed telephone calls and wrote letters to NYCHA staff to introduce individual Hasidic families as model prospective tenants. Around the same time, the *New York Times* reported that plans to build the second Southside public housing development, Independence Houses, were back in full swing—and that the Hasidim would be given preference as tenants there (*New York Times* 1963). Many Puerto Ricans in the Southside also were interested in the new apartments in the two developments. Their experience with the application process, however, proved much different from that of the Hasidim. Simply getting applications proved difficult, and NYCHA gave out conflicting information to many Puerto Ricans about income eligibility requirements (Price 1979, 138–41). When Jonathan Williams and Independence opened in late 1964, about 75 percent of the apartments in the two developments went to Jewish tenants—about evenly split between older Orthodox Jews and more recently arrived Satmar Hasidim—20 percent to Puerto Ricans and 5 percent to African Americans. This was the case even though at the time, the NYCHA waiting list for public housing in Brooklyn was over 90 percent Puerto Rican and African American.[3]

By the early 1970s, three more large, publicly subsidized housing developments were planned for the Southside urban renewal area, with a total of nearly seventeen hundred low- and moderate-income apartments. The Seneca Club's arrangement with NYCHA and the Satmar Hasidim continued, such that when tenant lists for two of the new developments were drawn up, each included an outsized majority of Hasidic tenants. At the Taylor-Wythe Houses, Hasidim secured upward of 60 percent of the apartments, Latinos about 25 percent, and African Americans 10 percent. At Bedford Gardens, 75 percent of the apartments went to Hasidim, the rest to Latinos and

3. Author's field notes on interview with Martin Needelman, project director of Brooklyn Legal Services Corporation A, July 7, 2006.

African Americans. At the third new development, which would eventually be named after the famed Puerto Rican baseball player Roberto Clemente, activists at Los Sures, Brooklyn Legal Services Corporation A, and four churches in the Southside were determined that the distribution of apartments would be different.

Los Sures versus United Jewish Organizations: The Williamsburg Fair Housing Lawsuit

Staff at Los Sures, along with Latino and African American residents of Williamsburg in general, had long grumbled about the rental outcomes at the local public housing developments (by the mid-1970s, the Puerto Ricans of the Southside were being joined in increasingly large numbers by Dominicans and members of other Latino groups). Following a series of peaceful street protests by Latinos and African Americans, Monsignor Bryan Karvelis, pastor of Transfiguration Catholic Church, led the establishment of a nonprofit organization to oversee the development of what would become Roberto Clemente Plaza.[4] Kent Village, Inc., was led by a board of directors that reflected the ethnic diversity of the neighborhood more accurately than had previous community sponsors: it included the pastors of the four local churches—three Catholic, one Lutheran—two rabbis representing the Satmar and Pupa Hasidic sects, and staff members from two of the churches' affiliated social service agencies.[5] To take charge of finding eligible low-income applicants for the completed apartments, Kent Village turned to Los Sures. In 1976, as Kent Village was about to break ground on Clemente Plaza, Los Sures established an informal agreement with city housing officials on behalf of the Williamsburg Housing Association to recalibrate the overall distribution of public housing apartments in the

4. Federal law required that all developments built on urban renewal clearance sites (i.e., using federal funds) have a "community sponsor" that would somehow represent the interests of "the community" in the redevelopment process. The success of this provision varied widely, with some sponsors representing well the interests of former residents of the clearance site, and others simply serving as fronts for site developers.

5. Personal communication from Cathy Herman, former Los Sures director of planning and development, June 20, 2006. Along with other information, Herman forwarded personal communications she had received from Douglas Moritz, the administrator of Los Sures from 1976 to 1982, and Wil Vargas, a staff member of the Southside Community Mission at Transfiguration Catholic Church, during the same period. Kent Village members were Monsignor Karvelis, Monsignor Agustín Ruíz, Father Matthew Foley, Reverend John Heinemeier, Rabbi Charnas, Rabbi Templer, Wil Vargas, and Wilbur Curtis.

Southside. The plan called for allocating 75 percent of Clemente Plaza's apartments to Latino and African American families and the remaining 25 percent to white—essentially, Hasidic—families.

Los Sures' standing with the city government as a trusted organizational partner for housing provision smoothed the way for this informal agreement. At the same time, however, Los Sures was pursuing a more contentious strategy that it hoped would effect a more permanent solution to NYCHA's apparent preference for Hasidic tenants over Latino or African American ones in the Southside's public housing. The Williamsburg Fair Housing Committee brought together a group of Puerto Ricans and African Americans from the neighborhood, including several members of Los Sures' staff and board of directors. These residents' incomes made them eligible for public housing, but their applications for apartments in the Southside developments had been denied. Brooklyn Legal Services Corporation A (Brooklyn A) worked with Fair Housing to develop a legal strategy challenging what the activists believed were NYCHA's discriminatory rental practices at the five existing Southside developments. In 1976, as construction began on Clemente, Fair Housing filed suit against NYCHA in federal court. The Southside's United Jewish Organizations (UJO), a by-now predominantly Satmar entity, responded with a countersuit over the informal agreement between Los Sures and city housing officials regarding the plan for tenanting Clemente.

After two years of litigation and negotiation among the various parties, a federal judge approved a consent decree worked out under court mandate between Fair Housing, the UJO, the Williamsburg Housing Association (and, by implication, Los Sures), NYCHA, and the federal Department of Housing and Urban Development (as the principal funder and overseer of all the developments in the urban renewal area). As part of the consent decree, NYCHA admitted to using illegal racial quotas in the renting of the five Southside housing developments it administered. This practice was explicitly underlined in the judge's opinion, as was the reversed ratio planned by the city and WHA/Los Sures for Clemente Plaza:

> Evidence adduced during the December 1976 hearing on the preliminary injunction and admissions by the NYCHA demonstrate that apartments at Jonathan Williams Plaza, Independence Towers and Taylor-Wythe Houses, as well as certain publicly financed apartments at 115–123 Division Avenue and at Bedford Gardens, were designated and rented in a manner calculated to achieve certain racial percentages on each floor of those developments and thus through the developments as a whole. These percentages were

approximately 75% white/25% non-white at Independence Towers, Jonathan Williams Plaza and Bedford Gardens, 90% white/10% non-white at 115–123 Division Avenue and 60% white/40% non-white at Taylor-Wythe Houses. It also appears that the HPD [the city's Department of Housing Preservation and Development] and the Williamsburg Housing Association intended that Clemente Plaza, which was completed only after this action was begun, be rented 25% to white families and 75% to non-white families.[6]

Pursuant to this finding of fact regarding the existence of illegal racial quota policies, the consent decree required NYCHA to adjust the tenant population at each of the six Southside developments, to achieve a more equitable balance between white and nonwhite families, and thenceforth to rent all available apartments on a colorblind basis. Specifically, the decree required NYCHA to decrease the proportion of units occupied by white families to 68 percent at Jonathan Williams, Independence, and Division Avenue and 35 percent at Bedford Gardens, and to maintain white occupancy at no more than 60 percent at Taylor-Wythe. At Clemente Plaza, whose initial renting had been halted by the countersuit filed by the UJO, the consent decree declared that 51 percent of apartments would go to Latino or African American families and 49 percent to white families. This agreement, affirmed by the court in 1978, marked a startling victory for the young Southside Latino organizations. Fair Housing, Brooklyn A, and Los Sures thus firmly established themselves as key organizational players representing the interests of the Southside's poor Latino residents in the broader fields that help determine the realities of everyday life in the neighborhood. The organizations' successful effort to harness the formal power of the courts to redistribute the Southside's public housing would be only the first engagement of this battle between Los Sures and the UJO for influence over the economic and political systems that shaped the availability of affordable housing in the Southside.

The Growth Machine Returns: Los Sures Playing Defense

By 1990, the Southside, along with the rest of New York City, stood poised on the crest of rising economic fortunes. For the first time since 1950, the decennial census recorded a significant increase in the city's population.[7]

6. *Williamsburg Fair Housing Committee v. New York City Housing Authority*, 450 F. Supp. 602 (S.D.N.Y. 1978).

7. One other increase in the city's population did occur during this period, between 1960 and 1970 (from 7.78 million to 7.89 million people), but this was a small change compared

Figure 2. U.S. Secretary of Housing and Urban Development Henry Cisneros visits Los Sures, mid-1990s. From left: unknown, David Pagán (executive director, Los Sures), Sally Hernandez-Piñero (commissioner, New York City Department of Housing Preservation and Development), Cisneros, U.S. Representative Nydia Velasquez, city councilman Victor Robles, Martin Needelman (executive director, Brooklyn Legal Services Corporation A). Photo courtesy of Los Sures.

Crime began a stunning and continuous fifteen-year drop. Average wages climbed, pulled by the expansion of the upper-income population and its swelling take-home pay. Unemployment fell—though partly as the perverse result of growing labor force detachment and a massive jump in the incarceration rate among poor African Americans and Latinos. By this time, Los Sures had become a fixture both in the Southside and in the city's housing policy circles. The organization had planned, financed, built, and rehabilitated over three thousand units of affordable housing, continually developing new ways to provide the Latino residents of its neighborhood with affordable places to live.

As the pool of available city-owned buildings and land shrank with every completed project, however, Los Sures found it harder to put each new one together. In addition, many long-term Latino renters in the

to the growth between 1980 and 1990 (7.07 to 7.32 million people), and then between 1990 and 2000 (7.32 to 8.01 million people).

neighborhood found their homes increasingly coveted both by members of the fast-growing Hasidic population and by property owners looking to cash in on the neighborhood's newfound attractiveness to higher-income housing seekers. Throughout most of the 1990s, Los Sures fought against these new housing pressures by relying on the organizational strategies it had used successfully during the three decades of the growth machine's absence from the Southside. But these approaches proved less and less effective in the face of rapidly changing market conditions in the neighborhood. Rather than continuing to expand the supply of affordable housing available to low-income Latino residents, Los Sures found itself mostly playing defense.

By the time of my fieldwork, which began in 1997, Los Sures was a mature organization with six operational divisions: tenant organizing, property management, planning and development, social services, economic development, and administration. Among these, the organizing unit boasts the most direct link to the group's origins. In its earliest days, even before it was incorporated, Los Sures' work consisted of identifying dilapidated buildings experiencing problems with their landlords, convincing tenants to collaborate in pursuit of better conditions, and then helping the tenants work together to demand or implement changes, including taking over management or ownership of the building themselves. This approach—drawing power from tenant participation, then leveraging it with the organization's skills and professional relationships—remains at the heart of the organizers' work. Each Monday morning, Barbara Schliff, director of the organizing unit, gathers her staff together to review the upcoming week's schedule, as described in the following excerpt from my field notes:

> Barbara tells Jerry, Lydia, and Rosa that we'll have the meeting now, even though Marilyn and Debbie aren't back yet [from housing court]. We all go into Barbara's office and sit at the big table. She asks for everyone's [tenant] meetings. Rosa has 265 South 2nd Street (35 units), where there's a rent strike, and they're going to do a walk-through with Brooklyn Legal Services to see if the repairs have been done. She also has 364 South 1st Street (30 units), where there's also a rent strike, and the landlord is supposed to be doing repairs. Lydia has 341 South 5th Street and 454 Bedford Avenue, where inspections have been done, they've gone to court, and the landlord has been ordered to make repairs. Jerry has 330 Rodney Street (4 units), which has very bad conditions and a very bad landlord, and where Los Sures has had a lot of problems organizing the tenants; even with bad conditions, the rent is

very high [by Los Sures' standards]—$650 to $700 for an apartment—since there are no rent regulations. He's trying again to organize a rent strike. Jerry also has 210 Roebling Street (35 units), a 7A building, where Los Sures is in more of a management role. There, Jerry will mostly be collecting rents and seeing if there are any complaints. Barbara has 104 Division Avenue, an HDFC [Housing Development Fund Corporation, a low-income tenant cooperative], where the two Hasidic tenants who bought out previous tenants have now finally moved in. . . . Barbara takes people's days for "intake," that is, the day they will sit at the front of the office and deal with whoever comes through the door looking for help. Today is Lydia; Jerry takes Friday; Rosa takes Wednesday. Barbara writes them on the calendar, says she'll get Debbie and Marilyn to do Tuesday and Thursday. The rest of the meeting is about when people will take comp [compensatory] time; Barbara has told me that the organizers work odd hours and often in the evenings, so in order to keep their schedules at about 40 hours a week, they take comp time. Everyone arranges for their days off: Lydia on Wednesday—her husband has off that day, *"y tengo que aprovechar"* ["and I have to take advantage of that"], she says—Rosa on Friday. Everyone's schedule is complex, with [housing] court dates, tenant meetings, days off, etc., but it is all worked out.[8]

Although the organizers' strategy of working with tenants remains the same as in its early years, the parameters within which Los Sures fights for decent, affordable housing for low-income Latinos have shifted significantly. In the 1970s, Los Sures' primary foes were the private landlords who had turned their backs on the Southside. By 1990, however, the organization faced very different conditions. The Hasidic community's extremely high birth rate (the Satmar average ten children per family) has led to a doubling of their population every ten years, creating enormous pressure for additional housing in the Southside. What during the 1980s had been a trickle of artists filtering into the neighborhood's abandoned industrial lofts had now become a flood. And as the twentieth century entered its last decade, young college graduates who could no longer afford skyrocketing Manhattan real estate costs started discovering the neighborhood, just one subway stop across the East River. These ambassadors of gentrification made all of Williamsburg a new target for the growth machine, nearly fifty years after it began its suburban dalliance. At Los Sures, the defensive struggle had begun.

8. Author's field notes, July 7, 1997.

In the Trenches with the Organizers of Los Sures

Despite the mounting pressures on the Latino residents of the Southside, in the late 1990s gentrification posed less of an immediate threat than did the Hasidim. Gentrification was concentrated in Williamsburg's Northside, along the subway route that runs across Fourteenth Street in Manhattan, through the trendy East Village, and then under the East River to Williamsburg. Pressure from the Hasidim, however, was insistent and immediate, particularly for the numerous Latino residents scattered throughout the majority-Hasidic section of the Southside. Hasidic housing seekers employed a variety of techniques to gain control over additional housing units in the neighborhood, and organizers at Los Sures found it intolerable that all the work the organization had done over the years to improve and expand affordable housing for local Latinos should be rolled back by Hasidic expansionism. Much of the organizers' time was spent helping Latino tenants resist Hasidic efforts to displace them.

One type of housing developed by Los Sures had proved particularly attractive to the Hasidim: the low-income tenant cooperative, better known by its official name, the Housing Development Fund Corporation, or HDFC. The HDFC housing form was created in 1966 through an amendment to the New York State Private Housing Finance Law (article XI, sections 570–82). As part of the wider effort during this period to find ways to create both affordable housing and new property tax revenues, the HDFC legislation offered a new method of moving abandoned, tax-delinquent properties acquired by the city back into private ownership. Most buildings that became HDFCs were located in poor, crime-ridden neighborhoods, where finding regular buyers usually proved impossible. Los Sures and other neighborhood housing organizations suggested another option: let the tenants of the buildings themselves become owners. Numerous abandoned properties in poor neighborhoods like the Southside became HDFCs some years after being seized by the city. In each case, a community-based housing organization helped tenants conduct moderate rehabilitation and form a tenants' association, and the city then sold the building to the tenant association for a nominal fee (Leavitt and Saegert 1990). Working with tenants throughout the 1970s and 1980s, Los Sures created thirty-eight HDFCs in the Southside. In the late 1990s, these buildings housed approximately a thousand residents—mostly Latinos—in some three hundred apartments.

As in any co-op, residents of HDFCs own shares in the buildings that contain their apartments and pay monthly maintenance fees to the co-op's management association (as opposed to paying rent to a landlord). When the city sold an in-rem property to a newly founded HDFC, the terms of sale prohibited resale of the shares for at least ten years. HDFC bylaws spelled out this condition, along with a restriction on the income of any person looking to buy shares in the co-op. The original share price in most of the Los Sures HDFCs was extremely low: usually $250 per apartment.[9] Monthly maintenance fees also were and continue to be very low: in 1997 the average monthly maintenance for a two-bedroom apartment was about $250. Thus, HDFCs offer one of the few truly low-cost housing options in New York City. Similar apartments in rent-controlled buildings in the Southside now easily rent for $700 per month; on the open market, they usually go for twice that. Even with such low maintenance fees, however, the HDFCs in the Southside consistently met their tax obligations to the city. This feat owed in part to the significant work that Los Sures organizers put into the regular operations of the HDFCs they worked with; indeed, many HDFCs in other New York neighborhoods faced major tax arrears and were in danger of going into receivership once again (Leavitt and Saegert 1990).

Due to the work of Los Sures and other neighborhood housing organizations in negotiating HDFC regulations with policy makers, coaxing funds out of the city budget to support HDFC rehabilitation, organizing tenants to purchase their buildings, and helping shareholders manage their properties, the mostly Latino residents of HDFCs in the Southside reaped substantial benefits. Not only do their apartments provide long-term, affordable housing in well-maintained buildings, but the HDFC arrangement generates significant housing equity for shareholders. Hasidic housing seekers frequently approached Latino HDFC residents, seeking to purchase their apartments. The staff at Los Sures reported that these buyout offers were tempting for older residents who wanted to retire, and a few had sold their apartments to Hasidic buyers. The going rate in 1997 was about twenty thousand dollars, a small sum in the the Southside housing market even then, but a substantial nest egg for a low-income couple seeking a retirement home in Puerto Rico or the Dominican Republic. At the time of my fieldwork, Los Sures was becoming increasingly concerned about HDFC buyouts, which threatened to put truly low-cost housing out of the reach of Latino residents. Hasidic buyers were particularly suspect at Los Sures because staff there believed they undermined the collective, democratic

---

9. The $250 share price was set by the city's housing department in consultation with the city welfare agency. Many potential HDFC shareholders were receiving public assistance, and a one-time, lump-sum payment for the HDFC share proved a cost-effective way for the welfare agency to secure permanent, low-cost housing for its clients.

governance of the low-income cooperative and were interested in taking over the entire building for Hasidic families.[10] Los Sures decided to seek funding for a project to work with the HDFCs to prevent such sales. By establishing uniform procedures and reasonable maximum prices for the sale of HDFC units, Los Sures hoped to preserve the HDFCs for low-income Latinos.[11]

Another common problem faced by low-income Latino tenants in the Southside involved illegal harassment by landlords who hoped to get current tenants to vacate their apartments. This technique has a long history in New York City real estate and in the Southside has been used not only by Hasidic property owners who prefer to rent to Hasidic tenants, but also by non-Hasidic landlords hoping to replace low-income Latinos with higher-income young professionals. After displacing longtime tenants in rent-controlled buildings, these landlords can renovate their apartments, claim release from rent-control regulations, and charge whatever rent the newly hot market will bear.[12] The organizers at Los Sures worked with tenants in buildings throughout the Southside who had complained of harassment by both types of landlords.

To help low-income Latino tenants resist and put a stop to landlord harassment, the Los Sures organizers relied on New York City's extensive system of housing, building, fire, and health code regulations. The Municipal Housing Code specifies minimum standards for health, safety, fire protection, light, ventilation, cleanliness, repair, maintenance, and occupancy in all of the city's residential dwellings. In addition, the buildings, fire, and health departments regulate a range of safety and health conditions in residences. During my fieldwork, I heard many, many stories of tenant harassment from the Los Sures organizers. One day, for example, I was walking through the neighborhood with Lydia Bonilla, an Americorps vol-

10. Author's field notes, May 30, 1997.

11. As part of my volunteer work at Los Sures, I helped to write a grant proposal for this project to the New York Foundation. The proposal was successful, securing a grant of $35,000 for the project. Using these funds, the organization developed and began implementing the new policy.

12. New York City's rent control and rent stabilization laws, administered by the New York State Department of Housing and Community Renewal, dictate strict procedures by which building owners may set and raise rent levels in their apartments. Rents may be raised much more quickly if an apartment is vacated and rented to a new tenant (under a "vacancy lease") than if a tenant or immediate family member remains in constant tenancy. The goal of most building owners is to raise the rent as quickly as possible to $2,000 per month, the threshold at which an apartment is eligible to be removed permanently from rent control or rent stabilization. This removal process, called "vacancy decontrol," also requires that the current tenant vacate the apartment and that the newly unregulated apartment be rented to a new tenant. Thus, building owners have multiple incentives to remove current tenants from rent-controlled and rent-stabilized apartments.

unteer working with the Los Sures organizing unit. Pointing to a two-story brownstone house with an odd, one-story gray concrete extension that jutted above the rest of the buildings on the block, Lydia said it had been her first building when she started at Los Sures. An elderly Latina woman was living on the second floor, and the owner, a Hasid, was pressuring her to move out. When she refused, he illegally started building the extension directly above her apartment. The woman's ceiling cracked, allowing water to pour in when it rained, and the daily construction made so much noise she could barely stand to be at home. Lydia worked with the woman for about a month, stopping the work several times by finding absent permits, permit violations, noise violations, and so on, but after a while the woman couldn't take it any more, and moved out.[13]

The Los Sures organizers feared that ongoing Hasidic displacement of Latinos from the neighborhood would bring about the destruction of their community. They also felt that their particular, close knowledge of the neighborhood's rapidly changing housing supply gave them a rare, accurate, timely understanding of the challenges the Hasidim posed to the Southside and its Latino residents. Early in the fieldwork period, as I spoke with Barbara Schliff about the work of Los Sures, she raised the specter of displacement, acknowledging that her analysis of the situation might sound alarmist to an outsider: "You probably think I'm paranoid," she said to me, "but this really is a big issue, and it's happening. There is harassment [of Latino tenants] all the time, and we [the Los Sures organizers] spend so much of our time running around trying to stop it."[14]

Barbara was not alone among the staff at Los Sures in attributing many of the Latinos' housing difficulties to the Hasidim. On one of my regular volunteer visits I chatted, as I often did, with organizer Debbie Medina. That day she was mulling over what to advise tenants in one of her buildings, which had been destabilized by the recent demolition of a Hasidic-owned one-story garage with which it shared a wall. The damage put 100 South Eighth Street at risk for a city-ordered evacuation. Based on her many years' experience battling harassment, housing code violations, and illegal construction by the Hasidim, Debbie had reservations about following Los Sures' standard procedure to salvage the building. Although Barbara, her supervisor, was encouraging her to work with the city to vacate the building, get it repaired, and then reinstate the tenants, Debbie worried that as soon as the tenants moved out, the building's owner would find some way to get

13. Author's field notes, May 19, 1998.
14. Author's field notes, May 30, 1997.

the city to condemn it. If that happened, the Latino tenants would lose their homes with no compensation, and the lot could be rebuilt as a new development for Hasidim. Debbie was seriously considering advising the Latino tenants to stay in the building until the owner offered to buy them out—that way, she said, "at least they'll get some good money for their troubles."[15]

The hostility among the Los Sures organizers toward the Hasidim, while fortified on a near-daily basis by their experiences protecting Latino tenants from harassment, ultimately is rooted in the 1978 consent decree regarding public housing allocation in the Southside. In that ruling, the federal courts had made official what Los Sures staff and other members of the Williamsburg Fair Housing Committee had charged for years: that the Hasidim, with the active assistance or benign neglect of government housing agencies, were gaining unfair, illegal advantage in the competition for affordable housing in the neighborhood. Having established this fact with regard to public housing, it was but a small step for the Los Sures organizers to see the same process at work in the Hasidim's overall orientation to their housing and community needs.

Indeed, this belief had been reinforced repeatedly by revelations about the Hasidic community's abuse of public funds and systems. In 1986, for example, the Beth Rachel School for Girls, a Hasidic yeshiva and the largest religious girls' school in the world, began sending four hundred students to receive federally funded remedial classes inside the Southside's Public School 16. While parochial school students are entitled to these services, the yeshiva went one step further: it arranged for the girls to receive their classes in a segregated setting, in nine classrooms located behind a specially constructed partition that separated them from the school's own 150 students (most of them Latino) in remedial classes (*New York Times* 1986; Perlez 1986). Although a federal judge initially upheld the arrangement, an appeals court struck down that ruling, declaring the partition unconstitutional.[16] Thirteen years later, the principal of the same Hasidic yeshiva pled

15. Author's field notes, August 4, 1997.

16. The P.S. 16 incident turned out to be the precursor to a much larger effort by the Satmar Hasidim to establish a segregated public school setting for their special needs children. A long-running court case concerns the Satmar Hasidic village of Kiryas Joel, located about fifty miles north of Williamsburg, where the Satmar established a settlement in the early 1970s (Knight 1974). With the state government's assistance, the Satmar secured their own public school district, with boundaries exactly contiguous with the village's, where 99% of the residents are Satmar. The district is eligible for federal and state education funding, including supplementary Title I funds for low-income students, and funding for special needs students. The constitutionality of the school district has been challenged in federal court repeatedly, and the case has been heard once at the Supreme Court, and denied a second hearing there.

guilty to fraud for partnering with the local school district in a nearly twenty-year corruption scheme: the school district had provided no-show parapro-fessional jobs to Hasidic women, who kept the health insurance and other benefits for themselves but turned over their Board of Education paychecks to the yeshiva principal, who used the funds to run his school. A total of $4.3 million in salaries and $1.9 million in benefits had been stolen from city and state coffers.[17] The Southside's Hasidim also have been dogged by charges of welfare fraud, as in 1996, when an investigation by the New York *Daily News* charged that "dozens" of Hasidic tenants in three of the South-side's public housing developments held substantial financial resources that, had they been disclosed, would have disqualified them from public housing eligibility (G. B. Smith 1996). Occasionally, allegations like these have been borne out in evictions from public housing or demands to pay restitution to the government for improperly obtained welfare payments. More often, however, nothing seems to happen, an outcome that only fu-els the sense among neighborhood Latinos, including the organizers at Los Sures, that the Hasidim receive preferential treatment from many quarters.

The Growth Machine Returns:
The United Jewish Organizations Goes On Offense

Throughout most of the 1990s, as the Hasidim aggressively sought addi-tional housing for their fast-growing population, they largely confined their efforts to their traditional area of settlement in the Southside, south of the aptly named Division Avenue. By the late 1990s, however, the pressure of a population that was doubling in size every ten years could no longer be confined by this boundary. Conditions in the Southside housing market had also changed, and the United Jewish Organizations (UJO) had begun moving to recalibrate the informal agreements that had long structured the

---

Each declaration of the district's unconstitutional status has been answered by New York State with the passage of special legislation designed to sidestep the particulars of each court ruling (Berger 1995, 1996, 1998, 1999; Dao 1994; Foderaro 1999; Greenhouse 1994; Hernandez 1997; Kolbert 1989, 1990; Lyall 1992; *New York Times* 1997).

17. Steinberg 1999. In 1999, Rabbi Hertz Frankel pleaded guilty to federal charges of con-spiracy and received a sentence of three years' probation and a one-million-dollar restitution fee. Employees of School District 14 were also charged with crimes; three eventually pled guilty to embezzlement charges, while the other died in the midst of plea negotiations. By the time of the indictment, William Rogers, the superintendent who had presided over the scheme for eighteen of its twenty years, was deceased, as was his successor, Mario DeStefano, who had continued the illegal activities during his first two years as District 14 superintendent.

Hasidic-Latino housing battle. This came as a shock to the organizers at Los Sures, who had viewed the borders of their organization's city-sanctioned, traditional service area as inviolate. To meet the UJO challenge, Los Sures turned away from its standard housing defense procedures—which relied on the power of bureaucratic regulations—and took its battle to the court of public opinion and politics.

During my first week in the field, most everyone I met talked about a large demonstration that had been held by the Latinos of the Southside about a week earlier. Activists with the newly resurgent Fair Housing Committee, aided by staff at Los Sures and Brooklyn Legal Services Corporation A, had organized the march in response to new demands by the Hasidim for greater control over the future of housing development and occupancy in the neighborhood. According to my field notes, Barbara Schliff, head of the organizing unit at Los Sures and an active member of Fair Housing, told me that the UJO had recently sent a letter to Mayor Rudolph Giuliani, demanding that it share control with Los Sures over any new housing development in the Southside, including units being built in the areas traditionally controlled by Los Sures.[18] A few days earlier, when I had interviewed David Pagán, the administrator of Los Sures, I recorded in my field notes that he too had mentioned this letter, which was written on UJO stationery and signed by that organization's executive director, Rabbi David Niederman. Copies of the letter were sent to a number of local elected officials and city agency directors (a Los Sures staff member gave me a copy). The letter states in part:

> The following recommendations were finalized at a UJO leadership meeting after the briefing [by former Deputy Mayor Fran Reiter on the progress of the Williamsburg Housing Task Force]. . . .
>
> 2. B. UJO should be a participant all [sic] housing efforts in Williamsburg, including in the Southside Urban Renewal Area. This should include participating in discussions on apartment sizes and design, as well as active participation in marketing. . . .
>
> 2. C. The first $3,500,000 of the Cross Subsidy fund [city funds collected through the sale of vacant land in Williamsburg and designated for subsequent low-income housing development in the area] was allocated to Los Sures. Seventy five percent of the remaining funds should be allocated to the UJO, and the rest to Los Sures.

18. Author's field notes, May 27, 1997.

2. D. HPD [the city's Department of Housing Preservation and Development] should now move immediately to begin design and construction for Partnership Housing in the Broadway Triangle [an area of Williamsburg that lies within the traditional service area of Los Sures], identifying UJO as co-developer. . . .

4. The Mayor's office should identify funding the UJO could be eligible for, to form a working, professional staff, to develop housing, and a plan for community development within the South Williamsburg community [a moniker recently appended to the Hasidic section of Williamsburg, previously referred to as the Southside]. I estimate that approximately $350,000 annually would be required to undertake this effort.

Each of the cited provisions of the letter refers to some aspect of the long history of politically parceling out the Southside's city-owned land and publicly subsidized housing among Latino and Hasidic organizations. Over the years, efforts to control the distribution of housing in the neighborhood had been shepherded, contested, and mediated by myriad government agencies and by Los Sures, the Fair Housing Committee, the UJO, the federal courts, and a succession of mayors, among others. Along the way, certain tacit agreements had been established alongside the formal regulation of other concerns. The letter from UJO challenged many of these informal understandings, making what Fair Housing, Los Sures, and many Latino residents believed to be unfounded claims on housing resources that they thought rightfully belonged to neighborhood Latinos. Members of Fair Housing, recently embroiled in a new battle with NYCHA over the allegedly discriminatory allocation of public housing units in favor of the Hasidim, read the UJO's demands as yet another volley aimed at Latino claims on affordable housing in the Southside. They decided to respond with a strategy that had served them well at several key moments in the past: a public protest. With a march through the streets of the Southside, Fair Housing hoped to demonstrate that the Hasidim were not the only group in the neighborhood with the political muscle to make demands on the mayor's office.

Staff at Los Sures estimated that the march, held on May 14, 1997, drew nearly a thousand participants. While I could not confirm this figure, the New York *Daily News* did find the event important enough to cover in the next morning's paper (Gonzalez 1997). Two participants in the march described it to me on separate occasions within two weeks of its occurrence. I recorded both their accounts in my field notes:

Debbie [Medina, a Los Sures organizer] says she wishes I had been there to see the march, that it was a really powerful show of strength from the [Latino] community. Marilyn [Rivera] and Lydia [Bonilla, both of Los Sures] agree. Debbie says it's really important to do things like the march, to bring out the people and let the Hasids and the city see that they [Latinos] need to be taken seriously. It did get a little scary for a minute there, when the Hasids blocked the street, but everyone held it together and they ended up taking another route. Which she doesn't think they should have had to do, since they had told the police [before the march] what the route would be.[19]

John [Mulhern, of Nuestros Niños child care center,] says that the march was heading toward the schoolyard at P.S. 16, which takes up a whole block and can be approached from either of two routes. One street was blocked by a Hasidic bus, because it was the street where the Satmar rebbe lives, but the marchers only knew that the street was blocked, and didn't like that, since they had approved that route with the police. John says that it would be a big insult to march past the rebbe's house, and that he thinks the marchers didn't know that, or maybe didn't even know that the rebbe lived there. A large group of Hasidim had gathered near the bus, and as the marchers tried to go down the street, there was the beginning of an ugly confrontation. Fortunately, the two sides and the police got things under control fairly quickly, and the marchers ended up taking the other route to the schoolyard.[20]

Fair Housing certainly would not have been pleased if the march had degenerated into violence. The high tension the march spawned, however, drew the ever-roaming gaze of city officials to the Southside. Given that New York City neighborhoods must continually compete for the limited attention of city officials, the anxiety produced by the march gave Fair Housing and the Latinos of the Southside an opportunity to try to capitalize on their political momentum in a mayoral election year.

City officials' concern with the increasingly visible tensions between Latinos and Hasidim in the Southside expressed itself in the local police precinct's greater attention to Fair Housing's activities in the period immediately following the march. At a Fair Housing meeting I attended about two weeks after the march, members seemed pleased that their work was garnering this notice. Carmen Calderón, a Fair Housing leader, reported that Inspector Díaz

19. Author's field notes, May 29, 1997.
20. Author's field notes, May 30, 1997.

of the Ninetieth Precinct in the Southside had contacted her earlier that day, wanting to know if Fair Housing was planning a demonstration or act of civil disobedience on June 4. Alice Silva, a Fair Housing leader and a member of the Los Sures board of directors, chimed in that she had received the same call. Both women reported to the meeting that they had sarcastically told the inspector that they did not know why he was calling them, since he had previously painted them as rabble-rousers with no real leadership role in the neighborhood. After some discussion, the group decided they would neither confirm nor deny that Fair Housing was in fact planning an event for June 4, thereby leaving the police to grapple with uncertainty.[21]

During the rest of this meeting the members fleshed out an idea for the June 4 event: a community forum to which they planned to invite Mayor Rudolph Giuliani. Anticipating that the mayor would decline their invitation, the group planned a skit in which a stand-in for the mayor would stand mute as Fair Housing members peppered him with questions about his plans to address the housing and other needs of Latinos in the Southside. The stand-in's silence, in their vision, would represent Giuliani's failure to respond to Latino concerns—not only the housing questions raised by the UJO letter, but also questions related to education, environmental justice, police-community relations, and so on.[22]

On June 4, about an hour before the community forum was scheduled to begin, I joined members of Fair Housing outside Transfiguration Catholic Church, the site of the event. It was clear that the group's activities were still being closely monitored by city officials, because a major police presence was massing on the blocks surrounding the church. This was much to the surprise and delight of Fair Housing members, as I recorded in my field notes:

Carmen [Calderón] is standing with me and her sister, and says that she was told that 176 officers are on alert tonight for this meeting, with orders to arrest people if they step out onto the street to march. She says this with a smile, showing both incredulity at the size of the police response and a kind of pride that Fair Housing is generating this hubbub. . . . A van pulls up, carrying the sound system for the meeting. The driver of the van, a Latino man in his 40s, gets out and says, "Yo, they've got about a million cops waiting on the corner over there. I've never seen so many cops in my life!" . . . Two vans carrying about ten officers each pass by the front of church. A car with high-level cops in it goes by. Then a car with two detectives, and another car with more

21. Author's field notes, May 29, 1997.
22. Author's field notes, May 29, 1997.

high-level cops, including a man someone identifies to me as Inspector Díaz. Next are two community affairs officers, both Black or Latino, wearing light blue windbreakers with what appear to be bullet-proof vests under them. There is, again, amazement and pride [among the members of Fair Housing] at the police turnout. . . . Police officers begin deploying along the street in front of the school. They line up on both sides of the street, on the street side of the cars parked at the curb, one cop at every two-car interval, all the way down the block. More Hasidim are gathering in the streets, and more people are arriving for the meeting. It begins to look and feel something like a war zone. . . . Barbara [Schliff, of Los Sures and Fair Housing] observes, "Well, at least we're costing the city some money tonight."[23]

Despite the large police response, turnout for the mock forum was decidedly lower than at the march. Still, some 350 people packed the auditorium at Transfiguration. After some introductory remarks by Sammy Flores, a Fair Housing member, and two local religious leaders, Sammy called for the Giuliani skit to begin. Marilyn Rivera, an organizer at Los Sures, played the role of the mayor. Wearing over her head a paper bag with pictures of Giuliani's face stapled to it on three sides, she sat in a chair on the auditorium's stage while Sammy and Chris, two members of Fair Housing, asked a planned series of questions:

"Mr. Mayor, have you visited Williamsburg to speak with the Latino community?" "Giuliani" shakes his finger sideways, indicating "no." The crowd boos. "Mr. Mayor, have you met with representatives of the Latino community?" Again, "Giuliani" indicates "no." More boos. Sammy asks several more questions in this vein; there is the same response from "Giuliani," and the same boos—though getting softer—from the crowd. Chris takes over at the podium. "Mr. Mayor, are you planning to privatize our public hospitals?" "Giuliani" indicates "no," which is not the answer called for in the script. Marilyn is showing some confusion about what she's supposed to be doing. Chris asks, "Mr. Mayor, are you planning to displace Latinos and Blacks from public housing?" There is a pause, and "Giuliani" indicates "no." Again, this is the wrong answer. The crowd has gotten fairly silent. The skit is foundering. Nevertheless, Chris keeps asking questions. Finally, the skit ends. Some people have been leaving during it, slowly. Debbie [Medina] takes the microphone and says the people of Los Sures need to show the mayor that they count, and they should do so not by rioting, like the police seem to think they're

23. Author's field notes, June 4, 1997.

going to do, but "the right way": by registering to vote, signing petitions for other candidates, and voting in elections. She repeats this in Spanish.[24]

The members of Fair Housing hoped their skit would place the immediate issue of the Hasidic play for greater influence over the disposition of city housing development resources into what they saw as its broader context: the mayor's general dismissal of the needs of the Southside's Latino community in favor of attention to Hasidic interests. Although city officials clearly feared that Latino anger over the UJO letter might boil over into a street conflagration, Fair Housing and Los Sures sought only to channel Latino dissatisfaction into political expression. As a strategy for addressing the rapidly changing housing situation in Los Sures, however, replacing the mayor was a long-term and uncertain approach. Even if Giuliani lost his reelection bid, there was no guarantee that his successor would act any differently. With this calculus in mind, other key actors in the Southside were developing a very different analysis of the Latino-Hasidic conflict and moving to seek a more secure resolution to the housing crisis in the Southside than the one pursued by Fair Housing.

A Political Solution? The Memorandum of Understanding

For many years, the conditions of the Southside housing market had allowed Los Sures to develop affordable housing one project at a time. In the 1970s, there were so many abandoned buildings and city-owned vacant lots in the Southside that the organization could pick and choose among them, partnering with city government, banks, and construction companies to acquire sites, package financing, stipulate building specifications, secure the necessary permissions, and contract with a builder. Even in the 1980s, as the ongoing rebuilding of the neighborhood meant fewer spaces for redevelopment, Los Sures continued to focus, at any given time, on only a few discrete projects—one in construction, one or two in development, some initial ideas about where the next would be. By the end of the 1990s, however, the Hasidic housing scramble and the accelerating interest of the growth machine in Williamsburg demanded a more sweeping vision.

The Los Sures organizers now had their hands full running from building to building to help scattered groups of tenants in dire need of their knowledge, skills, and connections to the housing bureaucracy to stop

24. Author's field notes, June 4, 1997.

harassment and attempts at eviction. The organization's housing development team was likewise struggling to complete its latest projects in a context of sharply rising costs and cuts to government housing funds. As part of the Fair Housing Committee, staff members at Los Sures understood the importance of developing a broader strategy to address the housing crisis, but their commitment to communitarian practices of decision making meant this effort would take time—another commodity in short supply among the Latinos of the Southside.

Even as Fair Housing was carrying out its protest and political organizing activities in the late 1990s, three of the Southside's local elected officials were quietly working with the mayor's office on a large-scale housing and redevelopment agreement that purported to address the interests of both Latino and Hasidic residents. Just four days after Fair Housing's community forum, at which Mayor Giuliani had been lampooned for neglecting the Latinos of the Southside, a small item ran on a back page in the *New York Times*:

> In an effort to help reduce both an acute housing shortage and long-running tensions between Hispanic and Hasidic residents of Williamsburg, Brooklyn, the Giuliani administration has approved a $25 million plan to generate scores of new housing units in the area. (J. Sexton 1997)

The article reported that the Giuliani plan would provide funds for Los Sures to build eighty-two two-family houses "in the Hispanic part of the neighborhood." The Hasidic community would, at the same time, benefit from zoning changes in the area adjacent to the traditional southern boundary of its settlement, which would allow the conversion of numerous old industrial buildings into residential condominiums. In addition, the plan called for the construction of a new child care center in the Southside, to be run by a local Latino CBO much beloved in the neighborhood. The impetus for the plan, the article stated, was to "seek to end a stalemate on the future of housing in the overcrowded, often emotionally volatile neighborhood." As the article's author noted, however, the plan was hardly made without an eye to its political ramifications: "It also has political benefits for the Mayor in an election year, perhaps enhancing his efforts to win support from Hispanic voters and solidifying his standing among the politically potent Hasidim" (J. Sexton 1997).

Although the *Times* reported on the plan in early June, there seemed to be little immediate awareness of it at the Latino-serving organizations in the

Southside. When I arrived at Los Sures on the day following the article's publication, I asked Cathy Herman and Barbara Schliff what they knew about the plan, but they had not heard about it.[25] When I reported that Los Sures had been designated as the sole developer of eighty-two two-family houses slated for the Southside urban renewal area, Cathy and Barbara seemed satisfied. Over the summer, however, discontent began brewing at Los Sures and among members of the Fair Housing Committee. Although both groups felt vindicated that Los Sures had won the fight for development rights in one of the few remaining parcels in the Southside urban renewal area, they voiced concern that the eighty-three houses they would develop there (the *Times* article was off by one) would make only a small dent in the housing needs of the neighborhood's Latinos. They feared that the Latino community was being bought off relatively cheaply; the Hasidim, it seemed, stood to gain much more from the deal. Debbie Medina, an organizer at Los Sures and an active member of Fair Housing, referred to the eighty-three houses as "crumbs from the mayor."[26] Indeed, although the plan would enable Los Sures to produce 166 units of subsidized housing, the *Times* article reported that the agreement's rezoning provisions would allow the Hasidim to "develop as many as 1,600 market-rate condominiums" (J. Sexton 1997).

On September 15, 1997, three months after the initial *Times* article appeared, the mayor's office made a splashy public announcement of the plan. It was now referred to as a Memorandum of Understanding (MOU) between the Latino and Hasidic communities on the future of housing development in the Southside. A press release from the mayor's office stated, in part:

> Mayor Rudolph W. Giuliani today joined with [state] Assemblyman Vito J. Lopez and [city] Councilmen Victor L. Robles and Kenneth K. Fisher [all of whom represented parts of Williamsburg] to sign an historic housing agreement for Williamsburg, Brooklyn that ends a decades-old impasse between Jewish and Latino communities in that area. . . . A letter of agreement, signed by the Mayor and three lawmakers, will allow the City to move forward with a plan to create new low-income and market rate housing and a new day care facility. It will also provide funding for land-use and environmental studies which will pave the way for future housing and economic development in the area.[27]

25. Author's field notes, June 9, 1997.
26. Author's field notes, July 16, 1997.
27. Press release announcing memorandum of understanding; document in author's possession.

The press release went on to summarize four "major components" of the plan. Two were aimed explicitly at the low-income Latino constituents of Los Sures and Fair Housing: the subsidized development—by Los Sures—of eighty-three two-family houses for moderate-income families, and the construction of a new day care center for children of low-income families, to be located in the heart of the Southside. A third component of the plan dealt with the rezoning of several different areas of the Southside, for the purpose of "produc[ing] several hundred units of market rate housing over the next five years and hundreds more over the next 15–20 years." Although the areas to be rezoned were not specified in the press release, the full text of the MOU—which I obtained from a staff member in one of the study organizations—gives general boundaries: the Broadway Triangle (MOU provision 4), South Williamsburg (provision 8), Flushing Avenue and the area surrounding the Williamsburg Bridge (provision 9), and a vacant industrial area west of Kent Avenue (provision 10).[28] Although the Flushing Avenue site lies outside the traditional boundaries of the Southside, the other four targeted sites have been hotly contested by Latinos and Hasidim for many years.

With the announcement of the MOU, Los Sures and the Fair Housing Committee found themselves effectively outflanked by a set of actors with better access to the mayor's office, a key site of land-use decision making. Los Sures and Fair Housing had hoped to postpone important decisions on housing issues in the Southside until after the upcoming mayoral election by using the techniques of ad hoc protest and electoral mobilization, with the ultimate goal of unseating the incumbent mayor—and hoping for different treatment from the next one. In contrast, the Southside's local elected officials—Assemblyman Lopez and Councilman Robles on behalf of the Latinos, Councilman Fisher for the Hasidim—had hammered out a plan that relied on the insider politics of preelection horse-trading. The mayor himself hoped to come out with a compromise he could sell to voters from both groups; as he described the agreement, "nobody gets exactly everything that they want or as much as they want. But everybody is being treated fairly and equitably" (Shin 1997).

Over the next several months, Los Sures, Fair Housing, and several other Southside Latino organizations would strongly dispute this characterization, embarking on a protracted fight over the rezoning provisions of the MOU. The stakes of this battle were particularly high for Los Sures. As the organization summed up its own situation in a commemorative report marking its twenty-fifth anniversary:

28. Memorandum of understanding; document in author's possession.

Los Sures anticipates tremendous changes in the Williamsburg area in the next decades. The waning of the older industrial businesses, the possible incursion of market rate housing in the Southside, combined with budget cuts in rent subsidy programs and the continued assault on tenant protections *threatens to transform our community into one that the current Latino residents may neither recognize or be able to live in.* Consistent with our mission, Los Sures will continue to fight for the right to be an active participant in the shaping of the future of the Southside (Southside United Housing Development Fund Corporation 1997; emphasis added)

The MOU marked a key turning point in the social and economic organization of the Williamsburg landscape. While many Southside Latinos read the MOU as simply another attempt to divide up the Southside between Latinos and Hasidim, in fact the agreement heralded the receding significance of the sparring between these two groups in shaping the future of all of Williamsburg. The duel between the Latino and Hasidic organizations had taken center stage during New York City's lean years, when Williamsburg had no place on the agenda of the growth machine. In the throes of the city's economic transformation, Williamsburg had nothing to offer growth entrepreneurs. Both Williamsburg's residents and the city's economic elites watched helplessly as the area's once-surging manufacturing base shrunk to a shadow of its former self and residents' exodus to the suburbs picked up speed. The pitched Latino-Hasidic battle in effect amounted to a desperate struggle over the relatively slim pickings that the growth machine left behind; the two groups' ability to make much from little is a testament to the ingenuity of their organizations and their people. During the 1990s, however, the interests of capital returned to Williamsburg. The MOU, signed in 1997, proved to be the first critical step in the growth machine's ultimately successful effort to reshape Williamsburg in its own image.

Handmaiden of the Growth Machine: Land-Use Regulations in Williamsburg

Zoning regulations are among the most important factors governing land use and development in urban and suburban areas. These regulations determine what kinds of usages and buildings are permitted in a particular geographic area, which may stretch over many miles or be confined to one lot on a city block. Three main usages exist in New York City's current Zoning Resolution, which dates to 1961: residential, commercial, and industrial. Within each of these categories, subcategories correspond to specific types of usage (for example, single-family homes versus large apartment houses in a residential district) and regulate such characteristics as the height of buildings, the density of occupancy on a site, and the amount of parking required. Zoning regulations aim to keep noncompatible land uses separated, to protect open space, and generally to control the pattern of development within the city. Zoning law has been used, for example, to prevent the location of a pollution-producing factory close to a concentrated residential area, to require that buildings be set back a certain distance from the street, and to mandate that a high-rise apartment building provide adjacent outdoor space for its occupants' use.

As a mixed-use neighborhood, Williamsburg long contained a range of zoning, including pure residential, pure industrial, and variously mixed residential-industrial-commercial areas. In many of the neighborhood's industrial zones, however, factories had closed down over the years, casualties of the transformation of the New York City economy away from manufacturing. The Hasidim had been pushing the city to rezone some of these areas for residential—or mixed residential, commercial, and community—use. With UJO's encouragement, owners of some of the industrial-zoned lots in the Hasidic section of the Southside also began to seek permission to convert them to residential use, and by the late 1990s, Los Sures and the UJO were battling over zoning.

In New York City, there are two ways to change the allowable land use, building height, or building density designated for a particular lot: a one-time zoning variance, or a permanent change to the city's Zoning Resolution. A variance is by far the easier option, as it requires a minimal bureaucratic process: application to the local Community Board (an appointed body of up to fifty nonsalaried members charged by the city government with overseeing activities within one of New York City's fifty-nine Community Districts), and approval by the city's obscure, five-person Board of Standards and Appeals. A variance allows a property owner to build outside the existing zoning regulations of a site. In the case of the Southside's Hasidim, variances usually involved permission to build residential facilities in areas zoned for industrial or commercial use, or to build residences larger than those allowed by current residential zoning. An application to change the Zoning Resolution, in contrast, must pass through the city's arduous Uniform Land Use Review Procedure (ULURP); this entails four distinct levels of approval, with public hearings at each step—much greater scrutiny than is required before granting a zoning variance.

During the time of my fieldwork, the monthly meeting agenda of Brooklyn's Community Board One (which covers Williamsburg and neighboring Greenpoint) frequently included variance applications, many of them for lots in the Hasidic area of the Southside. At the April 8, 1997, Community Board One meeting, for example, variance applications for three such lots were made: 254–260 Wallabout Avenue, 401 Marcy Avenue, and 83–113 Lorimer Street/112–144 Middleton Street. The board approved the first two, while the last, a composite lot covering nearly an entire block, was denied.[29] Once a variance application passes the Community Board, it then goes to the city's Board of Standards and Appeals for final approval. Variances have allowed many property owners to circumvent existing zoning regulations in the Southside in a piecemeal fashion, and the organizers at Los Sures resent this. For example, when I told Barbara Schliff, head organizer at Los Sures, that Community Board One meetings always seemed to have variance applications on the agenda, she nodded, replying: "This is how they [the Hasidim] do it; they rezone the land building by building, so that you don't really notice what's going on."[30]

The regular granting of variances in the Hasidic section of the Southside has increased substantially the concentration of Hasidic families there. Not only do variances allow property owners to tear down existing structures, displacing current tenants, they also allow the construction of buildings with more—and larger—apartments than previously existed on the sites. Developers in the Southside often build to the specific, unusual needs of the Satmar Hasidic population, including apartments large enough to accommodate the average Satmar family size of twelve, and dual kitchen facilities to ease the demands of complying with kosher dietary laws. These apartments do not suit well the housing needs of most Latino families—or of anyone else—whose smaller size leads to their de facto exclusion from an increasing number of residential buildings in this section of the Southside.

In mid-1997, the issue of zoning variances in the Southside began to take a back seat to the city's imminent plans to undertake large-scale changes to its Zoning Resolution for the area. Changes to the Zoning Resolution are always preceded by large-scale, city-sponsored study of the impacts of rezoning. Section 197-a of the New York City Charter decrees that Community Boards may submit to the City Council a formal set of recommendations for dealing with any number of land-use, zoning, economic, social, and other issues facing their communities. As stated in the city's *197-a Plan Technical Guide*:

> At their best, 197-a plans can force consensus within a community about its future direction, challenge conventional wisdom among decision-makers,

29. Author's field notes, April 8, 1997.
30. Author's field notes, May 27, 1997.

and lead to significant shifts in land use policy.... [A] 197-a plan offering general land use goals, flexible enough to adapt to changing conditions, will most likely achieve the community's long-range planning objectives, and become a useful guide for [city] agencies making decisions about the study area. (New York City Department of City Planning 1997)

Community Board One had embarked on the multiyear process of producing its 197-a plan in 1993. That year, four community-planning workshops were held at locations throughout the Williamsburg-Greenpoint district, including the Latino and Hasidic sections of the Southside. The workshops aimed to collect input from the different sections within Community Board One's jurisdiction in order to put together a comprehensive plan for the entire area.[31] The many residents who volunteered their time to work on the Community Board One 197-a plan took seriously the city's official position that a completed plan would be treated as a strong participatory effort to wrangle with the district's competing interests and put forth a series of well-thought-out recommendations for the future.

Around the time that Community Board One produced the first draft of its 197-a plan, however, New York's Department of City Planning (DCP) put in motion its own effort to make zoning changes in the Southside. In June 1997, the city made public its first proposed change to the Zoning Resolution in the neighborhood: the rezoning of a thirty-block area surrounding the Williamsburg Bridge. Los Sures and the other Latino organizations opposed this rezoning plan, arguing that it would open the door to market-rate housing developers and push out the remaining industrial businesses in the area. They argued that these changes would negatively impact the Latinos of the Southside, who would be displaced by rising rents in buildings near new, high-cost developments, and would lose an important local source of employment. The UJO, in contrast, supported the proposal—mostly because it would open the door for additional rezoning in their section of the Southside, for which they were already preparing.

The DCP plan for rezoning around the Williamsburg Bridge caused a furor at Los Sures and among members of Fair Housing, as well as at El Puente, a Latino community organization and alternative high school with offices next door to Los Sures. These groups charged that the bridge rezoning would speed the displacement of the Latino community from the Southside, and—even worse—that DCP had developed its plan without their

---

31. In early 1998, residents of Greenpoint decided to split off from the overall Community Board One planning effort and develop their own 197-a plan.

input as community representatives. The DCP plan thus realigned the concerns of the Southside Latino organizations. If their initial reaction to the Memorandum of Understanding had been that the Hasidim were, once again, being given an unfair advantage, they now confronted the far more sobering thought that the bridge rezoning presaged a seismic shift in the social and economic organization of their neighborhood. Los Sures and the other groups were beginning to understand the extent of the growth machine's designs on Williamsburg, but with the Hasidim vocally supporting the bridge rezoning, the old tensions still simmered. The Southside's fight against the bridge rezoning would thus be fought on two fronts: the familiar terrain of Latino-Hasidic conflict, and the new frontier of the growth machine's return.

When Los Sures, Fair Housing, and El Puente complained loudly about the bridge rezoning proposal, DCP hastily called two public meetings to present the plan to the community. The first meeting, held on the Northside of Williamsburg, was announced just hours before it took place. As a result, nobody from the Southside attended. A second meeting, announced in advance, was held on September 29, 1997, at a newly opened arts center in the Southside—neutral territory between the Latinos and the Hasidim. Two representatives from DCP presented the rezoning proposal, then opened the floor for questions. The audience of about forty people seemed united in its opposition to the plan, though no Hasidim appeared to be present. Representatives from El Puente and Los Sures decried the city's disregard of their ongoing work on the Community Board One 197-a plan, arguing that any changes to the neighborhood's zoning regulations needed to account for many local issues besides housing. Local residents complained that the bridge rezoning plan had been developed "in secret," without requests for input from the Southside's Latinos.[32] Despite the tense mood in the room, the DCP staff gave little indication that they were sympathetic to the concerns raised by these and other speakers.

Realizing that this public hearing signaled that ULURP was now under way for the bridge rezoning proposal, staff from Los Sures and El Puente decided to work together to press for the Latino Southside's interests during the review process. This decision to collaborate was significant, as Los Sures and El Puente, despite operating out of adjacent buildings on South Fourth Street, had been divided by long-standing tensions. The two groups, along with representatives of other local organizations and some local residents, formed an alternative rezoning coalition that worked through most of the

32. Author's field notes, September 29, 1997.

winter of 1997–1998 to combat the DCP plan. Starting with the 197-a plan already drafted by Community Board One, coalition members sought to develop a full-fledged 197-a plan for the Southside, with special attention to the Williamsburg Bridge area. They articulated this goal repeatedly over the next four months at the various public ULURP hearings being held to review DCP's proposal. Rezoning just one small area of Community Board One, they argued, would be detrimental to the overall development of the district. This small-scale rezoning not only would shift dramatically the market value of both the rezoned section and the surrounding areas, but also would leave the rest of the neighborhood in land-use limbo. Members of the alternative rezoning coalition argued that if the bridge rezoning proposal were approved, the city would move on to consider land-use issues in other districts, without further consideration for the many other elements of the Community Board One 197-a plan.

Tick-Tock Goes the ULURP Clock

The first public declaration of the alternative rezoning coalition's arguments occurred on October 28, 1997, when Community Board One held its public hearing and vote on the DCP proposal, as required by ULURP. That night, the rezoning coalition held a march from the block of South Fourth Street where both Los Sures and El Puente are located, to the site of the Community Board One meeting, the Swinging Sixties Senior Center, at 211 Ainslie Street, some fifteen blocks away. When we left from Los Sures, there were about seventy-five people in the group, including most of the members of the rezoning coalition—Debbie Medina, Carmen Calderón, Marilyn Rivera, Paula Rojas, John Fleming, Gino Maldonado, Axel, and Adela—as well as students from El Puente's high school and a group of older residents from some of the Los Sures buildings. The walk seemed to take a very long time, and the group dissipated somewhat as marchers advanced at different speeds, but people were generally cheerful, chatting with each other and asking questions about the meeting. I was walking with Barbara Schliff, from Los Sures and Fair Housing, who seemed a bit subdued, and we stopped every so often to wait for some of the older women who were bringing up the rear. When we finally arrived at the senior center, everyone gathered in order to make a grand group entrance into the meeting room.[33]

An ordinary Community Board One meeting usually has fewer than fifty people in attendance (including board members). On this night, the room

33. Author's field notes, October 28, 1997.

was packed with close to two hundred. The board's Land Use Committee made a short presentation of the DCP proposal, then allowed individuals and organizations that had signed up in advance to deliver short arguments for or against the proposal. Cathy Herman, Director of Planning and Development at Los Sures, stated the official Los Sures position against the proposal, employing the argument developed by the alternative rezoning coalition. She distributed printed copies of her testimony to members of the board and audience:

> In 1996, staff of Los Sures met with members of other community organizations in order to study the Department of City Planning's proposed re-zoning of our community. Several meetings were held with the goal of developing a consensus. . . . On September 16th [1997], Los Sures received a copy of the Department of City Planning's latest Proposed Change in Zoning for the area immediately around our office here in the Southside [the Williamsburg Bridge area]. . . . When was this proposed change formulated and published? Los Sures had understood from conversations and correspondence with the Mayor's Office that we would be consulted about proposed zoning changes for our immediate service area. This map is significantly different from the previously published proposed zoning change, dated May 1996. . . . Los Sures was assured that we would be consulted on the Proposed Zoning Change, and receiving short notice that a Public Hearing would be held does not really constitute a dialogue. Time is needed to talk and to discuss this Plan which could have such an impact on the future direction of the Southside. Consequently, we ask Planning Board #1 and the ULURP Committee to disapprove of the Department of City Planning's Proposed Zoning Plan at this time.[34]

Following the rest of the public comments on the proposal, the Land Use Committee issued its recommendation: that the board either modify the proposal or, if it could not agree on modifications, that it turn down the proposal in its entirety.

Community Board One is composed of representatives from the three main ethnic groups in the Williamsburg-Greenpoint district: Latinos, Hasidim, and middle-class whites (who live mostly in Greenpoint and the

---

34. "Comments o[n] the City Planning Commission Proposed Change in Williamsburg Bridge Rezoning," delivered by Cathy Herman, October 28, 1997; document in author's possession.

Northside of Williamsburg). It was clear that the Latino board members would vote against the DCP plan and the Hasidic board members would vote for it. Thus, the non-Hasidic white board members became the swing votes. Discussion on the proposal began, which I recorded in my field notes:

One of the [non-Hasidic] white board members asks a question about a modification that the Land Use Committee proposed. Marty [Needelman, a member of Community Board One and the Los Sures board of directors, and executive director of Brooklyn Legal Services Corporation A] starts to give an answer, which quickly gets into details that I can't quite follow. The board member who asked the question looks satisfied. Then one of the Hasidic board members, Rabbi Weber, stands up and says that it's very important to approve the plan as it stands, because the housing need is so great in Williamsburg, and the plan will not do any of the things that people against the plan are saying it will, like push up rents. On the contrary, he says, because there will be more housing, there will be less competition, and therefore rents will fall. Marty and some of the other board members—some Latino, some white—shake their heads at this, and there is skeptical murmuring from the crowd.... As the discussion goes on, it seems like some of the white board members are agreeing with the Los Sures position. The Hasidic board mem bers seem to be getting worried, because every now and then one of them jumps up and heads out to the hallway with his cell phone in his hand. This happens about three or four times.... Finally, the chair calls for a vote on the proposal. The district manager [a salaried staff person who oversees the activities of the Community Board] polls each board member individually, and as it starts to look like the proposal is going to lose, one of the Hasidic board members jumps up again to make another call. The final vote is narrowly in opposition to the proposal. When the Chair announces that the proposal is NOT approved by Community Board One, there is cheering from the Latino members of the crowd.[35]

The Hasidim badly wanted to see the Williamsburg Bridge rezoning proposal pass, not so much for its immediate effects—the blocks targeted for rezoning were not in the traditional Hasidic area of the Southside—as for the larger rezoning process it would set in motion: the provision of the Memorandum of Understanding that called for the bridge rezoning (provision 9) specified that rezoning would take place concurrently in the area around

35. Author's field notes, October 28, 1997.

Flushing Avenue, the traditional southern border of the Hasidic area. The Hasidim already were starting to build residences in this industrially zoned part of the neighborhood by using zoning variances (Liff 2001a), but passage of the bridge rezoning proposal would open the way for a wholesale rezoning, which promised to greatly accelerate housing production.

Following its rejection by Community Board One, the bridge rezoning proposal moved on, as mandated by ULURP, to the office of Brooklyn borough president Howard Golden. In his written analysis of the proposal, Golden clearly demonstrated his support of the growth machine's interest in developing new, unsubsidized housing in Williamsburg, and he elided the displacement concerns of the Latinos of the Southside. Golden recommended that the bridge rezoning be approved, filing his comments with DCP on December 10, 1997.[36] With that, the proposal moved on to the City Planning Commission, the first authority to consider the proposal that could actually make a binding decision on it. As required by ULURP, the Planning Commission held a public hearing, where the thirteen commissioners heard testimony from a large number of people both in favor of and against the plan. Eight members of the Los Sures/El Puente alternative rezoning coalition spoke, urging the Planning Commission to vote against the rezoning proposal. Most of them highlighted the process issues that had been central to the anti-rezoning argument all along. Jesús Ortega, a staff member at Los Sures and a member of the alternative rezoning coalition, asked the commissioners to consider the draft of the 197-a plan that the alternative rezoning coalition had been working on all winter. Upon hearing that this document would be ready in about three weeks, the commissioners agreed that they would like to see it.[37]

While all of the speakers against the bridge rezoning proposal argued, like Jesús, that the input of the Latino community had been excluded, several of the seven Hasidim who spoke in favor of the proposal disputed this claim. Rabbi Leib Glanz, director of the Southside's United Talmudic Academy, referred in his comments to the Memorandum of Understanding signed by local elected officials from the Southside, professing confusion

---

36. It should be noted that the borough president approved the proposal with one slight modification: the removal from the proposal of a parking lot across the street from the Domino Sugar manufacturing plant, which that large employer argued needed to remain industrially zoned in case it decided to expand the plant. Despite this effort to protect the plant, which had operated in Williamsburg for nearly 150 years and was the neighborhood's largest employer, Domino's parent company, American Sugar, closed it down in 2004, after years of downsizing and labor strife.

37. Author's field notes, January 7, 1998.

as to why Los Sures was fighting the bridge rezoning proposal.[38] Claiming that Los Sures had originally supported all the provisions of the MOU, Glanz suggested that the organization must have "lied" about this, since it now opposed the project.[39] Glanz's comments point up the rift between Assemblyman Lopez and Councilman Robles, the elected officials who negotiated the MOU on behalf of the Latinos of the Southside, and the members of the alternative rezoning coalition, who disagreed with the MOU from the moment it was released. This intra-Latino conflict had manifested itself a number of times since the MOU signing ceremony in September 1997, and it reflected a serious difference of opinion regarding the process of decision making.

Members of Los Sures, El Puente, and Fair Housing were committed to the messy, time-consuming process of consensus building, as demonstrated by their months-long collaboration on the revised 197-a plan for Community Board One, and their repeated complaints to city officials about being excluded from discussions on the bridge rezoning. After a visit I made to the Los Sures offices just after the Brooklyn borough president's November hearing on the rezoning proposal, I recorded in my field notes an exchange I had with Barbara Schliff and Cathy Herman about the growing conflict. They acknowledged that the alternative rezoning coalition's stance was causing Los Sures real grief with their local elected officials, but emphasized the importance of staying true to the processes of participatory decision making:

I say to Cathy and Barbara that I've heard Los Sures is having problems with Vito [Assemblyman Lopez]. Cathy says that it's true, that he keeps yelling at David [Pagán, administrator of Los Sures] in public meetings, but that they're just trying to get on with their work. The one who's not even talking to them is Victor [Councilman Robles], he's so mad. I ask if there's anything Vito can do to hurt Los Sures, and she says not really, since they've pretty much already had most of their funding that Vito has an influence over pulled out from under them over the last couple of years. . . . Barbara says that Vito can't stand the fact that Los Sures is going against the rezoning plan after he's come out supporting it and after he's signed the Memorandum of Understanding. But, they [Los Sures] continue to argue that when David agreed to the MOU, he was under the impression that the rezoning plan called for consultation

38. Glanz is identified in the New York *Daily News* story about potentially fraudulent claims of public housing eligibility among the Hasidim as simultaneously residing in public housing and owning a $187,000 home in Williamsburg (see above and G. B. Smith 1996).

39. Author's field notes, January 7, 1998.

with Los Sures and the rest of the community, and was related to the 197-a plan that they've been working on for some time. Plus, Vito is saying that David said in some meeting that he supported the rezoning plan, but that is simply not true. And that, she says, is why David is continuing to support her and the rest of the organizers in the anti-rezoning efforts they're doing.[40]

For his part, Assemblyman Lopez was incensed by the persistent refusal of Los Sures to knuckle under and accept the provisions of the MOU, which he firmly believed represented the best the Latinos of the Southside could hope for in the prevailing Williamsburg real estate climate. His own views about the most effective way to negotiate for advantage within the competitive city made Los Sures' dissension from the MOU particularly galling, especially given the fact that Lopez recognized the importance of Los Sures' housing work on behalf of his constituents, and had collaborated with the organization on various projects. I witnessed Lopez's irritation with Los Sures during a visit to his annual retreat for community organizations and leaders from his Williamsburg-Bushwick district. On the first evening of the retreat, I stumbled across Lopez's informal, late-night chat session with top-level staff from a number of the district's organizations—including David Pagán, the head of Los Sures. I recorded the following discourse by Lopez in my field notes:

Vito says to me that as a graduate student, there's something I should know about politics. "The most important factor in politics is loyalty. The second most important is respect." Angela [Battagglia] and Chris [Fisher, Lopez's two top deputies] nod their heads. Vito continues, saying that the way to get things done in politics is to make sure you have all your supporters together; that way you can make deals and bring things into the district. He says some people don't think that's the way to do it, that they can just take help from someone, then "shit all over you" when they feel like it (this is surely a thinly veiled reference to Los Sures and Fair Housing on their anti-rezoning work). Some people don't agree with how he operates, and that's fine, but they can't expect him to keep helping them, and keep putting up with their attacking him. He says people like Debbie [Medina, a Los Sures organizer] and Barbara [Schliff, lead organizer at Los Sures] say they're entitled to say what they think, oppose him when they think he's wrong, and "that's fine, they're entitled." But, at the same time, they come to him and ask for help. They think they can say, "Vito's no good," and that he'll keep on helping them. Well, if they have the "right" to attack him, he too has the right to challenge them, and if they

40. Author's field notes, November 21, 1997.

lose their reputation—and a lot of people, especially in city and state government, where the money comes from, will listen to a [nonprofit organization's] local political representative—then they're going to be in a lot of trouble. David [Pagán, head of Los Sures] is sitting quietly through all of this, though it's clearly directed at him, or at least his organization.[41]

Lopez's comments at the retreat strangely echoed what one of the Hasidic supporters of the bridge-area rezoning proposal had said to the City Planning Commission at the ULURP hearing just two days earlier. I recorded in my field notes the strikingly similar understanding held by members of the Hasidic community on how to make things happen in the city:

> The next speaker is Rabbi Joseph Herskovitz. He says the Latino leaders [Assemblyman Lopez and Councilman Robles] agreed to the MOU, so why are there these problems now with people in the [Latino] community? Why don't the Latino people trust their leaders? "In our [Hasidic] community" he says, "if our leaders tell us something is good, well, even if we have questions, we say 'OK, it's good.' That's what leaders are all about."[42]

The fight over the MOU and the bridge rezoning plan, while hewing in part to the familiar Latino-Hasidic political divide, also revealed a split among Latino interests over how decisions regarding the future of the Southside should be made. In the end, the members of the alternative rezoning coalition lost the rezoning battle on both counts. The City Planning Commission passed the DCP rezoning proposal on February 4, 1998, with the modification of maintaining the existing industrial zoning of an eleven-acre lot owned by Domino Sugar. On March 18, the City Council also approved the DCP plan, with some additional slight modifications. For the Hasidim, the vote signaled a sort of previctory victory: now that this provision of the MOU had been implemented, their much-anticipated rezoning plan for the Flushing Avenue area could proceed. For the Latino elected officials, the alternative rezoning rebellion was successfully put down. Gracious in victory, Assemblyman Lopez and Councilman Robles helped negotiate a last-minute effort by the alternative rezoning coalition to remove four key blocks from the version of the DCP plan passed by the City Council.[43]

---

41. Author's field notes, January 9, 1998.
42. Author's field notes, January 7, 1998.
43. These blocks contained privately owned sites where Los Sures and El Puente already had development plans in process, for low-income housing and a new school building, respectively (Waldman 1998). The blocks' zoning was maintained as M1-1 to prevent their owners

The bridge rezoning turned an important page in the Southside's history. As the end of the century neared and passed, the Latinos of the Southside saw their decades-long political feud with the Hasidim take a back seat as plans germinated for the growth machine's exploitation of the city's newest redevelopment frontier. Eight years after the signing of the MOU, the city proclaimed a massive reorganization of the Williamsburg-Greenpoint district's land-use regulations, opening the way to large-scale, luxury redevelopment of the area, particularly along the once-industrial waterfront. As Mayor Rudolph Giuliani's press release announcing the MOU in 1997 had promised, that document had in fact set the stage for producing "hundreds more [units of market-rate housing in Williamsburg] over the next 15–20 years." Although Giuliani did not stay in office long enough to see his plan come to fruition (term limits forced him to step down in 2001), the vast Williamsburg-Greenpoint rezoning he first set in motion stands as a major landmark of the first term of his successor, Michael Bloomberg.

Epilogue: The Two Sides of the Growth Machine

On March 23, 2005, the New York City Council passed legislation to rezone nearly two hundred blocks along the waterfront of Williamsburg and neighboring Greenpoint, opening the door for this once heavily industrial area to become the city's newest residential jewel. A few days later, on the home page of the Department of City Planning Web site, an aerial photograph of Williamsburg-Greenpoint that had served as the initial link for visitors looking for information about the rezoning plan was plastered diagonally with a banner announcement in red type: "Approved!" Eight years had elapsed since the initial step on the path toward this massive feat: the 1997 Memorandum of Understanding signed by Mayor Giuliani and three of the Southside's elected officials. Two things were notable about the final 2005 rezoning legislation. First, a massive mobilization by community groups from Williamsburg and Greenpoint, including Los Sures, El Puente, and the Fair Housing Committee, had forced some changes to the original proposal as it wended its way through the public review process. Second, although the two key documents informing the 2005 rezoning—the 1997 MOU and the Williamsburg 197-a plan, finally completed in 2002—had included the Hasidic section of the Southside, by the time DCP

---

from selling to high-end residential developers (low-income housing produced by nonprofit developers is the only residential use allowed in M1-1 zones). The M1-1 zoning was later removed from these blocks in the 2005 overall rezoning of Williamsburg-Greenpoint.

presented its comprehensive rezoning proposal for review, this piece of the neighborhood had disappeared from the plan.

Between 1997 and 2001, the Hasidim had played all their political cards in a successful play to slip out of the jaws of the growth machine as it clamped down on the Southside. Assisted by a happy accident of geography—they occupied the southernmost section of Williamsburg, separated by the Latinos of the Southside from the gentrification creeping down from the Northside—the Hasidim locked down control over housing opportunities in their traditional area of settlement. They then turned south, away from their long fight with the Latinos, away from the grasping arms of the growth machine, to meet their continuing housing expansion needs. The Latinos of the Southside were not so lucky. The 2005 rezoning plan covers much of their traditional area of settlement, placing longtime Latino residents at far greater risk of displacement as high-end housing development proceeds, pushing up rents in the surrounding areas. The Hasidic approach to politics kept them one step ahead of the forces of capital. In contrast, the Latinos would be forced to rely on the scrappy political skills they had honed during their years of fighting in the role of the underdog. Faced with the plan for massive rezoning of their neighborhood, the Latino organizations in the Southside joined with some forty other groups from Williamsburg and Greenpoint to extract a few concessions from the growth machine.

A Political Escape from the Growth Machine

Following the passage of the Williamsburg Bridge–area rezoning in 1997, the UJO moved swiftly in pursuit of the MOU provisions that would directly benefit its constituents: the rezoning of large tracts of land within and adjacent to their traditional area of settlement in the Southside, south of Division Avenue. The first fruits of their efforts materialized on February 10, 1999, when the City Council passed Resolution 614, an amendment to the Williamsburg Urban Renewal Plan. This provided for two tracts of land on the western edge of the Hasidic area to become eligible for the public investments provided by an urban renewal designation. One day later, these same two tracts of land were rezoned by the City Council from industrial to residential usage (New York City Council Resolution 617). Together, these two pieces of legislation would facilitate the publicly assisted construction of residential housing on the two sites.

Two years later, the Hasidim secured their next set of rezoning benefits. This effort proved far more complex and encountered strong opposition from the Latinos of the Southside along the way. First, in July 2001, the

City Council passed an amendment to the city's Zoning Resolution, adding to the law section 62-736, which allows the City Planning Commission to modify the city's requirements for waterfront development sites with respect to lot coverage, building height and setback, and distance between buildings (Resolution 2023). Then, on December 11, 2001, the council passed four resolutions concerning one of the most coveted city-owned properties on the Williamsburg waterfront: the former site of the Schaefer Brewery, which had closed down in 1976, the last nail in the coffin of north Brooklyn's once-vibrant beer manufacturing industry. Resolution 2140 rezoned the site from industrial to mixed residential and commercial use. Resolution 2141 granted a special permit, as provided for in the recently passed section 62-736 of the Zoning Resolution, allowing increased bulk (more apartments in a bigger building) and a decreased setback (distance from the building to the street) for buildings constructed on the site. Resolution 2142 conveyed certain development designations to the site that allowed the city's Department of Housing Preservation and Development to select a developer to construct two residential towers there—one of fifteen and the other of twenty-five stories—with 350 apartments and ground-floor retail space.[44] The final resolution, 2163, waived for the site certain landscaping requirements specified in the Zoning Resolution.

The Department of City Planning proposals that would eventually become the latter three resolutions became public knowledge when the city commenced ULURP with a presentation to Williamsburg-Greenpoint's Community Board One. The language specifying the particular configuration of the buildings to go on the site—the proposal that became Resolution 2142—raised the suspicions of Los Sures and the Fair Housing Committee that a fix was in for the development of the city-owned property. As had been the case with the Williamsburg Bridge rezoning four years earlier, the Latino organizations felt they had been excluded from the city's planning for a site in which they too had a long-standing interest:

> Los Sures, joined by the neighborhood's Latino politicians and activists, is angry about a planning process they claim was done behind their backs. . . . Until last summer [2001], the proposal [for the Schaefer site] was shrouded in mystery. When HPD [Department of Housing Preservation and Development]

44. The resolution provides for the site to become an Urban Development Action Area, to be used for an Urban Development Action Area Project. These are urban renewal designations that allow city funds to be spent for site clearance and preparation, in anticipation of a private developer building on the site.

introduced its plan to Community Board 1 last April [2001]—as the first step in the land use approval process [ULURP]—to change the zoning on the property from manufacturing to residential use and to get permission to build a high-rise on the site, the agency's presentation had one gaping hole: it did not include the community sponsor and the developer, say board members and others present. (Pacenza 2002)

By the time the above-quoted article was written, it had become public knowledge that the city had selected Williamsburg's United Jewish Organizations as the community sponsor and developer for the project. Information also was emerging about the floor plans for the buildings, which were scheduled to include numerous very large apartments—six and seven bedrooms. Given that few New York City families—aside from the Satmar Hasidim—have so many members as to necessitate such large apartments, Latinos in the Southside complained that residents with smaller families would be effectively excluded from a large portion of the building. This statistical likelihood was especially important to Los Sures and Fair Housing, since 40 percent of the Schaefer apartments were slated to be reserved for low-income families. As had been the case with the Williamsburg Bridge rezoning, however, the Department of City Planning proposals went on to pass the City Council over the objections of the Latino organizations.

Although the Schaefer site redevelopment project was a real prize for the Hasidim, their most important set of rezoning benefits had come earlier that year, in May 2001. City Council Resolutions 1911 and 1912 opened the door for the Hasidim to expand across their traditional southern boundary, Flushing Avenue. The Hasidim had long been wary of crossing Flushing Avenue, the dividing line between Williamsburg-Greenpoint's Community Board One and neighboring Bedford-Stuyvesant's Community Board Three. Not only did they have few relationships with the members of Community Board Three—and no seats on the board, in contrast to Community Board One—but the potential for complicated racial dynamics with this historically African American neighborhood likely gave them pause. Nevertheless, by the end of the 1990s, the Hasidim simply were too pressed for space to leave the area directly south of their traditional settlement untouched. The May 2001 City Council resolutions rezoned an irregularly shaped fifteen-block stretch of Flushing Avenue from industrial to residential use. In addition, the council established a Special Mixed-Use District over several blocks within that rezoned area; such a district allows for a combination of residential, commercial, and industrial use—including schools and congregations, two major organizational needs of the Hasidim. The Flushing

Avenue rezoning did indeed raise the ire of African American residents of Bedford-Stuyvesant, who charged that the resulting housing would be racially segregated—the same argument that Latinos in the Southside had been making about the Schaefer brewery site and the Los Sures low-income cooperatives.

Politics Faces Capital: The 2005 Williamsburg Rezoning

2001 was a big year in rezoning, not only for the Hasidim but also for the rest of Williamsburg. That year, Mayor Giuliani gave his final State of the City address, in which he promised to move forward a number of changes in the city's land-use regulations. He specifically mentioned the Brooklyn waterfront as an area with a rising interest in land-use issues (Liff 2001b). His announcement was contemporaneous with the long-awaited completion of Community Board One's 197-a plan for Williamsburg. The plan offered a wide-ranging analysis of the conditions of Williamsburg's waterfront and inland areas, covering three distinctly named sections of the neighborhood: the Northside, the Southside, and the newly christened "South Williamsburg" (the Hasidic area of the Southside). It also made a long series of recommendations regarding local housing, business development, open space, employment, and other issues.

Although the idea of a 197-a plan is to allow residents of an area to put forward their own analysis and recommendations for their community's future, such a plan is never implemented without careful review by the Department of City Planning. In most cases, what is billed as a "community plan" has been modified significantly by DCP, bringing it into line with the agency's existing goals and projects in the area. DCP subjected both the Williamsburg 197-a plan and a separate Greenpoint 197-a plan to numerous revisions before sending them on to the City Planning Commission for consideration and approval. The City Planning Commission adopted the revised 197-a plans in 2002, thereby enshrining more growth-oriented versions of the original proposals as official "community plans" for the neighborhoods.[45] These two official 197-a plans thus became the basis for a more intensive DCP study of a large section of the Williamsburg-Greenpoint waterfront area, undertaken to consider the possibilities of implementing a large-scale rezoning there.

---

45. Community Board One's original proposal was included as an appendix when DCP published the certified Williamsburg 197-a plan (New York City Department of City Planning 2002).

After nearly three years of study, on September 30, 2004, DCP submitted its applications to make changes to the city's Zoning Resolution and Zoning Map in regards to a nearly two-hundred-block area of Williamsburg-Greenpoint (New York City Department of City Planning 2004a). The department envisioned a sweeping transformation of the decaying industrial waterfront and its adjacent upland areas into a new center for residential development in the housing-starved city. Since the time of Robert Moses, the city and its real estate interests had not advanced a program of such scope, which if adopted would reshape a vast section of the city in one fell swoop (with the possible exception of Battery Park City, the huge housing development on the Hudson River in lower Manhattan, which opened in the late 1980s). As the waterfront rezoning proposal moved through ULURP, it encountered enormous resistance from the residents and organizations in much of Williamsburg and Greenpoint. Los Sures and the other Latino organizations from the Southside joined forces with Community Board One and some forty other neighborhood groups to form the North Brooklyn Alliance, presenting a united front against the rezoning proposal.

Following the ULURP hearing at Community Board One, the board voted on December 6, 2004 to *disapprove* the DCP application. The board's Waterfront Committee then submitted to DCP a thirty-two-page document detailing alternative rezoning recommendations (Brooklyn Community Board One Rezoning Task Force 2004). The most important of these included mandating that 40 percent of new housing developed in the rezoned area be reserved for low- and moderate-income families, and that 50 percent of these units be allocated to current residents of the area served by Community Board One; that a new Special Mixed-Use zoning designation be developed that would incorporate stronger protections for manufacturing uses within mixed residential/manufacturing areas; that the height and bulk regulations for buildings on the waterfront be significantly reduced and setback regulations modified; that additional parkland be included in the overall project; and that private developers of waterfront properties be required to ensure public access to the waterfront itself. The Brooklyn borough president also recommended disapproval of the DCP application and supported Community Board One's efforts to use the rezoning to create greater support for light manufacturing uses, lower-density residential development, more guaranteed affordable housing, and additional open space (Borough President of Brooklyn 2004).

In response to the concerns of the community, DCP took the unusual step of issuing a modified rezoning application that addressed a number of the specific alternative recommendations made by Community Board One and superseded the original application (New York City Department of City Planning 2004b). The most significant changes included reducing slightly the maximum building heights and densities allowed on the waterfront; introducing a new inclusionary housing provision to the Zoning Resolution, which would allow residential developers to build somewhat higher and more densely if their structures included affordable units; adding five acres of parkland to the rezoned area; maintaining manufacturing zoning on several blocks that the original plan had targeted for residential use; and modifying the setback and alignment provisions for buildings on or approaching the waterfront. At the public hearing of the City Planning Commission, members of the North Brooklyn Alliance continued to speak out against the modified application, charging that it still did not contain sufficient protection for light manufacturing usages; that the building heights and densities on the waterfront were still excessive; and—most importantly for the Latino organizations of the Southside—that the voluntary nature of the affordable housing incentives left local residents at the mercy of developers, who could opt to develop no affordable housing units at all.

On March 14, 2005, the City Planning Commission approved the modified rezoning application, with a few additional changes. The commission further reduced the maximum building heights and densities allowed on the waterfront; maintained the original manufacturing zoning of a few additional blocks; and increased somewhat the incentives available to developers to include affordable housing in their residential projects in the rezoned area (New York City Department of City Planning 2005). These changes still fell far short of the alternative recommendations put forward by Community Board One and the North Brooklyn Alliance, particularly on the issue of guaranteeing low- and moderate-income housing. The City Planning Commission, however, stated unequivocally that it would not require developers to include affordable housing in their projects:

> Testimony was received at the public hearing recommending a mandatory affordable housing requirement. . . . The Commission notes that, while there is a strong demand for new housing in Greenpoint and Williamsburg today, waterfront sites are subject to a range of exceptional costs, and that this waterfront represents a new and untested market where changes in market conditions could affect the feasibility of new housing development. The Commission heard considerable testimony regarding the difficulty of designing a mandatory inclusionary housing program that would provide effective incentives to private developers in a range of market conditions, and the risk that a mandatory inclusionary housing program without such incentives

would impede housing development in the event that market conditions decline from their current high levels. The Commission also notes that requiring inclusionary housing as a condition of the residential development proposed in Greenpoint and Williamsburg would be outside the scope of this action. (New York City Department of City Planning 2004b, 83)

The commission likewise declined to include antiharassment provisions in the rezoning language, stating that an effort to codify such protections for low-income residents at risk of displacement would also be outside the scope of their authority (New York City Department of City Planning 2004b, 84).

The efforts of the North Brooklyn Alliance to reshape the designs of capital on Williamsburg and Greenpoint through political engagement yielded certain concessions in the rezoning plan. It is notable that the comparatively middle-class, professional interests in Greenpoint and the Northside of Williamsburg achieved greater success in their efforts to preserve open space and waterfront access than did the low-income Latinos in the Southside who sought to secure their number-one priority: affordable housing. Despite the insistence of developers and the City Planning Commission that the inclusionary housing provisions of the DCP's modified plan will produce large numbers of affordable units as residential redevelopment proceeds, it remains to be seen if developers will in fact take advantage of the affordable housing incentives. Furthermore, it will never be known if a mandatory affordable housing provision would in fact have proved workable for real estate developers seeking profits in the neighborhood. After all the efforts of Los Sures and the other Latino organizations to formulate and press for the alternative rezoning recommendations, only time will tell if the Latino presence in the Southside will survive in the aftermath.

This story of Williamsburg's decline, rehabilitation, and gentrification begins and ends with the growth machine: its abandonment of the neighborhood in the 1950s and its voracious return half a century later. In between, it is a story about the possibility of neighborhood organizations' changing something about the conditions in which poor people live, and about the limitations on that potential. Los Sures helped develop an innovative response to the destruction wrought by capital's flight from Williamsburg, creating housing for a group of people who, over time, became the Latino community in the Southside. But Los Sures found it increasingly difficult to implement its long-standing strategies for producing affordable housing in the context of the city's rising economic fortunes. The political side of the growth machine offered some openness to influence in its willingness both to respond to the threat of disruption posed by the Fair

Housing Committee and to engage in insider dealing with local elected officials—negotiations that resulted in the small Latino gains laid out in the Memorandum of Understanding. To the extent that the capital side of the growth machine is indifferent about exactly where and how it generates its profits, the political side can suggest equally profitable alternatives for the particulars. Still, the Hasidim, organized around a single central authority, were able to use this aspect of the growth machine to greater advantage than the geographically and organizationally scattered Latinos. Working through their aptly named United Jewish Organizations, the Hasidim were able to shape the details of the growth machine's operation in a way that benefited them substantially. In contrast, Los Sures, El Puente, and Fair Housing effectively hit the political wall, and the growth machine rolled over them.

The importance of politics to the growth machine's operation cannot be denied. At the same time, however, the Hasidim enjoyed an additional advantage: despite their high rate of individual poverty, as a community they have access to significant sources of capital. This is related to the Hasidim's tightly organized approach to finding new housing, as discussed in a *New York Times* article on their early forays across the traditional southern boundary of their Southside settlement:

> The developer [of a converted factory just across the southern border of Community Board One], Hank Camuso, said that after meeting Rabbi Nie-derman [executive director of Williamsburg's United Jewish Organizations], he agreed to rehabilitate the property specifically for the Hasidim. . . . The benefit, for Mr. Camuso, was the assurance that most units would be sold to reliable buyers with almost no advertising. To enable Hasidim to buy the units, which began at $145,000, United Jewish Organizations arranged generous financing terms with banks. Buyers had to put down only 10 percent of the purchase price. The financing arrangement highlights a contradiction. Many Hasidim have little money, yet they have an increasing ability to make the [housing] market meet their needs. The explanation is that they are concentrated and organized, with well-defined demands, as manufacturers of kosher products learned long ago. (Waldman 1997)

Perhaps the story of Williamsburg would have turned out differently if the Southside Latinos had also been able to add the punch of capital to their organizational and political skills. The distinct trajectories of the Latinos and Hasidim of the Southside reveal some important lessons about the possibilities of reconnecting poor urban neighborhoods to the broader economic and political systems of the city through the actions of community-based organizations. The fundamental circumstance that drives these possibilities is the state of the growth machine's interest in a particular part of the city: does this or that neighborhood offer potential for land-use intensification and the extraction of profits by real estate and/or business interests?

At the level of organizational action, the question is whether a CBO can influence the growth machine on either of its two sides—capital or politics. If the growth machine were based simply on the power of capital and the organizations that maneuver it—purchasing land, structuring debt, buying out competitors, and so on—the playing field would admit only those possessing capital. As the discussion of the 2005 Williamsburg-Greenpoint rezoning clearly shows, however, government is a necessary component of the growth machine because of its unique powers to regulate land use; without the participation of the Department of City Planning, the City Planning Commission, and the New York City Council, Williamsburg-Greenpoint could never have been transformed into an area for high-end residential redevelopment. The thirst of capital to move into this area thus would have remained unslaked. Government actors of course respond to the needs and desires of capital, but they also have some accountability to the public; after all, elected officials must be voted into office before they can influence or control the actions of government agencies, and they must subsequently stand for reelection.

The potential for CBOs to influence the capital side of the growth machine is quite limited. Both the tax code and society's normative expectations frown upon CBOs, as nonprofit organizations with public service missions, accumulating substantial quantities of discretionary assets. While some nonprofit organizations can claim such resources—universities, hospitals, and major museums, for example—CBOs are among the poorest organizations in the nonprofit sector, in line with their near-total focus on serving poor people and poor places.[46] Most of the opportunities for CBOs to impact the growth machine, then, come on the side of politics. As the story of the Southside's housing struggles during the 1960s and 1970s shows, when private and public developers ignore a neighborhood, a variety of CBO engagements with government and private-sector actors can produce positive results. So, for example, Los Sures convinced the city government to allocate public resources to rehabilitate, on a modest scale, properties that private landlords had abandoned in the Southside; this improved housing conditions for poor Latino residents. At the same time, the United Jewish Organizations worked out deals with the local political

46. See the extended definition of a CBO in chapter 1, n. 3.

machine to secure disproportionate numbers of apartments for Hasidim in the new Southside public housing developments. Later on, as Los Sures entered into housing development, it partnered with banks and private-sector builders to construct new types of housing that, with the support of government subsidy programs, had become relatively low-risk enterprises.

When the growth machine's interest in Williamsburg returned, however, the political opportunities for CBOs shrank. The real estate interests that set their sights on Williamsburg were well-versed in the bureaucratic machinations of profit-seeking, with vast knowledge about how to coordinate the organizations that control capital with the structures of government regulation. This is the very essence of the growth machine. As capital's pressure on government increases, CBOs have less political room to press their own concerns. The public interest represented by government takes on a more private character when the growth machine moves into high gear, and if CBOs are to protect their own constituents' interests, they too must become more privately oriented. The story of the Hasidic success in maneuvering the political side of the growth machine between 1998 and 2004 demonstrates the difference that a privately oriented approach to politics makes. The next chapter explores this issue further.

CHAPTER THREE

A Voice in Politics

What is "politics"? In a general sense, politics can be thought of as the process of negotiation and compromise among competing interests that underlies how most things get done. Thus, we see politics not only in the halls of government, but also at the office, in schools, at church, within families, and in many other settings. Of course, the relative power of competing interests deeply affects their bargaining positions, and great power imbalances largely obviate the need for politics in the sense of negotiation and compromise. In most situations, however, the way things turn out can be shaped—at least partially—by political action undertaken by interested parties.[1] In the previous chapter I examined the various ways in which Williamsburg's Latino and Hasidic community-based organizations engaged in politics in their nearly forty years of struggle to produce affordable housing. In the most recent round of that fight, the arcane politics of zoning and land use proved key to their differential ability to maneuver around the returned growth machine; CBOs representing both groups engaged in political activity directed toward influencing the 2005 rezoning, but the strategy pursued by the Hasidim, along with their greater access to private capital and more fortuitous geographic location, produced decided advantages in the housing field.

As the sociologist Manuel Castells has observed, urban politics largely focus on a competition for critical resources: along with affordable, quality housing, residents of poor urban neighborhoods need parks, clean streets, safety, quality education, and so on (Castells 1977). Poor neighborhoods usually lose out in this competition, finding themselves with substandard

---

1. This interplay of structure and agency in collective outcomes is what the sociologist Charles Tilly has famously called "contentious politics" (Tilly 1986; Tilly and Tarrow 2006).

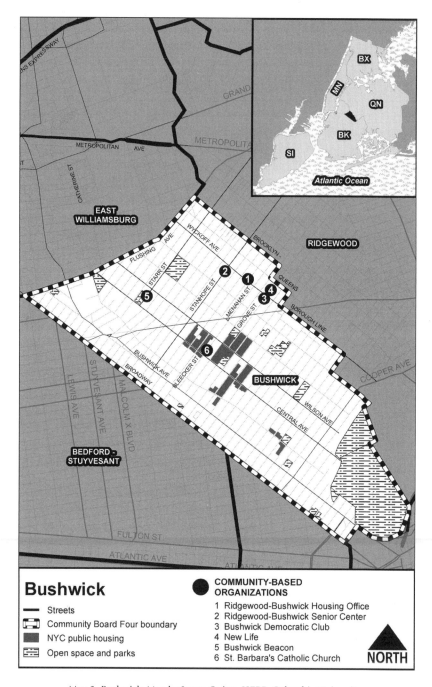

Bushwick

— Streets

▢ Community Board Four boundary

■ NYC public housing

▤ Open space and parks

COMMUNITY-BASED ORGANIZATIONS

1 Ridgewood-Bushwick Housing Office
2 Ridgewood-Bushwick Senior Center
3 Bushwick Democratic Club
4 New Life
5 Bushwick Beacon
6 St. Barbara's Catholic Church

▲ NORTH

Map 3. Bushwick. Map by James Quinn, ISERP, Columbia University.

housing, few if any green spaces, irregular trash collection, high crime rates, and failing schools. The story of Los Sures and the United Jewish Organizations captures the response of Williamsburg's Latinos and Hasidim to the devastated housing conditions of their neighborhood. The two CBOs' unique solutions to that problem involved significant political engagement with the city's housing bureaucracy and other actors in the housing field. The present chapter examines the distinctive uses of politics by two CBOs—the Ridgewood-Bushwick Senior Citizens Council and Saint Barbara's Catholic Church—in a second poor Brooklyn neighborhood: Bushwick, which lies just east of Williamsburg.

In a general sense, both the Ridgewood-Bushwick Senior Citizens Council and Saint Barbara's Catholic Church are interested in the same thing: they want to redress the decades-long neglect of Bushwick by government and the private sector. The two CBOs understand that efforts to accomplish that goal must be directed externally. The powerful government and private-sector actors they seek to influence are rarely located within Bushwick itself. As a result, both have turned to politics as their fundamental tool for facilitating poor Bushwick residents' access to a range of critical resources. Their approaches to politics, however, could not be more different. Ridgewood-Bushwick and Saint Barbara's offer distinct analyses of how Bushwick's neglect can be reversed, and thus pursue vastly different sets of political practices.

Ridgewood-Bushwick focuses its political efforts on government decisions about where to spend public money. Specifically, it targets the contracts through which government agencies allocate funds to nonprofit organizations to provide social services for needy residents. To win these contracts, Ridgewood-Bushwick both demonstrates its competence as a service provider and applies political pressure to the elected officials who control key elements of the contracting process. Ridgewood-Bushwick's strategy accepts the general trend toward government's turning over social provision tasks to private organizations, and it seeks to capture as many of the available government dollars as possible. A certain form of politics proves crucial to this effort. Ridgewood-Bushwick sees its clients as potential voters and works hard to ensure that they reliably turn out to represent the organization's interests in the voting booth. The result is what I call a *private politics of distribution*, where Ridgewood-Bushwick clients' limited form of political action helps the CBO win contracts, which in turn gives those clients greater access than other Bushwick residents to the resulting services.

In contrast, Saint Barbara's pursues what I refer to as *public goods politics*. At bottom, this approach attempts to take politics out of the hands of bureaucratic organizations—government agencies, nonprofit service providers, for-profit corporations, and the like—and place it in the hands of citizens. For Saint Barbara's, "politics" entails, not simply the distribution of government money, but an opportunity to move failing status quo approaches to public problems toward more successful solutions. We need bureaucracies to run public services, such as housing, education, health, transportation, and security. But entrenched interests can often turn these organizations' focus toward self-preservation rather than effectiveness. This is where informed citizens, like those Saint Barbara's cultivates, play a role: they strive to convince elected officials, corporate CEOs, and other powerful actors that current approaches to specific issues are failing but that by working together with citizens—and as citizens—they can develop and implement new, successful strategies. Saint Barbara's itself never takes on implementation, as Ridgewood-Bushwick does; this operational focus would be outside the proper realm of its public goods politics. Instead, Saint Barbara's works to reconfigure current public service systems to produce better results for all.

Bushwick, the Forgotten Neighborhood

The first time Bushwick was forgotten in post–World War II New York City came as a blessing. At the height of Robert Moses's reign as development czar, Bushwick remained virtually untouched: he ran no highways through the neighborhood, razed no buildings for urban renewal projects, built almost no public housing there.[2] While Moses was tearing up Williamsburg to make room for the Brooklyn-Queens Expressway, displacing families and businesses in droves, the mostly Italian American residents of Bushwick went on with their daily lives largely undisturbed. They continued to have easy access to the still-plentiful factory jobs on the Williamsburg waterfront, as well as in brewing and garment manufacturing concerns within Bushwick itself. Their houses and apartments escaped Moses's axe, keeping many extended networks of family, friends, and neighbors in Bushwick well into the 1960s. When the African American and Puerto Rican migrants began arriving in the early part of that decade, Bushwick's better-quality housing stock and largely intact social structure meant higher rents and property

2. Moses did eventually set his sights on Bushwick. In 1964 he announced plans to build the Bushwick Expressway through the neighborhood, in order to feed suburban traffic to the Williamsburg and Brooklyn Bridges and onto his proposed, ill-fated Lower Manhattan Expressway. When fervent citizen protest eventually killed the latter project, the Bushwick Expressway also disappeared.

prices, ensuring that these new arrivals were of somewhat greater economic means than their co-ethnics who settled in the cheaper, less well maintained apartments of Williamsburg and neighboring Bedford-Stuyvesant. As a result of all these factors, Bushwick entered its phase of decline at least a decade later than the adjoining neighborhoods.

As the 1960s progressed, and as urban renewal demolition proceeded apace in Williamsburg and Bedford-Stuyvesant, many poor African American and Puerto Rican residents displaced from those areas began settling along the edges of Bushwick. Poverty increased in these areas, and in 1966 the administrators of the city's Community Action Program placed Bushwick on their list for a second round of antipoverty community action agencies, should federal funds become available to expand the program (Institute of Public Administration 1966). When these funds materialized in 1967, a Bushwick Community Corporation was set up on the southwest side of the neighborhood, close to its border with the mostly African American Bedford-Stuyvesant. The service-providing organizations funded by the CAP and supervised by the Bushwick Community Corporation also were concentrated in this more heavily black part of the neighborhood, with a few in the more Puerto Rican northwestern section, adjacent to Williamsburg.

This distribution of CAP resources in Bushwick caused a certain resentment among the Italian Americans in the still predominantly white, eastern sections of the neighborhood, which bordered all-white Ridgewood, Queens. They increasingly complained that the city government was forgetting them—this time to their detriment—while giving at least some consideration to their black and Puerto Rican neighbors. In particular, they worried that the housing destruction plaguing the African American and Puerto Rican areas of Bushwick was headed in their direction. By the early 1960s, fires—both accidental and deliberate—were becoming epidemic in these sections of the neighborhood. Lamentably, Bushwick's housing stock proved especially susceptible to fires. Many of the three- and four-story wood-frame row houses that lined Bushwick streets had common cocklofts—a sort of half-attic—through which fires could spread rapidly to adjacent houses. The risks and consequences of fires were worsened by the city's cuts in fire protection; fewer engine and ladder companies were available, and those that remained had less manpower (Wallace and Wallace 1998). Residents of Bushwick's more affluent sections cried out that their barely stable neighborhood would soon become an impoverished, dilapidated ghetto unless the city intervened.

This competitive complaint echoed throughout the white working-class neighborhoods of New York City during this period. Many middle- and lower-middle-class whites—those with greater financial resources—had already left for the suburbs. The white working class, however, remained tied to their old neighborhoods by both sentiment and finances (declining city property values made it difficult to finance a suburban move by selling the old house). By the late 1960s, their low-volume grumbling had become a clamor loud enough for mayor John Lindsay—running for reelection—to hear. During his first term, the Republican mayor had set up "Little City Halls" in three tension-filled, predominantly African American and Puerto Rican neighborhoods: an effort to provide residents with easier access to the city agencies charged with solving local problems (A. E. Clark 1966, Knowles 1967). Just prior to the 1969 election, he proposed expanding this nascent program to several white working-class neighborhoods (Bennett 1968, 1969). The Democratic political establishment cried foul, charging that Lindsay was simply seeking political advantage in an increasingly racially divided city. Political commentators warned that Lindsay could not govern the city if he continued to neglect the needs of the white working class. Typical were these bold remarks in a *New York Times* analysis following Lindsay's narrow reelection:

"Of all the groups in society, the white working class is less on the move," said Irving Levine, director of urban projects for the American Jewish Committee, which has made several recent studies of the white worker.

"They see themselves stuck forever with an unbelievable lack of options," he went on. "They see no programs directed at them or their kids, they see their taxes rising and neighborhood services getting worse, they see the intelligentsia on television depict them as bigots and backlashers and they're furious and can only shout: 'Allright, I'm a bigot if that's what you want.' They want to be recognized, they want to be told that they exist, and not as a negative force."

"They do represent failures in the great American sweepstakes in that they have been economically upgraded and have not shared in the credit card goodies of our culture," said Dennis Clark, a product of a working class Irish neighborhood in Philadelphia and a staff member of Temple University's Center for Community Studies.

"But there is also a dimension of sadness, a pathetic failure about them, an estrangement from their original vitality," he said. "The [white] ethnic groups represent people set adrift from another culture. They represent insecurity in many ways, and a great deal of nervousness about never having made it in their own country or in the United States. There is, therefore, a lot of free-flowing aggression against neighboring [nonwhite] groups." (Weinraub 1969)

Bushwick had been passed over in the preelection "Little City Halls" expansion, but in 1972 the neighborhood was finally *not* forgotten. The mayor, in his continuing quest to establish localized city offices, against the will of the Democratic-controlled City Council and Board of Estimate, created his Office of Neighborhood Government. This experimental program gave five white, working-class areas undergoing racial change "district managers": city employees who were responsible for coordinating the activities of various city agencies—police, fire, sanitation, and so on—in their respective neighborhoods.[3] This increased municipal attention to the issues and problems facing Bushwick was accompanied by new city funds to begin addressing them.

Bushwick's path to greater interaction with city officials and funding structures was thus very different from Williamsburg's. While the Latinos and Hasidim of Williamsburg's Southside built their own organizations, drawing on initial public investments to cajole (or force) city government into innovative partnerships, the residents of Bushwick mostly waited until the city government came to them. The Bushwick organizations seeded by the CAP in the late 1960s largely failed to sustain themselves after funds for that program expired, as evidenced by a 1974 Columbia University study of the neighborhood that commented on the dearth of local organizations and the concomitant low participation of local residents in organizational life of any kind (Friedman, Bloom, and Marks 1974). These conditions presented an opportunity to build new community-based organizations in Bushwick when the city began offering new and sustained resources. One program that was getting under way as the CAP organizations declined proved uniquely transformative of Bushwick's relationship to city government. A seemingly innocuous effort by the city to provide community centers for the elderly became, in the context of rising concern over the fate of senior citizens left behind by their newly suburbanized children, a source of significant public dollars in Bushwick.

Filling the Organizational Void: The Ridgewood-Bushwick Senior Citizens Council

In 1970, a young social worker named Vito Lopez got a job working for New York City at Bushwick's recently opened community center for the

---

3. The Office of Neighborhood Government also assigned district managers to West Tremont (the Bronx), Washington Heights (Manhattan), Crown Heights (Brooklyn), and the Rockaways (Queens) (Carroll 1972).

elderly. Lopez hailed from the predominantly Italian American neighborhood of Bensonhurst, Brooklyn, and had been trained in the community organizing program at Yeshiva University's Stern School of Social Work. His grandfather was a Spaniard who migrated to Italy, where he married an Italian woman, then immigrated with her to the United States, settling in one of Brooklyn's many Italian neighborhoods. Lopez grew up in this milieu, firmly attached to his Italian American roots and distant from his Spanish ones. He proved an excellent match for the mostly Italian American elderly who took part in the activities of the Bushwick Senior Center, one of the few city-run efforts in this neighborhood before 1972.

Within this neighborhood that city government consistently forgot, the low-income elderly population was among the most forgotten. Lopez began putting his community organizing skills to work with Bushwick's senior citizens, prefiguring the lessons that the rest of the neighborhood would soon get from the Bushwick Office of Neighborhood Government about the relationship between claiming the city's attention and getting its agencies to act. Lopez's goal was to make even stronger claims on the city government by organizing the neighborhood's elderly to speak the language politicians understand best—voting. The *New York Times* reported on one of Lopez's early sorties in this campaign, when he and some of his center's clients participated in a 1971 public hearing about the conditions of the elderly in Brooklyn:

> There were no shouts of "Right on!" or "Power to the people!" but more than 100 elderly persons assembled in Brooklyn's Borough Hall were angry about what they felt was a serious neglect of the problems of the aged. One after another they told of long waits for decent housing, for nursing homes, and for medical facilities to be built. . . . Vito Lopez, a young staff member of the Bushwick Senior Center, urged not only for a coalition [among the elderly and the professionals who serve them] but also the formation of a political party for senior citizens. "When you start to vote, then the politicians start to worry," said Mr. Lopez, who was enthusiastically received. (Johnson 1971)

While Lopez clearly had a political vision for his organization from early on, the Bushwick Senior Center had started out like most of the other senior centers around the city. Opened by the city government in 1970 and located in a city-owned building on Stanhope Street in Bushwick, it offered a basic set of services to local residents over the age of sixty-five: nutritious hot lunches for twenty-five cents (about half the cost of meal production); educational and recreational activities, from art and dancing to sewing and English classes; delivery of meals to the homebound; assistance with applications for government benefits, such as Social Security and Medicare; and opportunities to socialize with others.

Before long, however, Lopez was to change the shape of his organization. Bit by bit, he found new sources of public funds—city, state, and federal monies targeted to the needs of the elderly—to expand the center's offerings beyond those covered by the basic city contract. In the course of his research, he also repeatedly came across public funding streams that could support programs to benefit Bushwick's younger residents. To take advantage of these opportunities, in 1973 Lopez founded an independent, nonprofit, community-based organization, with the intention of bidding on government contracts to serve non-elderly residents of Bushwick.[4] Recognizing that the mostly Italian American constituency of the senior center lived not only in the easternmost section of Bushwick, but also in the adjacent neighborhood of Ridgewood, Lopez gave his nonprofit a hyphenated name: the Ridgewood-Bushwick Senior Citizens Council. Its relation to the nominally independent senior center was cemented when, soon after its incorporation, the new CBO secured its first contract: to administer the city-funded Bushwick Senior Center.

From its inception, the Ridgewood-Bushwick organization shaped its programs on the basis of the availability of government funds to support them, choosing to focus on those few of the many problems facing its neighborhood that the government had, through its appropriations, recognized as meriting attention. By the mid-1970s, one of these was housing. Bushwick faced two critical, intimately intertwined housing issues: the fires that were more and more rapidly destroying its wood-frame housing stock and the efforts to prevent this "transitional neighborhood" from becoming a full-fledged ghetto. In other words, both residents and city officials wanted Bushwick to look less like its troubled Brooklyn neighbors to the west, Williamsburg and Bedford-Stuyvesant, and more like the still solidly working-class (and white) Ridgewood, to the east in Queens (Fowler 1973; Stankus 1972).

Ridgewood-Bushwick focused first on stabilizing the deteriorating, privately owned housing stock where many senior citizens from the neighborhood lived. In 1978, the New York City Department of Housing Preservation and Development (HPD) had just started its Community Consultant program, which provided funds for CBOs to work with landlords and tenants

---

4. The organization received its New York State incorporation in 1976 and its federal tax-exempt status from the Internal Revenue Service in 1978.

to improve existing housing in distressed areas. Ridgewood-Bushwick won one of these contracts, which provided enough funds to hire two full-time employees. Angela Battaglia, a young woman from the neighborhood who had recently graduated from Fordham University, had begun volunteering at Ridgewood-Bushwick a few months earlier. She had been introduced to Lopez by her father, who had encouraged her to pursue her interest in working with senior citizens within Bushwick rather than continuing to volunteer at a senior center on Manhattan's Upper East Side. After proving her mettle as a Ridgewood-Bushwick volunteer, Battaglia got the nod for one of the new paid positions. She and a second employee worked with local block associations and individual residents, providing information, advocacy, arson prevention tips, and other services called for by the city contract. After becoming more familiar with the neighborhood's housing needs, Battaglia realized that a more pressing issue was making certain that landlords could provide basic tenant services more regularly – adequate heat, hot water, repairs, and so on. When New York State announced the availability of new funds for weatherizing old buildings—replacing windows, adding insulation, upgrading burners, installing new boilers—Battaglia applied for a contract. By helping landlords improve the efficiency of their heating systems, Ridgewood-Bushwick lowered their costs of providing appropriate heat and hot water and improved tenants' access to these critical services. Next, Battaglia turned her attention to the increasingly problematic issue of annual rent increases. As rents rose, many senior citizens, who lived on small, fixed incomes, could not afford them. Landlords, however, needed the additional money to continue providing building services. Ridgewood-Bushwick helped seniors apply for the New York State Senior Citizen Rent Increase Exemption (SCRIE) or federal Section 8 housing subsidies so that tenants could afford rents and landlords could maintain their buildings appropriately.[5]

At each step in the development of its housing programs, Ridgewood-Bushwick sought out government funds, secured a contract, and hired employees—often local residents—to implement the services, all of which facilitated its growth as an organization. The relative absence of other community-based organizations in Bushwick, particularly in the eastern sections of the neighborhood where it worked, meant Ridgewood-Bushwick faced little competition. As the Italian American population dwindled, it was mostly replaced by Latinos, especially Puerto Ricans and Dominicans. Ridgewood-Bushwick was able to adapt to these newer populations by

5. Author's field notes on interview with Angela Battaglia, June 30, 1997.

sticking to its core vision of locating public-sector resources and using them to expand its services and build loyalty to the organization.

The Ridgewood-Bushwick Philosophy: Helping People

Ridgewood-Bushwick aggressively pursues government funding. Given the low incomes and lack of private capital among Bushwick residents, public funds provide one of the relatively few secure sources of support for the area's low-wage and unemployed workers, retirees, and welfare recipients. "Helping people," as founder Vito Lopez puts it, is the first principle in Ridgewood-Bushwick's careful plan to maximize the availability of these resources. This foundational philosophy features prominently in Ridgewood-Bushwick's printed materials, as well as in the actions of its staff. The organization's mission statement, for example, concludes with the following promise:

> If you need help in Ridgewood, Bushwick, or any of the communities that we serve and your particular problem is not listed [in our directory of services], please call the department that specializes in the area you are concerned with. If we cannot help you directly, we will find the person that can.[6]

This official sentiment was repeatedly realized during the course of my fieldwork at Ridgewood-Bushwick, with Lopez himself as one of its primary promoters. In private settings and public statements that I observed, Lopez consistently identified helping activities as the core of his work. One Christmas Day, for example, I joined close to 150 other volunteers working on Ridgewood-Bushwick's massive holiday celebration for local senior citizens. While some drove around the neighborhood in pairs, bringing hot meals to five hundred homebound seniors, the rest of us did prep work in the kitchen, or served what seemed like endless plates of manicotti, meatballs, sausages, salad, and fruit to the three thousand seniors who claimed a space at one of the long tables in the senior center's dining room—if only long enough to polish off their food before someone else clamored for their seat. During a brief break from my work in the kitchen, I chatted with Lopez, who was standing in the entrance hall, attired in his usual dark suit

---

6. Ridgewood-Bushwick Senior Citizens Council n.d.; emphasis added. Most of Ridgewood-Bushwick's programs and services are located in and serve residents from the Bushwick neighborhood. At the time of my fieldwork, the organization also operated two community centers for the elderly in adjacent areas of Queens. Since then, Ridgewood-Bushwick has taken on elderly service centers in other parts of Brooklyn and Queens.

and tie, sucking on a hard candy while greeting arriving volunteers and seniors. "Other people talk and complain" about problems in Bushwick, he said, "but I get out there and *do* things for people."[7]

Lopez embodies the "helping people" philosophy—no surprise given that he originated it. But it is remarkable how his orientation pervades the organization. At the Ridgewood-Bushwick Housing Office, where I conducted most of my fieldwork with this group, the "helping people" philosophy was much in evidence. Substandard housing remains widespread in Bushwick; though conditions have improved considerably since the neighborhood's nadir in the late 1970s, the community continues to face the problems presented by aging housing stock and unscrupulous landlords who have severely neglected their properties. Drawing on a variety of government low-income housing programs, the Ridgewood-Bushwick Housing Office develops new housing and rehabilitates existing stock, building or renovating multifamily rental properties, two-family homes for sale, and supportive housing developments dedicated to senior citizens. The office's tenant organizing work focuses on assisting tenants in buildings where private owners are not providing adequate services, using tactics such as documenting housing code violations, taking landlords to housing court, and organizing rent strikes. The actual strategies are similar to those employed by Los Sures in Williamsburg's Southside—although Los Sures emphasizes the pursuit of social justice while Ridgewood-Bushwick promotes the principle of "helping people."

To give one example of the Ridgewood-Bushwick approach, one hot summer's day I accompanied Carmen Bonilla, a tenant organizer, on a visit to one of the privately owned buildings where she was working with tenants to procure necessary repairs. The building was in bad shape, with broken mailboxes, a rickety stairway, missing chunks of flooring, holes in interior walls, a leaking roof, no electricity in the hallways, and a flea infestation in the basement, among other problems.[8] The process of forcing repairs requires extensive documentation of the conditions, plus extended follow-up to monitor progress or, in the event there is none, to begin proceedings against the landlord in housing court. In the midst of our reconnaissance, Carmen took a break from snapping pictures and writing notes to hold a meeting with the tenants, with whom she had been attempting to organize a rent strike. Sometimes, especially in the early stages of putting together a rent strike, tenants are suspicious of the process. That

7. Author's field notes, December 25, 1997.
8. Author's field notes, July 23, 1997.

Figure 3. The housing office of the Ridgewood-Bushwick Senior Citizens Council, 217 Wyckoff Avenue in Bushwick. Photo by Heather Wollin.

was the case in this building, where Carmen was meeting some resistance. At the meeting, tenants expressed both displeasure at the condition of their building and suspicion regarding Carmen's motives for trying to organize improvements. I recorded in my field notes how Carmen relied on the core Ridgewood-Bushwick philosophy to respond to their concerns:

> An older woman, Magda, starts complaining that not all the tenants in the building contribute to the common gas and electricity expenses, so why should she contribute, since she'll just be paying for the others? She gets very upset and starts cursing. Her daughter, Lila, and another young woman join in. Shouting ensues. Carmen shouts over all of them, saying they have to think about their kids' safety, and eventually they calm down. Carmen says that the tenants have to get together and collect the money for these two bills. The tenants seem to agree to do so, but I wonder if they really will. Carmen winds up the meeting by recapping the plan: pay these bills, get the 7A administrator in, evict the tenants not paying rent, fix up the apartments, rent to new tenants. The tenants seem to understand and approve, but there is still lingering discontent over the payment of the bills. As Carmen finishes, Lila says, "What I want to know is, why are you doing this, what's in it for

you? Nobody does things unless it gets them something." Carmen looks at her, pauses, then says, *"I do it to help people."* Lila looks a little skeptical, so I say, "It's her job to do this." Carmen agrees with me. One of the other women says, "Yeah, it's her job; people have all kinds of different jobs, and this is hers." Lila looks appeased.[9]

This exchange is particularly interesting because it demonstrates a kind of disconnect between Carmen's sense of an adequate explanation for her work and the rationale that actually satisfied the disgruntled tenant. Carmen's impulse was to rely on an articulation of the organization's "helping people" philosophy to respond to a direct challenge of her motives. For her, "I do it to help people" constituted an answer to Lila's suspicions that was both honest and obvious. For Lila, however, it was neither. In supplying a different explanation—"it's her job"—I was attempting to reframe Carmen's response in another language, yet without changing its meaning. My reinterpretation of Carmen's explanation—prompted by my own discomfort with the tenants' suspicions of her—appeared to make an impact on Lila, especially when it was expanded upon by another tenant. Carmen herself agreed with this interpretation of her work, but the fact that she did not invoke the "job" rationale on her own illustrates the extent to which she accepts and embodies the "helping people" philosophy of Ridgewood-Bushwick.

Staff members at the Ridgewood-Bushwick Housing Office continually emphasize how their work assists individual residents of Bushwick. Success is measured by the number of individuals and families who move into safe, high-quality apartments in the buildings developed by Ridgewood-Bushwick. As Angela Battaglia, the housing office director, put it in an informal conversation at the opening ceremony for a new Ridgewood-Bushwick senior citizen building: "This is what our work is really about, isn't it? Giving homes to people."[10] Similarly, Ridgewood-Bushwick's tenant organizing work is understood as a process of improving individual apartments, and then whole buildings, but only occasionally goes beyond the focus on individual assistance to address broader neighborhood concerns. This is not to say that Ridgewood-Bushwick sees only individuals or lacks a conception of how the broader organization of society impacts its ability to help people. On the contrary, Ridgewood-Bushwick actively engages the political systems of the city in ways that transform its efforts to "help people"

9. Author's field notes, July 23, 1997. Emphasis added.
10. Author's field notes, July 2, 1997.

locally into political clout that reaches far beyond the boundaries of its neighborhood.

How Politics Helps People

When Vito Lopez began expanding the services of the city-run senior center, then founded and built up the programs of the Ridgewood-Bushwick Senior Citizens Council, he recognized that benefits flowed both from providing more services to local residents and from employing local people as organizational staff. Over the years, Lopez has built a devoted following of clients and employees at the two linked organizations (and a number of others that were added later). Bushwick residents, poor and living in a neighborhood where few local service organizations existed (Friedman, Bloom, and Marks 1974), had previously had little access to the kinds of human services the growing enterprise provided. At the same time, the area had long faced high unemployment rates, so residents were always on the lookout for job opportunities. Ridgewood-Bushwick's active pursuit of government contracts to support additional programs thus turned service seekers into clients and job seekers into employees as the organization grew during the late 1970s and early 1980s.

It was in these years, as he witnessed again and again the link between political influence and access to public funds, that Lopez realized the importance of running for elected office. He got his chance in 1984, when the New York State Assembly seat for the Fifty-fourth District, covering Bushwick and parts of Williamsburg, became vacant. The sitting assemblyman, Victor Robles, left the seat to run in a newly established district of the New York City Council (where, as we have seen, he would become involved in the redevelopment of Williamsburg a decade and a half later). Lopez was able to use the base of support he had developed at Ridgewood-Bushwick to win the Assembly seat, which he continues to occupy today. Immediately following his election, Lopez resigned as executive director of Ridgewood-Bushwick, but he continued to maintain extremely close ties to the organization, employing his newfound political clout on its behalf. To this day, although he holds no formal position within the organization, Lopez operates as the de facto leader of Ridgewood-Bushwick, collaborating closely with executive director Christiana Fisher and housing office director Angela Battaglia to set organizational priorities, programs, and strategies.

The tight connection between Ridgewood-Bushwick and Assemblyman Lopez strongly impacts the organization's financial picture. Many CBOs in poor places get most of their financial support from government sources, through city, state, and federal contracts to deliver services ranging from housing support and assistance to the elderly to child care and supplemental educational programs. Although bureaucratic procedures are in place to ensure that contracts are awarded on the basis of merit, there is play in the system. As in any governmental process, politics regularly become part of the equation. A key factor in this political drama is that decisions about awarding government contracts are almost always made *outside* of the neighborhoods where CBOs like Ridgewood-Bushwick operate. Thus, to the extent that CBOs are dependent upon government contracts to continue providing services and to survive as organizations, they have a built-in incentive to try to influence those bigger systems that decide how contracts are disbursed.

Government agencies charged with allocating funds for CBO-provided services usually fall under the direct control of the executive branch, which means that these executives—the mayor, the governor, the president—have significant capacity to control contract decisions. Powerful members of the legislative branch, like Lopez, also may influence these decisions as part of their bargaining with the executive to pass policy changes or other legislation. Both executives and legislators need to win elections in order to stay in office and thus can be vulnerable to organized electoral pressure. Some CBOs stay far away from politics, preferring to let the merits of their work drive decisions about contract awards. Other CBOs develop arm's-length relationships with potentially influential elected officials. A few CBOs ally themselves closely with specific politicians, in pursuit of a mutually beneficial relationship. Ridgewood-Bushwick falls into this last category, via its intimate tie to Assemblyman Lopez.

In the heyday of the political machine, close relationships between local elected officials and voters in their district were commonplace. These relationships were based on an exchange of valuable goods. Elected officials distributed food, coal, legal assistance, government jobs, and other resources to needy local residents. In return, residents gave one of the few resources they controlled: their votes on Election Day. Tammany Hall, which ruled New York politics for eighty years, epitomized this model of governance in the nineteenth and early twentieth century, while Chicago's six-term mayor Richard J. Daley provides a more contemporary example. Today, the strong political party organizations that made the machine possible have mostly disappeared, the result of a dramatic decline in the resources they control; civil service reform, for example, has significantly reduced the number of jobs under the direct control of party organizations (Erie 1988; Freedman 1994; Moynihan and Wilson 1964). The last several decades

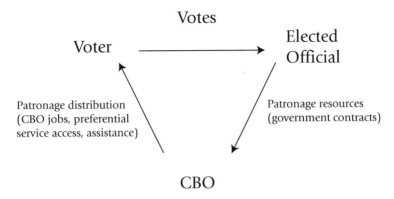

Figure 4. Triadic exchange.

have seen a concomitant decline of party organizations (Erie 1988; Guterbock 1980; Jones-Correa 1998; Ware 1985). In contrast, CBOs have seen the resources under their control expand as public services have been increasingly privatized—that is, contracted out to private organizations rather than delivered directly by government agencies and employees (Salamon 1995).

When public funds flow to a particular CBO, it is able to offer resources to local residents. These include, in addition to the housing, day care, youth development, drug treatment, and other services the CBO has contracted to provide, jobs in the organization itself. CBOs in poor urban neighborhoods like Bushwick are thus structurally positioned to reprise the role of the political machine—despite the consensus among most social scientists that the machine is dead (Erie 1988; Freedman 1994; Gordon 1968; Guterbock 1980; Moynihan and Wilson 1964). Like the machine, today's CBOs can organize voters to affect the allocation of public resources (service contracts) and can direct those resources to specific persons within neighborhoods (patronage). The political machine organized voters by distributing patronage as part of a direct exchange between voter and party. Ridgewood-Bushwick, like other nonprofit organizations incorporated under section 501(c)3 of the Internal Revenue Code, is legally prohibited from engaging in this kind of exchange (or in partisan politics generally); a CBO that did so would jeopardize its nonprofit status and thus its eligibility for many of the contract awards it relies on. My research shows, however, that CBOs can engage in a more complicated, and technically legal, exchange of resources for votes—a three-way, indirect transaction involving not just the CBO and the client/voter, but also the elected official (see fig. 4).

In this triadic exchange, the CBO serves as the fulcrum through which patronage resources are distributed and client/voters are organized. The CBO thus becomes a necessary component of the primary exchange between the political entity—the elected official—and the individual client/voter. Unlike their counterparts in the era of the political machine, today's elected officials themselves no longer directly control patronage jobs or other significant divisible benefits. Instead, the CBO holds and distributes benefits to client/voters—but the elected official is the conduit through which these resources come to the CBO. In essence, community-based organizations—offering as they do jobs in the CBO and its related enterprises; preferential access to CBO services; and other kinds of assistance, including help with navigating public service bureaucracies—are structurally positioned to replace political party organizations.

The idea that CBOs can be practitioners of a "new machine politics" must be understood in the context of a wider set of political and organizational practices: the systemic operation of the contracting regime, which transcends the boundaries of poor neighborhoods like Bushwick. Figure 5 provides a diagram of these relationships. The bottom half of the diagram revisits the local relationships just described, highlighting the CBOs' intermediate position between client/voters and elected officials. The top half shows the broader political system within which the triadic exchange is embedded. Here, the lower-level electoral districts in which CBOs are located (e.g., city council, state legislature, and congressional districts) connect to higher, aggregated levels of the city, state, and national polity. Some of the exchanges represented are direct; the nonprofit CBO, for example, provides services in exchange for participation from client/voters. Other transactions involve intermediate steps and exchanges, as when CBOs engage in electoral organizing in order to obtain from district-based elected officials the government resources they will in turn distribute. The exchange relations specified in the diagram can vary in magnitude, but strengthening one tends to raise the overall level. For example, a CBO with a strong electoral organizing capacity can help a district-based elected official deliver a large reliable voting constituency to political higher-ups, which in turn can lead to higher levels of government contracts going to the CBO (see fig. 5).[11]

---

11. For a full theoretical discussion, see Marwell (2004b). Compare to Burstein and Linton (2002), who argue that social movement groups are more likely to affect public policy when their activity contributes to the electoral efforts of politicians, and Fiorina (1981), who demonstrates that congressional representatives who assist their constituents ("constituent casework") reap electoral benefits from doing so.

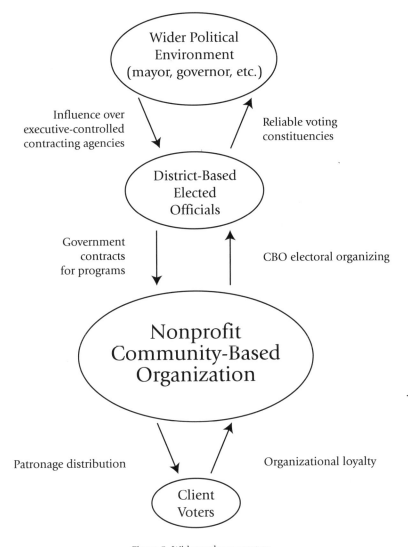

Figure 5. Wider exchange system.

Ridgewood-Bushwick relies on Assemblyman Lopez to use his political clout to help secure government contracts and other forms of public financial support for the organization. In turn, Lopez taps into Ridgewood-Bushwick's staff and client networks to create and command a reliable voting constituency. This constituency serves Lopez in two ways. First, it ensures his own reelection (Lopez has won most of his elections with 90 percent of the vote). Second, it provides him with a political resource to trade within the broader system of city, state, and national politics. Candidates for higher-level political office—mayor, governor, senator, even president—improve their chances when they accumulate blocs of voters organized and directed by others. Although today's political wisdom argues that votes won correlate with campaign funds spent, campaign strategists increasingly recognize the power of grassroots organizing as an alternative (or additional) way to turn out votes (e.g., Nagourney 2002). The Christian Coalition and other conservative organizations, for example, have used this strategy with great success. As a representative of one of the poorest political districts in the country, Lopez has very limited access to campaign donations from his constituents. He concentrates instead on building and maintaining a reliable voting constituency: a (relatively) large core group of voters that turns out regularly to support selected higher-level candidates. By reliably delivering his constituency, Lopez gains increased access to the government resources that winning higher-level officials control.[12] By organizing clients and staff into a reliable voting block, Ridgewood-Bushwick is thus able to pressure higher-level political actors to make favorable contract allocation decisions. The first step in this process, however, is to bind local residents tightly to the Ridgewood-Bushwick organization itself.

Helping People Help the Organization

In an influential 1979 article, political scientist Charles Hamilton argued that CBOs could never serve as effective political agents because they were bound by law to distribute their services without requiring that service recipients reciprocate in any way (Hamilton 1979). This condition of receiving government service contracts meant that rather than developing reciprocal patron-client relationships, as had the nineteenth-century political machine, CBOs could only foster "patron-recipient" relationships. Whereas the patron-client system regularly produced electoral victories for the machine, thereby ensuring party control over the distribution of public resources, the patron-recipient relationship hamstrung CBO efforts to organize voters. Because the interests of CBOs were not represented within the electoral arena, wrote Hamilton, the populations they serve—mostly poor people of color—would "always be in demand-making, benefit-seeking,

---

12. Incumbents running for reelection are, of course, in a better position than challengers in this system; incumbents can make a down payment of resources in return for future political support, while challengers can only trigger resources after political support has been delivered and the election won.

and invariably subordinated positions" (Hamilton 1979, 226). Neither the organizations nor their constituents could thus wield any leverage over the elected officials who make decisions about how to spend and distribute public resources. Ridgewood-Bushwick's cultivation of the triadic exchange, however, has allowed the organization to take up precisely the electoral role Hamilton claimed CBOs could not attain. While following the letter of the nonprofit law, Ridgewood-Bushwick nurtures a particular kind of reciprocity among its service recipients and staff, creating a set of local residents whose private interests overlap with those of the organization. This process results in a kind of privatization of the organization itself, with unattached "clients" becoming more like contributing "members" to the Ridgewood-Bushwick enterprise.

How does a CBO like Ridgewood-Bushwick cultivate this kind of reciprocity? Most fundamentally, this task requires that the CBO communicate to its clients that the organization expects something in return for its services. Clients might be urged to participate in a tenant organization in exchange for the CBO's pressuring landlords for building improvements; to attend CBO-sponsored public events intended to increase resident involvement in its programs; or to contribute to CBO fund-raising activities, such as anniversary dinners or street fairs. Cultivating reciprocity does present some formidable challenges, as CBOs that engage in such work are caught between the need to follow the letter of the law and the desire to effectively fulfill their missions. As noted above, financial support to CBOs usually is contingent upon service recipients being free of obligation to the CBO. This is particularly true for publicly funded services, which must follow governmental rules requiring equal access and nondiscrimination, but these conditions usually apply to foundation- and corporate-supported services as well.

At the same time, a core aspect of CBOs' work is understood to be the construction of lasting relationships between CBOs and local residents. Indeed, the last decade's discussions among CBOs, government, and foundations concerning how to improve conditions in poor neighborhoods have centered on the belief that relationship building—often shorthanded as the formation of "social capital"—should be a primary function of CBOs, and reciprocity between CBOs and local residents has been seen as key to this process.[13] Given the CBO legal environment, however, it is difficult for

13. See, e.g., Briggs, Mueller, and Sullivan 1997; Chaskin 2001; Scully and Harwood 1997; Stone 1996; U.S. Department of Housing and Urban Development 2000; Walsh 1997; Warren 2001.

CBOs to enforce reciprocity (Briggs, Mueller, and Sullivan 1997; Chaskin 2001; Saegert, Thompson, and Warren 2001). An important difference nevertheless remains between the organizational practices of CBOs that *attempt* to cultivate reciprocity and those that do not. Furthermore, some CBOs, like Ridgewood-Bushwick, are more insistent than others in articulating their reciprocal expectations.

Ridgewood-Bushwick cultivates reciprocity with its clients in many ways. One example can be seen in the organization's housing development work. Using a combination of federal, state, and city contracts and tax subsidies, Ridgewood-Bushwick develops, builds, and manages subsidized housing for low-income families and senior citizens. All of this government-subsidized housing is required to be distributed to income-eligible renters or buyers based on a lottery: the availability of housing units must be publicly announced (for example, in local newspapers), standard applications filed with a government agency, and winners randomly selected. Even within these bounds, however, there is ample room for Ridgewood-Bushwick to skew the results of the lottery toward its own clients. (During the course of my research, informants also described how other local housing organizations, including Los Sures and the United Jewish Organizations, engaged in similar practices.)

The lottery process begins with the announcement that a CBO is in the process of constructing new housing, with a certain number of apartments to be made available. While sophisticated, persistent low-income housing seekers may have learned independently when and where to look for public announcements of new housing, individuals with connections to the particular CBO are much more likely to find out about such developments and to request applications. CBO clients also benefit from assistance in completing the forms. Applications for government-subsidized housing are quite complicated, and those that are incomplete in any way are excluded from the lottery. Assistance from Ridgewood-Bushwick staff helps to increase the proportion of valid applications submitted by individuals affiliated with the organization. The informational and assistance benefits offered by Ridgewood-Bushwick, and other CBOs, thus ensure that its clients are overrepresented in drawings for any subsidized housing development it builds. The high value of housing resources in New York City's increasingly tight and expensive market encourages strong reciprocity toward Ridgewood-Bushwick from residents of its housing developments. Fieldwork repeatedly confirmed that residents of buildings built, managed, or organized by Ridgewood-Bushwick are among the most reliable participants in its organizational activities.

Ridgewood-Bushwick also cultivates reciprocity through the numerous social gatherings, parties, and trips that it sponsors. While these events lack the material value of a subsidized apartment or house, they nonetheless offer frequent occasions for clients to relax, socialize, dance, drink, and generally have a good time. From the organization's perspective, these events serve as regular opportunities to reinforce the connections between Ridgewood-Bushwick and its clients, while simultaneously coaxing clients into involvement in the organization's activities and underlining the central role played by the organization in making Bushwick a more congenial place to live. Major events on the Ridgewood-Bushwick social calendar include Thanksgiving and Christmas dinners, summer picnics and block parties, and a winter weekend retreat. More impromptu get-togethers for staff members' birthdays, weddings, births, baptisms, and so on also take place.

The Thanksgiving and Christmas events are the longest-standing Ridgewood-Bushwick gatherings. Both began in fulfillment of the original mission of the Bushwick Senior Center to assist local senior citizens. When Vito Lopez was still the center's director, he noticed that the families of increasing numbers of seniors had moved away, leaving them alone on the holidays. One year, he decided to host a Thanksgiving dinner at the center. That first time, Lopez cooked and served a turkey to twelve seniors who had no place else to go.[14] By the late 1990s, as we have seen, Ridgewood-Bushwick was serving full Thanksgiving meals to nearly three thousand elderly residents of the area, in an astounding community mobilization that continues today. Volunteers do much of the work, preparing meals to be served at the senior center party and delivered, by volunteers, to homebound senior citizens, many of whom are ill or infirm and live alone. Christmas Day brings the same routine, with a party at the senior center and a cadre of volunteers delivering meals and visiting for a few minutes with the homebound.

The holiday events offer an opportunity for a wide range of Ridgewood-Bushwick affiliates to come together in collective celebration. The festive mood and honorific treatment of local residents—seniors and volunteers alike—help cultivate loyalty to the organization. As the seniors sit at long tables festooned with holiday colors, many dressed in their best outfits, volunteers provide table service, grandly delivering meals from the kitchen. At the end of the day, Assemblyman Lopez gathers the volunteers together to thank them for their hard work and to remind them of the joy their

---

14. Author's field notes, December 25, 1997.

efforts have brought to local residents.[15] The same is true of other social gatherings Ridgewood-Bushwick sponsors, including block parties, summer picnics, and special events. The opening of a new subsidized housing development, for instance, might include a ribbon-cutting ceremony, a tour of the building, lunch in the beautiful back courtyard, and a dessert of celebratory house-shaped cookies. Twice every summer, Ridgewood-Bushwick sponsors a free bus trip to a pristine state park eighty miles from Brooklyn, where residents are met by local politicians and CBO staffers wearing funny aprons and dishing up freshly grilled steaks. For many Bushwick residents, who lack the resources to arrange and pay for such events themselves, Ridgewood-Bushwick is a constant, caring presence that makes important contributions to their overall quality of life.

Scholars, community service practitioners, and public policy makers alike generally approve of organizational activities that cultivate resident participation, as this indicates residents' involvement in neighborhood affairs, and serves as a mechanism for the creation of "social capital." But these events can also be understood as serving the needs of the organization, by strengthening its importance in the lives of the residents. As Ridgewood-Bushwick successfully encourages reciprocity with local residents, it also shrinks their perspective. Once won over by Ridgewood-Bushwick and its considerable benefits, these clients may develop a narrow interest in the fortunes of the organization itself, rather than those of the wider neighborhood or the city as a whole, or even a notion of the public good. Ridgewood-Bushwick's privatized orientation has an immediate goal: the transformation of loyal organizational participants into a reliable voting constituency—a necessary component of the organization's efforts to win additional government service contracts. At the same time, however, the organization's particularistic distribution of publicly funded benefits raises important questions about the overall system that encourages this development. These murky issues, however, are irrelevant if Ridgewood-Bushwick cannot turn its loyal participants into reliable voters.

Turning Clients into Voters

Holiday parties and help with housing lottery applications, among many other activities, are critical for Ridgewood-Bushwick's cultivation of client reciprocity, but they are not sufficient to attract the government contracts that determine the organization's ability to provide services in Bushwick.

15. Author's field notes, December 25, 1997; December 25, 1998.

That task requires that adherents to the Ridgewood-Bushwick enterprise be converted into something else: reliable voters. This process has two components. First, clients and staff must understand the role of politics in the fortunes of the organization; they need to be aware of the wider environment that links their receipt of jobs and services to their acting in the electoral arena. Second, Ridgewood-Bushwick must convince decision makers within the wider political environment—from the mayor and governor to the officials in charge of city, state, and federal agencies—that it has control over the members of its voting constituency. This ultimate test is a single one: Ridgewood-Bushwick is in control if it can regularly turn out its voters in elections. Ridgewood-Bushwick fulfills these two components through three sets of activities: (1) continually educating its client-voters about how contracts are allocated by city, state, and federal agencies; (2) regularly exhibiting the Ridgewood-Bushwick constituency to decision makers within that wider political environment; and (3) winning elections on the district level.

EDUCATING CLIENT-VOTERS. Ridgewood-Bushwick has two sets of client-voters: its staff and the local residents who receive its services. As in political machines, some of the most reliable adherents are those individuals who are employed by the organization itself. Ridgewood-Bushwick currently comprises over fifty separate programs and organizations, offering cradle-to-grave services. To deliver all of these services, Ridgewood-Bushwick employs a large staff, which continues to grow rapidly: from a handful of employees at its 1974 founding, to fifteen hundred during my fieldwork in 1998, to over two thousand by 2005. Their jobs span a wide range, including superintendents at Ridgewood-Bushwick–managed apartment buildings, tenant organizers, GED teachers, receptionists, social workers, home attendants, and others. These men and women are a key resource for Ridgewood-Bushwick's efforts to build a reliable voting constituency, as many of them—not coincidentally—live and vote in the district. If a Ridgewood-Bushwick employee cannot vote in local district elections, his or her job is wasted patronage. There is strong recognition of this fact among employees, so much so that workers who move out of the area often maintain their voter registration at the address of a family member who still lives in the old neighborhood.[16]

16. This is not to say that all Ridgewood-Bushwick employees are local residents. There are some professional jobs—housing development, legal assistance, accounting, social work—that often are filled by outsiders. It is important for Ridgewood-Bushwick that qualified workers fill

In addition to counting on staff members' votes, Ridgewood-Bushwick relies on its employees to help get out the vote in the neighborhood. The organization's nonprofit, tax-exempt status prohibits it from engaging in partisan electoral activities. Its employees, however, retain the right to partisan political involvement on their own time. Careful to stay within the letter of the law, employees who work on the arduous tasks of grassroots campaigning do so through the Bushwick Democratic Club, a by-now well known heavy hitter in Brooklyn politics, housed in a spare, two-room storefront down the street from the Ridgewood-Bushwick Housing Office. In the early months of the campaign season, a core group of Ridgewood-Bushwick employees gathers after regular working hours at the club to build lists of regular voters and make pre–Election Day phone solicitations.[17] On Election Day, nearly two hundred campaign volunteers, mostly Ridgewood-Bushwick staff but also clients of the organization, gather at the club at 6:00 a.m. to begin a long day of door-to-door canvassing to pull voters out to the polls.

For the Ridgewood-Bushwick staff, the relationship between being an employee and participating in the organization's political work is well understood. Ridgewood-Bushwick is officially closed on election days, freeing up staff members to work at the political club. There is a strong sense of expectation that they will join in, as I learned from a staffer at the housing office when I asked him, a few weeks before one election, what Ridgewood-Bushwick employees would be doing with their day off. When he told me that everyone would be down at the Bushwick Democratic Club, I was surprised and asked, "That's not required, is it?" "Of course not," he replied, with a slight smirk and an ironic tone—clearly implying that it was indeed required. When I asked what would happen if an employee did not show up at the Democratic Club, he admitted that while a person would not necessarily lose her job, neither would it be a feather in her cap in subsequent hiring or retention decisions.[18] Fieldwork on that election day and several

---

these jobs because organizational competence is a necessity for CBOs if they want to continue receiving government contracts. I myself—a relatively unknown quantity but, as a graduate student, identified as someone with a high level of education—was offered jobs at Ridgewood-Bushwick numerous times. The total number of jobs filled by outsiders, however, is relatively small, and some Ridgewood-Bushwick professionals are also local residents.

17. Most political campaigns in New York City purchase voter lists that indicate which registered voters have voted in recent primary and general elections. Campaigns usually target these voters for preelection mailings and phone calls, and door knocking on Election Day itself. The Bushwick Democratic Club compiles and maintains its own lists rather than purchasing them.

18. Author's field notes, October 18, 1997.

others during the study period confirmed that many Ridgewood-Bushwick employees—on this day acting as members of the Bushwick Democratic Club—spent upward of twelve hours going door to door in the neighborhood to pull out voters for favored candidates. Many of the doors they knocked at belonged to people who were clients of Ridgewood-Bushwick. With a familiar face handing out palm cards and asking for their vote, many of these residents promised to make it to the polls before the day was out.[19]

Ridgewood-Bushwick staff members have multiple opportunities to learn about the relationship between engaging in electoral politics and securing government contracts to fund organizational activities. Their daily job tasks are embedded within a continual discussion about government funding and the political processes that affect contract allocations. Ridgewood-Bushwick clients are less exposed to these exchanges, but they are important targets for the organization's electoral work. The organization primarily utilizes public forums to educate these client-voters about the connections between political activity and service availability. These forums include gatherings to mark the commencement of new Ridgewood-Bushwick services, as well as ongoing coverage of the CBO's work in its community newspaper, the *Bushwick Observer*. Every month, ten thousand free copies of the paper are distributed throughout the neighborhood.

During my fieldwork, I observed numerous events celebrating the opening of new Ridgewood-Bushwick services. These events always featured Assemblyman Lopez as the keynote speaker and were frequently attended by people from the wider political environment as well. Ridgewood-Bushwick organizational leaders, as well as Assemblyman Lopez, invariably reminded the assembled client-voters of the important role that political activity played in service delivery. At the ribbon-cutting ceremony for a new Ridgewood-Bushwick senior citizen housing development, for example, I was impressed by the turnout of both local residents and elected officials on a steamy July morning. Inside a large white tent set up on Bleecker Street in front of the new building, named Plaza de los Ancianos ("Senior Citizens' Plaza" in Spanish), some two hundred elderly Bushwick residents sat on white folding chairs while an overflow crowd of about fifty younger people stood out in the sun. Colorful helium balloons were lashed to the tent poles and floated up along the ceiling as Assemblyman Lopez addressed the crowd. Next to him stood Angela Battaglia (Ridgewood-Bushwick's housing director), U.S. senator Alfonse D'Amato (Republican of New York), and three Democratic officials: Brooklyn borough president

19. Author's field notes, November 4, 1997; November 3, 1999.

Howard Golden, and City Councilmen Victor Robles and Martin Malave-Dilan. Lopez thanked Battaglia for her hard work, saying that she deserved much of the credit for the new building, but that all of the elected officials present that day had also helped with the project. He was happy, he said, to work with all of them to bring new resources into Bushwick.[20]

Events such as these represent one opportunity for Ridgewood-Bushwick client-voters to make the connection between services and politics, as politicians line up to associate themselves with the much-needed resources provided by the organization. Articles in the *Bushwick Observer* often make these connections even more explicit. An analysis of the *Observer* from April 1997 to December 1999 indicates that the newspaper's articles fell into three main groups. The smallest category—about 25 percent of all articles—comprised items of general community interest. The second group—about 47 percent—addressed programs and services provided by Ridgewood-Bushwick. The third category of articles—about 28 percent—covered Assemblyman Lopez. This last category, in particular, communicates the important role that Lopez plays in bringing benefits to Bushwick residents, as well as the political clout he wields. The cover story of the March 1998 issue, for example, begins: "On February 4, 1998, history was made in Bushwick as [New York State] Gov. George E. Pataki made an unprecedented visit and tour of the community. The Governor, who was invited to visit and tour the area by Assemblyman Vito Lopez, arrived with many of his top commissioners." This and similar stories are part of the client-voter education process employed by Ridgewood-Bushwick as it works to turn its loyal participants into reliable voters.

DISPLAYING THE CONSTITUENCY A second key piece of Ridgewood-Bushwick's political work is to communicate to officials who make decisions about public service contract allocations that Assemblyman Lopez and the CBO he founded have a large and responsive set of potential voters. Many Ridgewood-Bushwick events, such as the ribbon-cutting ceremony described above, do double duty, providing opportunities for both client-voter education and constituent display. Perhaps the most important of these display events is the annual retreat held by Brooklyn Unidos, one of the many organizations under the Ridgewood-Bushwick umbrella. At the retreat, the embeddedness of the triadic exchange in the wider political environment is most clearly visible.

20. Author's field notes, July 2, 1997.

Figure 6. Photo, autographed by state assemblyman Vito Lopez, of participants in the 1998 Brooklyn Unidos retreat in Pawling, New York. Photo courtesy of Brooklyn Unidos.

Brooklyn Unidos is a coalition of some 350 neighborhood "leaders" from Bushwick and Williamsburg, including members of tenant associations, block associations, low-income cooperatives, parent-teacher associations, and clients and staff of local CBOs. Brooklyn Unidos operates under the nonprofit umbrella of Ridgewood-Bushwick, but, in another example of role fluidity at the organization, is managed by staff members from Assemblyman Lopez's district office. In addition to monthly meetings, at which high-ranking city and state political figures regularly make appearances, the highlight of the year at Brooklyn Unidos is its three-day retreat, held at a nonprofit conference center in upstate New York. The formal goal of the retreat is to allow Brooklyn Unidos leaders a period of concentrated interaction with policy makers and government officials who administer public service programs of significance to people in Bushwick and Williamsburg. The most important informal goal is for Assemblyman Lopez to put his voting constituency on display for government agency representatives, who then report on the retreat to their respective department heads and elected officials. The retreat helps facilitate the triadic exchange: client-voters receive benefits, Lopez displays his constituency to government officials, and government officials connect Lopez's political strength to their future decisions about government contract allocations.

Two types of events held during the retreat contribute to this process. During the day on Saturday and Sunday, Brooklyn Unidos members attend workshops that address issues of concern to their neighborhood work, such as affordable housing, welfare reform, or domestic violence. Each work-shop features a panel of speakers, a mix of high-ranking public agency officials and representatives of local CBOs. Lopez himself usually mod-erates each panel and makes sure to comment on the significance of the gathering for both panelists and Brooklyn Unidos members. At one re-treat I attended, the first workshop of the weekend drew a full house, with some 160 people filling the chairs in the main conference room by 10:00 a.m. on Saturday. At the front of the room, Assemblyman Lopez stood to introduce the panelists seated along the table to his left: Veronica White, CEO of the New York City Housing Partnership, a major public-private developer of affordable housing; Richard Roberts, commissioner of New York City's Department of Housing Preservation and Development, the city agency responsible for affordable housing; Joseph Lynch, acting commis-sioner of New York State's Division of Housing and Community Renewal, the state housing agency; Bill Traylor, vice president of the Local Initiative Support Corporation, a primary syndicator of tax credits for subsidized low-income housing; and Cece Tkaczyk, executive director of the Neigh-borhood Preservation Coalition of New York State. After introductions, Lopez moved straight to his main point: that the Brooklyn Unidos mem-bers were "important enough for all of these important people to give up their Saturday for you—and Joe Lynch even brought his wife with him."[21]

The triadic exchange is in clear view here. Ridgewood-Bushwick has or-ganized a group of nearly two hundred local residents who are sufficiently committed to their work to give up an entire weekend to the retreat. Lopez presents this constituency of client-voters (designated as "leaders") to a group of public officials who represent the mayor, governor, and other rel-evant political players. Lopez's remarks make it clear that he is responsible for the organization of these client-voters—and of many more who answer to those in attendance. The Brooklyn Unidos members see how Lopez has brought these top-level agency officials to meet with them, thereby demonstrating his access to the decision makers who provide the govern-ment contracts that pay for CBO jobs and services. Furthermore, Lopez's speeches remind the client-voters of the role that voting plays in delivering these resources.

The workshops are a key feature of the conference because they em-body the triadic resources-for-votes exchange. At the same time, the con-ference serves as a patronage benefit to the client-voters, thereby reinforc-ing their loyalties to Ridgewood-Bushwick and to Lopez. As with many of

21. Author's field notes, January 10, 1998.

Ridgewood-Bushwick's social events, the main benefits of the conference are the leisure activities. First, there is the simple fact of a free weekend in the country for a group of people who have few opportunities for such activities. Lopez covers the entire cost of the retreat (conference rooms, lodging, food, transportation, etc.) out of his Assembly "member-item" budget.[22] In addition, the Brooklyn Unidos retreat is well known for its parties. There are four parties during the weekend: one on each of the bus trips to and from the conference center, one on Friday night, and one on Saturday night. On the bus trips, Brooklyn Unidos members share food they have prepared and mix drinks from an impromptu bar set up in the aisle of the bus. The Friday and Saturday parties feature a disc jockey brought along from Brooklyn, flashing lights, alcohol (beer on Friday night, liquor on Saturday), and lots of dancing. Both parties continue into the wee hours of the morning, but people always make it to the workshops the next day.

The Brooklyn Unidos retreat is only one example, albeit a highly illustrative one, of the ways in which Ridgewood-Bushwick and Assemblyman Lopez work together to organize client-voters, and to parlay that voting constituency into influence within the wider political environment. Top elected officials not only send their agency leaders to the Brooklyn Unidos retreat, but also make regular appearances at other Ridgewood Bushwick events and facilities. During their election campaigns, for example, Mayor Rudolph Giuliani appeared at the Ridgewood-Bushwick picnic at a state park in Long Island, Governor George Pataki traveled to the Ridgewood-Bushwick Senior Center to speak about his health policy proposals, and (former) U.S. senator Alfonse D'Amato was the featured speaker at the opening of a new subsidized housing development built by Ridgewood-Bushwick. During the 2000 U.S. presidential campaign, Democratic candidate Al Gore paid a visit to the organization, as reported on the front page

22. Each member of the New York State Legislature receives a quantity of public funds to distribute to nonprofit organizations in his or her district. Assemblyman Lopez spends the majority of his member-item funds on the annual Brooklyn Unidos retreat. At the 2000 retreat, for example, Lopez stated that he had spent forty thousand dollars for the weekend (author's field notes, February 19, 2000). The importance of member-item funds to legislators who seek to build machine-politics CBOs like Ridgewood-Bushwick is underlined by an ongoing political battle in New York State. In 2001, state senator Pedro Espada (Bronx) switched his party affiliation from Democrat to Republican. His publicly stated reason was that since Republicans controlled the state senate his member-item funds would increase significantly if he switched parties (Perez-Peña 1997). It was later learned that Espada had channeled over four hundred thousand dollars in member-item funds to a CBO of which he was the executive director. Public outcry led to the funds being returned, but Espada remains embroiled in a legal fight over his party switch. He continues to maintain that he wants to be a Republican because of the additional resources it brings into his district.

of that year's October edition of the *Bushwick Observer*. Clearly, Ridgewood-Bushwick and Lopez have the attention of important players in the broader political system of the city and state.

WINNING ELECTIONS Proving the effectiveness of its ability to mobilize its constituency is the final piece of Ridgewood-Bushwick's political work: converting its promising display of client-voters into actual electoral victories. During my fieldwork, Assemblyman Lopez's political club was recognized by elected officials and the media as a contributor to one citywide electoral victory—Mayor Rudolph Giuliani's 1997 reelection—and as the force behind the winning candidates in three critical district-level elections: a 1999 state judicial election, a 2000 state district leader election, and a 2001 city council election. At a meeting of Brooklyn Unidos two days after the 1999 judicial election, which pitted Lopez's candidate against a candidate backed by the district's rival Hasidic Jewish population,[23] Lopez drove home the importance of his organization's win:

> Vito says that [Election Day] was a "very, very successful day" for the organization [Ridgewood-Bushwick, the Bushwick Democratic Club, and Brooklyn Unidos]. The Hasidim lost, and they lost badly.... He says that the victory is only the beginning of a larger struggle, in which they have to find out who their friends are. Candidates have to choose sides, and if they want the support of one of the more impressive Democratic organizations in the city, they [the candidates] are going to have to play with [Lopez and his organization].... He says that you can't expect things to move your way without understanding the politics of what's going on. A political favor means that when there are two hundred requests for public money, and only two get funded, the people who are owed a favor get one of those two. At work today, he had three high-level people from the mayor's office call to talk to him about what Bushwick needs. He says he's not sure if he wants to take that step [of getting so close to Giuliani, the Republican mayor], since it's a little scary, but this is the kind of recognition the organization is getting now.[24]

The reward for engaging in these three types of political work is a steady flow of government contracts to Ridgewood-Bushwick. During the fieldwork

23. New York City has multiple and overlapping districts for a wide variety of elected offices. Judicial districts are usually very large—in this case large enough to encompass both Lopez's Bushwick state assembly district and the section of Williamsburg dominated by the Hasidim.

24. Author's field notes, November 4, 1999.

period, Ridgewood-Bushwick received millions of dollars in contract revenues for a wide variety of projects. These included the organization's third federally funded Section 202 supportive housing building for senior citizens. Most neighborhoods are lucky to win one of these highly competitive contracts, but Ridgewood-Bushwick opened its third such building in 1997. In 2000, Ridgewood-Bushwick won an extremely unusual, twenty-six-million-dollar contract to build and operate a 216-bed nursing home in Bushwick. This contract was facilitated by New York's governor, George Pataki, who allowed it to be funded through the New York State Dormitory Authority. Also in 2000, Ridgewood-Bushwick won a new contract to operate its own legal assistance program for low-income individuals needing help with civil cases. Most recently, following my exit from the field, Ridgewood-Bushwick received a multimillion-dollar contract to operate a charter school, contracts to develop and manage a fourth Section 202 senior housing building, and a contract to build and run a new youth center. These important new contracts were in addition to the ongoing contracts that fund over 90 percent of Ridgewood-Bushwick's regular seven-million-dollar budget.

Ridgewood-Bushwick's emphasis on expanding its pool of public funds by winning additional government contracts fundamentally shapes its orientation to the broader political field of the city. To the extent that more contracts result in improvements to its neighborhood—replacing vacant lots with subsidized housing, building a local merchants' association to fight crime and attract more shoppers, establishing a nursing home in an area with virtually no other long-term care for the elderly—Ridgewood-Bushwick's activities generate public benefits for the neighborhood. Despite these contributions, however, Ridgewood-Bushwick's top priority is on maintaining what is essentially a private (albeit nonprofit) organizational enterprise. By "helping people"—providing local residents with needed services or employing them—Ridgewood-Bushwick ensures their loyalty and commitment, as well as the CBO's health and expansion. Sociologists Walter Powell and Elisabeth Clemens have argued that relieving nonprofit organizations of the tax burden carried by for-profit firms is "ostensibly justified by the expectation that nonprofits will produce public goods that would go underproduced in their absence or on the grounds that production exclusively through the marketplace would exclude some members of society" (Powell and Clemens 1998, xvi). Ridgewood-Bushwick's on-the-ground practice, motivated by its central concern with securing government contracts, presents a challenge to this assumption. The organization deliberately targets the benefits of its work to a partially exclusionary set of beneficiaries: those local residents who pledge their loyalty—and deliver their votes—to the Ridgewood-Bushwick enterprise.

Not all CBOs pursue the Ridgewood-Bushwick course of action, which I call a *private politics of distribution*. Indeed, Bushwick itself is home to another CBO whose approach to politics could not be more different. Saint Barbara's Catholic Church works with its parishioners and other local residents to build a more publicly oriented form of political power in Bushwick. Their work embraces a broad notion of citizenship in society by aiming to expand the pool of opportunities for all residents of Bushwick, and for that matter, of the city as a whole. Like Ridgewood-Bushwick, Saint Barbara's understands the importance of orienting its activities with reference to organizations whose economic and political powers transcend neighborhood boundaries. Its commitment to what I call *public goods politics* explicitly seeks out the organizational sites of power on specific issues, then aims to combat it with the power of its own constituency. Whereas Ridgewood-Bushwick sizes up the political system as it is, then carves out its own instrumental place within it, Saint Barbara's attempts to shift the underlying operation of the system itself, thereby reconfiguring the political field that its constituents—and hundreds of thousands of other city residents like them—confront on an everyday basis.

Citizens' Power in Bushwick: Saint Barbara's Catholic Church

Saint Barbara's Catholic Church was built by German immigrants to New York, who by the end of the nineteenth century had established a large and successful beer brewing industry in north Brooklyn. Many of the brewery owners lived in Bushwick, and they desired a church that reflected both their Catholic origins and their significant wealth. In 1893, after a massive fundraising campaign, they got their wish, inaugurating an ornate church worthy of inclusion in the American Institute of Architects' *Guide to New York*. Legend has it that one brewer, Leonard Eppig, gave so much money to the campaign that he convinced the Brooklyn diocese to name the church after his daughter, Barbara. The twin bell towers of Saint Barbara's reach high into the sky, visible from almost anywhere in Bushwick. Together with its school building, convent, and rectory, Saint Barbara's covers about two-thirds of the square block bounded by Central and Wilson Avenues on the north and south, and Bleecker and Menahan Streets on the east and west.

The Italian immigrants who flooded into Bushwick in the first decades of the twentieth century joined their German neighbors at Saint Barbara's and soon became the great majority in the parish. In thriving midcentury

Bushwick, Saint Barbara's busily carried on the usual masses, baptisms, weddings, and funerals, ministering to its solidly working- and lower-middle-class flock. By the mid-1960s, however, the fire epidemic that would devastate Bushwick in so many ways had begun. In 1968, over two thousand fires struck Bushwick, nearly half of them causing structural damage to residential and commercial properties.. Ten years later, during the first six months of 1977, Bushwick faced eight hundred fires, nearly a third of them officially designated as "suspicious" (Sanchez 1990). The decade was particularly hard on the area immediately surrounding Saint Barbara's, which fell victim not only to fires but also to late-arriving urban renewal clearance. All around the church, these scourges left little but burned buildings and vacant lots.

In 1971, New York City tore down all the buildings on the square block just south of Saint Barbara's in preparation for the construction of much-needed public housing. Thirty-three businesses were forced to close and 277 families—nearly a thousand people—lost their homes (Gottlieb et al. 1977a). It took nearly nine years for the promised public housing to open, and for most of that time the land lay fallow, attracting illegal garbage dumping, junkies, and even packs of wild dogs (Albert Davila 1984; Gottlieb 1979). On the block just north of the church, between 1972 and 1977 all but four of its thirty-eight three- and four-story residential buildings burned to empty shells (Gottlieb et al. 1977b). When a citywide blackout hit in the summer of 1977, the massive looting and destruction that took place on Broadway, the commercial strip just a few blocks southwest of Saint Barbara's, only made that street look more like the rest of the neighborhood. In the midst of all this, the block occupied by the church was one of the few to escape physically unscathed.

As housing disappeared from the blocks surrounding Saint Barbara's, the people followed suit. By 1979, the congregation had dwindled from a high point of fifteen hundred regulars at Sunday mass to fewer than fifty (La Rosa 1987). Along with the departing congregants, most of them Italian American, went the financial contributions that had helped sustain the church's physical plant. In the mid-1980s, after nearly a decade of waiting, some nine hundred units of low-density public housing finally opened on the lots surrounding the church (Gottlieb 1993), and the development's mostly African American and Latino residents began to revive the Saint Barbara's congregation. As the pews filled up again on Sunday mornings, it became clear that the prolonged period of neighborhood devastation had taken its toll on the church facilities. By the time Monsignor John Powis became pastor of Saint Barbara's in 1989, the sanctuary had sustained

Figure 7. Saint Barbara's Catholic Church, 138 Bleecker Street in Bushwick. Photo courtesy of bridgeandtunnelclub.com.

serious structural damage, to say nothing of its more cosmetic decline: dirty marble, leaky windows, faded paintings, worn-out fixtures. The state of the church reflected the conditions of Bushwick as a whole, which still grappled with high levels of crime, large swaths of substandard housing, unsafe and poorly functioning schools, and a range of related social problems. Father

Powis, a veteran of struggles in New York's poor neighborhoods, girded himself for his new challenges.

The parish system of the Catholic Church gives this ancient institution some key similarities to the contemporary community-based organization. Each parish, like Saint Barbara's, serves residents of a particular geographic area. Although the primary mission of the parishes is spiritual, many also provide services to local residents in need, including soup kitchens, homeless shelters, legal services, food and clothing pantries, and child care. Until the late 1990s, religious congregations were barred from directly receiving government funds that were available to support the delivery of these and similar kinds of services.[25] Many religious groups, however, established affiliated nonprofit service organizations that adhered to the constitutional mandate of the separation of church and state, and so were eligible to receive government monies. Such groups run the gamut from very large nonprofits, such as Catholic Charities, to small CBOs like the Southside Mission, the service arm of Transfiguration Catholic Church in Williamsburg's Southside. Indeed, in poor urban neighborhoods like Williamsburg and Bushwick, local churches—particularly Catholic churches—often function in many of the same ways as nonreligious CBOs.[26] The pastors of both Transfiguration and Saint Barbara's have long seen their service to the poor as part of their parishes' core spiritual mission.

Saint Barbara's itself does not run a formal nonprofit affiliate, but the church plays an integral role in a number of ongoing service and community organizing activities in Bushwick. From their office in the church rectory, Father Powis and two other members of the church staff counsel parishioners and other local residents on immigration and citizenship laws, help them file paperwork for public benefits, distribute a small amount of clothing and food, and try to troubleshoot the myriad other problems of people who come through the church doors seeking help. In one of his more controversial moves, Father Powis has allowed members of two of New York City's major youth gangs, the Latin Kings and the Ñetas, to hold meetings at the church. At the time of my research, he was hopeful that

25. The 1996 federal welfare reform legislation included the first "charitable choice" provision passed by Congress, and subsequent federal social assistance legislation has also included such provisions. These provisions order state governments to not discriminate against religious congregations in choosing contractors to deliver federally funded social services.

26. The CBO parallel is far from universal among urban congregations, especially non-Catholic congregations. For an illuminating discussion of urban churches that have few ties to the low-income neighborhoods where they are located, and thus little in common with CBOs, see McRoberts (2003).

his support would strengthen the gangs' interest in turning their members toward positive youth development activities.[27] Saint Barbara's also works with a group of independent CBOs that rent space from the church in the buildings that once housed its convent and school. Linked together in a cooperative structure called "Saint Barbara's Plaza," these CBOs provide service referrals, operational tips, and moral support to one another as they go about their daily work in early childhood education, women's economic development, family support, health promotion, and other service areas. Once a month, Father Powis convenes the Plaza CBOs to foster ongoing communication and discuss emerging concerns facing the neighborhood.

Amid all the activities to which it provides support and encouragement, Saint Barbara's is most directly involved with a citizens' organizing effort that targets not only Bushwick, but the equally poor Brooklyn neighborhoods to its east, Brownsville and East New York. The East Brooklyn Congregations federation organizes church members—including parishioners at Saint Barbara's—across the three contiguous neighborhoods to combat blight, poor public services, unemployment, educational failure, and a host of related issues. An affiliate of the national nonprofit Industrial Areas Foundation (IAF), East Brooklyn Congregations runs a tiny staff out of an office in an East New York public housing development. The IAF is the legacy of Saul Alinsky, the well-known community organizer from Chicago. Alinsky's ideas have been synthesized into the IAF's core principle of organizing: transforming people from disconnected, disenfranchised subjects into powerful, public citizens who can create social change (see, e.g., Gecan 2002; Rooney 1995; M. R. Warren 2001). The IAF believes that change results from meaningful, public relationships between people. Members of a congregation, residents of a neighborhood, or students in a school become a collective of leaders when they build relationships with each other, then draw on their mutual trust and respect to create a plan for change in which they are all invested. Change comes when these leaders build public relationships with powerful individuals from the government and private sectors who can help transform their visions into reality. This "relational culture" (Gecan 2002) is really about everyday citizens claiming power: the power to reshape their world, and to improve the lot of others like themselves.

In 1978, IAF sent an organizer to East Brooklyn Congregations to commence eighteen months of building relationships among the members of

---

27. Author's field notes on interview with Father John Powis, August 4, 1997.

some twenty churches, Catholic and Protestant, in Brownsville and East New York. These efforts took place just a few miles from where Vito Lopez had already initiated his growing enterprise, but they had little else in common with Ridgewood-Bushwick. Whereas Lopez hewed to his "helping people" philosophy, gathering grateful clients into a growing political muscle, EBC aimed for a citizen-centered form of issue identification, strategy development, and action implementation. Once EBC's series of relational meetings had produced solid commitments from a wide range of East Brooklyn residents to work for social change, the group commenced several concrete projects. Over the next ten years, EBC leaders garnered numerous neighborhood investments by the city government,which replaced thousands of missing street signs, repaired long-dilapidated parks and playgrounds, renovated the local subway stations, and built two new neighborhood health centers (Gecan 2002). EBC accomplished its most visible change—building and selling nearly three thousand single-family homes to local residents of modest means—through an innovative collaboration with the private sector and the city.

Although the center of EBC's work in its early years lay in Brownsville and East New York, by 1983, Saint Barbara's had brought Bushwick into the federation (Gecan 2002, 138). The connection was strengthened when Father Powis, who had been a founding member of EBC during his 25-year tenure at Our Lady of the Presentation Catholic Church in Brownsville, moved to Bushwick. When he arrived at Saint Barbara's in 1989, Father Powis was committed to expanding the church's involvement with EBC. He recognized that Saint Barbara's parishioners lamented the physical condition of their church, one of the most spectacular in Brooklyn. This was particularly true of longtime parishioners, who had lived through the worst years of Bushwick's—and Saint Barbara's—decline. With this concern in mind, in 1990 Saint Barbara's undertook a project that, while meeting the IAF criterion of addressing an issue strongly felt by the parishioners themselves, seemed to overreach the goal of providing an easy victory: the renovation of the church. The church finance committee estimated that a complete renovation would cost $550,000. Having never previously sought subsidies from the Brooklyn diocese to pay its bills, the finance committee was loathe to request such assistance now. Father Powis realized the potential that a parishioner-focused fund-raising campaign could have for building his congregation's leadership capacities and sense of efficacy, so he and the finance committee worked out a plan. Half the money would come from a low-interest loan from the diocese, and parishioners would donate the other half (Maire 1997).

Father Powis and a group of Saint Barbara's leaders began reaching out to parishioners, talking with them about the fund-raising campaign. Needless to say, these talks could not ignore Bushwick's extremely difficult socioeconomic conditions: in 1990, the area's median household income was $21,246 (just over half the citywide figure), its official unemployment rate was 16 percent (nearly twice the city's rate of 9 percent), and over 40 percent of the population had incomes below the poverty line (New York City Department of City Planning 2005). Was there really a spare $275,000 floating around in Bushwick? Amazingly, after one-on-one meetings with hundreds of parishioners, the answer to that question turned out to be "yes." Some three hundred members of Saint Barbara's committed themselves to donate $720 over the course of two years: about a dollar a day (Maire 1997). Other parishioners donated smaller amounts, contributing to the cause in a less structured but nonetheless important fashion. The donations slowly added up, the loan from the diocese came in, and renovations commenced. By December 1993, just in time for Saint Barbara's hundredth anniversary, the task was completed. Twenty-five stained-glass windows, the century-old work of German craftsmen, shone brilliantly over the heads of the church's now mostly Latino and African American parishioners. Bright colors and new gold leaf leapt out of the magnificent wall paintings. The intricately carved wooden pulpit had been lovingly restored. The huge dome of the church, which had suffered major structural damage due to water leakage over the years, rose sturdily, light streaming in from the windows along its base. A brand-new baptismal font was installed next to the simple altar, while elaborate marble statues of Jesus and numerous saints gleamed all around the church.

The renovations project fulfilled the fundamental IAF organizing principle: by building relationships among themselves in pursuit of their common goal, the Saint Barbara's parishioners had opened the door to their own power. They themselves had identified a problem, planned a solution, and implemented it successfully. Their revitalized spiritual home stood as testament to their vision and hard work. With this victory, the Saint Barbara's parishioners crossed an important threshold in becoming involved citizens of their community, and then turned their efforts toward other aspects of what IAF organizer Michael Gecan calls "the public's business" (Gecan 2002).

Organizing to Reform Public Education in East Brooklyn

During the course of Saint Barbara's fund-raising campaign, the Bushwick church also was also becoming involved with a new EBC project that

affected all of the federation's member congregations: public education reform. Parents involved with EBC in Brownsville, East New York, and Bushwick alike complained vociferously about the poor quality of their children's schools. The schools' reading scores documented the high level of
failure in these areas—in 1989, only 50 to 60 percent of elementary school
students in the three districts were reading at grade level (*New York Times*
1989a, 1989b)—and parents themselves could see that their children were
not mastering even the most basic of academic skills (Maire 1997). Conditions at the two large city high schools that served the EBC neighborhoods—
Thomas Jefferson and Bushwick High Schools—were plagued by dismal
graduation rates and escalating violence. EBC parents' anger about their
children's educational failure dwarfed their frustration with other potential
issues, such as crime, public transportation, sanitation, or health care. In
line with the IAF principle that anger underlies the most effective organizing
efforts, EBC decided to launch an educational reform effort.

An initial effort to reform the area's existing high schools proved futile,
leading EBC to change strategies: the organization would create two small,
alternative high schools in which it would partner with the city's central Board
of Education to establish the schools' structure and curriculum, recruit
students, and oversee operations (T. A. Ross 1996). One of these two "EBC
High Schools for Public Service" would be located in Bushwick, the other
in East New York. After enormous struggles with the Board of Education,
the teacher's union, and other segments of the educational bureaucracy,
the two EBC high schools opened in 1993.

At the same time, some leaders at Saint Barbara's were expressing great
dissatisfaction with the quality of the local elementary and junior high
schools. In those years, New York City's high schools were administered by
the central board, while locally elected community school boards ran the
elementary and junior high schools in each of the city's thirty-two local
school districts.[28] In 1990, Sister Kathy Maire, who had joined the Saint
Barbara's staff in the same year as Father Powis, decided to "see if there was
enough anger" around the issue of educational failure in Bushwick's local
school district to "organize it."[29] Sister Kathy recruited fifteen leaders from
Saint Barbara's to hold one-on-one meetings with six hundred Bushwick
residents, some of them parishioners at Saint Barbara's, some not (Maire
1997). As the leaders reported to Sister Kathy, residents' anger about the

28. In 2003, Mayor Michael Bloomberg abolished the community school boards and
recentralized the school system under direct mayoral control.
29. Author's field notes on interview with Sister Kathy Maire, July 22, 1997.

Bushwick public schools came through strongly in their meetings, but nobody had a clear idea of where the capacity to make change in the schools resided. Parents blamed teachers, principals, the local community school board, the district superintendent, the bilingual education program, the mayor, the city, and numerous other culprits for their children's failure to learn and for the lack of safety in the schools. This unfocused anger was ripe for the EBC organizing approach, and Sister Kathy began working with leaders in the newly christened Bushwick Parents Organization to break that anger into manageable chunks that could be mobilized into "actions."

An IAF-style "action" begins by identifying the source of control over a discrete problem. This means locating an actual *individual* who has the power to make and enforce a decision to do something specific about the problem. Once this person is known, all phases of an action are directed toward presenting him or her with a simple, dichotomous question: We know that x is an important step in addressing our problem, and that you control x. Will you do it? Recent accounts of IAF organizations in New York and Texas tell stories of many of these kinds of actions (e.g., Gecan 2002; Rooney 1995; M. R. Warren 2001). For example, Gecan tells the story of a group of EBC leaders from East New York who determined that the extended closure of a local public pool and park complex cruelly left children and teenagers with no place to play or cool off during the hot summer months. They secured a meeting with the city commissioner in charge of parks, and asked him only one question: When do you plan to reopen the Betsy Head Park and Pool? Frustrated by the leaders' refusal to converse about any other topic, the commissioner lost his temper in the most outrageous way, screaming and cursing at them. Then, apparently anxious about what the EBC leaders might tell the press, the commissioner got to work: three days after the meeting, construction crews appeared at the pool, and it reopened six months later (Gecan 2002, 55–57).

In contrast to this example, where the target of the action was clear, a major part of the challenge confronting Sister Kathy and the Bushwick Parents Organization lay in figuring out *to whom* they should direct their actions. Bushwick residents' unfocused anger about education issues mirrored the often-impenetrable public schools bureaucracy. Undaunted, Sister Kathy reconfigured this barrier into an integral part of building an educational reform action.[30] First, small groups of four or five Bushwick Parents leaders attempted to meet with the principals of the district's elementary and junior high schools. In response to the leaders' overtures, however, the district

---

30. Author's field notes on interview with Sister Kathy Maire, July 22, 1997.

superintendent, Felix Vazquez, decreed that only individual parents could meet with a principal, and only to discuss their own child: no "political groups" would be allowed in the schools. The Bushwick Parents leaders then held a series of meetings with the superintendent himself, stressing their rights as parents to discuss general school matters with school administrators. After several months of pursuing the point, the superintendent finally relented. The herculean efforts required of Bushwick Parents members just to win the right to meet with their children's school principals, however, turned out to be what Sister Kathy called "a perfect tool for educating the parents about how they were not welcome in the schools."[31]

Over the next three years, Bushwick Parents struggled mightily and achieved some small victories.[32] They held meetings with the principals of all five elementary schools in District 32. They conducted a facilities audit of each of these schools, documenting the enormous problems in their physical plants, including the absence of even a single working toilet in one school's boys' bathrooms. After setting up a meeting with the Division of School Facilities, Bushwick Parents procured an agreement for multiple repairs. When the agreement was not implemented, the group went to the press. Their story received coverage in the New York *Daily News* and the *New York Post*, and the repairs were completed shortly thereafter. After all this work, however, Bushwick Parents still had not made any progress on addressing the academic issues at the heart of their concerns. The group next decided to turn its attention to the issue of bilingual education in the Bushwick elementary schools.

Not Enough Anger: Bushwick Parents and Bilingual Education

Bilingual education has a long and complicated history in New York City. In 1973, a Puerto Rican advocacy group called Aspira ("Aspire") filed suit against the New York City Board of Education for abridging the rights of Puerto Rican students to secure a basic education, as guaranteed by New York State law. The suit turned on the fact that the city's public schools offered education only in English, a language that the vast number of recent migrants from Puerto Rico did not understand. *Aspira v. Board of Education* was a class action on behalf of the 182,000 Puerto Rican students who were required by the state to attend school, only to receive unintelligible

---

31. Author's field notes on interview with Sister Kathy Maire, July 22, 1997.

32. The following account is drawn from the author's field notes on an interview with Sister Kathy Maire, July 22, 1997.

instruction. After eighteen months of adversarial challenges between the city's lawyers and the Puerto Rican Legal Defense and Educational Fund (which represented Aspira), the parties arrived at a consent decree stipulating the implementation of bilingual education classes for all students who spoke only (or primarily) Spanish. Bilingual education enabled hundreds of thousands of Spanish-speaking students to attain a level of education they otherwise would not have been able to achieve. Since the mid-1990s, however, bilingual programs in New York City and elsewhere have come under fire. Critics charge that bilingual education is no longer fulfilling its stated purpose—to teach children English and move them into English-only classes—but is confining them to a second-class education.

During her years working with Bushwick Parents, Sister Kathy had heard many stories of parents' and children's bad experiences with New York City's bilingual education program. For example, students with Spanish surnames had routinely been placed in bilingual classes when they entered school, even if they had been born in New York and spoke little or no Spanish. Once a student was on the bilingual track, parents found it notoriously difficult to move the child into English-only classes. Many advocates blamed this problem on the higher per-pupil allocations given to individual schools for bilingual-program students. Since a reduction in the number of bilingual students means a loss of resources to the school, there is a disincentive to transfer the children out of bilingual classes. The prolonged placement of children in bilingual education has been confirmed recently by a study showing that less than 50 percent of students in New York City's bilingual classes exit these classes within three years, and that nearly 20 percent remain in bilingual classes for more than nine years (Mayor's Task Force on Bilingual Education 2000). Most poignantly, perhaps, many parents and former bilingual students lament how children's use of English with their peers and in other aspects of everyday life clashes with their Spanish-language classroom instruction; the result, many claim, is language confusion and a failure to learn either language well enough to succeed in school.[33]

About a year before I began fieldwork at Saint Barbara's, Sister Kathy had turned Bushwick Parents' focus to the issue of bilingual education. She had worked with a number of Bushwick Parents leaders to get their children out of bilingual classes, and now planned to have these leaders organize other local parents to do the same.[34] The first step in this process called for

---

33. Author's field notes on interviews with Sister Kathy Maire, July 22, 1997, and Alberta Williams, January 8, 1998; author's field notes, January 28, 1998.

34. Author's field notes on interview with Sister Kathy Maire, July 22, 1997.

returning to the root of all IAF-style organizing efforts: the relational meetings called "one-on-ones" (Gecan 2002; Rooney 1995; M. R. Warren 2001). A one-on-one is designed to let two people meet, discuss their lives and concerns, begin to understand each other's goals and motivations, and start the process of building trust. One-on-ones help reveal which concerns are commonly held and how much interest there is in doing something to change them. Building an IAF-style "citizens' power organization" does not require that its leaders agree on everything. On the contrary, debate among different viewpoints is an essential part of the organizing process, as it allows leaders to acknowledge their disagreements and then come to a true consensus for action. One-on-ones are the crucial foundation of this process.

Getting one-on-ones done at Bushwick Parents proved a significant challenge. One of the group's primary recruiting sites was a CBO that belonged to Saint Barbara's Plaza called the Maura Clarke–Ita Ford Center (MCIF).[35] Two Irish American Catholic nuns, Sister Mary Burns and Sister Mary Dowd, founded MCIF in 1993 to teach basic education and employment skills to poor women. Bushwick Parents held biweekly meetings at MCIF, immediately following the center's classes, in hopes that MCIF students—many of whom had school-age children—would become involved with the group. One of the MCIF staffers was Alberta Williams, a stout, serious African American woman in her fifties who was a longtime parishioner at Saint Barbara's, and had been involved with organizing efforts at the church since they began.[36] Alberta was leading the Bushwick Parents recruitment effort at MCIF but often found the task of encouraging public citizenship among the women to be an uphill battle.

One day at MCIF, as the noon dismissal time drew near, Alberta and I entered the center's GED classroom, a rear corner of which also served as the organization's administrative office. Seven Latina and African American women, ranging in age from early twenties to late forties, sat in scattered desks and chairs. Upon seeing Alberta, one of the women groaned audibly, complaining that she wanted to go home and did not want to take part in the Bushwick Parents meeting. Alberta fixed her with a half-smile and a stare, then asked everyone to gather around the large table in the middle of the room so we could talk more easily. As all the women complied, Alberta handed out a sign-in sheet, then asked how they were doing with their one-on-ones. There was silence. The women stared down at the floor,

35. MCIF is named for two nuns who were murdered in El Salvador by right-wing paramilitary forces in 1980.

36. Author's field notes on interview with Alberta Williams, January 8, 1998.

or exchanged quick glances across the table, making sure not to look at Alberta. She repeated the question. This time, several of the women offered excuses. "I was going to do it with my neighbor," said one woman, "but she canceled on me at the last minute." Another protested to Alberta: "I was supposed to meet with you to practice it." Alberta nodded, then remarked calmly that the women really needed to hold some one-on-ones and that she was happy to schedule practice sessions with them if they wanted.

For the remainder of this meeting, as well as a number of subsequent Bushwick Parents meetings I attended during the late winter and spring of 1998, Alberta tried to tap into whatever "cold anger" the MCIF students were feeling about the dismal performance of the Bushwick public schools. In IAF parlance, cold anger refers to a certain kind of citizen outrage—outrage that can be transformed into sustained, deliberate, collective action to change a specific malfunction in the public sphere. One day, for example, to give the women a more concrete sense of how bad the Bushwick schools were, Alberta informed them about the wretched scores the schools had posted in the yearly citywide reading and math tests—some of the worst scores in the city, with only 20 to 40 percent of students performing at grade level.[37] At another meeting, to get the women to recognize the kind of lip service the schools paid to parent involvement, Alberta recounted her experience of attending a PTA meeting at her granddaughter's school: the first fifteen minutes were spent talking about how, when a child knocks a glass of milk off the table, it can be used as an opportunity to teach the responsibility of cleaning up after making a mistake; the rest of the meeting was spent making Valentine's Day decorations out of construction paper and pipe cleaners.[38]

Although sometimes the women seemed interested in the information, or appreciated the chance to talk about things that had happened to them, Alberta's repeated educational efforts seemed to yield little fruit in terms of bringing the women into roles as leaders and public citizens. When Sister Kathy came to MCIF in the late spring to hold a Bushwick Parents meeting herself, she asked the women to talk about how they felt their children were doing in school, and how they thought their lives were going more generally. The vast majority of the women who answered stated briefly that things were mostly going smoothly for their families—a condition under which it becomes impossible to organize using the IAF strategy.[39]

37. Author's field notes, January 28, 1998.
38. Author's field notes, February 11, 1998.
39. Author's field notes, May 7, 1998.

This lack of cold anger was underlined for me one day when Sister Mary Burns asked me to pitch in with Sister Kathy's efforts to recruit new members to Bushwick Parents. A few weeks after I began my fieldwork at Saint Barbara's, Bushwick Parents had managed to send a strong contingent to a citywide training conference for organizers interested in reforming bilingual education. The conference had been very energizing, and Sister Kathy felt the time was ripe to really push the Bushwick Parents members to get their one-on-ones going. In particular, she was counting on two women, Milagros Hilario and Iris Rijo, who had gone to the training conference. Both Milagros and Iris were MCIF students and regular attendees at Bushwick Parents meetings, and I already knew them. When I arrived at MCIF for one of my usual Wednesday morning volunteer sessions, Sister Mary sent me off to the Saint Barbara's rectory, where the two women were supposed to be meeting to commence a set of one-on-ones.[40] Arriving at the rectory, however, I discovered that the sisters' optimism about the state of Bushwick Parents appeared rather unfounded.

Neither Milagros nor Iris showed up to meet me. After waiting about forty-five minutes, I called Milagros at her home to see if she was planning to come. She was surprised to hear from me, saying that she did not know anything about the supposed meeting with Iris. She invited me to come over to her apartment, where she said we could figure out what to do next. I walked the two blocks from Saint Barbara's to Milagros's building, a slightly run-down, four-family brick house in a row of similar attached buildings stretching neatly down the block. Of the four buzzers jerry-rigged to the door jamb, only hers had a name affixed to it. Milagros opened the door dressed in a nightgown, bathrobe, and slippers and asked me to pardon her appearance. Inside her spotlessly clean first-floor apartment, Milagros apologized for the mix-up, then telephoned Iris to confer about the one-on-ones. Both women expressed confusion about what Sister Kathy wanted them to do and said they felt very uncomfortable going out to talk to other parents when they had only a vague notion of what the topic of conversation should be. As Milagros and I talked further, it became clear that she and Iris both felt that conducting the one-on-ones was a task for Sister Kathy—not for them.[41]

The idea that an external organizer like Sister Kathy should shoulder this relationship-building work violates the very foundation of the IAF's

40. Author's field notes, February 18, 1998.
41. Author's field notes, February 18, 1998.

approach. The IAF strategy relies on group insiders' claiming public power and organizing their peers to create social change: in this case, Milagros and Iris, as parents of children in the Bushwick schools, reaching out to other parents to inform them of the problems surrounding bilingual education and the local school district more generally. It was this model that had led to the identification of elementary education as a key issue in Bushwick, via the six hundred one-on-ones conducted by fifteen Saint Barbara's leaders back in 1990. Now, however, the model was breaking down. No Bushwick Parents leaders had emerged who were willing to take on the one-on-ones, and even the two women identified by Sister Kathy as best equipped for the job showed little interest. Over the next few months, these difficulties continued, and the one-on-ones never got off the ground.

As lead organizer of EBC, Sister Kathy's work involved several different projects in East New York, Brownsville, and Bushwick. Bushwick Parents was only one of these, and she seemed stretched too thin to work very effectively with the group. In an effort to address this problem, EBC decided in early 1998 to hire an organizer who would work only with Bushwick Parents. Finding the right person proved difficult and time-consuming, but a few months after Milagros and Iris declined to take on the one-on-ones, a young Latina woman was hired. She did not stay long, however. After meeting her one day in April of that year,[42] I never saw her again. Sister Kathy told me several weeks later that she had quit.[43] The difficulty of finding effective organizers can plague a group like Bushwick Parents. Unlike Ridgewood-Bushwick, where paid staff carry out the service work that binds local residents to the organization, Sister Kathy and other IAF organizers rely on volunteer leaders to mount social change efforts. A good organizer motivates these everyday leaders to work effectively, inspiring other neighborhood residents to recognize the power and abilities possessed by each and every one of them. Once infused with a sense of their own capabilities, residents become the IAF's "public citizens"—and theoretically, this mass of powerful people renders organizers like Sister Kathy less important. Without the spark of a good, focused organizer, however, it is difficult to ignite the fire of resident action, as the case of Bushwick Parents demonstrates.

The difficulties faced by Bushwick Parents did not escape the notice of the staff at MCIF. Indeed, figuring out how to make Bushwick Parents work more effectively was a frequent topic of conversation for them. As an outsider observing Bushwick Parents, my presence sometimes prompted

42. Author's field notes, April 29, 1998
43. Author's field notes, June 17, 1998.

these discussions, but it was clear that Sister Kathy, Sister Mary, Alberta and the other MCIF staff members also talked about it when I was not there. One explanation they developed seemed to focus on how the women involved with Bushwick Parents lacked various characteristics necessary to be successful at organizing work. Alberta, for example, compared Bushwick Parents to a group of Saint Barbara's parishioners who had been involved in organizing work for many years, concluding that the Bushwick Parents leaders did not really understand the organizing approach and exhibited too much "passivity" in the face of obstacles.[44] Sister Kathy worried that the women taking classes at MCIF had too hard a time just keeping their lives together to have energy left over to be angry about their situations—anger being the necessary fuel for the organizing fire.[45] Alberta, however, also recognized a broader explanation for the problems at Bushwick Parents.

Another Side of Organizing at Saint Barbara's

In addition to locating the cause of the Bushwick Parents leaders' lack of enthusiasm in their personal characteristics, Alberta tied the group's difficulties into the broader history of Saint Barbara's involvement with organizing work. She noted that many of the most active and established leaders at Saint Barbara's had begun their organizing efforts in the early 1980s, working with Father Powis's predecessor, Father Edmund Brady. This group included many older, long-term residents of Bushwick—and longtime Saint Barbara's parishioners—most of whose children were grown. This meant they had less interest in the educational issues that were the central focus of Bushwick Parents.[46] In addition, few of the Bushwick Parents leaders were actually parishioners at Saint Barbara's—many told me they belonged to Pentecostal churches in Bushwick or elsewhere[47]—a fact that Alberta linked to their limited commitment to Bushwick Parents.[48]

Alberta's analysis of the problems at Bushwick Parents returned to the core principles of the IAF, which organizes from a congregational base precisely to leverage members' already established, ongoing relationships. From this perspective, the Bushwick Parents project was, perhaps, doomed from the start. In addition, Sister Kathy's turning of Bushwick Parents

44. Author's field notes, May 13, 1998.
45. Author's field notes on interview with Sister Kathy Maire, July 22, 1997; author's field notes, May 13, 1998.
46. Author's field notes, May 13, 1998.
47. Author's field notes, January 29, 1998; March 25, 1998; April 8, 1998.
48. Author's field notes, May 13, 1998.

toward educational reform challenged the IAF strategy of selecting "actionable" issues: issues where the lines of authority can be clearly determined and responsible actors accurately targeted. The New York City educational bureaucracy represents an enormous, apparently intractable challenge—one that has perplexed successive mayors and challenged even the larger, more disciplined EBC organization during its earlier forays into public education reform. The chances that a small and relatively inexperienced group like Bushwick Parents could find a way into this highly complex bureaucracy seemed limited.

As Bushwick Parents pursued educational issues during the 1990s, a group of older, more experienced Saint Barbara's leaders chose instead to pursue a range of smaller tasks, taking on issues where they could clearly identify and pressure the responsible parties—a strategy more in line with the IAF organizing philosophy. Recalling the difficulties EBC had faced when opening its two alternative high schools, the experienced Saint Barbara's leaders—a group that included Alberta—shied away from the educational focus of Bushwick Parents. Instead, they selected other issues that affected the quality of life in Bushwick and also appeared more readily winnable.

One such campaign grew out of Saint Barbara's leaders' anger over a decision by the New York City Fire Department to remove street-corner call boxes from Bushwick and other neighborhoods around the city. The call boxes had long served as city residents' first line of defense against fires, but in 1995 Mayor Giuliani and the fire department decreed them superfluous. When they initiated a citywide removal project, however, they failed to reckon with the particularly grisly history of fires in Bushwick. Local residents remembered well that 1970s Bushwick had claimed the dubious distinction of being the most burned-out neighborhood in the city. They reacted vituperatively to the retiring of the fire-call boxes, and Saint Barbara's leaders spearheaded a drive to restore them to the city's street corners. Recruiting members of the city council to their cause, they ultimately secured an agreement from the mayor to reactivate all boxes in neighborhoods where more than 10 percent of the population lacked telephones (which included Bushwick).[49] Invigorated by this victory, these leaders went on to attack other issues, such as maintenance problems and erratic mail delivery in the nearby Hope Gardens housing project, and the absence of a traffic light at a crucial intersection next to Saint Barbara's.

In the latter campaign, for about seven months beginning in the fall of 1997, Father Powis and parishioners from Saint Barbara's made a weekly

49. Author's field notes, May 13, 1998; Kennedy (1996).

pilgrimage after mass to the corner of Central Avenue and Menahan Street, half a block from the church's main entrance. I participated in several of these vigils, following my occasional visits to Saint Barbara's services. On one Sunday in May, Father Powis ended the service with his usual reminder to all to join in the vigil for the traffic light:

> Father Powis tells the congregation to remember that at least one person has been killed by a speeding car at the corner of Central and Menahan, and that the neighborhood's children and senior citizens are in danger there every day. He then leads the recessional down the central aisle, heading straight for the church's double doors. He's carrying all his priestly paraphernalia, the deacon has a large wooden cross, the altar boys are following them. People start to file out from the pews, falling in behind them. Out in the street, Father Powis leads about two hundred people down to the corner. He prays for the city to install the light, to protect the parish and the neighborhood. A man and a woman, in their forties and fifties, respectively, make short speeches about the dangers of the corner without the light. The whole thing takes about fifteen or twenty minutes, and then people start to disperse.[50]

This particular vigil turned out to be one of the last. A little over a week later, I ran into Father Powis, who told me the city had finally agreed to install the traffic light. Though he wasn't sure when this would actually happen, given the city's often glacial pace, in this case things moved quickly. Later that same week, as I arrived at MCIF for my regular volunteer session, I witnessed a city maintenance crew hard at work setting up the light.[51]

Organization vs. Organizing: Harnessing Politics for Neighborhood Improvement

Contestation within the field of politics helps determine where and how the financial and regulatory resources of government and the private sector are parceled out within cities. This distribution significantly impacts the set of opportunities and quality of life available to residents of particular places, such as Bushwick. Both traditional political practices, like citizen voting, and more creative strategies fueled by organized action in response to particular pressing problems are part of the political field. Both the Ridgewood-Bushwick Senior Citizens Council and Saint Barbara's Catholic

50. Author's field notes, May 17, 1998.
51. Author's field notes, May 27, 1998.

Church actively engage this field, whose boundaries stretch far beyond their Bushwick neighborhood. The two groups put forward very different visions for both the role of organizations as political actors, and the character of the benefits these organizations should produce. Ridgewood-Bushwick's private politics of distribution butts up against Saint Barbara's public goods politics in the battle for both the allegiance of local residents, and the attention of outside government and private-sector actors.

Everyday practices at Ridgewood-Bushwick reveal its commitment to an understanding of the city that approximates what sociologist Charles Perrow would call a "society of organizations" (Perrow 1992). That is, Ridgewood-Bushwick views itself as one of myriad bureaucratic organizations—in neighborhoods, in government, in the economy, in the public sphere—attempting to achieve certain goals through interaction with other organizations that control certain resources and powers. Given this perspective on the social world, Ridgewood-Bushwick invests in building an organization aimed at persuading elected officials of the benefits of acceding to its demands. By creating and deploying its reliable voting constituency, Ridgewood-Bushwick speaks to elected officials in the language of votes—the very currency of elected office. Furthermore, Ridgewood-Bushwick's demands are couched in terms to which elected officials can easily respond; the organization does not ask for major reconfigurations of vast political or economic systems, but only for government contracts that allow it to provide services, maintain loyal organizational adherents, and turn out voters. In this sense, it reprises the organizational form of the latter-day political machine, drawing public resources toward itself for distribution to its "members."

Saint Barbara's, on the other hand, rejects the idea that in order to change the way that economic and political fields operate, it must build a privately oriented organization of its own. A fundamental tenet of groups that have adopted the Industrial Areas Foundation organizing model is that the power to create change lies in its leaders. Rather than privileging the top of a bureaucratic hierarchy, these groups define leaders as individual citizens who, working together, can reclaim the public voice central to the idea of democratic governance. Thus, the East Brooklyn Congregations organizing federation to which Saint Barbara's belongs has only four full-time employees, while the national IAF has a similarly tiny staff. The point is to organize citizens to act publicly, not to establish a permanent organization whose direction, as much organizational theory has demonstrated, can easily fall prey to the challenges of simple organizational survival. Indeed, one longtime IAF organizer conceives of the group's fundamental premise—its "relational culture"—as inherently opposed to "bureaucratic culture," wherein the internal machinations of large organizations lead to outcomes that more often serve the organization itself than the citizens to whom they are presumably accountable (Gecan 2002).[52] While Ridgewood-Bushwick is content to maneuver—and has found considerable success—within the existing rules of a bureaucratic system, Saint Barbara's wants to replace the dominance of organizations with the dominance of organized citizens exercising voice.

These contrasting views, of "organization" versus "organizing," have important implications for what individual neighborhood residents can learn about the possibilities of political action from Ridgewood-Bushwick and Saint Barbara's. At Ridgewood-Bushwick, Assemblyman Lopez is the singular leader, setting the organization's direction and calling on its "members" to mobilize in a narrow version of political participation that serves the organization's strategic ends. Saint Barbara's, in contrast, aims to have many leaders, whose relationships with each other create the foundation for making carefully bounded political claims. One consequence of the Saint Barbara's strategy is that effective leaders, like Alberta Williams and the other older leaders at the congregation, have a far deeper understanding of how the bureaucratic systems they are working to change function, and how to locate the points at which they are vulnerable to organized citizens. In contrast, while Ridgewood-Bushwick's client-voters have certain pieces of this knowledge—particularly about how the government contracting system works—it is far from clear that they would be able to analyze and create "actions" in the way that leaders at Saint Barbara's do. Saint Barbara's and the broader IAF movement seek to reinsert the claims of citizens into a decision-making environment that has become increasingly dominated by organizations that cater to their own interests. At the same time, however, Ridgewood-Bushwick demonstrates that organizations with clear private orientations can produce real material benefits for poor people and places.

The actual achievements of Ridgewood-Bushwick and Saint Barbara's have much to do with the former's highly effective organization-building and the latter's fragmented, and at times anemic, implementation of the IAF organizing philosophy. Creating the kind of systemic change to the political field that leaders at Saint Barbara's and the IAF envision is a long, arduous

---

52. It is worth noting here that Perrow (2002) explicitly argues that the proliferation of *private* organizations, especially corporations, is largely responsible for the society of organizations' having concentrated more and more power and wealth in the hands of a few private interests with little or no public accountability.

process. The idea is to use small, "winnable" actions—like getting the traffic light installed in front of the church—to build a strong constituency of informed leaders equipped to tackle other issues that have greater impacts on the lives of Bushwick residents. Taking on the highly complex problem of public education in Bushwick seems to have mismatched the capacity of the Saint Barbara's leaders with the scope of the problem. In contrast, Ridgewood-Bushwick sets its sights more modestly. Rather than aiming to fundamentally reshape the operations of the political field—a task that may in fact require a more concrete vision than leaders at Saint Barbara's or EBC possess—Ridgewood-Bushwick instead demonstrates great expertise at drawing resources within the field as it is currently configured.

One important additional factor is the competition between the two organizations over how to integrate Bushwick into the city's political field. The fact that Ridgewood-Bushwick and Saint Barbara's operate within the same geographic space plays a role in the differential success of their approaches, and the two groups are clearly hostile toward one another. Ridgewood-Bushwick has long held the dominant position in Bushwick, as its private politics of distribution approach has allowed it to bring enormous amounts of public resources into the neighborhood and to attract widespread resident support. Operating within the Ridgewood-Bushwick shadow, it has been difficult for Saint Barbara's to wield much power on its own—though it should be noted that Bushwick Parents did eventually see some of their bilingual education reform goals realized, when Mayor Bloomberg committed in 2000 to make a series of changes in that program (Holloway 2000). Furthermore, in East New York and Brownsville, where few organizational competitors exist, the larger EBC organization is a powerful political voice.

CHAPTER FOUR

A Path to Work

If a place to live is one of our most basic needs, every household requires the fulfillment of two fundamental tasks: generating income, to pay for shelter, food, clothing, and so on, and managing the domestic front—raising children, cleaning, cooking, and other work necessary to the functioning and very survival of family members. Today, most people's income comes from paid work. Getting people into jobs, however, does not rely on the uncomplicated logic often attributed to employment: an exchange of labor and wages between employee and employer. Rather, this seemingly simple transaction is embedded in a range of agreements entered into by organizational actors. Government agencies, for example, set the minimum wage; unions negotiate salary rates and benefits through collective bargaining; firms decide, among other things, where to locate (e.g., Fligstein 2001; Western 1998). Once jobs become available in particular places, at certain wages, with set working hours, requiring specific skill sets, individuals' family responsibilities may or may not allow them to take those jobs. Paid work and domestic reproduction thus go hand in hand, and all of the organizational players involved in these complementary tasks can be considered as part of the same field.

When circumstances require that all adult members of a family generate income—as in single-parent families that lack other sources of income or two-parent families when the wages of one parent are not sufficient to meet family needs—the demands of paid work often conflict with domestic duties. Alternative arrangements thus become necessary. One primary strategy is to involve family members other than parents in income generation or domestic tasks, as when a grandparent provides child care while parents work or an adult sibling provides a regular supplemental source of income. When families have few financial resources—as is all too common in neighborhoods like Williamsburg and Bushwick—these arrangements can become quite complex, with parents and their children involved in multiple exchanges within extended family networks. Extended family members or close friends—"fictive kin"—may provide substitute child care, a parent may collaborate with other relatives to purchase food and prepare meals for a larger group, a set of adult siblings may rotate responsibility caring for an elderly parent, and so on (e.g., Newman 1999; Stack 1974).

To supplement family resources, citizens of most contemporary societies can obtain assistance in generating income and caring for the home front from formal organizations, including the government and any number of private enterprises, both for-profit and nonprofit. Governments provide income to certain groups of people, most prominently the elderly and retired workers but also, under variable conditions, the temporarily unemployed, the disabled, and dependent children. Firms also provide income to individuals who are not current employees, primarily through retirement pensions but also as payments during fixed-time absences from work, such as maternity leave. On the domestic side, private organizations often provide services to families who cannot (or choose not to) meet these responsibilities within the family; such organizations include restaurants, child care centers, household cleaning services, nursing homes, and others. While higher-income families usually purchase such services with their own money—and thus have greater flexibility in choosing particular service providers—low-income families may be eligible for government assistance to defray certain costs.

In a world where meeting the twin responsibilities of making money and discharging domestic duties has become considerably more complex than in the past, community-based organizations form a key piece of the survival system for lower-income families. For one thing, CBOs serve as important sources of employment for neighborhood residents. From Los Sures in Williamsburg to the New Life Child Development Center in Bushwick, CBOs create jobs and provide an environment that eases residents with limited employment histories into paid work. Although many CBO jobs are low-paying or part-time—characteristics widely considered to define "bad" jobs—they often are appropriate for the skill levels of local residents. CBOs also organize the provision of several critical domestic-sphere services that make it possible for adult family members to engage in paid work in the first place: taking care of children and assisting elderly relatives with daily living tasks are the most important of these. We shall see, for example, how the Nuestros Niños Child Development Center in Williamsburg's Southside enables hundreds of local parents to hold paid jobs, secure in the knowledge that their child care arrangements are both reliable and safe. In the following pages, I detail some of the ways that CBOs connect local residents to paid work, both by creating opportunities to earn money and by helping to fulfill domestic responsibilities.

Market Substitute: Community-Based Organizations and Job Creation

As community-based organizations emerged in poor urban neighborhoods in the early 1960s, they were acutely aware of the difficulties their residents faced in getting jobs, starting businesses, and otherwise generating income. With the restructuring of the U.S. urban economy under way, the decline in low-skill, relatively well paying manufacturing employment hit residents of lower-income neighborhoods like Williamsburg and Bushwick particularly hard. Unemployment rose as the local factories that employed many residents closed down, leaving more and more families without stable incomes. Many local businesses succumbed, squeezed by rising costs and declining receipts as the amount of cash circulating within neighborhood economies was constricted. Newly formed CBOs saw the writing on the wall: as economic times got worse, private capital would increasingly flee, taking with it local residents' opportunities to work and earn their own money. Over the course of the 1970s, this prophecy proved true: New York City's unemployment rate soared from 4.9 percent in 1970 to a peak of 11.1 percent in 1976. In Brooklyn, the statistics were even worse. By 1976 the borough's unemployment rate reached 12.2 percent, and until 1990 Brooklyn had the dubious distinction of being the most unemployed borough in the city (New York City Department of City Planning 2003).

Within this difficult economic climate, New York City CBOs began working to create jobs for residents of their neighborhoods. Their approach to economic development in high-unemployment, inner-city ghettos applied some of the same principles that underlay the federal Area Redevelopment Act of 1961. That legislation, nearly ten years in the making, sought to target federal funds to areas of the country where industries had substantially reduced their workforces or moved away entirely, leaving a massive employment vacuum in their wake. Coal mines in West Virginia, for example, had been increasingly automated, and the textile industry had moved from New England to the southern states (Kremen 1974). Economic development CBOs in the nation's cities also drew on ideas, long extant within the African American community, about the importance of "separate development"—

creating an economic, political, and social system exclusively populated and controlled by African Americans (Halpern 1995).

In 1966, New York's senators, Robert F. Kennedy and Jacob Javits, directed federal funds to a small group of nonprofit organizations aimed at generating capital and jobs within poor neighborhoods, then channeling those dollars into local transactions to strengthen the neighborhood economy. The senators' inspiration to support these "community development corporations" (CDCs) came from activists in the largely African American neighborhood of Bedford-Stuyvesant, Brooklyn, who were already working informally on this strategy. With new federal dollars in hand, the activists incorporated a new 501(c)3 organization, christening it the Bedford-Stuyvesant Restoration Corporation (BSRC).[1] The group set about pioneering many community economic development strategies in which local residents, foundation funders, and government agencies alike placed high hopes.

Although CDCs are today best known for their housing development work, they initially pursued the creation of self-sufficient neighborhood economies. In addition to special support from the federal government, private funders like the Ford Foundation backed the CDC model on the premise that these organizations would have the potential to mount economic and other development projects on a scale unmatched by other neighborhood entrepreneurs (Faux 1971). The BSRC brokered loans for local business owners, developed a large neighborhood shopping center, and in 1968 won what appeared to be a major victory: an agreement from the IBM corporation to locate a production facility in Bedford-Stuyvesant, with a majority of employees to be drawn from unemployed local residents. Although the BSRC made some progress with its economic development agenda in its early years, the task ultimately proved much more difficult than the group's organizers had anticipated.

By the mid-1970s, the BSRC and fledgling CDCs across the nation were reevaluating their approach to neighborhood development, moving away from the increasingly apparent difficulties of business ventures toward an emphasis on housing development, which had proven to be more secure (Halpern 1995). At the same time, rising national unemployment spurred Congress to pass legislation creating new public works programs. In 1973, passage of the Comprehensive Employment and Training Act (CETA) gave CBOs the opportunity to develop new approaches to supporting neigh-

---

1. Senators Kennedy and Javits sponsored a 1966 amendment to the Economic Opportunity Act of 1964 to create the Special Impact Program, which appropriated funds for the BSRC and a few other similar organizations across the country.

borhood residents' work aspirations and efforts. Unlike previous public works programs, in which public service workers were assigned only to government agencies, CETA also provided for worker placement in non-profit CBOs (N. E. Rose 1995). In Brooklyn, emerging CBOs like Los Sures and Ridgewood-Bushwick often relied on CETA workers. The placement of CETA workers in CBOs was consistent with government and private-sector demands that public service employees do work that was "socially useful" and did not displace existing public or private sector workers. These placements offered opportunities for unemployed local residents to gain work experience, while also contributing to CBO efforts to improve the physical and social conditions of their neighborhoods.

President Ronald Reagan ended CETA in 1981, part of his sweeping effort to privatize many public services and shrink the size of the federal government. As part of this trend, government at all levels increasingly contracted with nonprofit organizations to provide social assistance services previously administered directly by government agencies and employees (Marwell 2004b; Salamon 1995; S. R. Smith and Lipsky 1993). Financed by government contracts, CBOs have since taken on numerous social provision tasks, in the process creating jobs that are somewhat more permanent than CETA placements. Some characteristics of these jobs benefit residents of low-income neighborhoods who might otherwise remain unemployed. These jobs are located near residents' homes (Kain 1968, 1992); require skill levels that match residents' current capacities or can be attained with short-term training (Kasarda 1989; Wilson 1987); treat residents' specific knowledge of their neighborhoods and local people as an asset (Kretzmann and McKnight 1997); and valorize the often unrecognized contributions of low-income people, especially women, to neighborhood improvement work (Naples 1998; Susser 1982). On the negative side, many of these jobs only add to the low-wage labor market, with its problems of low pay, part-time hours, limited career mobility, and few or no fringe benefits. However, given the high rates of unemployment in Williamsburg and, especially, Bushwick—in the year 2000, 10.6 percent and 17 percent, respectively, compared to 9.6 percent citywide (New York City Department of City Planning n.d.)—the CBO contribution to employment should not be minimized.

What Kinds of Jobs?

Jobs at CBOs come in all shapes and sizes and require a wide variety of skills. Upper-level positions—executive directors, program directors, financial officers—are filled by individuals whose advanced skills could easily transfer to similarly responsible and comparably compensated jobs with other nonprofit groups or in the business world. At the middle levels, necessary skills are tied more closely to particular job tasks. Some positions require specific education or certification (for example, teachers and assistant teachers in child care classrooms, social workers, or building superintendents), while others call for skills that are more likely to have been learned over time on the job (such as tenant organizers, job developers, or youth counselors). Local residents with limited education and few skills often fill entry-level jobs at CBOs; their lack of formal training is usually compensated for by their willingness to learn on the job and a familiarity with the organization's mission and staff. CBO clients sometimes become entry-level staff as well, usually following a period of volunteer involvement with the organization. In some cases, individuals find a career ladder within a CBO, as long-term employment with the organization leads to their learning new skills and being recognized as reliable and valued workers. These individuals thus are well-positioned to take advantage when new, higher-level jobs emerge within the organization.

A frequent critique of staffing patterns at CBOs is that, over time, these organizations become increasingly professionalized and employ fewer local residents. Individuals who have never resided in Williamsburg or Bushwick do indeed hold some of the top-level jobs at CBOs in these neighborhoods. Vito Lopez, the founder and first executive director of the Ridgewood-Bushwick Senior Citizens Council did not live in Bushwick, nor does his successor, Chris Fisher, who has held the position since 1986. Michael Rochford, the executive director at Saint Nicholas Neighborhood Preservation Corporation in Williamsburg (Saint Nick's), first came to the organization as part of a group of students from the Pratt Institute, an urban planning school in the Fort Greene neighborhood of Brooklyn. He did not then live in Williamsburg, nor has he since. The first several administrators of Williamsburg's Los Sures did hail from the neighborhood, but David Pagán, who has held the top job for the last fifteen years, lives in Queens.

Other top officials at Williamsburg and Bushwick CBOs, however, do have long-term residential ties to the neighborhoods. John Mulhern, the ex-priest who founded the Nuestros Niños Child Development Center, has lived in Williamsburg's Southside since the late 1960s. He and his wife, Luz Maria, raised their three children in the neighborhood, while John oversaw the growth and development of thousands of other local youngsters who passed through Nuestros Niños. Zully Rolán grew up in Williamsburg, spent a number of years working at Saint Nick's before heading to a position at the city's Department of Housing Preservation and Development, and returned in 1996 to take the job of director of Saint Nick's Housing Division. At Ridgewood-Bushwick, the second highest-ranking staff member, Angela Battaglia, has deep family roots in Bushwick, stretching back to the time when the neighborhood was heavily Italian American. She is currently the director of Ridgewood-Bushwick's Housing Office, and her story exemplifies how a local with few specific skills can move up the organizational hierarchy of a CBO.

Born and raised in Bushwick, Angela is a trim, efficient woman in her midfifties, perpetually in motion. She first got involved with Ridgewood-Bushwick in the mid-1970s as a volunteer.[2] After graduating from Fordham University and working for two years at an export company, she quit the job, disillusioned by what she felt was its lack of redeeming social value. She used her free time to volunteer with senior citizens at a CBO on Manhattan's Upper East Side, not realizing that Ridgewood-Bushwick was doing the same kind of work right in her own backyard. One day on a Bushwick street, she ran into an old friend of her father's, who told her about Vito Lopez and his organization. Angela immediately decided to volunteer there instead. After a few months, Vito Lopez hired her part-time through CETA, since she had by then been unemployed long enough to qualify for that program. He put her in charge of Ridgewood-Bushwick's nascent housing program, even though, as Angela put it, "I was terrified, since I had absolutely no experience in housing." About a year later, when a new city contract came through at Ridgewood-Bushwick, Vito hired Angela full-time. She thus moved into a paid position of significant responsibility for which, by her own admission, she had no apparent qualifications. Nonprofit organizations often tap inexperienced yet bright individuals to take on major tasks, and Angela's subsequent achievements heading up the organization's housing program more than attest to her strong professional capabilities. As a result of the experience and visibility Angela attained at Ridgewood-Bushwick, in 1996 she was appointed by Mayor Rudolph Giuliani to the New York City Planning Commission, a part-time position that carries an annual salary of forty thousand dollars and makes binding decisions on land-use issues throughout the city.

At the Nuestros Niños child care center in the Southside of Williamsburg, local residents, especially local women, fill most of the jobs. In each of the school-age classrooms at the organization's three facilities, a head teacher and an assistant teacher care for between twenty and twenty-five children in

2. This account is drawn from the author's field notes on an interview with Angela Battaglia, June 30, 1997.

Figure 8. Nuestros Niños Child Development Center, 384 South Fourth Street in Williamsburg. Photo by Heather Wollin.

the hours after school. During school vacations (including summertime), a part-time teacher's aide helps cover a full ten-hour day of care. In its preschool classrooms, where city regulations require a lower staff-to-child ratio, three adults always supervise each group of fifteen children. Nuestros Niños thus employs some seventy-five women as teachers in its programs, though only the preschool teachers work on a full-time, full-year basis. In addition, the organization requires administrative and support staff to run its programs, and most of these are full-time positions. They include one executive director; one assistant director; a director of school-age programs at each of the three sites; three enrollment workers, located at the main site on South Fourth Street; and a receptionist, janitor, and cooking staff at each facility. All together, there are about twenty-five of these positions at the organization.

Finally, there is the family day care program. Nuestros Niños currently supervises nearly one hundred local women, each of whom provides care for two to five children in her home. Each "provider mother" has passed through training certification at Nuestros Niños, and her home has been inspected and licensed by the city's Department of Health as a family day care facility. For most provider mothers, family day care work is their primary or sole source of income, the equivalent of a home-based business. After the 1996 welfare reform legislation, a number of former welfare recipients received training as family day care providers at Nuestros Niños and subsequently became part of the organization's family day care network. In addition to employing nearly a hundred women as provider mothers, the family day care program employs a full-time program director and two full-time program aides. The latter are responsible for placing children with appropriate providers; they also monitor the providers' compliance with family day care regulations, including approving the nutritional content of children's meals and making unannounced home visits.

In total, then, Nuestros Niños provides over two hundred full- and part-time jobs in child care. Most of the employees are local women, including quite a few whose English-language skills would make it difficult for them to find jobs in English-monolingual settings. The familiar environment at Nuestros Niños, however, makes it easier for them both to discharge work responsibilities and to complete their required on-the-job certification hours; nearly everyone speaks Spanish, and a coworker is always ready to take the extra time to translate or explain a strange word or new concept.

Barriers and Preferences: How CBO Jobs Meet Workers Where They Are

If one important function of CBOs is to connect local residents to jobs, then the upper-level employees who already possess transferable skills represent the least of these organizations' concerns. Much as the CBOs value having local residents in upper-level positions, their priority is to incorporate potential workers with little work experience and few or no skills. As numerous studies of low-wage workers and the unemployed have shown, getting a job becomes ever more difficult as individuals grow older without acquiring educational credentials, specific job skills, or work histories (e.g., Munger 2002; Neckerman and Kirschenman 1991; Newman 1999; Oliker 1995; Stier and Tienda 2001). Many analyses of how to engage the long-term unemployed in regular work argue that unfamiliarity with basic work attitudes—"soft skills"—are a primary barrier: problems include tardiness, absenteeism, inappropriate language, unprofessional dress, and a lack of respect for authority. A somewhat different interpretation comes from ethnographic research on low-skill workers who leave formal employment for unemployment or informal economic activity. These studies emphasize the *discomfort* that individuals feel in workplaces whose routines and employees reflect formal, "corporate" attitudes toward social interaction and the organization of work (Bourgois 1996, Duneier 2000, Sullivan 1989, Venkatesh 2006).

In contrast to these uncomfortable or unfamiliar work surroundings, CBOs offer the residents of poor neighborhoods an employment environment where they experience relative "ease" (Bourdieu 1984) in their relationship to work, clients, coworkers, and even bosses. The idea of an "indigenous" organization—one made up of local residents rather than professionals from outside the neighborhood—is often evoked as a rationale for using CBOs to provide services to low-income people more effectively and sensitively. Moreover, in the case of paid work, "indigenous" CBOs offer a workplace that sidesteps some of the problems persistently identified as barriers to work among the poor.

For example, particular clothing is required for jobs at many workplaces—in some cases formal clothing (suits, ties, dress shoes), in others uniforms. Purchasing these items may strain low-income workers' budgets, and they are unlikely to use this clothing during their nonwork time. Some CBO employees, especially those who have regular contact with city officials, foundation staff, judges, or other people from outside the neighborhood do maintain professional dress norms. Others, however, dress in ways that make them indistinguishable from CBO clients, and the clothing, accessories, and hairstyles they wear at work mirror what they wear when they are not working. At a CBO in Williamsburg or Bushwick, for example, a female staff member may be just as likely to be wearing tight jeans, a tank top, and a gold nameplate necklace as is her client. While not self-conscious, this mode of self-presentation generally reinforces CBO employees' ability to relate to their clients and other neighborhood residents as members of the community. Furthermore, supervisors do not treat these forms of dress as a signal of employees' inability to perform their job tasks. While job-readiness programs for long-term unemployed individuals and welfare recipients often emphasize the importance of professional dress norms, the casual environment of many CBOs means that dress does not usually create a barrier to work.

Perhaps more importantly, CBOs can sometimes solve the problem of unemployed workers not possessing the skills necessary to take advantage of available employment opportunities—what sociologists and economists refer to as "skills mismatch." CBOs often try to develop the work skills of clients and other neighborhood residents by encouraging them to volunteer at the organization. By becoming a member of a tenants' association, assisting for a few hours a week in a day care classroom, manning a booth at a street fair, or otherwise participating in the CBO's activities, local residents get to know the organization, its mission and programs, how it operates, and its staff members. This volunteer activity can serve as a kind of skills training, particularly for a job in the CBO itself, but potentially in another workplace as well.

For example, on one of my first days conducting fieldwork at the New Life Child Development Center in Bushwick, I met Lina, whose daughter was enrolled in the organization's morning Head Start session. An energetic and cheerful New York–born Puerto Rican woman in her midtwenties, Lina was volunteering in one of the center's classrooms while her daughter attended the program in another classroom. A few months later, after I settled into a regular volunteer assignment in one of the Head Start classrooms, I saw Lina again. Shortly before noon, she walked into the classroom pushing the lunch cart, wearing kitchen whites and a scarf around her hair. As she positioned the cart in its regular spot by the window, she looked around the room, saw me, smiled, waved, and came over to say hello.

Lina proudly recounted her ascent up a certain kind of career ladder at New Life. Her involvement with the organization had begun as a client, and she later became an occasional volunteer. When the CBO became certified as a welfare-to-work site, where mothers could perform the twenty weekly hours of "work activities" required by the city in return for public assistance payments, she began spending more time at New Life. At that point, Lina's "volunteer" work took on double duty: it was something she did on her own volition, and it also fulfilled her workfare mandate. In the course of this work, Lina learned many of the routines at New Life and impressed teachers and supervisors with her energy and reliability. When a position on the kitchen staff opened up, Lina was hired and became, as she called it, a "regular worker."[3]

While this trajectory into employment worked well for Lina—and for a number of other people I got to know at the Williamsburg and Bushwick CBOs—the practice could also cause problems for the organizations. There were always more CBO volunteers interested in permanent jobs than the CBO could accommodate, and this sometimes created resentment among those who were not hired. This was particularly true of CBOs that sponsored workfare programs, where the few cases in which a workfare participant got a permanent job raised expectations that other workfare participants could follow the same path. In a series of focus groups I conducted with workfare participants at New Life, for example, many of the women voiced the expectation that after completing their "work experience" assignments there,

3. Author's field notes, June 30, 1998.

they would become regular employees of the CBO.[4] This view clashed with the welfare-to-work program's basic idea: that the hours participants spent at New Life would somehow prepare them for jobs in other places. CBOs thus walk a delicate line, serving as a source of training and employment for some local residents but being unable to meet the overall demand for jobs from the large numbers of unemployed in their neighborhoods.

In an effort to better meet this demand, while remaining cognizant of the need to match jobs to local residents' skills, some CBOs have created ventures that explicitly focus on providing jobs to residents. In Williamsburg, the Saint Nicholas Neighborhood Preservation Center (Saint Nick's) operates two such efforts. One, the East Williamsburg Valley Industrial Development Corporation (EWVIDCO), works to improve and fortify the environment for businesses located in a section of the neighborhood designated by the city as an "in-place industrial park." Industrial parks provide hiring and investment tax credits, as well as discounts on utility costs, to businesses located within their boundaries. EWVIDCO manages these benefits for the East Williamsburg Industrial Park, while also working with the local police precincts to improve safety in the area; monitoring the state of infrastructural concerns such as road repair, street lighting, and sanitation; and offering informational seminars to local businesses. Saint Nick's started EWVIDCO to help preserve the job base in Williamsburg, thereby fostering work opportunities for local residents. To help this process along, one of EWVIDCO's central activities is maintaining a hiring pool to match local workers of varying skills to above-minimum wage jobs available in the industrial park. These job-matching services are free to local businesses, and sometimes include wage subsidies.[5]

Saint Nick's also runs a home health care agency, which provides in-home attendants to frail or incapacitated Williamsburg residents who need assistance with nonmedical life tasks such as cleaning, cooking, shopping, bathing, and personal grooming. While providing a much-needed service to local senior citizens and the disabled, this venture also offers jobs to some fourteen hundred residents of Williamsburg and the surrounding area, making it one of the largest employers in north Brooklyn. For the many Williamsburg residents—mostly women—with limited education, job skills, and in some cases English proficiency, home attendant work offers a form of employment that draws on the domestic skills they already have. This was

4. Author's field notes, October 30, 1997; November 11, 1997; November 20, 1997; January 22, 1998; January 23, 1998.
5. Author's field notes, June 16, 1997.

the case with a woman I sat next to one day at a Parents' Association meeting at the Williamsburg Beacon, a youth and family support program also run by Saint Nick's. As we waited for the meeting to begin, I struck up a conversation with Ana, a reserved Dominican immigrant in her fifties, whose granddaughter attended the Beacon. When she mentioned that she worked part-time for Saint Nick's as a home attendant, I asked how she liked the job. "It's easy for me," she said, noting that she took care of her father before he died, and that he needed a lot of the same things her clients do. Ana especially enjoyed seeing her clients' moods shift when she arrived: many of them spent most of their time home alone, and Ana's company perked them up considerably. "I've always been the kind of person who likes to help people," she said, smiling gently. "This job lets me do that."[6]

Ridgewood-Bushwick also runs a large home health care program, employing some twelve hundred Bushwick residents as home attendants. Both Saint Nick's and Ridgewood-Bushwick provide potential employees with the three-week training required to become certified as a home attendant. This short-term investment in job skills, plus the large client base maintained by the CBOs, means that most neighborhood residents who begin the home attendant training complete it and are placed in assignments soon thereafter. Home attendant work can be burdensome, however, particularly given the variability of clients' demands and the emotional labor required. One year at Ridgewood-Bushwick's Christmas party, for example, I listened while Nilsa, one of the CBO's home attendants, told a group of us about her "crazy day" with one of her clients. He was an elderly man who lived alone and had been showing signs of mental deterioration. That day, when Nilsa came upstairs from taking out the garbage, he had disappeared. She ran out into the street looking for him, worried because he had left without putting on his shoes. A couple of people on the street told her they had seen the man go by—shoeless—so Nilsa began to run. After about two blocks she finally spotted him, then had to chase him down, as he appeared oblivious to her calls for him to stop. When she finally got him back to the apartment, she tended to his dirty, cut feet and worried about how much longer she could continue to work with him, as his condition seemed to be getting much worse.[7]

Notwithstanding difficulties like these, the home attendant jobs provide a source of income for many Williamsburg and Bushwick residents who otherwise would have few ways to earn money. Most home attendants

6. Author's field notes, November 20, 1997.
7. Author's field notes, December 29, 1997.

work part-time, but many of them prefer this arrangement, as they have numerous domestic responsibilities to attend to as well. Thus, although many analysts would consider working as a home attendant a bad job because of its low wages, part-time hours, and lack of opportunities for advancement, the job is well matched to many local residents' skill levels and their need to balance income generation with domestic responsibilities.

Employment in a CBO does more than avoid some of the issues that have been identified as barriers to work. As the discussion of home attendants begins to illustrate, CBO jobs also respond to *preferences* of local residents. In the case of home attendants, part-time hours allow these employees to attend to their own household tasks while generating some income. CBO jobs are also located close to residents' homes, which not only avoids the problem of securing reliable transportation and the burden of long commuting time but again allows workers greater flexibility in attending to domestic duties. For example, on a number of occasions when I was accompanying Carmen Bonilla, a tenant organizer at Ridgewood-Bushwick, on her visits to apartment buildings where she worked with tenant associations, she called her elderly mother to let her know we would be stopping by for lunch.[8] Carmen's mother lives in the Bushwick-Hylan Houses, a large public housing development on the border between Bushwick and Williamsburg. Carmen and her six siblings grew up there, and two of her sisters moved into their own apartments in the development when they had families of their own. The group of siblings shared responsibility for checking in on their mother, who lived alone.

For Carmen, an enormously personable, dedicated, and fun-loving Puerto Rican woman in her late forties, working in the neighborhood where many of her family members lived allowed her to keep in close contact with them during the workday. Carmen served as an important source of assistance not only for her mother but for her unemployed sister and several young nieces and nephews who lived in Bushwick. This kind of family accessibility was important to many of the employees of the CBOs I studied. Working in their own neighborhoods, CBO employees were reassured that they could quickly arrive to pick up a sick child from school or attend to an elderly parent's emergency, and then return to work easily once the matter was resolved. In addition, the family-friendly environment at most CBOs meant employees sometimes brought their children or grandchildren to work with them when other arrangements could not be made. One day at

8. Author's field notes, July 15, 1997; September 16, 1997; February 10, 1998.

Nuestros Niños, for example, Amantina Duran's daughter Trudis arrived with her three-year-old son in tow:

> Amantina introduces the little boy to me as Avery, her grandson. She asks him if he can say hello to me, and he looks up at me, but can't quite manage it. Trudis tells him *"véte con abuela"* ["go stay with Grandma"], tells Amantina she'll be home later, and leaves, saying good-bye on her way out. Amantina asks Avery if he's hungry, he nods, and she heads out of the office to the kitchen to find him a snack.[9]

Such compatibility with domestic responsibilities is one preference that many employees can satisfy by working in a CBO. Many CBO workers also value working in an organization with a genuine commitment to bettering the community. As the sociologists Ida Susser and Nancy Naples have pointed out, many low-income women who become involved in community improvement work see it as an extension of their family responsibilities—community and family merge into one (Naples 1998; Susser 1982). Beginning with the public works jobs funded by the federal CETA program, CBOs have been able to financially compensate community-oriented residents for their contributions to CBOs and the local social infrastructure more generally. Although CETA lasted for only eight years, the growth of the CBO sector through the privatization of social service provision has made possible the continued compensation of community workers, and on a somewhat more stable basis. This structure has allowed CBOs in Williamsburg and Bushwick to offer employment to local residents who find great satisfaction in earning money through a form of work to which they feel strongly committed.

While the constant connection to family and community provided by a job in a CBO thus solves certain kinds of employment barriers and satisfies certain preferences of low-skilled workers, the minimal separation between paid work and the domestic sphere can also present challenges. Carmen Bonilla, for example, found that living in the neighborhood made it nearly impossible to ever get away from her organizational responsibilities with Ridgewood-Bushwick. Early in our acquaintance, she explained to me why, after residing in Bushwick nearly her whole life, she had moved away a couple of years earlier. Local residents she was working with knew where she lived and would show up at her apartment at all hours to ask for help. The

---

9. Author's field notes, July 7, 1997.

lack of privacy, and stress of seeming to always be at work, became un-
bearable, and Carmen finally moved to another Brooklyn neighborhood,
about a half-hour's drive from Bushwick.[10]

Staff members at other CBOs in Williamsburg and Bushwick reported
similar challenges. Tenant organizers at Saint Nick's and Los Sures, employees of Nuestros Niños, and youth workers at the Bushwick and Williamsburg Beacons often ran into clients or potential clients during nonwork
hours. This proved especially difficult when CBOs' limited resources prevented staff members from being able to help residents who desperately
needed assistance. At the New Life Child Development Center, where few
employees actually lived in Bushwick, these non–work-time encounters
were minimized. This may have contributed, however, to employees' lack-
ing the kind of unity and familiarity with clients that was evident in most
of the other CBOs in the study.

The Stability of CBO Jobs: Contracts versus Third-Party Payments

A central vulnerability of any job lies in the uncertainty concerning an
employer's ongoing ability to support the costs of that job. Like most
service organizations, the largest budget item for CBOs is staff salaries—for
child care workers, home attendants, tenant organizers, youth counselors,
social workers, and others. As nonprofit organizations, CBOs have little
capacity to generate capital, and as organizations serving the poor, CBOs
usually cannot rely on their clients to pay for their services. Instead, they
depend upon external sources of funds. The most common source by far is
the government: city, state, and federal agencies award contracts to CBOs to
carry out a wide range of social provision services. These contracts specify
the type of service to be provided, the minimum number of clients to be
served, the kinds of employees who will deliver the service, and a range
of other issues. Contracts are awarded through a competitive process, in
which CBOs submit bids for the work, as well as evidence of their expertise
and past performance in the area. The duration of CBO contracts varies,
but most run between one and three years.

The contract-based nature of many CBO jobs means that positions may
disappear when the contract expires. A government agency may decide to
stop supporting a certain program, or budget cuts for a particular area of
service may give rise to increased competition among CBOs for the dollars
that remain. When a contract to a CBO is lost or discontinued, employees'

---

10. Author's field notes, July 15, 1997.

salaries paid for by that contract must be found elsewhere—or employees lose their jobs. At Los Sures, which built up its organization during the 1970s and early 1980s using both federal CETA monies and city Community Management Program contracts, the end of these programs posed a major challenge. These funds had long supported tenant organizers and employees involved in building renovations, allowing Los Sures to pressure the owners of increasing numbers of the neighborhood's distressed buildings to provide appropriate maintenance, and to take over, renovate, and help tenants manage buildings that had been abandoned. Without CETA and the Community Management Program, funding for tenant organizing proved particularly difficult to maintain. By the time of my research, Los Sures was struggling to cobble together support from other sources to meet the costs of maintaining a full staff of organizers.[11] For example, when funds that had supported the salary of one organizer were cut at the end of 1996, the best Los Sures could do was to reassign that employee's tasks to a participant in the federal VISTA volunteer program, Lydia Bonilla. After completing her year of service during 1997–1998, however, Lydia left the organization, and funds to replace her did not materialize.[12] In an ongoing scramble, parts of the organizers' salaries were folded into other contracts, drawn from fees that Los Sures collected on development and management projects, and supplemented by occasional grants from private foundations.

CBOs that rely on government contracts to pay employees can also be vulnerable to shifting political winds. As I discuss in detail in chapter 3, because contracting is a government function, it contains important political dimensions. Of all the CBOs in Williamsburg and Bushwick, Los Sures suffered the greatest such political impacts. The persistent challenges that its organizers raised around housing issues in Williamsburg's Southside left that unit of Los Sures particularly vulnerable: Barbara Schliff, the lead organizer, blamed the organization's ongoing conflict with the Southside's politically powerful Hasidim for the loss of a longtime city contract that had supported organizers' salaries. Although Los Sures, Saint Nick's, and Ridgewood-Bushwick had all received funds from the city's Community Consultant Program for over a decade, she said, in the late 1990s, Los Sures was the only one of the three to lose its contract.[13] Indeed, CBO vulnerability to political fights is structurally embedded in the contract system,

11. Author's field notes on interview with David Pagán, administrator of Los Sures, May 23, 1997.

12. Author's field notes, October 18, 1999.

13. Author's field notes, May 30, 1997.

and was particularly pronounced during the time of my research, when Rudolph Giuliani was mayor of New York. While Giuliani was in office, a number of incidents arose in which his administration was accused of pulling CBO contracts as a result of political disagreements between the organizations and the mayor (Barry 1998). Whether as a result of politics, budget cuts, or a move from one type of program support to another, government contracts—the bread and butter of most CBO budgets—often prove to be a risky source of payroll funds.

In recognition of this risk, some CBO job creation schemes have turned to a more secure alternative source of funding: payments from third parties in a noncontractual relationship. The home health care enterprises at Saint Nick's and Ridgewood-Bushwick rely on this type of payment, which helps explain the continued growth of these efforts and the relative security of home attendant jobs. Home attendant services are paid for by individual clients' Medicaid, Medicare, or private insurance benefits. As long as a client's coverage remains in place, the services he or she receives will be paid for. In addition to matching home attendants looking for placements with clients in need of services, Saint Nick's and Ridgewood-Bushwick also manage the submission of claims and receive direct payments from the state and private insurers. Out of these funds, the CBOs pay the home attendants' wages, salaries of the administrative staff, and overhead costs (e.g., space rental, office supplies, and taxes).

Third-party payments, by attaching CBO service payments to individual clients, avert some of the vulnerabilities of jobs underwritten by government service contracts that must periodically be renewed. Indeed, most health care organizations, both nonprofit and for-profit, depend on third-party payments—Medicaid, Medicare, and private insurance—to meet a large proportion of their costs. As my research in Williamsburg and Bushwick drew to a close, Ridgewood-Bushwick was applying this model to a new project in its neighborhood: a state-of-the-art, 216-bed nursing home. Although the costs of building the facility were covered by a New York state contract, its ongoing expenses—including the cost of supporting the three hundred new jobs it created in Bushwick—were to be covered by third-party payments from individuals' health care insurance. At Saint Nick's EWVIDCO project, part of the money needed to support staff salaries comes from another kind of third-party payment: membership dues paid by businesses who belong to the group. While these third-party funds must be supplemented by contracts and other sources, they lend some financial stability to the jobs in this part of the CBO.

As CBOs of all kinds struggle to create and maintain jobs for neighborhood residents, a subset of these organizations provide working families with critical domestic-sphere help: a reliable, affordable source of child care. Historically, organized, nonfamilial child care in the United States has always been linked to parents'—especially mothers'—imperative to work. The child care and youth development CBOs of Williamsburg and Bushwick thus play a critical role in making sure that parents are able to show up at work consistently, knowing that their children are being supervised by qualified adults in a safe environment.

Family Supplement: Raising Children outside the Home

The earliest child care facilities in the United States emerged in the mid-nineteenth century to supervise the children of mothers who had been widowed or abandoned, and thus needed to work to support their families (E. Rose 1999). Nonfamilial child care was so frowned upon during this period that these facilities accepted children only from single mothers in the most desperate situations—those with no relatives to help out and no source of financial support apart from their own labor. During the Great Depression, when many men faced chronic unemployment, wives often found themselves becoming the main source of family economic support. The Women's Division of the Federal Emergency Relief Administration (FERA) established a number of income-generating enterprises for women, such as sewing cooperatives, food canning projects, and various human service jobs. As women went out to work, many placed their children in nursery schools that the Works Progress Administration (FERA's successor) had created to employ out-of-work teachers, nurses, and dieticians (Cohen 1996; E. Rose 1999). Unlike the earlier child care facilities, whose main function was simply custodial—a place for working mothers to leave their children under some semblance of supervision—the WPA nurseries often drew on the skills of their professional staff to make educational activities a part of the children's day.

By 1942, with the nation at war and the economy surging, staff at the WPA nursery school program returned to their regular jobs, and most of the nurseries closed down. As wartime manufacturing needs grew rapidly, however, women were called to enter the workforce in large numbers. They needed places to leave their children while they worked, and in the name of the war effort, Congress appropriated funds from the 1940 Lanham Act to build and operate thousands of child care facilities in "war-impacted" areas across the nation (Cohen 1996; Gatenio 2002). Although New York City was home to major war production facilities—especially the Brooklyn Navy Yard—it was excluded from access to Lanham Act child care funds (Levine and McCabe 1965, 29). In the wake of the success of the WPA nurseries, however, New York's mothers and child advocates clamored for expanded access to child care services from the city.

In 1941 New York's mayor, Fiorello LaGuardia, established the Mayor's Commission on the Wartime Care of Children, which shortly led to the appropriation of state and city funds to staff child care programs in the city's churches and community centers. Spurred on by the recommendations of the commission, LaGuardia oversaw New York City's development of a publicly funded child care system that remains in place today: a network of private, nonprofit organizations that contract with the city to care for the children of low-income, working parents (Gatenio 2002; Levine and McCabe 1965). At present, New York City's Administration for Children's Services oversees this network, which is the largest municipal child care system in the United States, serving approximately seventy-five thousand children annually (New York City Administration for Children's Services 2001). Even this level of government-subsidized child care, however, falls far short of meeting the needs of New York's low-income, working parents. A recent study indicates that New York City has an additional forty-six thousand children—some 60 percent of the number currently served—who need and are eligible for subsidized child care, but for whom no provider is available (City of New York 2003).

While early efforts to provide nonfamilial child care were a response to increased demand for mothers' participation in the workforce, by 1960 a second rationale for providing child care outside the home was emerging. New research findings on young children pointed to the importance of the first few years of life as key in their physical, intellectual, and social development. The Head Start program, begun in 1965 as part of the War on Poverty, focused attention on the developmental needs of three- to five-year olds from very low-income families. Head Start's philosophy argued that poor children came to their first day of school already disadvantaged, with fewer cognitive, social, and emotional skills than their better-off peers, as poor children's home environments allegedly did not provide the kinds of stimulation that best foster brain development. Head Start targeted families receiving welfare, as well as poor working families, in an effort to improve the children's early development and lay the foundation for greater success in school and the labor market (Cohen 1996). This proved to be one of the few moments where the primary rationale for nonfamilial child care focused on the benefits to children rather than on pushing mothers into the workforce.

The developmental focus of Head Start soon was adopted by organized child care programs more generally, due in no small measure to the greater number of middle-class women entering the labor force and their concomitant expanded use of child care facilities (Steinfels 1973). As national attitudes about the appropriate productive roles of women shifted—from an emphasis on domestic tasks to a growing acceptance of and demand for generating income—nonfamilial child care became less controversial, and support for government income assistance to nonworking, single mothers declined. Changes in welfare programs followed, as the federal government began requiring mothers receiving welfare payments to work in exchange for their benefits (N. E. Rose 1995). By 1980, when Ronald Reagan's picture of the "welfare queen" cemented public opinion against recipients of public assistance, demands for work by low-income mothers with children surged. The 1988 Family Support Act required welfare recipients to work, but only if they could find a suitable child care provider, which would be paid for by federal child care subsidies (Cohen 1996). The 1996 welfare reform legislation explicitly acknowledged child care as one of the most difficult barriers facing low-income parents required to work (e g , Fuller et al. 2002; Meyers 1995; Newman 1999; Oliker 1994, 1995; Strawn and Martinson 2000), and appropriated unprecedented sums for child care to support women transitioning off public assistance. Thus, the growing demands on low-income women to earn money were increasingly supplemented by government assistance directed toward the critical domestic responsibility of child care.

The widely increased availability of public funds to pay for child care, however, has not been accompanied by a significant commitment to ensuring that the care is of high quality. This is despite the repeated warnings of child advocates that low-quality child care often compromises children's developmental progress. In New York City, for example, most of the subsidy expansion in post–welfare reform child care came in the form of vouchers that recipients could exchange for care. Some of these vouchers were routed through the city's oversight agency for licensed child care providers, the Agency for Child Development (ACD), but more were distributed through the city's welfare agency, which does not require that they be used for licensed care. Between 1996 and 1997, for example, ACD distributed some 9,000 vouchers that families could use to obtain *only* licensed child care (New York City Administration for Children's Services 2001, 19). (While the number of vouchers increased, the number of available spaces at the licensed facilities with ACD contract remained largely stagnant, tightening an already highly competitive market.) Over the same period, the city's welfare agency, the Human Resources Administration, allocated 16,500 vouchers—nearly twice as many as ACD—as part of individual welfare cases (New York City Administration for Children's Services 2001, 31). These welfare-related vouchers were designated to pay for care from informal, unlicensed providers, including relatives, friends, and neighbors. This practice marked a departure from the city's long history of maintaining professional standards in its subsidized child care programs (Gatenio 2002).

Raising Nuestros Niños

It's 11:45 a.m., lunchtime at Nuestros Niños, a developmental child care center in the Southside of Williamsburg. Downstairs in the main kitchen, rolling metal carts of hot food are on their way to the classrooms on the upper floors, where teachers and teachers' aides will serve platefuls to the preschool children sitting quietly at their low tables. As they place each item from the menu on the plates, the adults ask the children to identify it: "ham!" "*plátanos!*" "beans!" "carrots!" they call out in unison. The classrooms where the older children will arrive after school closes for the day are still quiet. But by this time next month, when school is out for the summer and the older children will spend full days at Nuestros Niños, the kitchen staff will be twice as busy.

As I sit filing some papers in the first-floor family day care office, John Mulhern, the sixty-something executive director of Nuestros Niños, sticks his head in: "Lunchtime!" he calls out to me and Amantina Duran, Ana Cruzado, and Sonia Raices, three members of the family day care staff. Smiling, we all put down our work and head leisurely to the small staff kitchen down the hall, where our own metal cart awaits. We pick up plates from the cart and help ourselves to the food. Amantina chides John gently for taking only ham and bread, leaving all the vegetables behind. John sits at the table sheepishly, as the other women shake their heads and make noises in support of Amantina. Within a few minutes, we all have joined John at the table, eating and chatting, enjoying the break and the company.[14]

Nuestros niños is Spanish for "our children." Three decades before I set foot in this highly regarded Southside child care center, John, who grew

---

14. Author's field notes, June 9, 1997.

up in a New York Irish family, arrived in the neighborhood to take up the post of assistant priest at Transfiguration Catholic Church. Since graduating from seminary, he had been performing pastoral duties in Puerto Rico. With Transfiguration newly dominated by Puerto Rican migrants, the diocese sent John to the parish, where his Spanish language skills and experience ministering to Puerto Ricans promised to be valuable. Three years later, John fell in love with one of his Puerto Rican parishioners and left the priesthood to marry her. The couple settled in the Southside, during the time when the area was suffering through the worst of its housing abandonment and arson problems, and the population was declining rapidly. Determined to help stabilize the neighborhood, John and Luz Maria bought a house on Hewes Street, less than two blocks from Transfiguration.[15]

Despite having left the priesthood, John remained very attached to the parishioners at Transfiguration. He wanted to remain involved in parish work, but the diocese prohibited any spiritual ministering by ex-religious. John's former colleagues at Transfiguration, however, knew that he could contribute to the work of the church in other ways. In 1971, Sister Peggy Walsh, a nun assigned to Transfiguration, had begun a series of parenting workshops at the church.[16] Appreciative of what they had learned at Sister Peggy's workshops, five of the mothers some of whom were providing informal care for the children of their working friends or neighbors—asked her if she could establish a more permanent child care setting along the lines of the workshops. Sister Peggy agreed, and set up *la escuelita* ("the little school") on the first floor of the church's convent.

With the volunteer help of the mothers, *la escuelita* cared for seven or eight young children. It quickly became clear, however, that the need for child care in the Southside far exceeded this number, as many families depended on both parents' wages from work outside the home. The pastor of Transfiguration, Father Bryan Karvelis, knew that John had connections in city government and asked him to try to find city funds to direct toward the neighborhood's child care needs. In early 1973, John was successful. After securing a promise from the city to make funds available later that year, he hired a few local mothers to help him staff the program and rented a building on South Fourth Street. Knowing their children were in the hands of trusted friends and their beloved ex-priest alleviated working

15. Author's field notes on interview with John Mulhern, May 23, 1997.
16. The following account of the early years of Nuestros Niños is drawn from the author's field notes on a May 25, 2004, interview with Amantina Duran, one of the mothers involved in the organization during its genesis in Transfiguration Catholic Church.

mothers' worries; this was not some impersonal child care provider but rather a collective enterprise taking care of *nuestros niños*. The arrangement quickly took root, and in 1975 John incorporated Nuestros Niños as an independent nonprofit organization. With a board of directors composed of local clergy and activists, he began administering the care of 120 children under a contract from the city's Agency for Child Development.

Beg, Borrow, and Steal: Creating Child Care for Low-Income Families

Low-income parents require reliable, affordable child care if they are to maintain their attachment to work, generate sufficient income to support their families, and perhaps move up to better-paying jobs that will afford them and their children more options in life. Nuestros Niños faces an array of challenges in helping parents access such child care, and it resolves these challenges through organizational strategies that allow it to maneuver smoothly through New York City's publicly subsidized child care system. By 1997, when I started conducting fieldwork at Nuestros Niños, the organization had expanded from its original ACD contract serving 120 children at the South Fourth Street center, to contracts covering 300 children at two separate facilities in the Southside, plus seventy-five family day care homes caring for an additional 300 children from the neighborhood.[17] Still, the organization's waiting list for families seeking care had hundreds of names on it. Even before the 1996 welfare reform, which pushed many single mothers into the workforce, Nuestros Niños had faced greater demand for care from working parents than it could accommodate. With new federal mandates that all recipients of Temporary Assistance to Needy Families (TANF) be working or engaged in "work activities," the need for child care had surged in the Southside, and the staff at Nuestros Niños was on the front lines.

John and most of the Nuestros Niños staff live in the Southside, leaving them open to constant entreaties—not just during working hours—from families in desperate need of child care. John was always looking for opportunities to help his neighbors meet this challenge, so when I began fieldwork at Nuestros Niños, he asked me to work on a small expansion project he was trying to get off the ground. He was hoping to commandeer two largely unused community rooms in apartment buildings a few blocks away, enough space to accommodate forty additional children in the orga-

17. Since I concluded my fieldwork at Nuestros Niños at the end of 1998, the organization has taken over administration of another local child care center and added twenty-five family day care providers to its operation, meaning nearly one thousand children are in its care.

nization's after-school child care program. This was not a large number, to be sure, but would cover forty children whose parents otherwise would rely on improvised, unstable arrangements or no care at all. As he explained the project to me, John remarked that Nuestros Niños was always trying to find ways to help the parents in the neighborhood, and that he constantly "begs, borrows, and steals" from the center's teachers to get them to squeeze a couple of extra kids into their classrooms.[18]

The soaring post–welfare reform demand for child care had, as we have seen, led New York City to move away from its traditional commitment to subsidizing only licensed, professional child care. City welfare administrators were most concerned with procuring some form of custodial care for recipients' children. As a result, they neither mandated any kind of quality standards nor attached sufficient funds to welfare-related child care vouchers to ensure that care would be of the kind universally supported by child care experts and child advocates (Gatenio 2002). At Nuestros Niños, the staff was acutely aware of the importance of quality care for all children. One day, as I sorted applications for the forty potential new after-school slots, John came to check on my progress. I had about a hundred applications in front of me and asked him what I should do with the ten or so duplicate applications I had found. While I had been ready to simply throw them away, consolidating what seemed to me excess paper, John told me to staple the duplicates together. Filing multiple applications, he said, "shows the parents are really taking an active role looking for care, which means they really need it, they haven't found any alternative." When I asked him what happens to the children for whom there is no space at Nuestros Niños, John said they might find a spot in one of the three other child care centers in the neighborhood, but usually they get care from a relative, friend, or neighbor—an alternative, he said with a grimace, that meant "it's probably not the kind of developmental care we hope they'll get."[19]

A few days after this conversation, I accompanied John and two other Nuestros Niños staff members to a meeting at the office of New York City mayor Rudolph Giuliani, where we met with two members of Deputy Mayor Fran Reiter's staff. This was in early June 1997, as the mayor turned his attention to the long-simmering tension between the Southside's Latinos and Hasidim over access to housing in the neighborhood (see chapter 2). The two items on our meeting agenda were resolving a leasing problem with Nuestros Niños' South Fourth Street building and getting an update

18. Author's field notes, June 2, 1997.
19. Author's field notes, June 2, 1997.

on the new Nuestros Niños facility that the city was planning to build on South Second Street. After hearing out the deputy mayor's staff and thanking them for their assistance on these two long-term components of the child care effort in the Southside, John deftly raised the short-term expansion plan on which I had been working. Although new ACD contracts for child care facilities are very hard to come by, given the largely fixed budget for this piece of the city's child care programs, John took advantage of his momentary audience with the deputy mayor's staff to float his idea. He noted that the area of the Southside where he would set up the new program had no school-age care available, and that Nuestros Niños would have no trouble filling all the slots. Should the city produce an ACD contract, he could guarantee that the organization would have the program up and running by the fall. The deputy mayor's staff listened and nodded, then told John they would bring the idea to Nicholas Scoppetta, who was then commissioner of the city's child services agency.[20]

As I found out a few days later, John's timing was politically astute—no surprise for this self-confessed political junkie and one-time city council candidate who counts local state Assemblyman Vito Lopez among his closest friends. As recounted in chapter 2, on June 8, three days after our meeting with the deputy mayor's staff, the *New York Times* reported on a major agreement brokered by Mayor Giuliani that attempted to meet the demands of the Southside's competing Latinos and Hasidim (J. Sexton 1997). Although the focus of the agreement, spelled out in an official memorandum of understanding,[21] lay squarely on housing issues, the city also gave the official go-ahead for the new Nuestros Niños center on South Second Street—an attempt to sweeten the pot for the Latinos of the Southside. John's request for an additional, small ACD contract to provide forty more children with care had thus sought to piggyback on the Southside's unusual moment of leverage with the mayor. His opportunistic attempt to squeeze a few more child care slots out of the city captures the essence of Nuestros Niños' commitment to its core mission of supporting work and child development among the Southside's low-income Latino residents.

Over the next several months, John and I worked on the expansion project, hoping our advance legwork would increase the chances of getting a city contract to support these two classrooms. We lined up the necessary staff, assessed the conditions of the spaces, secured the support of the tenants who lived in the two buildings, and pulled together the names of

---

20. Author's field notes, June 5, 1997.
21. Memorandum of Understanding; document in author's possession.

close to fifty children from the Nuestros Niños waiting list. Our efforts ultimately proved fruitless, however, as the plan ran up against the reality of
the city budget and the receding political urgency of the Southside Latino
community in the wake of the mayor's September press conference on the
Memorandum of Understanding (see chapter 2). Indeed, government budget limitations are the most significant impediment to providing child care
via organizations like Nuestros Niños. The New York City comptroller's
office estimates that between forty-eight thousand and one hundred thousand children eligible for city-subsidized child care are not receiving it.
Compare this to the thirty-three thousand children who currently receive
center-based care paid for by ACD, and the additional forty-two thousand
children whose care the city pays for in either licensed family day care
homes or informal, unlicensed settings (City of New York 2003; New York
City Administration for Children's Services 2001). In this context of extreme competition for child care vouchers and slots in child care centers,
establishing and maintaining these pathways to child care proves critical
to both parental work prospects and children's development.

Who Pays? Organizing the Financing of Child Care for the Poor

As befits a form of child care organized by and for parents whose economic
situation requires full-time work from all of the adults in a household,
Nuestros Niños and other ACD-sponsored child care centers provide care
that matches traditional full-time work schedules. Nuestros Niños opens
at 8:00 a.m. and closes at 6:00 p.m., allowing parents time to drop off
their children, commute to their jobs, put in a typical 9:00 a.m. to 5:00
p.m. workday, and return to pick up their children before closing.[22] During the school year, Nuestros Niños operates full-day care for preschool
children and serves school-age children (up to age twelve) from 2:30 to
6:00 p.m. When school is out in the summertime, school-age children also
receive full-day care. Daily life at Nuestros Niños is devoted to meeting
the twin challenges of facilitating parental work and helping fulfill families' child-raising responsibilities. The former task involves efforts by the
organization's staff to coordinate the complexities of New York City's public child care bureaucracy on behalf of parents, while the latter revolves
around setting and attaining appropriate standards of care for the children.

22. A new challenge facing child care providers is to accommodate off-hour work schedules,
such as second and third shifts, which are increasingly common in a twenty-four-hour service
and production economy. Nuestros Niños currently offers no such care.

As any working parent knows, and any number of studies of low-income working parents have demonstrated, if child care arrangements fall through or become too expensive, absence from work is inevitable. A child care facility like Nuestros Niños often proves a more reliable source of care than an informal arrangement with a relative or friend, thereby ensuring that parents' employment is not jeopardized by child care problems. At the same time, however, formal, licensed care involves substantial costs, which low-income families cannot pay on their own. A key function of Nuestros Niños thus lies in helping families maintain their eligibility for the public subsidies that cover the costs of care at the center. In New York City, families with incomes below 100 percent of the federal poverty line (adjusted for family size) are eligible for a full subsidy from the Agency for Child Development (ACD), meaning they have no out-of-pocket expense for care. ACD also serves moderate-income families, whose incomes range up to 200 percent of the federal poverty line, by providing partial subsidies and requiring parents to contribute on a sliding scale (up to no more than 10 percent of family income) to the costs of their children's care (Fender et al. 2002). Subsidies apply to both center-based and family day care at Nuestros Niños, though absolute costs for family day care are lower. At Nuestros Niños, most families receive a full subsidy; less than 5 percent of the organization's revenues come from parent fees.

The eligibility certification process for child care is similar in many ways to eligibility determinations for other forms of public assistance, such as welfare payments, food stamps, Medicaid, or subsidized housing. Applicants are required to fill out government forms requesting assistance, and to provide proof of address, income, family size, social security numbers, and so on. As numerous studies of welfare recipients have shown, public assistance application and recertification processes often function as barriers to receiving benefits: one missing piece of paperwork, or a blank space on an application form, can delay or even completely derail the process. To avoid such problems, New York City's ACD child care centers have established arrangements with the city to centralize and streamline the eligibility determination process for the families they serve. I learned about this critical role played by child care CBOs one morning at Nuestros Niños, when I arrived for my usual volunteer session and was surprised to see a large group of mothers crowded into the waiting area. When I asked Sonia Raices, one of the family day care workers, about it, she told me that the mothers were there to complete their ACD recertification. Every few months, a city eligibility worker makes the trip out to Nuestros Niños to collect the family documentation necessary to determine whether or not

ACD will continue paying for care. Families receiving care under Nuestros Niños' ACD contract need to be recertified regularly, and staff members who coordinate and oversee recertification in conjunction with the city eligibility worker spare parents the uncertainty of this process.[23]

Managing this uncertainty proves especially critical for families whose circumstances change over time; they may still qualify for public subsidy but under a different category that requires different proof of eligibility. For example, a mother might be in a welfare-related job training program that lasts eight weeks, during which time she is eligible for city-funded child care. When the training program ends, however, she loses that eligibility, and the provider is supposed to pull her child out of care. If, several weeks later, the mother finds a low-wage job, her child again becomes eligible for care—but by then her slot at the child care CBO may have been assigned to somebody else. This scenario has negative consequences for everyone involved: the mother, the child, and the CBO. If the mother lacks access to child care at the moment a job is offered, she will not be able to accept the job. If the child is constantly shifted among child care settings, social and cognitive development are disrupted. And the CBO's challenge is to keep its slots filled as mothers swirl through the various eligibility categories associated with training programs, mandatory welfare-to-work assignments, and jobs. Amantina Duran, a staff member at Nuestros Niños, explained to me that the organization often juggles the eligibility system on behalf of its clients, thereby both supporting parents in their struggle to remain attached to the workforce, and providing continuity of care to their children.[24]

This kind of slippage between the formal rules governing subsidy eligibility and their actual implementation—what organizational sociologists call "loose coupling" (Weick 1976)—takes place across the boundaries of different organizations (child care CBOs and the city child care agency) and economic sectors (nonprofits and government). The ongoing, stable partnership between the city child care agency—which pays for low-income parents' work-enabling child care—and Nuestros Niños—which performs the daily service provision—facilitates this kind of play in the eligibility system. Nuestros Niños has proved itself to the city over the years as a reliable partner, and the organization's city eligibility worker allows the CBO to work out the details of individual families' cases without demanding unwavering compliance.[25] In a system that benefits from denying assistance

23. Author's field notes, August 4, 1997.
24. Author's field notes, June 2, 1997.
25. Author's field notes, June 9, 1997.

to applicants, saving money when applications are denied, this represents a significant accomplishment.

In addition to helping families maintain their child care subsidies throughout the year, each July Nuestros Niños provides a significant subsidy of its own to parents. The bulk of the funds the organization uses to pay its center-based and family day care staff comes from an annual contract appropriation from ACD. The contract divides the total sum allocated to Nuestros Niños into monthly payments, but none of these payments can be released until the annual contract is processed by the city. At the start of each fiscal year, ACD finds itself behind in approving the annual paperwork, which leaves child care CBOs like Nuestros Niños without funds to pay salaries. The problem is well known within the organization, and every July John reminds his staff that when the city's fiscal year changes over, their salary checks will likely be at least a few days late.

In 1997 the city proved particularly inept at renewing its ACD contracts, and it was nearly a month into the new fiscal year before funds were released to Nuestros Niños and the city's other child care CBOs.[26] In the interim, staff at Nuestros Niños carried on working as usual, providing full-day care to nearly seven hundred children without pay. This contrasts sharply with the procedures followed by government agencies when budget appropriations are delayed and stopgap spending bills are not passed to cover short-term costs. In 1995, for example, the federal government was shut down due to an impasse between Congress and President Clinton over the size and provisions of the year's budget. With no funds available to cover employee salaries, all but essential personnel were furloughed until a budget agreement was reached (Van Natta 1995; Wines 1995). Although this only took a few days, federal employees were not allowed to work during that time. In contrast, the staff at Nuestros Niños continued caring for their young charges for an entire month rather than throw their parents' working lives into an uproar.

Raising the Next Generation of Workers

In addition to freeing parents for work outside the home, childcare CBOs play a critical role in the development of the next generation of workers. Schools in New York's low-income neighborhoods have notoriously dismal records of fostering the academic achievement among their students. Moreover, economically stressed families often find it challenging

26. Author's field notes, July 28, 1997.

to provide the secure and nurturing home environments that optimize children's overall development. The lessons children learn from child-care CBOs thus make an important contribution to their sense of values, academic achievement, self-esteem, ability to relate to peers, respect for authority, aspirations, and many other attitudes and skills that affect their future prospects in the labor market. Faced with so many opportunities to make an impact on the lives of the children they care for, the child care CBOs of Williamsburg and Bushwick make different choices about where to direct their energies. These choices reflect a long-standing tension in the early childhood community about the relative importance of academic and social development.

While educational attainment is among the most important predictors of future employment and income prospects, a sole focus on academic skills does not account for the myriad challenges young people face in constructing a path to self-sufficient adulthood. These challenges are even greater for low-income youth, who have access to fewer familial and other resources to aid them in their development and to protect them when they make mistakes. All of the CBOs in Williamsburg and Bushwick that care for children understand the importance of fostering all aspects of their development. Should they forget, the government agencies that regulate child care providers and contract for their services mandate that CBO programs attend to children's social, emotional, physical, and cognitive dimensions. At the same time, however, individual CBOs make important choices about which aspects of development they believe matter most for children's progress to-ward adulthood, and the adult responsibilities of paid work and family.

Nuestros Niños, perhaps because a core of its clientele consists of pre-school children, focuses squarely on the emotional development of its charges. The organization places utmost value on the cultivation of meaningful personal relationships—especially between staff members and children, but also among staff members themselves. The goal is to reproduce the staff's clear ideas on how a life caring for children should be conducted. The daily pace at Nuestros Niños is unhurried, with ample time between work and learning tasks for both children and adults to come to know each other better, reflect on their own situations, and appreciate their common bond. Even within the bureaucratic structure of a publicly funded developmental child care organization, the staff at Nuestros Niños succeeds in creating a space that feels like home.

Executive director John Mulhern had carefully cultivated this special atmosphere, which he felt was an important element of his organization's success with children. Demonstrations of love, caring, and trust abounded at Nuestros Niños, taught to and modeled for children by the adult staff. As Mulhern explained to a group of college students visiting Nuestros Niños one afternoon: "I try to hug a hundred kids a day, because kids need to know that they're important, that people pay attention to them, that they can count on people."[27] His statement, in today's climate of fear regarding the quality of child care and the very real possibilities of child abuse, caused some consternation in his audience, as the following excerpt from my field notes shows:

> One of the Latina students asks him if he's serious about the kid hugging, because she knows that her sister would never let a person in his position hug her kid: "Nobody touches my sister's kids, unless they're family." John says that of course there is an appropriate way to do these kinds of things, and that he always hugs kids in public, often in front of their parents. He says there's no reason that anyone would hug someone else's child in private, and that it would be inappropriate to do so. But he would also tell the student's sister that she needs to lose that attitude, that kids benefit from the attention and affection of other adults, and she needs to be more open to that. The students seem satisfied with this answer.[28]

Nuestros Niños has been teaching these lessons of trust, caring, and respect throughout its long history. The children who spend time within its walls carry these emotional lessons with them into the wider world, beneficiaries of its familial embrace.

In contrast to the emphasis on emotional development at Nuestros Niños, the Williamsburg Beacon maintains a laserlike focus on the development of academic skills among the first- through eighth-graders in its after-school program. The Williamsburg Beacon is one of eighty youth and family support centers sponsored by New York City's Department of Youth and Community Development in neighborhoods throughout the city. Since 1991, when it started the Beacon program, the city has contracted with CBOs to provide a range of educational, social, recreational, and communal activities to local residents, with a focus on comprehensive youth development (C. Warren, Feist, and Nevarez 2002). All of the Beacons are housed in city public schools, but CBOs, not school administrators or city agency representatives, are in charge. A Williamsburg CBO, the Saint Nicholas Neighborhood Preservation Corporation (Saint Nick's) runs the

27. Author's field notes, July 14, 1997.
28. Author's field notes, July 14, 1997.

Williamsburg Beacon, which is housed in the former Eastern District High School, on the corner of Grand Street and Bushwick Avenue.[29]

The Williamsburg Beacon's spotlight on children's cognitive development came only after a risky decision by Saint Nick's executive director, Michael Rochford, to shake up the program. Toward the end of 1997, Michael hired a Williamsburg native, Eddie Calderón-Melendez—who at the time ran a highly successful Beacon in the Bronx—to fill a new Saint Nick's position, as director of youth and family programs. Eddie's position included overall responsibility for the Williamsburg Beacon, as well as for a number of Saint Nick's other youth-oriented programs that were already operating or being developed for future implementation. Shortly after Eddie's arrival at Saint Nick's, the then-director of the Williamsburg Beacon, Frank Alvarado, was fired.[30] Eddie took over as Interim Director of the Beacon, and moved rapidly to implement a new, academically focused program of activities.

Working within a tense situation leading up to and following Frank's dismissal, Eddie immediately began replicating the highly successful program he had implemented at the Phipps Beacon in the Bronx, which not only had won him the position at Saint Nick's, but also had established him as a sought-after national authority on youth development programs. The core of the Williamsburg Beacon's after-school program became a highly structured, literacy-based curriculum, explicitly designed to improve the academic skills of the children by engaging them in fun learning activities. As the following excerpt from my field notes shows, on a visit to the

29. The history of the Williamsburg Beacon is complex. In 1991, when the city first solicited bids for the Beacon program, a CBO called Neighborhood Women of Williamsburg-Greenpoint won one of the ten original contracts. Because of difficulties with the District 14 Community School Board, however, the Williamsburg Beacon was denied operating space in any of the local elementary or junior high schools, where all Beacons were supposed to be housed. After two years, the Williamsburg Beacon was permitted to open in the local public high school (Eastern District High School), which was not controlled by the community school board. At that time, Saint Nick's operated a program through the Beacon, but did not run the overall operation. In a controversial 1995 move, Saint Nick's responded to grumblings from various CBOs and individuals in Williamsburg that Neighborhood Women was not using the Beacon contract to the best advantage of neighborhood residents. When the Beacon contract came up for renewal, Saint Nick's submitted a competing application to the city, which selected Saint Nick's—ousting Neighborhood Women. Relations between the two Williamsburg CBOs remain tense, and Neighborhood Women's profile has declined precipitously.

30. This was the culmination of a weeks-long, increasingly ugly struggle between Frank and Michael. Michael handled the near-crisis and brought it to a clean resolution using a skillful combination of community-organizing and bureaucratic-power techniques. See chapter 5 for an extended discussion of these events.

Williamsburg Beacon shortly after the new program's implementation, I found a well-functioning academic environment:

> I go to Eddie's office, say hello, and ask if I can see some of the classrooms. He says I'm more than welcome, tells me that they've changed a bunch of the rooms they're using, and gives me the room numbers for a couple of the after-school program groups. I go to the first room. Inside, two new staff members—about twenty or twenty-two years old—are working with a group of about twelve kids. They are discussing a book about Native Americans, and the kids are making masks that relate to the story. There are lots of books and other materials in the classroom. Everyone seems quite engrossed with what they are doing. . . . I go to another classroom, and see much the same scene. These kids are a bit older, and they are doing a writing assignment. A couple of them are acting out a bit, but generally the room is under control and the kids seem to be interested in the work.[31]

Under the previous director, I had never seen this kind of attention to children's cognitive development at the Williamsburg Beacon. These changes point up the importance of staff interests and qualifications in choosing what aspects of child development garner the most attention in a child care CBO. Eddie clearly saw academic skills as the foundation of a successful child care program, though his curriculum also provided room for children to exercise creativity, work collaboratively, and develop leadership abilities—all key components of a wider youth development philosophy. While his predecessor at the Williamsburg Beacon had come from a youth recreation background, Eddie himself had been trained in a broader approach to youth education and development and was completing his doctoral degree at Columbia University's school of education. In line with his training, Eddie also emphasized the importance of staff capacity, setting high expectations for his after-school program counselors, and training them extensively in how to implement the Beacon's new academic curriculum.

Finally, the Bushwick Beacon focused on a third aspect of child development, which had great salience in Bushwick's high-violence environment: personal safety. Like the Williamsburg Beacon, the Bushwick Beacon was established with one of the original ten contracts let by the city in 1991 for this new youth and family support program. The Bushwick Beacon has been run since its inception by the YMCA of Greater New York and is

31. Author's field notes, February 17, 1998.

housed at Intermediate School 111, on the corner of Starr Street and Wilson Avenue.[32] All of the Bushwick Beacon staff, from the director to the after-school program counselors, talked to me repeatedly about the importance of the Beacon as a place where young people could feel safe: protected from teasing, pressure to engage in petty crime or other negative behaviors, and violence.[33] While an evaluation of the Beacon program citywide pointed to the provision of safe space for young people as an important function of all Beacons (C. Warren, Feist, and Nevarez 2002), the Bushwick Beacon also grappled with its location in the middle of an area that, during most of the 1990s, was well known as one of the most active drug markets in Brooklyn (Maher 1997).

In 1994, drug dealers murdered a neighborhood antidrug activist in a park two blocks from the Bushwick Beacon. Despite an increased police presence, drugs still were sold freely in the park at the time I was conducting my research. In addition, small local gangs sold drugs out of stores on two corners of the block where the Bushwick Beacon was located. Rory Morlos, the Bushwick Beacon's director, acknowledged that he could not rid the area of drug trafficking and other gang activity completely. Instead, he had worked over the years to establish relationships with the gang members—for example, by allowing them to field teams in the Bushwick Beacon's football and basketball leagues—with the result that they almost never conducted their less desirable activities in high-traffic areas surrounding the Beacon. Although there was a shooting at the Bushwick Beacon the year it opened, in subsequent years the building, programs, and staff have been largely respected and left alone by the gangs. Rory estimated that close to 90 percent of the children and youths who attended the Bushwick Beacon lived in the surrounding ten-block area. The prevalence of drug activity and related violence in these children's lives meant that securing their safety took precedence over all other developmental efforts by Beacon staff.

One apparent downside of the Bushwick Beacon's attention to providing a safe and welcoming environment, however, was the staff's seeming unwillingness to place too many demands on the youngsters who par-

32. At the time of my research, I.S. 111 was one of the worst-performing public junior high schools in New York City. It had been placed in a special "Chancellor's District," where all the worst-performing schools were supposed to receive extra attention and resources to improve students' outcomes. As of this writing, I.S. 111 has been broken up into several "small schools," all housed in the same physical building.

33. Author's field notes, September 9, 1997; October 27, 1997; December 23, 1997; February 10, 1998.

ticipated in the program. For example, there was no structured academic program at the Bushwick Beacon, only occasional halfhearted attempts by the staff to help children with their homework. In addition, some staff at the Bushwick Beacon explicitly voiced the opinion that an academic focus was not appropriate for an after-school program. Elvira Medina, the Bushwick Beacon's after-school program director, explained to me that children needed a break from academic work after school, and that it was her job to attend to other aspects of their development during that time.[34] Although this perspective fits with a comprehensive approach to youth development, it presumes that children are receiving a solid education during their time at school—something that students at Bushwick's public schools could rarely expect.

Child care CBOs in Williamsburg and Bushwick take on part of the challenge of preparing local children for their future engagement with paid work and family responsibilities. In the best-case scenario, these CBOs contribute to a joint enterprise with sturdy families and quality schools to foster children's social, emotional, physical, and cognitive development, thereby assuring their successful transition to adulthood. Most children in neighborhoods like Williamburg and Bushwick, however, face challenges that make CBOs' efforts an uphill battle. With only 20 to 50 percent of students in Williamsburg's and Bushwick's public schools reading at grade level, for example, child care CBOs rarely get to provide supplemental cognitive development opportunities; rather, they must take on the challenge of compensating for the poor performance of their charges' schools. In 2003, the Williamsburg Beacon decided to reconfigure this arrangement by adding a charter school to its program offerings: the charter school serves children in grades nine through twelve and has an extended school day (8:15 a.m. to 5:30 p.m.) and school year (eleven months of school). At Nuestros Niños and the Bushwick Beacon, program emphases are also geared toward staff's sense of the important developmental challenges local youngsters face, all with an eye toward seeing children successfully manage the rocky path to adulthood.

Between A Rock and a Hard Place: Community-Based Organizations and Work

In the 1950s, Williamsburg and Bushwick were still places where residents could find decent-paying, regular work, often in the manufacturing in-

---

34. Author's field notes on interview with Elvira Medina, September 29, 1997.

dustries that lined the Brooklyn waterfront and reached eastward along the borough's industrial corridor. The precipitous decline of manufacturing as a mainstay of the U.S. economy, however, did not spare these two hardworking neighborhoods, as the empty and converted factory buildings found throughout Williamsburg and Bushwick attest. Williamsburg still maintains a significant light manufacturing sector, which employs just over 8 percent of the local workforce—by far the largest share of manufacturing jobs in any Brooklyn neighborhood (New York City Department of City Planning n.d.). But as in the rest of New York City, manufacturing jobs are far outnumbered by jobs in health, education, social services, and community services. Seventeen percent of Williamsburg residents and 21 percent of Bushwick residents work in these kinds of jobs (New York City Department of City Planning n.d.).

Most of the jobs that CBOs in Williamsburg and Bushwick have created are in this sector. Social scientists would characterize many of them as "bad" jobs due to their part-time hours, low wages, lack of a career ladder, and vulnerability to termination if the government contracts that cover employees' salaries lapse or are discontinued. At the same time, however, CBO jobs have a number of characteristics that fit neighborhood residents' skill levels, preferences regarding work environment, needs for job flexibility to meet various domestic responsibilities, and desires to work on behalf of the community. For residents with limited education and few job skills, CBO jobs can often provide a much-needed, if far from ideal, source of income. They also maintain residents' commitment to regular work, a challenge that many scholars and policy makers identify as a source of continued and even intergenerational poverty (Murray 1984; Newman 1999; Stier and Tienda 2001; Wilson 1999).[35] It should be noted that full-year, full-time work in some of these jobs can still leave a family below the official poverty line. In fighting within larger economic and political fields for the resources to create these jobs, CBOs have made a Hobson's choice: to help local residents scratch out a living at the low end of the labor market. In a climate of high unemployment and inferior workforce preparation by the public schools, however, it is unclear what other avenues CBOs might pursue.

For Williamsburg and Bushwick residents who do work—inside and outside the neighborhood, at CBOs, private firms, or government agencies—child care CBOs are a critical piece of the equation that keeps them working. While many families make informal child care arrangements with relatives

35. For a critique of these and related ideas, see Wacquant (2002).

or friends, such providers may prove unreliable, causing parents to miss work and jeopardizing their continued employment. Moreover, a child care setting that does not attend to the totality of a child's development—and this is especially true for young children—will compromise the child's ability to learn. This subsequently affects how far he or she will go in school, and thus perhaps the type of job and level of income he or she will be able to attain in the future. Since our society agrees that paid work is the primary—even sole—path to generating income, threats to worker reliability and the acquisition of education and job skills put families at risk. Child care CBOs help low-income families avoid these difficulties by providing a reliable supplemental child care provider, continuity of developmental care for children, and a system that facilitates government payments for child care services with minimal disruption. Demand for government-subsidized child care, however, still far outstrips supply, and there is little that CBOs like Nuestros Niños, the New Life Child Development Center, and the Beacon programs can do to change that.

In Williamsburg and Bushwick, jobs and child care are like affordable housing: low-income families must rely on the luck of the draw, pouncing on a job, child care slot, or affordable apartment if one becomes available, or else waiting for government to dedicate additional funds to subsidize these much-needed services. CBOs play two critical mediating roles in this nail-biting waiting game. On one side, CBOs help individual residents get jobs, child care, and apartments by virtue of their insider knowledge about when these critical commodities will be available and how to expedite individuals' access to them. On the other side, they exert themselves within the larger systems that set the terms of supply: CBOs advocate for additional funding, proffer new ideas to increase production, and in other ways seek to restructure field-level arrangements so as to advantage the needy residents of their neighborhoods. This understanding of the role of CBOs in improving the quality of life and life chances of the poor has little to do with scholars' and policy makers' conventional wisdom about neighborhood organizations: that their value lies in their offering residents a place to connect to their neighbors, which theoretically leads to collective self-improvement. I examine the role of resident participation in CBOs in the following chapter.

CHAPTER FIVE

Organizations and Participation

The last three chapters have told a number of stories abut how the community-based organizations of Williamsburg and Bushwick engage with larger fields of action—housing, public resource distribution, paid work—in the ongoing pursuit of opportunities for local residents to become and remain integrated with key economic, political, and social systems. All of these stories turn on CBOs' bureaucratic relationships to sites of field-level negotiation and decision making, most of which lie *outside* the poor neighborhoods that CBOs, and their constituents, call home. The agreements CBOs obtain through these interactions create conditions that make possible the improved integration of poor neighborhoods and their residents into the structures of contemporary economic, political, and social life, thereby enhancing social order in the city and beyond.

Most discussions of locally based organizations in urban neighborhoods have emphasized how these groups tie local residents to one another by cultivating shared norms, a "sense of community," or a unified local identity.[1] This view relies on a central tenet of the Chicago ecological tradition: that discrete geographic subdivisions of the city integrate and order their residents via the "social organization" (Thomas and Znaniecki 1918) of a coherent "moral order" (Park 1915) within a particular physical space. The contribution of neighborhood organizations to this process is thought to be holding and transmitting norms and community identity, and bringing together neighborhood residents previously unknown to one another.

1. On shared norms, see Guest and Oropesa (1984), Kasarda and Janowitz (1974), Sampson and Groves (1989), Simcha-Fagan and Schwartz (1986), and Wilson (1987); on the "sense of community," Ahlbrandt (1984), Briggs, Mueller, and Sullivan (1997). Chavis and Wandersman (1990), Saegert, Thompson, and Warren (2001), and Silverman (2001, 2002); and on unified local identity, Carr (2003), Hunter (1974, 1985), and Suttles (1968).

Through these two processes, neighborhood organizations disseminate the "moral order" to organizational participants, and thence more broadly to area residents. Neighborhood organizations also have been understood as part of a more general process of trust formation within urban neighborhoods; organizational participation and informal interpersonal interaction together are said to create a climate wherein residents can actively enforce local norms without fear of retribution (Sampson, Morenoff, and Earls 1999; Sampson, Raudenbush, and Earls 1997).

These interrelated ideas about the creation, transmission, and enaction of norms within urban neighborhoods ultimately take the individual as their focus; the collective process is important primarily because it affects how individuals behave. This theory posits that to the extent that individuals are integrated into local norms, they will contribute to sustaining social order in the neighborhood. Outside the context of urban-focused research, community and voluntary organizations also are considered important for the effects they have on individuals. Participation in various kinds of organizations is said to increase individuals' sense of personal efficacy, to provide them with social support and companionship, to teach them skills, and to reinforce core ideas about the importance and feasibility of democratic governance (e.g., Putnam 1993a, 2000; Skocpol and Fiorina 1999).

This emphasis on organizations as sites within which individual behavior is shaped—albeit through collective process—runs counter to the approach I have been advancing throughout these pages. I do not deny that the CBOs in Williamsburg and Bushwick have individual participants, or that these individuals accrue some of the benefits that the aforementioned theories of participation claim. For many of these CBOs, however, resident participation more importantly serves as a means to an organizational end: mustering the bureaucratic clout necessary to shift the arrangements of the economic and political fields in which these organizations operate. The individually held products of interpersonal interactions within the community, then, are not these CBOs' main concern; rather, they are interested in how resident participation creates a resource that the organization can then deploy within relevant fields of action (cf. Edwards and McCarthy 2004). Although this perspective on participation may seem old-fashioned, it is consistent with my general position on the question of social integration and social order in the city: that integration into the non-locally organized systems of contemporary economic, political, and social life is just as important to poor people's life chances as how well they relate to their neighbors.

This chapter explores the different dimensions of participation found in the CBOs of Williamsburg and Bushwick, focusing on the interplay between organizational goals and the forms of individual participation that different CBOs cultivate, encourage, and downplay (e.g., Clemens and Minkoff 2004; Lichterman 1996; Polletta 2002). Some Williamsburg and Bushwick CBOs do in fact emphasize participatory forms that aim for individual transformation, and are less concerned with enhancing the organization's capacity to exert pressure within wider economic and political fields. Other CBOs encourage forms of participation that stabilize the organizations' existence—a necessary first step if a CBO is to bargain within fields to improve the set of opportunities available to local residents. For example, many CBOs use participation to help individuals develop life skills, or cultivate forms of participation that contribute to internal conflict resolution. Both these pursuits facilitate legitimacy for the organizations among local residents and external funders, which contributes to organizational survival. And finally, some CBOs explicitly seek to channel resident participation into strategies for making demands on powerful external actors. The specific forms of participation that various Williamsburg and Bushwick CBOs activate complement these organizations' distinct theories of how participation can strengthen their position within the economic and political fields in which they operate.

Organizational Participation and Individual Transformation: The *Fraternidades* of Transfiguration Catholic Church

Claims that "faith-based organizations," such as churches, mosques, or synagogues, can be uniquely effective social service providers are rooted in the idea that religious faith can transform an individual's self-concept, worldview, choices, and actions. At Transfiguration Catholic Church in the Southside of Williamsburg, a particular form of participation in the organization emphasizes the transformative power of faith, beginning with the character of a parishioner's personal relationship to God and Jesus, followed by striving to transpose that fundamental relationship into the individual's interactions with others. Of all the forms of organizational participation I observed in this study, Transfiguration's approach most closely embodies the idea that neighborhood organizations model and transmit specific norms and identity to local residents. Indeed, this form of participation enacted the kind of small-scale concern with family, church, and neighborhood predicted by theories of "social organization" (Thomas and Znaniecki 1918) and local community "moral order" (Park 1915). Active members of Transfiguration found deep meaning and human connection through the church's participatory structure. At the same time, however, the specific goals and dynamics of participation at the church sustained a certain contradiction with the hard-nosed, bureaucratic machinations often required to address the larger economic and political processes buffeting Southside residents.

Williamsburg's Southside contains three Catholic parishes, legacies of the area's nineteenth and early twentieth century waves of German, Irish, and Italian immigrants. Transfiguration currently boasts the largest congregation of the three: some fifteen hundred regular mass attendees drawn from a parish of ten thousand. Its current membership reflects the newer Latino migrations to New York, as well as the city's growing Puerto Rican out-migration: at the time of my research, the parish was approximately 20 percent Puerto Rican, 60 percent Dominican, and 20 percent Central American.[2] Given the whirlwind of church reorganization over the last thirty years, with urban parishes closing and the population of priests and seminarians shrinking drastically, the parishioners of Transfiguration have experienced an unusually stable environment. At the beginning of my research, Transfiguration's head priest had been with the parish for forty-one years. Monsignor Bryan Karvelis—Father Bryan to his parishioners—was beloved and respected not only by the members of Transfiguration but by nearly all of the Southside's Latino and African American population for his enormous dedication to the neighborhood and its people. He died on October 18, 2005, after nearly fifty years of service in the Southside.[3]

A veteran of the Catholic Worker movement, Father Bryan counted it a "tremendous blessing that Transfiguration is a very poor parish."[4] This particular understanding of the high level of poverty in the Southside, where approximately 40 percent of residents live below the federal poverty line, informed all of Father Bryan's personal religious practice, and, by extension, the manner in which he led his congregation. In his five decades at Transfiguration, Father Bryan took his vow of poverty extremely seriously, embracing it in ways that at times raised suspicion in the eyes of his diocesan superiors. For several years in his younger days, he lived outside the Transfiguration rectory, in a run-down apartment building nearby, so as to

2. Author's field notes on interview with Monsignor Bryan Karvelis, Transfiguration Catholic Church, July 9, 1997.

3 The Satmar Hasidim of the Southside suffered the loss of its own longtime religious leader six months later. Rabbi Moses Teitelbaum died on April 24, 2006, after twenty-seven years as the Satmar grand rebbe.

4. Author's field notes on interview with Monsignor Bryan Karvelis, July 9, 1997.

Figure 9. Transfiguration Catholic Church, 263 Marcy Avenue in Williamsburg. Photo by Heather Wollin.

better understand the trials of daily living that his parishioners faced. Since the early 1980s, he had shared the church's rectory with thirty-some young, single, mostly undocumented Central American men. He cooked his own meals—nearly unheard of for a Catholic priest who heads a parish—or accepted the home-cooked gifts of his parishioners. The Southside Mission, the church's affiliated nonprofit service agency, founded by Father Bryan in 1976, dedicates itself to assisting the very poorest and most disenfranchised of the residents of the Southside.

Father Bryan practiced a particular form of Catholic devotion, which he first learned during his seminarian studies. The practice is based on the teachings of Charles de Foucauld, an early-twentieth-century French Trappist monk who advocated the formation of small religious communities— "mini churches"—meant to recall the devotional organization and practice of the early Christians: "When two or three are gathered in my name, there am I in the midst of them" (Matthew 18:20). De Foucauld called these groups *fraternidades* (literally, "brotherhoods"). Among the Catholic seminarians, priests, and nuns who followed de Foucauld's teachings, living in *fraternidad* denoted an intimate communal setting for spiritual practice and material life, organized so as to produce the transformative love preached by Jesus. Small groups of four or five religious (of the same sex) shared living quarters, household duties, prayer, spiritual reflection, and service to the poor. Father Bryan first experienced this way of life during summer breaks from seminary, when he and several other seminarians extended the scope of the seminary's traditional service visits to poor urban neighborhoods to include living together in a local apartment and practicing the tenets of *fraternidad*.

Fraternidad's enrichment of Father Bryan's spiritual life was such that upon his 1956 assignment to Transfiguration as an assistant priest, he sought to continue its practice. After delicate negotiations with the parish's pastor, Father Bryan and two other male religious at the church received permission to take up residence in a run-down building in the Southside. A group of nuns assigned to Transfiguration moved into the same building shortly thereafter, to establish their own life in *fraternidad*. The religious life always had embraced key aspects of separation from the experience of the laity. Priests living outside the rectory were extremely unusual, nuns outside the convent even more so. The *fraternidad* ideal, however, turned this notion on its head. In order to truly share in Jesus' love with the residents of their poor parish, it was incumbent upon the *fraternidad* members to become a part of as much of the residents' lives as possible. Indeed, *only* through this intense communal experience could the *fraternidad* members become truly present to God and to the people of the parish whom they hoped to serve.

In 1964, Father Bryan became pastor of Transfiguration. A cornerstone of his ministry was the expansion of the *fraternidad* way of life to his parishioners. Although de Foucauld originally had envisioned *fraternidades* as a form of devotion only for religious—indeed, there were aspirations of creating a new Catholic order based on his teachings—Father Bryan was eager to offer the love and intimacy of *fraternidad* life to the laity as well. His motivation lay in the experience of migration that his (at that time) mostly Puerto Rican parishioners were grappling with, a form of uprootedness that Father Bryan felt was proving alienating and detrimental to their social, material, and spiritual lives (cf. Thomas and Znaniecki 1918). He turned to the *fraternidades* as a site within which to reconstitute the social ties of familiarity, support, and love that he believed many migrants lost upon their arrival in New York. In this sense, the *fraternidades* explicitly invoke an "Old World" construction of community, wherein individuals gain recognition from their fellows through ongoing, deeply personal relationships.

At the time of my research, some 350 Transfiguration parishioners—nearly a quarter of the number at a typical Sunday mass—were living the life of *fraternidad* in twenty small groups. Given the significant time commitment such participation entails, this figure is remarkably high. In order to become a member of a *fraternidad*, a parishioner first goes through a seven-month period of spiritual exploration to help her or him prepare for the demands of this way of living. The parishioner then selects an appropriate *fraternidad*, in consultation with Father Bryan and the *responsables* (leaders; literally, "responsibles") of the potential *fraternidades*. Each *fraternidad* meets once a week for communal prayer, spiritual reflection, and *la revisión de vida* (the examination of daily life). Meetings usually take place on weekday evenings and last two to three hours. In addition, each *fraternidad* spends two weekends a year at the Transfiguration parish retreat house in upstate New York. These retreats, which feature long periods of silent prayer and meditation, offer a more intense opportunity to experience the intimacy and love of *fraternidad* life. *Fraternidad* members also frequently volunteer at the Southside Mission's homeless shelter, serving meals and sharing conversation with its residents, or at Casa Betsaida, Transfiguration's hospice for people with AIDS. In all of these activities, the *fraternidades* emphasize the primary importance of an individual's personal relationship to God and to Jesus; this foundation allows members to be authentically present to the people around them, and thus to move ever closer to God. Participation in *fraternidad* life turns on individual transformation, the benefits of which then redound to the wider world.

Looking In on the Life of Fraternidad

During the early days of my fieldwork in the Southside, I heard bits and pieces of information about the *fraternidades* of Transfiguration, piquing my interest in these groups. One day, as I worked alongside Amantina Duran at the Nuestros Niños child care center, she mentioned something about going to a meeting of her *fraternidad* that evening. I told her I was very interested in the *fraternidades*, and asked if it might be possible for me to attend the meetings of her group so I could learn more about it. She replied that while she would happily welcome me, she needed to speak with the other members of the group first. She promised to let me know shortly what they decided. The following week, during my usual Monday volunteer session at Nuestros Niños, she invited me to come to my first *fraternidad* meeting, to be held on Thursday evening. We would meet at her home, then go together to the *fraternidad*.

On Thursday, I was running late. Amantina had asked me to come over at 6:30, but I had gotten caught up at a meeting at Southside Latino CBO and did not arrive until nearly 7:30. My lateness turned out not to be too problematic; my field notes recorded that while Amantina seemed "in a bit of a rush, [she] doesn't scold me as I apologize for being late."[5] As it turned out, I had arrived late not for the *fraternidad* meeting but for an event I had not even realized I had been invited to: dinner with Amantina's family. Ushering me up the stairs to their second-floor apartment, Amantina told me in Spanish—the language we always communicated in—that although the family had finished their meal, she had put aside some food for me. This extension of hospitality on the eve of my first contact with the *fraternidad* touched me, as I had not been expecting it at all. It proved to be only the first of several moments that evening in which my standard presentation of self in the field—as an intensely interested observer, ready to participate in whatever tasks might be asked of me, but guarded in revealing information about myself—would be jarred. The *fraternidad* setting, with its central premise of being present to one another through genuine interaction, would demand something more of me than I was accustomed to giving in the field.

At the top of the stairs, we entered the first floor of Amantina's spacious duplex apartment. Just recently, her family had been one of the lucky winners of a lottery for space in this new subsidized housing development on the western end of Division Avenue. The development's primary target group had been the Southside's Hasidic Jews, which meant that the units were unusually large—to accommodate the Hasidic families, which average ten children apiece. Amantina and her husband Natalio have five children, as well as one grandchild who lives with them. The new place thus provided

5. Author's field notes, July 10, 1997.

welcome relief from the small tenement apartments that had been their home for most of their time in the Southside. As we walked into the light, airy, eat-in kitchen, Amantina's husband stood at one of the two sinks, washing dishes. Amantina looked surprised when we said that we had never met; Natalio also works at Nuestros Niños, where I had been doing fieldwork for over a month. We finally figured out that Natalio and I had schedules that did not overlap: he works from 7:00 a.m. until about noon, while I had been coming in at about 12:30 p.m. Amantina then motioned me to the table, where a plate sat, covered by another plate to keep the food warm. As I pulled up a chair to eat, she and Natalio excused themselves to finish getting ready for the meeting.

Alone in the dining area, I tucked into *bistec encebollado* (steak with onions, seasoned with garlic and cumin) and green salad. One of Amantina and Natalio's sons, a first-year college student named Esteban, wandered into the kitchen for a brief conversation, then headed back out as his mother reappeared. When I mentioned to Amantina that Esteban and I had been talking about college and education, she anticipated the intimate interaction of the imminent *fraternidad* meeting, sharing with me some of her worries about how her son's schooling was going:

> She says it [Esteban's first year at the University of Connecticut] went pretty well, although it was difficult in some ways. She says there's not a lot of sup-port for students, and if you don't have friends who support your studying, it's hard to concentrate. Out of his three roommates and him, Esteban is the only one who is coming back next year; two failed out, and another is leaving because he didn't like it. Amantina is concerned that her son find a crowd that is study-friendly.[6]

As I was myself a student at the time, perhaps this frank discussion of Amantina's son's experience should be viewed as unremarkable, a simple exchange about matters on which I was presumed interested and knowl-edgeable. Within the context of a family meal and my invitation to share in the life of her *fraternidad*, however, the conversation took on additional significance. I was about to enter the space of Amantina's *fraternidad*, and though I did so on unusual terms—I was neither a Catholic nor a member of Transfiguration, nor had I gone through the customary seven months of spiritual preparation—this positioning appeared to induce a greater inti-macy between us. Indeed, as the evening continued, I learned a number of

6. Author's field notes, July 10, 1997.

personal details about the various *fraternidad* members, and felt compelled to share something about myself with them.[7]

Natalio joined Amantina and me in the kitchen, and we prepared to leave for the meeting. Natalio headed out first, to get the family's minivan, while Amantina collected her Bible and said good-bye to her two children, who were watching television in the living room. When Natalio pulled up to the curb a few minutes later, Amantina and I were still waiting for Heroina Ortega, the *fraternidad* leader, to join us. Heroina lives just two blocks away, in the Clemente Plaza public housing development. After about ten minutes of Natalio's slightly nervous waiting, Heroina finally materialized. A short, plump Dominican woman in her late fifties, with wispy light-brown hair, big glasses, and a beatific smile, Heroina apologized for her lateness as she climbed into the minivan with us. Amantina introduced me to her, reminding her that I was studying the Southside and its organizations and wanted to learn more about their *fraternidad*. Heroina welcomed me warmly, saying that the *fraternidad* members looked forward to having me at their meetings.

Amantina then inquired after Heroina's husband, who, she had told me as we waited for Natalio, had recently undergone brain surgery. Heroina responded with an optimistic and detailed report on her husband's condition. My field notes on this exchange comment that I felt rather awkward sitting in the midst of what seemed to be a very personal conversation between three old and dear friends. Apparently this did not bother Heroina or the others, however, as they talked freely, and I found that Amantina had given me enough background on the situation to allow me to follow the discussion. Again, the easy intimacy of the relationships of *fraternidad* appeared to include me in its embrace.

After driving east for a few minutes on Division Avenue, Natalio pulled to a stop in front of a somewhat forlorn, four-story tenement building, painted a rusty red. This section of the Southside, with a large industrial-looking building on the south side of the block unbalanced by the few

---

7. Why I revealed things about myself to the *fraternidad* members is a complex question, open to competing explanations. One interpretation is that the setting itself impelled me to approximate the tenets of *fraternidad* life, engaging in my own *revisión de vida* through open sharing with the *hermanos* and *hermanas* present. A second interpretation foregrounds my interests as a researcher conducting fieldwork; my utterances, then, would be understood simply as methods for establishing and maintaining a productive relationship with a set of informants in the field. I am inclined to favor the latter interpretation, though to the extent that I did not invent things about myself, either to mislead members of the *fraternidad* or to probe their thoughts on certain topics, there exists a certain ambiguity.

small-scale residential buildings opposite, reminded me of the mixed-use character of the neighborhood. We mounted the steps to the outer door, which had been propped open with a piece of wood, presumably in expectation of the *fraternidad* members' arrivals. This gesture suggested both that the intercom buzzer did not work and that the area is safe enough to allow unmonitored access to the building for at least a few hours. The lock on the inner door was broken. As we climbed to the third floor, I noted that while the building appeared to be in decent condition—no chipped paint on the walls, no missing or broken stairs, floors in good repair—it was still very much a tenement, the staircase and hallways narrow and dark. On the third-floor landing, our hostess, Cándida, a Puerto Rican woman in her fifties, greeted us and directed us to the rear apartment. I followed Heroina, Amantina, and Natalio inside as they exchanged cheerful greetings and kisses with Cándida. Cándida and I smiled at each other, but I was not introduced. My arriving in the company of the *responsable de la fraternidad* appeared momentarily adequate to justify my presence.

The door to Cándida's apartment opens into the kitchen, a room large enough to hold a table and four chairs at its center. The apartment has a railroad floor plan: the kitchen gives onto the living room, beyond which are lined up two additional rooms. Furniture crowds the living room: a matched sofa, loveseat, and overstuffed chair, all protected by plastic covers, as well as an old, wood-cabinet television set (hooked up for cable), a wooden coffee table, and a large fan. Dominating the wall above the television, a huge color portrait looks down on us: a bride and groom, probably Cándida's daughter or son, in an elaborate wood frame. Other family pictures, including school and graduation photos, cover the rest of the wall. Similar photographs are displayed on the coffee table and on the other walls. On visits to the homes of other *fraternidad* members for weekly meetings, I noticed a similar focus on family photos as a primary form of decoration, and was reminded that in my own home growing up the walls were hung with art; family pictures were confined to two flip-photo holders atop the piano in the living room, holding three-by-five-inch snapshots, and a few larger framed photos hung in the room my parents used as a study.

As we entered the living room, the six people already there rose to greet us. Since Amantina did not introduce me to anyone, I decided to do so myself. Each member of the *fraternidad* shook my hand and responded with his or her name; one woman, Milagros, kissed me on the cheek. There were two married couples in their forties, as well as two older women, alone; one appeared to be in her early sixties, the other closer to seventy. As we all settled down for the meeting, Cándida perched on the edge of the coffee table, which she had repositioned at the edge of the living room. Amantina insisted I take the overstuffed chair, which I did somewhat reluctantly, as it appeared to be the seat of honor in the room. Amantina then introduced me to the group, saying that I was conducting a study of the Southside, that I had asked her if I could come to see how the *fraternidades* operate, and that she was very happy to have me at their meeting. Everyone in the room smiled and nodded at me, then responded to Amantina's request to repeat their names and tell how long they had been members of the *fraternidad*. With these introductions completed, a brief pause ensued, marking the formal commencement of the meeting.

All of the *fraternidad* meetings I attended proceeded with the same format. First, an opening prayer circle. The hostess of that evening's meeting begins the circle by producing a small crucifix and reciting a brief prayer asking Jesus to forgive her sins. Several specific sins are named as part of the prayer, often "egoism" and an insufficient attention to silent prayer during the past week; other sins mentioned included lack of patience with family members or lax child-rearing practices. The prayer ends with the phrase *"le pido perdón a Jesús y a todos mis hermanos"* ("I ask Jesus and all my brothers and sisters to forgive me"). The other members of the *fraternidad* respond in unison: *"perdónala, Jesús"* ("forgive her, Jesus"). The hostess then passes the crucifix to the next person in the circle, who repeats the prayer and is forgiven by the other members. This process continues until each member of the *fraternidad* has prayed in this way. When my turn in the circle came, I simply passed the crucifix to the person on my other side; this never was remarked upon by any of the *fraternidad* members. Following the prayer circle, the group stands to recite the Our Father and the Hail Mary prayers, always in strong, emotional tones.

Sitting down again, the *revisión de vida* (examination of daily life) begins. One of the group members reads the first of two Bible passages designated by Father Bryan as material for that week's spiritual reflection, both in the *fraternidades* and at mass. Using the passage as a lens through which to view their own lives, group members discuss issues and challenges they currently face, and extend advice and succor to each other. When discussion spurred by this passage ebbs, the second passage is read and the process repeated. At the conclusion of the *revisión de vida*, the group stands again for the Our Father and the Hail Mary. The prayers are followed by the singing of one or two of the many folk hymns used at Transfiguration services. Heroina's voice always rang out loudest, but all the members joined in with heartfelt delivery. Hugs and handshakes then are exchanged all around, along with the wish *"que la paz esté con Ud."* ("may peace be upon you"). The hostess then serves her guests a modest snack, such as crackers with white cheese and guava paste, or home-style Dominican sweets produced by small local businesses, along with generic soda poured from large plastic bottles into thin plastic cups filled with ice. *Fraternidad* members munch on these offerings while chatting and joking. At about 10:30, two and a half hours after the beginning of the meeting, the members begin departing. They wish one another well until they see each other next. For most of the *hermanos*, this will not be long, as they are sure to run into each other at Sunday mass, if not sooner: during some volunteer work at the parish, on the street, or in a friendly visit at home.

I Am Present: Interaction, Spirituality, and Support in the Fraternidades

The central component of the *fraternidad* meetings is the *revisión de vida*. Here, the *hermanos* enact Father Bryan's vision of life in *fraternidad*: intimate sharing with an extended family of brothers and sisters in Jesus. During meetings I attended, the *hermanos* always spoke very openly about their difficulties both large and small, unburdening themselves while also receiving counsel and emotional support. The intimate setting of the *fraternidad* meetings required me to participate in a different way than I usually did at the other CBOs where I conducted fieldwork. In most other settings, I rarely had to present a totally independent self. I could either take on the role of the person I was with—as when I accompanied tenant organizers at Los Sures or Ridgewood-Bushwick on their rounds—or, when settings were more public, retreat into more of an observer role. In the context of the *fraternidad*, however, the entire point is for each participant in the group to become present to the other group members in a way that transcends the fleetingness of so many contemporary social interactions (cf. Wirth 1938).

I was introduced to this expectation at my very first *fraternidad* meeting. Through much of the meeting, I sat quietly, listening to the prayers and discussion without saying anything. Things seemed much as they had in the many other meetings I had observed at different CBOs and public venues in Williamsburg and Bushwick. The first Bible passage discussed in the *revisión de vida* was an excerpt from Saint Paul's letter to the Corinthians, in which he describes how Jesus had asked his apostles to spread his Gospel among the people, telling them that if people did not welcome their words they should simply "shake the dust from their feet" and keep going. Two of the *hermanos* gave quite literal interpretations of the passage, prompting

Heroina to step in and draw a broader lesson from it, as I recorded in my field notes:

> Heroina says that she thinks the passage has to do with patience in a general sense. Patience is very important to living, since you must be patient with all your loved ones, as well as with the general public, as you move through life. She says: "Patience is a dress that you have to put on in the morning, early every morning, and keep on wearing all day long." Patience is important with children, especially, but also with your husband or wife. If you are patient, and approach things with good humor, you can accomplish a lot, and help others to accomplish things as well.[8]

A long discussion ensued about the idea of patience, with several of the *hermanos* giving examples from their own lives, especially about their need to exercise greater patience with members of their families. The second Bible passage was then read, giving rise to only a few comments. At that point, Amantina turned to me to ask if I would like to share anything with the *hermanos*. I recorded my response, and the group's reaction, in my field notes:

> Amantina's request catches me by surprise, but I realize that I need to say something, as doing otherwise would appear rude and one-sided. I say that I've been listening carefully to what the group has been talking about, especially the issue of having patience. I say that I find it very hard to have patience with my husband sometimes, because he makes a mess in the house all the time and doesn't clean up.[9] I say that I've tried to not let it bother me, but then there's a big mess, and it needs to be cleaned up at a certain point. I wonder how you can have patience in such a situation. Everyone looks very interested in my story. Heroina says that this is always a problem in households, and it is important, first of all, to approach the situation with good humor. Yelling or making the person feel bad is not productive. Rather, I should try to slowly engage him in cleaning tasks, in partnership with me, or as a fun activity or joke. One way that she has found very helpful in dealing with this issue is to make a schedule of household tasks. That way, everyone in the household knows what's expected of them, and it's easier to do it. Tasks should be rotated so that everyone has to do everything. Also, this means that when, for example, it's my turn to clean the bathroom, which I

8. Author's field notes, July 10, 1997.

9. I was referring to my long-term boyfriend, with whom I lived but to whom I was not legally married. I used the Spanish term *esposo* in accordance with common usage among Puerto Ricans and Dominicans to describe a live-in partner even in the absence of legal marriage.

may hate to do and want to avoid, I can understand what it's like when he is faced with a task he hates and wants to avoid. A couple of the women agree that getting men to share in household tasks is very difficult. Amantina says that the schedule is a good approach. Heroina asks if my husband can cook. I say he knows how but doesn't do it very often. Amantina says that I should have him cook for me once in a while, even if it's just making something like tuna fish, because that's an important task. Heroina agrees, saying that *"una de las cosas más ricas para la mujer es que le cocine el esposo"* ("one of a wife's greatest pleasures is when her husband cooks for her"). Enrique says that he can't cook, sometimes can't even make coffee without burning it. Heroina says *"los hombres que no saben cocinar tienen que aprender"* ("men who don't know how to cook need to learn"), that her husband has learned how to cook, and it's very important to her that she doesn't always have to do it. Juan says that he cooks: he makes rice, and different meat dishes, and is working on his beans. Milagros [his wife] agrees, says his cooking is really quite good, and she appreciates it. The conversation on this then winds down, and Heroina thanks me for sharing with the group. I feel a little weird [about discussing my personal life with strangers], but mostly OK, since my question was a real one, and the advice I got was not bad.[10]

The reaction of the *hermanos* to my comments illustrates clearly the kind of interaction that the *fraternidades* offer to their members. Not only did the *hermanos* validate my mundane concern as real and important, they also claimed it as a shared experience, to which we could all relate. Heroina specifically reinforced the core *fraternidad* notion of shared experience as transformative when she suggested that by doing a particular household task that I hated, I would come to understand my partner's perspective better. She and the other *hermanos* then offered specific advice on how to improve the situation, including examples from how they dealt with the issue in their own lives. Although I felt somewhat uncomfortable during this exchange, which forced me to expose a small piece of my private life to the *hermanos*, my field notes also recorded a sense that by the end of the discussion, my discomfort was already beginning to work itself out. The genuine concern of the *hermanos* apparently helped to balance out some of the vulnerability I had felt.

The personal difficulty that I revealed at that first *fraternidad* meeting pales in comparison to many of the issues that the *hermanos* discussed with each other in this intimate setting. A few weeks later, one of the *hermanas* recounted a particularly harrowing experience she was going through. One

10. Author's field notes, July 10, 1997.

of her male relatives had recently returned home to the Dominican Republic and soon after disappeared from his house. His body was later recovered, showing evidence of torture, including some missing fingers. The man's wife and the rest of the family of course have been devastated by the event, and the *hermana* herself was having a very hard time with it. As she recounted this story, the *hermana* began to cry, and several of the other *hermanos* comforted her by stroking her arm and murmuring condolences.[11]

Here, the *fraternidad* offered a place of respite for the *hermana* to discuss a family tragedy. In revealing its intimate details, she moved seamlessly between her family of origin in the Dominican Republic and her *hermanos de la fraternidad* in New York. Indeed, this form of social support represents a key goal of the *fraternidades*: to create communities that explicitly recall the roles, responsibilities, and love of families. For the celibate religious, like Father Bryan, *fraternidades* stand in for the intimacies of family life. For lay people, the primary site in which to live the principles of *fraternidad* is the family itself. At the same time, however, the *fraternidades* offer another setting in which to pursue these ideals of interaction, spirituality, and support. There is a constant vigilance in pursuit of this form of interactive life, of seeking to move closer to God by being authentically present to people in everday life. As the following excerpt from my field notes shows, the *hermanos* are not shy about examining their shortcomings in this effort, and draw on each other's strength in an attempt to do better:

> Maria raises the issue of providing support to each other in New York. She points out that while nearly everyone in the *fraternidad* visited Heroina during the time of her husband's operation, none of them have been to see another woman—I don't catch her name, but it seems she is not a member of the *fraternidad*—who is also having problems. Amantina says that just because people don't visit doesn't mean they're not thinking of her, praying for her. Others agree, but the consensus is that at least some of them should go and visit anyway. The key issue is supporting others in their time of need, to let them know they have someone they can turn to for help and solace.[12]

The argument that regular, face-to-face participation in organizations can cultivate social support and transform individuals and their orientation to the world seems born out by my experience with the *fraternidad*. In addition to their weekly meetings, I also participated in a number of festive

11. Author's field notes, July 31, 1997.
12. Author's field notes, September 18, 1997.

and solemn events organized by the *fraternidad* members, including Sunday mass, a weekend retreat, the walking of the Stations of the Cross, and a celebration of the Last Supper. Each of these events served as another opportunity for *fraternidad* members to pursue a spiritual and moral life founded on being present to God and to people, and to reinforce the bonds that aid members in their efforts to achieve this.

Among the eight CBOs I studied—including Saint Barbara's Catholic Church—I found no other setting comparable to the *fraternidades* of Transfiguration. This unique form of participation has required not only the long-term, charismatic leadership of Father Bryan, but also the deep and extended pursuit of individual transformation by the *fraternidad* members themselves. The accumulation of these parishioners' work has conveyed the highest moral standing upon the church itself, as nearly everyone I met during my research had their own story about the honorable spirit and good deeds to be found at Transfiguration. At the same time, however, there seem to be limits to the effects this form of participation can exert. Because the focus of *fraternidad* life lies explicitly on the intimacy of interpersonal exchange, it is no surprise that such participation can profoundly affect individuals' sense of themselves and of their relationships and commitments to others. How this form of intimate connection might be transposed to relationships with organizational agents acting in pursuit of instrumental goals in economic and political fields is less clear.

Participation as a Path to Skill Development

The intensity of face-to-face interaction found in the *fraternidades* of Transfiguration was greater than that I observed in the participatory activities at other Williamsburg and Bushwick CBOs. But while these other groups rarely pursued the kind of individually transformative experience that the *fraternidades* provide, they did in many cases offer local residents a chance to learn skills that proved useful in their lives. For example, as discussed in chapter 4, residents who volunteer their time with CBOs often gain skills that make them more employable; sometimes volunteer work at a CBO leads to a paid job in the organization itself (cf. Naples 1998; Pearl and Riessman 1965; N. E. Rose 1995; Susser 1982). Participants in CBOs also can collect information and skills that will help them better navigate some of the bureaucracies that govern housing, education, the courts, government benefits, personal finance, and other aspects of their daily lives.

When individuals learn skills from CBOs, the organizations themselves also gain. Residents who have benefited from their CBO involvement create

204 / Chapter Five

legitimacy for the CBO within the neighborhood, demonstrating how the organization can improve individuals' situations. A positive local reputation in turn strengthens the CBO's position as the legitimate representative of local residents in the wider fields within which it operates. This field-level legitimacy proves critical for organizational survival, helping it to raise private funds, win government contracts, and be taken seriously as a voice in political matters. Survival, of course, is the first requirement for a CBO if it is to continue its work of integrating local residents into the complex economic, political, and social systems that organize contemporary life.

The Labyrinth of Owning a Home

Owning a home in New York City is no simple task. Managing a mortgage, paying the taxes, keeping up with changes in utility regulations, conforming to waste disposal requirements, shoveling snow from the sidewalk in time to avoid fines, finding the best deal on heating oil, and myriad other tasks confront city home owners. For shareholders in the low-income housing cooperatives that dot the streets of Williamsburg and Bushwick, add on the challenges of making collective decisions about everything, keeping maintenance ("rent") payments up to date, supervising the sale of apartments (shares) that become vacant, and many other tasks. The complexities of managing these cooperatively owned buildings can be daunting, especially for low-income, first-time property owners with low levels of education and sometimes a limited command of English. Both Los Sures and Ridgewood-Bushwick work with tenants in the cooperatives to teach them the management skills they need to run their buildings.

At Los Sures, the duties of the tenant organizing staff include regular attendance at bimonthly co-op association meetings, where organizers offer assistance with collecting rents, paying bills for maintenance and repairs, and staying up to date with tax liabilities and other regulatory requirements. The level of formality at these meetings varies. At some, three tenants watch the elderly president of their four-unit tenement co-op write checks for heating oil and water bills over coffee at her kitchen table, while in some larger co-ops, there is a more bureaucratized ritual of biweekly rent collection. Barbara Schliff, lead organizer at Los Sures, took me one day to a meeting of shareholders in the co-op at 104 Division Avenue. Entering the six-story, walk-up building, its plaster façade painted robin's egg blue, we passed through a wide lobby, then out the back fire exit and down some stairs. We reentered the building through a rear basement door, then wended our way through the large, rough concrete basement, making several turns, stepping over a large pipe, and finally emerging into a cool, damp, low-ceilinged room furnished with a large desk facing a group of mismatched chairs set in an improvised semicircle.

Evelyn Gonzalez, a Puerto Rican woman in her midforties with glasses and long, black hair pulled into a loose ponytail, sat at the desk, writing. Seven other people occupied the chairs, including Don Freddy, an elderly Puerto Rican man who sat upright, leaning on his cane, a straw fedora on his head, and a fidgety Puerto Rican boy of about twelve, running his Rollerblades back and forth along the floor as he sat. Barbara murmured to me that Evelyn was the president of the cooperative's tenants' association, then strode up to the front of the room to take the chair next to her. Greetings to Barbara rang out from the assembled tenants, and I slid into a seat at the back. Seeing this, Barbara shook her head, motioning me forward to a nearby chair. Somewhat self-consciously, I obeyed. Seated close to the desk, I watched with interest as Evelyn worked her way through a stack of money orders and checks, writing out receipts for each payment.

As Evelyn wrote, Don Freddy kept up a steady stream of cheerful chatter in Spanish, flirting with an older woman, who kept pace with his banter as the rest of the tenants listened and laughed. Enjoying the light mood in the room, I watched as Evelyn finished each receipt, then passed the corresponding money order (or check) to Barbara. Barbara then entered the amount into the building's rent book: a neat, handwritten record listing each apartment, its shareholder's name, the amount of the monthly maintenance payment, each payment made, and the remainder owed. If the tenant was in the room, Evelyn called him or her up to collect the receipt; if not, she put the receipt into a growing pile to her right. Since most of the tenants in the thirty-unit building were not at the meeting, Evelyn soon accumulated a number of receipts and called Don Freddy up to the desk, asking him to help her put them in order. Don Freddy pulled his chair up to the end of the desk, continuing to flirt, and sorted through the reciepts. In the midst of this process, one woman asked Evelyn to skip to her payment, so she could get her receipt and go home; Evelyn declined, reminding the woman that she writes each receipt in the order she received the payment. Sighing, the woman sat down again to wait her turn.

After about half an hour, all the receipts were written and only four of us remained in the room: Evelyn, Barbara, a stout Latino man in his fifties, and me. Barbara asked the man to stay for a few minutes, saying he needed to sign some checks to pay some building expenses. To protect against fraud, all checks from the co-op's account must be signed by two officers. Barbara and Evelyn looked over some bills, then wrote out two checks: to the building's fuel oil supplier and to the city of New York in payment of real estate taxes. The man signed the checks, then left. Looking satisfied, Barbara told Evelyn that the building is doing pretty well, with about six thousand dollars left in the cash reserve. Evelyn smiled, reminding Barbara that they had accumulated that reserve while getting up-to-date on their real estate taxes for the first time in many years. She also remarked on their good luck with the city's toilet rebate program, since that had put a hold on their water bill for about a year. The two women agreed that if not for that rebate program, the building would be in much worse shape financially.[13]

As is evident from this account, participation in running a co-op transmits concrete lessons in real estate management and collective decision making. Although Evelyn, the co-op president, evinced greater knowledge of the specific financial and management issues facing the building, the biweekly, public transactions of rent collection and bill payment offered any co-op resident the opportunity to take part in oversight of these tasks. Some residents simply showed up to drop off a money order and get their receipt—or sent a child to perform this errand. Others, like Don Freddy, contributed to the joint enterprise by assisting with some aspect of the process, while the man who cosigned the checks played a formal oversight role mandated by the co-op's internal management process. The residents' meeting demonstrates not only how certain tasks are managed within the organization, but also how co-op residents are integrated into external systems of property ownership and management, including both government (tax payments) and the private market (bank holding co-op's reserve account, fuel oil supplier).

Ridgewood-Bushwick's Housing Office tends to have a less hands-on relationship with the residents of the buildings whose tenants it has helped to form low-income cooperatives. This approach has worked well for some residents, who have become effective property managers in their own right. Linda Rosario, president of an eight-unit co-op on Stanhope Street in Bushwick, is one such example. I occasionally ran into Linda at Ridgewood-Bushwick events, where she would tell me about her ongoing efforts to upgrade her building. One day, she invited me to see the building for myself. Linda had recently installed a new security system, and as we walked into her apartment, she proudly pointed to the dual video monitors hooked up to cameras running constant surveillance at the front door. Sitting down on her sofa, she demonstrated how the placement of the monitors in her apartment allowed her to simultaneously watch television and keep an

13. Author's field notes, July 24, 1997.

eye on the building's entrance door and foyer. The security system offered co-op residents an extra amenity that many similar buildings in the neighborhood lacked—a service made possible by Linda's constant vigilance over the building's finances and safety.[14] Linda sometimes talked about looking for a job in real estate management, noting that she had learned a lot about this work as a result of her participation in the co-op. Although she had not, to my knowledge, ever worked at such a job, it seems that this would be a reasonable goal given the experience she had accumulated through her participation in Ridgewood-Bushwick's housing programs.

An Education about Education in Bushwick

In chapter 3, I discussed the efforts of Saint Barbara's Catholic Church and Bushwick Parents (a project of the East Brooklyn Congregations organizing federation) to make improvements to the notoriously bad public elementary schools in Bushwick. While these attempts to create systemic change proved sluggish and frustrating for parents, parishioners, and organizers alike, strategies to educate parents about the workings of the New York City school bureaucracy often yielded more success. Sister Kathy Maire, the lead organizer at East Brooklyn Congregations, tried many approaches to recruiting leaders for Bushwick Parents. At the time of my fieldwork, she was particularly targeting women in an adult education program housed at Saint Barbara's, on the theory that many of these women had school-aged children and would be concerned about the conditions in the local schools. Although efforts to recruit some of these women into committed leadership for Bushwick Parents ultimately yielded little fruit (see chapter 3), the women clearly appreciated learning about how the school system worked.

I had been volunteering at the adult education program in order to observe the work of Bushwick Parents. After about two months of tutoring various women in reading and English, Sister Mary Burns, one of the education program's codirectors, asked me to watch a presentation she was going to make to a group of students—also potential recruits for Bushwick Parents—about the public school reading and math scores recently released by the city. Sister Mary wanted me to observe her teaching techniques so I could make Spanish-language presentations to the students whose English was not good enough to understand her. Two weeks later, she ushered me into a classroom to present the scores and engage the women in a discussion of what they might do to find a better education for their children.

14. Author's field notes, February 11, 1998.

More than a little nervous, but confident in some of the techniques Sister Mary had used to communicate the information, I began the presentation.

First, I handed out copies of a table produced by the New York City Board of Education listing the reading and math scores at all nineteen elementary and junior high schools in Bushwick's Community School District 32.[15] The women seemed interested when I told them Sister Mary had asked me to talk with them about the scores in the Bushwick schools, and what the scores mean. I asked them to look at the figures in the table and to read them out loud together. After about six schools, I stopped them and posed a question: what does it mean to say that a school has 40 percent of its students reading at grade level? Nobody replied. Using one of the techniques I learned from Sister Mary, I asked ten of the women to come up and stand in the front of the class. Then I sent six of them back to their seats. I explained that 40 percent means that out of the ten women, only the four still standing knew how to read the way they should. There were nods of understanding all around the room, and when I asked what they thought about a school that has 40 percent of its students reading at grade level a chorus of "that's bad" went up. Turning to the table to find the scores for the schools their own children attended, the women read out a series of low numbers in grim voices.

I next pointed out that some of the schools' scores had increased in comparison to the previous year and asked why that might be. One woman suggested that the teachers were doing a better job, but nobody else offered an explanation. Following Sister Mary's example, I gave a simple lesson in statistics: the percentage of students reading at grade level can be increased if fewer bad students take the test. I explained that Sister Kathy and Sister Mary had heard reports about weak students being asked to stay home on test day and had been investigating the veracity of this claim. I repeated what Sister Mary had told me: that 10 percent of students had been absent from the school system on that year's test day, compared to only 5 percent the year before. Only a few of the women grasped the statistical implications of this change, and when one of them asked me to explain it again, another woman stood up and tried to take her through it. Although I was pleased by this woman's sense of engagement, she was not having much success, so I used another tactic to go over the statistics again. As I had watched

15. In 2003 Mayor Michael Bloomberg abolished New York City's community school district system, and with it the configuration of District 32 that existed during the time of my research. See chapter 3 for further information on this change.

Sister Mary do in her presentation, I wrote down six test scores on the blackboard, then calculated the average. Then I dropped the lowest score and calculated the average again; the light of comprehension went on in the women's eyes as the average increased.

The women expressed genuine shock that principals and teachers might attempt to massage the test scores this way. While I made sure to point out that Sister Kathy and Sister Mary were still investigating these allegations, the idea of score manipulation by school officials got all of the women talking. Several of them stated the obvious: that this practice made the schools look like they were doing better than they were. Another woman pointed out that children who are doing badly in school would suffer the most, as they become increasingly marginalized, pushed out as drains on the school's performance. Finally, one woman said that someone should do presentations like this one in all the schools, so that parents can understand what is happening. As I wrapped up the presentation, the women thanked me enthusiastically for talking with them. They had clearly learned some things about their children's schools that they had not previously known, and they had gained some small insight into how reported statistics may not always be what they seem.[16]

As these brief examples show, CBOs like Los Sures, Ridgewood-Bushwick, and Saint Barbara's can effectively teach new skills to residents of poor neighborhoods, improving their ability to navigate the complex bureaucratic environments that surround them. Without the Bushwick Parents organizing effort at Saint Barbara's, the women in the church's adult education program likely would never have picked up important information about conditions in the local public schools. Similarly, residents of Williamsburg and Bushwick would not have learned many critical details about owning real estate and meeting the city's housing regulations if not for their participation in the low-income cooperatives at Los Sures and Ridgewood-Bushwick. At the same time that individual residents benefit from these kinds of CBO programs, the organizations themselves enhance their reputations as sites of valuable information and resources in their neighborhoods. This reputational boost strengthens the position of CBOs as legitimate contenders within competitive economic and political fields. At both the individual and the field levels, then, the work of CBOs helps advance the integration of low-income, at-risk populations into the governing structures of our society.

16. Author's field notes, March 18, 1998.

Participation and Democratic Practice: Crisis at the Williamsburg Beacon

In his widely read book *Bowling Alone*, political scientist Robert Putnam contends that the face-to-face interactions that occur in small organizational settings cultivate individuals' disposition toward democratic problem solving and governance (Putnam 1993b, 2000). As the book spends little time discussing what participation in such organizations actually looks like,[17] Putnam does not consider the ways in which such interactions can cause difficulties for the selfsame organizations. Democratic participation can turn messy: its very nature is to encourage the expression of multiple opinions, which often contain very real conflicts. How organizations manage these conflicts has important implications for their reputations, as well as for their continuing commitment to incorporating constituents' interests and demands into their work. One particularly illuminating example of such a challenge occurred during my fieldwork at the Williamsburg Beacon, when tensions between the program's director and the executive director of the Beacon's sponsoring CBO, the Saint Nicholas Neighborhood Preservation Corporation (Saint Nick's), erupted into the open. This conflict elicited a contentious form of participation from the local residents who made up the Beacon's Parents' Association, but Saint Nick's confronted, defused, and ultimately repaired the relationship with the disgruntled parents, further cementing its strong reputation among neighborhood residents.

Saint Nick's took over the administration of the Williamsburg Beacon in 1994, hiring Frank Alvarado as the program's director. Frank, a Puerto Rican man in his forties, had grown up in Williamsburg and boasted some twenty-five years of experience working in youth programs in New York City. By the time I arrived at the Beacon, the program was serving upward of two thousand children and adults each year, in programs such as after-school child care, sports leagues and employment internships for teenagers, summer day camp, high school equivalency (GED) classes in Spanish and English, karate classes, and computer instruction and job placement assistance for adults. Both the Beacon and Frank enjoyed a good reputation among the East Williamsburg families that used the organization's services (see map 2).

Several months into my fieldwork, however, signs that all was not well at the Beacon began to emerge. At one of the monthly meetings of the Beacon Parents' Association, Frank closed his usual presentation on Beacon issues

---

17. For one excellent critique, see Boggs (2001).

and upcoming events by announcing that he was planning to leave the Beacon within the next three months. It was simply time to move on, he said, but he intended to work closely with the parents' group to make sure that they played an important role in hiring the new Beacon director. This seemingly innocuous statement turned out to be the opening salvo in an increasingly public disagreement between Frank and Michael Rochford, the executive director of Saint Nick's. Michael also was present at the meeting where Frank announced his impending resignation. As Frank concluded his remarks, Michael moved swiftly to clarify his own position in regards to the hiring process for the new Beacon director. Saint Nick's wanted the Beacon Parents' Association to have a strong voice in the selection process, said Michael. Saint Nick's would select three potential candidates for the director's job, then ask representatives from the parents' association to interview each one and report back to him on their preferences.[18]

Before that meeting, I had never seen Michael at the Beacon, and Frank had rarely mentioned either Michael or Saint Nick's, despite the fact that Michael was Frank's boss and Saint Nick's the Beacon's sponsor. Following Frank's resignation announcement, however, Michael started appearing at the Beacon regularly. At a Beacon Parents' Association meeting held about a month after Frank's announcement, Michael listened to discussion of the various agenda items, including a proposal for a new structure for the parents' association that I, as part of my volunteer assignment, had worked with several parents to develop. At the end of the meeting, I headed back to the Beacon offices in search of some information on a parent who had been nominated for president. Inside the office suite, the door to Frank's office was closed. This was unusual. One of the Beacon staff members saw me looking at the door, and told me Michael was inside. I recorded in my field notes what happened as the door opened and Michael and Frank emerged:

> Michael says, "So I'll see you tomorrow at the meeting, then." Frank, hands on his hips, shakes his head and says, "No, you won't." Michael asks him why not. Frank says he has an interview tomorrow and he won't be able to make it. Michael asks if they can schedule another time. Frank says no. Michael asks why he's being so uncooperative, he won't even give him a time to meet. Frank tells him he's simply not getting involved with that, it's not a Beacon activity. Frank is clearly agitated, and everyone in the room is watching the two of them, a bit nervously. Michael says he'll call Frank later, and leaves.[19]

18. Author's field notes, September 26, 1997.
19. Author's field notes November 20, 1997.

Despite this uncomfortable confrontation between Frank and Michael, things seemed to progress more or less normally at the Beacon over the next several weeks. My regular volunteer time there was spent in my usual array of tasks: preparing documents for the parents' association, calling parents to remind them of upcoming meetings, visiting with the occasional parent who dropped into the office, and chatting with the Beacon staff. On December 9, I received an unusual phone message. It was Martha Rodriguez, one of the more active parents in the parents' association, saying that she needed to speak to me urgently. Unable to call her that night, I reached her the next morning at her home. She told me that the parents at the Beacon were organizing a protest of Saint Nick's in response to Frank's departure, and that one of Frank's staff members had asked her to get me to attend a meeting that evening at the Beacon.[20] I promised to be there.

A little before 6:00 p.m., I walked into the wide, brown-tiled lobby of the school building that housed the Beacon. A large number of teenage boys milled around, nearly filling the space as they waited for the evening recreation programs to begin. Parents threaded through the crowd, their younger children in tow, heading home from the after-school program. Maneuvering farther into the lobby, I looked around for the Beacon staff member, but in vain. After a minute or two, I saw another Beacon staff member, a good friend of the person I was seeking. A moment later, this staff member saw me and pointed at me emphatically, as if waiting for me. As I recorded in my field notes, the staff member motioned me over:

[The staff member] says hello and hands me a flyer about the protest: "SAVE THE BEACON'S MISSION. The Williamsburg Beacons [*sic*] mission is to provide necessary services and resources to our children in the Williamsburg community. What has St. Nicholas done for our children? Parents, children, staff, co-locators, join us as we rally against Saint Nicholas to save the Beacons mission on Friday Dec. 12 at 4:00 p.m. Meeting place: Eastern District Plaza." I ask what the story is, and the staff member says they're going to do this protest on Friday, that they have support from [Councilman] Victor Robles, and "that's it." I ask what that means about Robles, and the staff member says that someone spoke to him, and that Robles said to "embarrass" Michael Rochford. As we're talking, the staff member is handing out flyers to people, telling some of them to keep it quiet. I ask what this meeting is about tonight, but the staff member doesn't know, saying that Michael called it to meet

20. Author's field notes, December 10, 1997.

with all the Beacon staff. The staff member tells me to find another Beacon employee to ask about it, so I go off to do that.[21]

By that time the crowd had cleared out a bit, and I saw the person I had originally been looking for standing near the front door of the building. As I approached, this staff member too pointed at me with enthusiasm. Leading me down the hallway and into Frank's office, the staff member told me that Frank had given Martha my number so she could call me. I asked what the meeting was about, but the staff member was unsure, saying that Michael wanted to meet with Frank and the rest of the Beacon staff. I inquired about the protest, which the staff member said was in response to things the staff had heard about Saint Nick's planning to reduce the size of the youth programs at the Beacon. The staff was organizing the protest so that people in the neighborhood will be aware of the planned changes and be able to mobilize to stop them. This staff member himself had called Councilman Robles, who gave the "go-ahead" for the protest. I told the staff member that since I was conducting research at the Beacon, I didn't feel comfortable taking part in the protest, but I would certainly observe it. The staff member seemed satisfied with that position, and just as I was about to ask another question about the protest, Michael walked into the office.

The account of Michael's arrival in my field notes indicates that I found his entrance jarring, but he handled himself smoothly, greeting all the people in the office. He asked me if I wanted to attend the meeting, and I replied that I did, if it was possible. Saying I was welcome, Michael walked into the assistant director's office to hang his coat in a locker. I felt a bit uncomfortable, and decided to head down to Room 262, where the meeting would be held. Out of the corner of my eye, I saw Michael come out of the office and follow me, but as I wanted to avoid looking too friendly with him in front of the Beacon staff, I did not turn around. Inside Room 262, an ordinary-looking classroom with neat rows of desks and little decoration on the walls, several counselors from the after-school program were sitting with five children whose parents were late picking them up. Michael sat down in one of the desks to wait. Parents slowly trickled in to retrieve their kids, and additional Beacon staff members arrived for the meeting. When all of the children had gone, Michael, fifteen staff members, and I remained.

Michael asked us to pull our chairs into a circle. He removed a small tape recorder from his briefcase, turned it on, set it on the desk in front of him, then asked us to introduce ourselves. After introductions, Michael

21. Author's field notes, December 10, 1997.

told us that he called the meeting because both Councilman Robles and the commissioner of the city's Department of Youth and Community Development (the city agency that funds the Beacon) had informed him of the planned protest of Saint Nick's by the Beacon staff. He said he wanted to talk to the staff about what the problem was, and that he was very sorry that Frank was not there, since he had specifically scheduled the meeting for a time he thought would be good for Frank. Motioning to the tape recorder, he noted that he was recording his own comments because he wanted to go on the record with them, but he said he would turn off the tape recorder if anyone felt it was necessary before they could speak freely. He wound up by asking if anyone could explain to him what their concerns were, what Frank's concerns were, or more generally what was going on.

Michael clearly was in crisis-management mode, as signaled by his use of the tape recorder. In calling this meeting with the staff, he placed himself in a somewhat hostile situation, but he recognized the necessity of facing the issue head-on. Well aware of the damage that could be done to the reputation of Saint Nick's by fast-moving rumors, he took steps to document as much of his interaction with the Beacon as possible, in anticipation of needing to back up his own version of events with concrete evidence. His efforts, however, produced very little at this moment. Much of the meeting consisted of an adversarial dialogue between Michael and the Beacon's assistant director, who had a very close relationship with Frank. Michael and the assistant director went back and forth about whether the protest had been initiated by parents or staff; whether or not Saint Nick's was planning to pull most of the children's programs from the Beacon and replace them with adult programs (the assistant director's claim, which Michael categorically denied); and whether it was appropriate for Frank—or any staff member with a complaint—to avoid discussing his concerns with his boss (in Frank's case, Michael). No staff member besides the assistant director uttered a word.

I recorded in my field notes that after about forty-five minutes, I began to feel that the mood in the room was deteriorating. Michael and the assistant director were locked in a frustrating indirect discussion of a missing third party—Frank—and Michael's tone had degenerated from sympathetic to lecturing. Michael seemed to be getting the same feeling that I had, because he wrapped up the meeting a few minutes later. He suggested that if the Beacon parents wanted to express their concerns about Saint Nick's, it might be a good idea to replace the scheduled protest with a meeting that he would lead personally. Around the room, a few heads nodded nearly imperceptibly, but no firm decision was taken. Michael then asked if anyone had anything they wanted to add, but seeing blank looks all around him he quickly thanked all the staff members for staying late, and adjourned the meeting.[22]

Despite this intervention by Michael, the protest by some of the Beacon parents took place as scheduled. When I arrived at the Beacon that Friday afternoon, a few parents were gathering on the front plaza. Michael was also there, to make one last attempt to dissuade the parents from this form of participatory action, which threatened his CBO's credibility. I was standing just inside the main doors of the building, watching the slowly growing group of parents from a distance, when Michael walked up from the direction of the Beacon offices and greeted me. He told me he wanted to meet with the parents to talk with them about their problems with Saint Nick's, and asked me if I might help facilitate that discussion. Feeling awkward, I reminded him of my researcher status and said I did not feel comfortable serving as an intermediary, which the parents might interpret as my endorsement of him. He nodded, understanding, and asked if I could suggest anyone specific who he might approach. Looking out at the assembled group, I suggested he try Sarah Tilgman, one of the more active members of the parents' association. Michael thanked me for the suggestion, commented that he only wanted the chance to communicate with the parents directly, rather than through Frank, and headed out to the plaza.

As I watched, Michael approached Sarah and the other parents. I could not hear what they said, but I could see that Michael directed most of his remarks to Sarah, who exchanged a few words with him. A few minutes later, Michael headed back inside. As he passed me at the door, I asked how the conversation went. He replied that he had requested a meeting with them, so they could hear Saint Nick's perspective on the Beacon situation, but that the parents told him they did not feel comfortable changing their plans to protest. With some chagrin, he said Frank had totally misrepresented Saint Nick's to the parents and the staff at the Beacon, and that this had created a very difficult situation. He hoped he would have the chance to talk with the parents soon. As Michael left, I headed out to see what the group was planning to do. It was already about 4:15, forty-five minutes past the originally scheduled time for the protest, and there was no apparent movement. I asked what Michael had wanted, and Sarah told me more or less the same story Michael had—adding that the parents did not want to meet with Michael, so they sent him away. Another woman chimed in that

22. Author's field notes, December 10, 1997.

she didn't trust Michael and wanted to get on with the protest. By about 4:30, the parents decided to move toward Saint Nick's.

About twenty parents—three African American women, one Latino man, and the rest Latina women—plus two Beacon staff members and myself walked the three blocks from the Beacon to the Saint Nick's offices. The Beacon staffers pulled their jacket hoods over their heads and looked at the ground so nobody would recognize them, telling me that Michael had decreed that all Beacon staff must be present at work that day. Once at Saint Nick's, confusion reigned. The Beacon staff members finally started a call-and-response chant—"Save the Beacon! / For our children!"—and one of the African American mothers suggested that the group conduct the chant while marching around in a circle. With the circle organized, the three African American women took turns leading chants—one of which was "Hell no! / Frank can't go!"—while the rest of the parents responded in chorus. A few people inside the Saint Nick's offices appeared in the upper-floor windows, and several residents of the neighboring houses stuck their heads out to see what was going on. Other than that, the protest provoked no response. After about half an hour of marching and chanting, the group tired and fell silent. Sarah Tilgman, using a bullhorn, then addressed a few words to the Saint Nick's offices about why the protestors were there, repeatedly asking, "What has Saint Nick's done for our children?" The group then decided to head back to the Beacon, where Michael had been, to address some of the protest to him. Following a few minutes of chanting outside the Beacon offices, a security guard emerged to tell the parents that Michael had returned to Saint Nick's. Soon after, the parents dispersed.[23]

The protest actually created less tension than the regularly scheduled Beacon Parents' Association meeting that took place about a week later. Michael continued his efforts to defuse the parents' dissatisfaction with Saint Nick's by attending the meeting with about ten members of the Saint Nick's staff and the Beacon Advisory Board. He spoke at length to the parents about Saint Nick's vision for the Beacon. After describing the history of Saint Nick's involvement with the Beacon, including the hiring of Frank as program director, Michael recounted the story he had told the staff the previous week: that Councilman Robles and the Department of Youth and Community Development (DYCD) had alerted him to a protest of Saint Nick's being planned by the Beacon staff. After noting that it was Frank's responsibility to communicate with him, the head of Saint Nick's, if there were problems at the Beacon, Michael summed up his remarks on

23. Author's field notes, December 12, 1997.

a low note: the incident had prompted DYCD to start an investigation of Saint Nick's and its Beacon program. He then invited questions from the parents, promising to stay until he answered all of them.

Michael's invitation brought forth many specific questions from parents about the Beacon programs. Most questions concerned the widely circulated rumor that Saint Nick's planned to cut back children's programs, including offering space to fewer children in the after-school program, and to replace children's activities with adult programs. Michael repeatedly denied that this was true, but he also acknowledged that program size is always limited by budget constraints and intimated that Frank had expanded some of the children's programs beyond what the budget could sustain. I recorded in my field notes that at one point in the meeting, Michael and Frank began fighting over the specifics of the Beacon budget:

> Frank keeps insisting that Beacon money is being spent improperly, such as on a job developer's salary even though she doesn't work at the Beacon full-time. Michael keeps insisting that this isn't true. As the two men go back and forth on this, people in the audience are starting to look uncomfortable. Finally, an older African American woman—a member of either the Beacon Advisory Board or the Saint Nick's board of directors—tells Michael and Frank: "you're losing this meeting." She says that the issues they're talking about now are not things that should be aired in public, and they need to stop talking about them and get together in private to resolve them. Michael says she's right, and that he's ashamed to be talking about it in this forum. Frank also agrees she's right. The woman suggests that the meeting wrap up now and says that Frank and Michael seem to have a directive from the group to build better communication and try to resolve the issues that are causing problems. There seems to be general agreement from the group on this.[24]

Although the parents' association meeting veered into dangerous territory, this airing of dirty laundry illustrated Saint Nick's particular skill both at creating the conditions for active participation by parents in the organization—even if that participation was directed against the CBO itself—and at resolving conflict through this same participatory process. Michael insisted on hashing out his disagreement with Frank in front of the Beacon parents. This allowed the parents to see, hear, and make their own judgments about both men's versions of recent events. To me, it also conveyed the impression that Michael did not intend to hide the dealings between

24. Author's field notes, December 18, 1997.

himself and Frank, and instead sought to invest the parents in the issues being disputed. All of these actions are consistent with Saint Nick's core commitment to ensuring that members of the community have access to information, encouraging them to formulate and express their own opinions, and involving them in a collective decision-making process. These are the basic components of a community organizing approach to working with people, and Michael turned to them in this moment of crisis, hopeful that a participatory process would prove fruitful.

As both a good organizer and a savvy administrator, however, Michael knew well how to balance organizing components with executive authority. By early January, it was clear to me that Michael's efforts to address his problems with Frank were operating on two parallel tracks. On the one hand, he worked hard to reach out to the disgruntled parents using organizing strategies. On the other, he restructured the Saint Nick's administrative apparatus, which eventually created an opening for removing Frank. As discussed in chapter 4, in the midst of the problems with Frank, Michael hired Eddie Calderón-Melendez to head up Saint Nick's newly created Youth and Family Program, under whose auspices the Beacon now fell. On the day of the January Beacon Parents' Association meeting, things seemed calm at the Beacon. Both Frank and Michael attended the meeting to introduce Eddie to the parents. Several days later, however, Frank was abruptly ousted from his position as Beacon director. While maintaining his title as director of the Youth and Family Programs, Eddie took over as interim Beacon director and moved swiftly to reorganize the program.

Part of his agenda was to rechannel the active participation by the parents from the Frank-Michael dispute into an effort that would help stabilize the Beacon and its reputation. He began by requiring all parents of children in Beacon programs to attend at least one meeting of the parents' association if they wanted their children to remain in the program. He also hired a number of new staff, trained them for a slew of new duties, and implemented a new, academically rigorous curriculum for the Beacon's main offering, the after-school program. Within a couple of months, Michael and Eddie brought the Beacon's crisis to a successful resolution. The programs improved, Eddie brought in an infusion of new private foundation support, parents began to express support for the new director, and the city's investigation produced nothing of consequence. What had begun as a contentious exercise of parents' participatory energies ended in a renewed relationship with an even stronger CBO. This conflict provides an important illustration of how internal power struggles in a participatory organization present a more complex management problem than in a traditional hierarchical organization. Michael's skill in acknowledging and valuing the concerns of Saint Nick's constituents, then weaving them into good crisis management and administrative decisions, eventually both enhanced the effectiveness of the CBO and won the continuing support of the neighborhood. Much as the teaching of skills lends CBOs additional legitimacy with local residents, CBOs' ability to weather crisis strengthens their position as they pursue better bargains in the economic and political fields that structure residents' opportunities and life chances.

Participation as an Organizational Resource

The previous three sections of this chapter have explored a number of ways that participation in neighborhood organizations produces benefits for individuals, including spiritual transformation, social support, skill and information acquisition, and the opportunity to engage in democratic problem solving. This section moves the discussion back to the level of fields, by considering how organizations foster and deploy resident participation in order to pursue field-level goals. The CBOs in Williamsburg and Bushwick actively cultivate different forms of resident participation, driven by different theories of how participation contributes to the attainment of organizational goals. The New Life Child Development Center and the Bushwick Beacon, for example, see little role for resident participation in strengthening their organizations and thus focus mostly on providing basic services. In contrast, the other six CBOs I studied all see important roles for resident participation in their efforts to reshape the fields where they operate. The ways in which they draw on this participation, however, are quite distinct.

As recounted in detail in chapter 3, Ridgewood-Bushwick operates with a clear view of how local residents can best contribute to its fundamental organizational goal: securing government contracts to provide services and jobs to Bushwick residents. Ridgewood-Bushwick assiduously cultivates two specific forms of resident participation that contribute directly to the contract procurement effort: displaying its constituency at key moments to government decision makers, and turning out enough voters to win district elections. All of Ridgewood-Bushwick's programmatic work with local residents, including organizing tenant associations, spearheading efforts to rid blocks of the drug trade, offering adult education classes, and developing affordable housing, represent intermediate steps toward this ultimate political goal (Marwell 2004b). Effective constituent display and the winning of elections require the involvement of large numbers of local residents. This means Ridgewood-Bushwick has no alternative to cultivating resident participation. But these forms of participation do not translate into democratic governance of the organization, as the work of Robert Putnam, for instance, implies (Putnam 1993a, 1993b). Instead, a small group at the top—Assemblyman Vito Lopez, executive director Chris Fisher, and housing office director Angela Battaglia—makes most of the substantive decisions about organizational operations.

In a different way, the Williamsburg Beacon also maintains tight control over resident participation in its activities. Eddie Calderón-Melendez, director of the Youth and Family Program at Saint Nick's, whose bailiwick includes the Beacon, arrived in the midst of a messy participatory episode that challenged the organization's legitimacy both in the neighborhood and with its primary funder, the city's Department of Youth and Community Development. After getting the situation under control, Eddie worked swiftly to set the boundaries for future parent participation in the Beacon. Early in his tenure at Saint Nick's, he described to me his philosophy of resident involvement in the organization, which I recorded in my field notes:

> Eddie says it's key that the parents who are in the program leadership understand the importance of their role. Especially when it comes to funders, who always want to see parent involvement in a program like this. He says he takes a lot of time to develop the right people as leaders, to teach them how to talk to funders, put on a strong face for the organization. Some parents are good at this kind of thing, and some aren't, and it's important to spend your time working with those who have the potential.[25]

Eddie proved to be a consummate professional. He brought top-quality standards to the Beacon's programs and its staffing. In the process, he also professionalized resident participation, turning parents into part of his increasingly successful effort to bring additional funding and resources into the organization and to establish it as a model program consistent with his national standing as a leader in youth development practice. Although his fund-raising efforts primarily targeted the private sector—philanthropic foundations and corporate giving programs—Eddie's general strategy had much in common with Ridgewood-Bushwick's. Both organizations created themselves with reference to their primary funders' criteria of success: the Beacon oriented itself toward foundations' ideas of "best practices" in program delivery, while Ridgewood-Bushwick opted for engagement with the political system that controls the government contracts on which it

---

25. Author's field notes on interview with Eddie Calderón-Melendez, January 29, 1998.

relies.[26] In the organizations' pursuit of these two divergent visions, resi-dent participation played important but distinctive roles.

A much different orientation to participatory action prevailed at Los Sures and its close partner, the Fair Housing Committee. Drawing on their long histories of successful confrontations with powerful government and private actors—especially their original legal victory in the racial discrimina-tion case against the New York City Housing Authority—Los Sures contin-ued to view large-scale public protest as the form of resident participation most important to achieving its organizational goals. Indeed, the symbiotic relationship between the formal Los Sures organization and the ad hoc Fair Housing Committee relied on a conjoint strategy frequently found among social movement actors: the agitations of a more radical group allow a more mainstream organization to make greater gains than it might have in the absence of the radical compatriot (Haines 1984, Jenkins and Eckert 1986). At the community forum organized by Fair Housing to demand greater attention from Mayor Giuliani to the housing needs of the Latinos and African Americans of Southside Williamsburg, the disruptive potential of Fair Housing was clearly signaled by the city's strong response. As re-counted in chapter 2, the enormous police force deployed by the city to monitor the community forum both surprised and delighted the Fair Hous-ing members, because it indicated quite clearly that the mayor was paying attention.

Los Sures' belief in the power of a mobilized, vocal constituency to sway public opinion and hence the city's decision makers has much in common with the political strategy of Saint Barbara's Catholic Church, as discussed in chapter 4. Like Los Sures, Saint Barbara's and its partners in the East Brooklyn Congregations rely on establishing direct and public relationships between an organized group of citizens and the individuals whose power in government bureaucracies or private firms can transform goals into reality. Although the Saint Barbara's approach relies on actions that are far more narrowly targeted than the diffuse protest activity favored by Los Sures, both groups honor the importance of participation as an enactment of democratic ideals of collective decision making. Furthermore, both Saint Barbara's and Los Sures aim to create changes that benefit a wide public—rather than the more narrowly defined set of organizational adherents to which Ridgewood-Bushwick orients its work.

The modes of resident participation cultivated by these Williamsburg and Bushwick CBOs often look very different on the ground, but in fact they

26. Cf. DiMaggio and Powell's (1983) notion of "mimetic isomorphism."

are all directed toward a single bottom line: enhancing the influence of each organization over the field-level decision making that produces systemic stratification and inequality within the city. For all these CBOs, power and resources flow from a clearly defined set of organizational actors and relationships that make up a field. Deploying distinctive theories of how resident participation can be used to press the necessary levers of power, each CBO attempts to coax fields into yielding their rewards. This field-level understanding of participation differs strongly from theories that focus on the changes in individuals that organizational participation can produce, as illustrated by the approach to participation found at Transfiguration Catholic Church.

At Transfiguration, the form of interpersonal interaction championed by Father Bryan, and practiced at its highest level in the *fraternidades*, undergirds the church's general orientation toward taking action in the world. Members of Transfiguration often take part in community meetings and activities organized by other Southside Latino CBOs, including some of the demonstrations planned by the Fair Housing Committee. The way in which many Transfiguration parishioners participate in these seemingly nonreligious activities, however, is fundamentally informed by their spiritual understanding of their place in the world. To become involved in efforts to assist directly those less fortunate, or to join with neighbors in a search for community improvement, is to be present to people and thus to move closer to God. Such interactions should always be respectful and encouraging of the formation of genuine relationships, for it is those interpersonal relationships that yield God's presence.

Thus, when Fair Housing staged the community forum in which it attacked Mayor Giuliani, many of the Transfiguration parishioners in attendance walked out of the meeting. Immediately afterward, John Mulhern, the ex-priest from Transfiguration who has remained a stalwart member of the church, got into a heated disagreement about the forum with Barbara Schliff, the lead organizer at Los Sures and a core member of Fair Housing. John argued that the skit about the mayor simply ridiculed him, accomplishing nothing more than inviting his ire; Barbara countered that the skit was a truthful portrayal of the mayor's neglect of the needs of the Southside's Latinos.[27] In the weeks following the forum, many Transfiguration parishioners expressed to Father Bryan their discomfort with the Giuliani skit, echoing Mulhern's dismay. Their negative response was so strong that Father Bryan called a meeting with Fair Housing and other Los Sures CBOs

27. Author's field notes, June 4, 1997.

to discuss it. For Barbara and for Debbie Medina, longtime organizers at Los Sures and activists with Fair Housing, the reaction from the parishioners at Transfiguration was a surprise, as the following two excerpts from my field notes show:

> Barbara tells me that Father Bryan told Fair Housing that since the meeting at Transfiguration, many people in the community have told him that they perceive Fair Housing as abrasive, rabble-rousing, overly radical, etc. He also said that the Southside is becoming divided and that something needs to be done to unite the different people working there. He says he wants to serve as mediator to bring the different factions together so that by the time the [mayoral] election comes around, the Southside can speak with one voice, even if there is factionalism behind closed doors. Barbara says she thinks this is a good idea, and that Fair Housing accepted his invitation, even though she doesn't think what Fair Housing did was so radical.[28]

> I asked Debbie what Father Bryan wanted with Fair Housing. She said he wanted to serve as a mediator between the different groups in the Southside, so that they could present a united voice to the public, even if behind closed doors they were fighting. She said he said that Fair Housing was perceived in the community as very abrasive, difficult to work with. She asked me, somewhat forlornly, bewilderedly, if I felt that the work they were doing was so far out, so abrasive, so hard to deal with.[29]

Barbara and Debbie both understood organizational participation (their own and others') as fundamentally oriented toward external actors who control the resources and power that Los Sures and Fair Housing need to ensure that the Southside's low-income Latino and African American residents have access to affordable housing. These organizations' theory of field-level decision making called for voicing noisy public demands, in hopes that city officials would, however reluctantly, pay more attention to the neighborhood, appropriate additional funds for affordable housing, and better enforce the consent decree Los Sures had won addressing discrimination in Southside public housing. For the parishioners at Transfiguration, however, change in the world happens through a different causal sequence. Amantina Duran, a coleader of the *fraternidad* whose meetings I attended, told me a few days after the community forum that she thought

28. Author's field notes, June 25, 1997.
29. Author's field notes, June 27, 1997.

that if the members of Fair Housing would just sit down with the mayor and his staff and calmly explain the housing needs of Williamsburg's Latinos, she was sure that the mayor would understand and help.[30] Amantina's proposed solution should not be understood as simple naivete, however. Rather, she sought to transpose the same form of genuine, caring interaction that undergirds *fraternidad* life onto the fight over affordable housing, thereby creating a foundation for positive change. To be sure, Father Bryan's call to Fair Housing and the other Southside Latino CBOs to put on a public face of unity recognized the harsh realities of the political world, but his effort also was acutely attuned to his parishioners' sense of relational disruption following the forum. Drawing on the "moral resources" (Edwards and McCarthy 2004) he himself had accumulated over more than forty years in the Southside, Father Bryan looked for a middle ground where all the local Latino CBOs could stand together.

Organizational Participation and Social Integration

The community-based organizations of Williamsburg and Bushwick are home to numerous forms of individual participatory behavior. In some cases, individual participation in these CBOs binds people together in close relationships of sharing and support. Participation has also taught neighborhood residents specific practical skills, such as how to manage a residential building, how to understand school performance statistics, or how to organize a community meeting. Some forms of participation reinforce the kinds of interpersonal interaction that foster a commitment to collective decision making, or are in fact organized around a particular issue that demands a collective resolution. All of these participatory outcomes take place within the boundaries of specific organizations, however, which raises important questions about the possibilities of translating these lessons of participation into other settings.

Urban sociologists usually argue that resident participation in local organizations contributes to the development of shared norms and identity among neighborhood residents—a "moral order," in Robert E. Park's terms (Park 1915, 1936). This hypothesis relies on one of two possible mechanisms: either individuals must transport the benefits of participation into the wider setting of the neighborhood, or larger numbers of local residents must participate in neighborhood organizations. In the former scenario, individuals must figure out how to duplicate the relationships, skills trans-

---

30. Author's field notes, June 23, 1997.

fer, or forms of interaction they have learned *inside* the organization to encounters with neighbors whom they meet *outside* organizational boundaries. If organizations serve as a kind of screening device, attracting people more inclined to these kinds of behavior in the first place and serving as a barrier to those who are not so inclined, then this replication process will prove daunting. If, on the other hand, the important task is to attract more individuals into organizational participation, the question of scale becomes important: at what point does an organization reach saturation in its capacity to build close relationships, teach practical skills, or foster particular forms of interaction?

If we consider the role of local organizations in urban neighborhoods as reaching *beyond* neighborhood boundaries, however, we face a different set of questions, which are linked to the issue of participation in a different way. The Williamsburg and Bushwick CBOs that draw on resident participation as a resource for their attempts to strike bargains within fields do so in an effort to facilitate local residents' integration into those fields. For example, Los Sures and the Fair Housing Committee organize resident demonstrations as part of their efforts to secure more affordable housing in their neighborhood. By directing these protests at players within the housing production field (but outside of Williamsburg), the CBOs attempt to negotiate a resolution that results in more of their low-income constituents having a decent place to live in an increasingly expensive city. Similarly, when Saint Barbara's parishioners gather for weekly vigils at the site of a dangerous street corner, they are attempting to influence players in the field of public resource distribution, where decisions about where to set up new traffic lights are made. To the extent that CBOs are successful in these efforts, they shift the economic, political, and social conditions that local residents face in their everyday lives, thereby contributing to their integration within these systems.

CHAPTER SIX

Conclusion

The classic question of urban sociology asks how we maintain social integration and social order in the rapidly changing human environment that is the modern city. From the Chicago School up to the present day, urban sociologists have examined these issues through the lens of the "community question," inquiring about how the interpersonal bonds presumed to underlie integration and order can be sustained in the context of huge populations, high density of residence, and the increasing fleetingness of social contacts. Although the community question once animated the entire discipline of sociology (Durkheim 1893; Park 1915, 1936; Park and Burgess 1921, 1925; Thomas and Znaniecki 1918; Toennies 1887), it has fallen into disuse in most subfields (Brint 2001). Urban sociologists, however, continue to turn to it as a major piece of their explanatory framework: they have lost, saved, limited, networked, and technologically reconceived community,[1] The idea has served as a particular touchstone for urban sociologists in the last two decades, as many turned to community in hopes of explaining cities' rising concentration of poverty and disturbing level of associated social problems.[2]

But as the early sociologists themselves knew full well, "community" is not the only way to conceptualize the necessary processes of social integration and social order. Indeed, much turn-of-the-twentieth-century soci-

1. See Fischer (1982), Gans (1964, 1967), Hunter (1974), Kasarda and Janowitz (1974), Sampson (1999), Toennies (1887), Wellman (1979), Wellman et al. (1997), and Wirth (1938).
2. See Briggs, Mueller, and Sullivan (1997), Brooks-Gunn, Duncan, and Aber (1997), Bursik (1988), Bursik and Grasmick (1993), Jencks and Mayer (1990), Morenoff and Sampson (1997), Morenoff, Sampson, and Raudenbush (2001), Sampson (1988), Sampson and Groves (1989), Sampson, Raudenbush, and Earls (1997), Small (2004), Wilson (1987), and Winship and Berrien (1999).

ological inquiry revolved around understanding the transition from informal, communally based forms of integration and order to formal, bureau-
cratically based forms—Ferdinand Toennies' famous distinction between
gemeinschaft (community) and *gesellschaft* (society) being the paradigmatic
(though much critiqued) statement (Toennies 1887). Why, then, have contemporary sociologists concerned with urban poverty been so focused on
"community" as the solution to problems of social integration and social
order in the city?

As discussed in chapter 1, the Chicago School's analytic framework of
"human ecology" set urban sociologists on this path nearly a century ago,
taking as the primary object of analysis the differentiation, in terms of social
and economic characteristics, between "natural areas" of the city. According
to this perspective, each "natural area" could be understood as a "community"
with its own "moral order" (Park 1915, 1936). The source of socioeconomic
differences between areas, then, was thought to be the variable capacity of
each community to exercise moral authority over its inhabitants (N. Anderson 1923; Drake and Cayton 1945; Hunter 1974; Shaw and McKay 1942;
Shevky and Williams 1949; Suttles 1968; Zorbaugh 1929). This simple idea
has wedded urban sociologists working in the ecological tradition to two
interrelated, foundational theoretical assumptions: first, that "community"
is the basis for achieving social integration and social order in the contemporary city, and second, that "community" is demarcated geographically.

Throughout this book I have argued strongly against the first of these
two assumptions and raised questions about the relevance of the second.
My primary goal has been to offer an alternative for theoretically ground-
ing empirical investigation of the problem of social integration and social
order in the city and beyond. I challenge the notion that, in contemporary
society, integration and order are produced principally within geographically bounded subareas of the city—the Chicago School's "natural areas," or
the "neighborhoods" of today's neighborhood effects researchers. Hence,
I do not assume that the interpersonal interactions that occur within spa-
tially defined communities should be the focus of antipoverty analysis or
policy making. Instead, I argue that integration and order derive substantially from the distribution of resources and opportunities within particular
fields of economic and political action—such as housing production, government spending, and employment—and thus that the competitive and
cooperative processes underlying this distribution should be a principal
focus of urban sociologists interested in poverty and inequality.

Individuals are socially integrated in modern society to the extent that
they have a real chance to take part in the bedrock components of the so-

ciety's way of life. In much of the contemporary world, this means, among other things, having a home, having a job, and having opportunities for safety, fulfillment, and advancement, rather than unending insecurity with no prospects for change (see, e.g., Bourgois 1996; Sullivan 1989; Young 2005). The greater the proportion of individuals who are socially integrated in this sense, the more stable the social order; under such conditions, social change—even explicit challenges to prevailing arrangements—will be incremental rather than revolutionary. The key question to ask, then, is: What elements of social structure impact the material opportunities on which social integration and social order are built? To the extent that recent urban poverty research addresses this question, its answer has been driven by the theoretical framework of network analysis. This approach argues that social structure resides in interpersonal relations and that social ties can produce resources for individuals and neighborhoods.[3] My discussion of community-based organizations instead takes up the relationship between social structure and resources at a different level: the economic and political fields that configure the distribution of resources over space and time.

Individuals may be well prepared or poorly prepared to take advantage of poverty-alleviating opportunities that present themselves in daily life, such as jobs, affordable housing, child care, health care, education, and so on. But if no such opportunities are available, even the most enthusiastic, hardworking, and competent individual will have little chance of escaping poverty.[4] Imagine, for example, a full-time, low-wage worker living in a place where a tight and expensive housing market demands that she spend over half her monthly income on rent. If the organizations whose practices create this particular outcome in the field of housing production instead found a way to produce lower-cost housing—as Los Sures and Ridgewood-Bushwick, in partnership with government agencies, private financers, and private builders do in Williamsburg and Bushwick—this worker would be less likely to find herself forced to choose between paying the rent, buying food for her children, keeping the electricity on, and filling the car's gas tank so she can get to work. With the household budget stretched beyond its limit because of the high costs of housing, this worker engages a daily struggle for survival. She has little chance of saving money to create some

3. See, e.g., Carr (2003), Coleman (1988), Granovetter (1973), Jencks and Mayer (1990), McLanahan and Sandefur (1994), Morenoff, Sampson, and Raudenbush (2001), Putnam (1993a, 2000), Sampson (1988), Sampson, Morenoff, and Earls (1999), Sampson, Raudenbush, and Earls (1997), Small (2004), and S. S. Smith (2005).
4. For a deeply informative discussion of what a life with almost no opportunities really looks like, see Young (2005). See also Stier and Tienda (2001).

cushion of financial security, to say nothing of developing assets through home or business ownership. Her children will venture out into the world without anything resembling a family safety net—a prospect all the more daunting when the public schools they attend have dismal track records and cuts in public youth programs mean they have no adult-supervised activities between the time that school gets out and their mother gets home from work.

The economic and political fields whose machinations distribute the wide range of opportunities that affect individuals' socioeconomic achievements in these ways thus represent a critical and nearly unexamined piece of the poverty puzzle (but see Beyerlein and Hipp 2005). An empirical discussion of fields requires a focus on formal organizations—the primary sites where the concatenation of distributive decisions that constitute field-level operations and outcomes are produced. I argue for an approach that apprehends both the workings of the individual organizations that compose fields and the content of transactions between organizations within a field. My particular empirical focus in this book has been on one set of organizations—community-based organizations working to improve the conditions faced by residents of poor places—but the perspective I am advocating could be engaged through empirical investigation of other types of organizations as well: government agencies, private firms, other nonprofit organizations, public-private partnerships, and so on.[5]

Urban scholars and policy makers have recently evinced a growing interest in the role of formal organizations in poor neighborhoods. The theoretical underpinnings of this interest, however, emanate directly from the ecological tradition: most contemporary discussions of neighborhood organizations (sometimes called "neighborhood institutions") consider their contributions to local social cohesion, community identity, or neighborhood defense.[6] These processes are frequently linked to theoretical discussions of "social capital," an approach that echoes earlier incarnations of the "community question." That is, the social capital framework assumes that the primary route to social integration and social order lies in fostering changes to the quantity, quality, and character of interpersonal social relations. Neighborhood organizations fit into this framework because they are thought to serve as a key location for transformations in how individ-

5. See, e.g., McQuarrie (2007), which examines the complete set of organizations in the field of low-income housing production in Cleveland.

6. See Briggs, Mueller, and Sullivan (1997), Guest and Lee (1983), Guest and Oropesa (1984), Hunter and Staggenborg (1986), Lee et al. (1984), Peterson, Krivo, and Harris (2000), Portney and Berry (1997), Silverman (2001, 2002), and Small (2002, 2004).

uals relate to one another. Given the ecological emphasis on interpersonal social relations within communities as the source of neighborhood conditions, local organizations thus are assumed to be particularly important for residents of poor places plagued by high levels of disorder, crime, and related social problems.

As the geographer James DeFilippis has observed about the social capital argument, however, it is very difficult—probably impossible—to create resources capable of alleviating poverty or fostering economic development out of the social connections of people who have few or no resources in the first place (DeFilippis 2001). This observation gains empirical support from a recent review of the "neighborhood effects" literature, which shows clearly that the effects of various measures of neighborhood-level "social capital" on poverty-related outcomes are mixed and weak (Sampson, Morenoff, and Gannon-Rowley 2002). In contrast, the effects of social ties on crime, public safety, and the supervision of potentially disruptive young people—Robert Sampson and colleagues' construct of "collective efficacy"—are strong and consistent (Morenoff, Sampson, and Raudenbush 2001; Sampson and Morenoff 1997; Sampson, Raudenbush, and Earls 1997). But these latter factors are not explicit indicators of poverty so much as associated social conditions.

While collective efficacy within a neighborhood helps decrease crime and other forms of acute disorder—undoubtedly important outcomes— this is not the same as reducing poverty. Realizing a more comprehensive form of social integration and social order in the city entails more than controlling crime; it demands the incorporation of materially excluded individuals into the forms of economic and political activity that hold the rest of society together. Recent research by Bruce Western and colleagues shows that the most coercive form of crime control—incarceration—has become a common step in the life course of members of the most economically and politically excluded group in U.S. society: young, African American men (Pettit and Western 2004; Western, Kleykamp, and Rosenfeld 2006). Sending increasing numbers of badly educated, unemployed, poor men to prison may indeed reduce crime, but prison is only a temporary means of producing social integration and social order. The emerging policy emphasis on "prisoner reentry" speaks directly to this reality, as government and CBOs have begun developing service programs intended to help ex-felons find not only social support but also education, jobs, health care, and other foundational components of material inclusion.

As I have argued throughout this book, an examination of the economic and political fields within which CBOs carry out their daily activities yields a more complete understanding of how social integration and social order are produced in contemporary society. In comparison to the early twentieth century, when the Chicago sociologists developed their ideas about urban neighborhoods as coherent communities integrating local residents into a moral order, the conditions in today's cities are more than ever the product of organizational and field-level practices. Economic, political, and social processes that in the past were more informally coordinated, and enacted on a smaller scale, are today embedded in far-reaching, complex sets of formal organizations whose fortunes are connected in fields of action shaped by competition, coordination, and domination. This means that neighborhood organizations attempting to reduce poverty cannot—and in fact do not—concern themselves only with the state of social relations inside neighborhood boundaries; rather, they consciously act as points of linkage to the economic and political fields operating in the city and beyond. It is through this connective work that neighborhood organizations contribute to social integration and social order, presenting otherwise excluded individuals with opportunities to join "mainstream" society, materially conceived.

This perspective on the role of contemporary CBOs reminds us of their founding impulse: an explicit concern with the material exclusion of poor people As products and descendants of the War on Poverty's Community Action Program, CBOs pushed forward an agenda entirely unlike that of earlier kinds of urban neighborhood organizations, such as the immigrant-serving voluntary associations analyzed by the Chicago School (Drake and Cayton 1945; Thomas and Znaniecki 1918; Wirth 1928; cf. Breton 1964) or the groups formed to resist neighborhood racial integration beginning in the 1950s (Molotch 1972; Sugrue 1996). The early immigrant-serving groups—burial societies, insurance collectives, cultural-preservation initiatives, and similar enterprises—sought social insurance and collective protection in a time of limited welfare-state services and xenophobic suspicion. Neighborhood defense groups tried to hold back the winds of urban demographic change, often disappearing when the populations they served decamped en masse to the suburbs. In contrast, CBOs birthed by struggles for civil rights and economic equality explicitly attempted to reshape the dominant institutional configurations of urban society (Cloward and Ohlin 1960; Moynihan 1969; Pollinger and Pollinger 1972). As part of the general movement for fundamental social change in that era, CBOs made their first forays into a variety of fields, pushing to reshape and extend those fields' boundaries to make room for members of groups that had been traditionally excluded: the poor, African Americans, Puerto Ricans, Mexican Americans, and women.

Much of CBOs' work to reshape fields and improve social integration has been directed toward the state, whose power and resources are frequently the target of other kinds of social movement action as well. As the momentarily more generous U.S. welfare state of the 1960s and 1970s shifted toward privatization after 1980, however, CBOs began to absorb many of the state's responsibilities. Taking on government contracts to provide all manner of social and human services to the poor residents of their neighborhoods, CBOs moved into a unique position between social movement orientations and state obligations (DeHoog 1984; Kramer 1982; Salamon 1995; S. R. Smith and Lipsky 1993). Some CBOs came to look almost indistinguishable from state agencies, while others largely refused to give up their movement tactics. Most CBOs, however, like those in Williamsburg and Bushwick, came down somewhere in the middle. Each individual organization made its own choices about how to deal with the sometimes conflicting challenges of meeting local residents' needs, conforming to contract demands, negotiating political hurdles, and advocating for ongoing social change.

Located between multiple players in a variety of fields, CBOs have become a particular kind of neighborhood organization: uniquely oriented to the external economic and political world, yet closely tied to specific geographic places and the local residents who are their constituents. The participant-observation method of research used to collect the data reported in this book proved well suited to the task of uncovering the connections of CBOs to economic and political fields operating beyond neighborhood boundaries—a location not usually considered the province of researchers interested in neighborhood-level actors. Future empirical work should continue to examine the situatedness of neighborhood organizations in fields whose operations transcend neighborhood boundaries, while at the same time paying attention to how CBOs can alter the conditions of daily life that residents of poor neighborhoods face.

As neighborhood organizations transmute themselves from communal collectives concerned with purely local conditions to bureaucratic players embedded in multiple fields of resource distribution and concomitant stratification, they form part of the general trend toward the formal organization of contemporary economic, political, and social life. As the opportunities and daily choices of poor individuals increasingly unfold in conditions set and negotiated by formal organizations, however, this study raises some sobering questions. It is in the nature of formal organizations to limit their products and benefits to those individuals who are understood to be organizational members—a concept at odds with the more public-goods

Figure 10. The author (center) with Assemblyman Vito Lopez (right) and Wayne Saitta (left), formerly of Brooklyn Legal Services Corporation A, now a justice on the New York State Supreme Court, Kings County. Photo courtesy of the author.

orientation of both communal life and the social movements that gave rise to CBOs (Powell and Clemens 1998). In chapter 3, I discussed this tension in the field of urban politics, as the Ridgewood-Bushwick Senior Citizens Council used politics to cultivate private benefits for organizational members, while Saint Barbara's Catholic Church fought to maintain a more public-regarding goal for political activity. The different forms of resident participation discussed in chapter 5 also illustrate the potential for CBOs to lean toward more privately oriented action, especially when CBOs that deploy tightly organized participation to attain their goals have more success in garnering scarce resources.

As private organizations, including CBOs, increasingly are charged with delivering social rights to citizens, these organizational processes should be critically examined. To the extent that the dynamics of private membership get under way in CBOs, contributions to the work of the group will increasingly be required for individuals to access the benefits collectively procured. As part of the general trends toward privatization, devolution, and marketization, CBOs thus are participating in what is becoming an ever more explicit rejection of the idea that the state must guarantee certain social rights of citizenship no matter what an individual's contributions. Rising economic insecurity in the United States is constraining the possibilities of universal social rights, as some clamor for the exclusion of those among us who shirk their responsibilities to the collective by behaving in socially unacceptable ways. Predictably, among that latter group, it is those with few economic resources who suffer most under the retraction of universal social rights, as they have little recourse except to the care of the state. In contrast, the wealthy have more options: wealthy individuals will never need to call on the state to bail them out of the consequences of their bad personal habits (such as drug addiction, chronic unemployment, or out-of-wedlock childbearing), and there are government safety nets to ameliorate corporate debacles and reckless management decisions such as the savings-and-loan crisis or the bankruptcy of private pension funds.

As community-based organizations continue working to enhance social integration and social order by creating opportunities for poor people's material inclusion in contemporary society, we should be mindful that in their negotiations within fields, CBOs routinely find themselves the least powerful players. Rather than bemoaning CBOs' (and other nonprofits') alleged abandonment of their social movement roots, scholars should seek to understand the field-level processes that both push CBOs into more formal structuring and disadvantage them in relation to their field-level competitors. Policy decisions that strengthen CBOs' power within fields might improve their ability to offer poor people opportunities for inclusion. At the same time, however, if policy is designed to shore up CBOs' negotiating strength within fields, this development must be accompanied by even greater attention to CBOs' accountability to the people in whose interests they claim to be acting.

Neighborhood organizations in poor places stand as one set of bureaucratic actors in our pervasively organizational society (Perrow 1992). Most urban sociological examinations of neighborhood organizations, however, do not take this perspective. Scholars generally have preferred to examine these groups in ways that are consistent with urban sociology's dominant ecological framework, considering neighborhood organizations' role in creating both individual-level outcomes and neighborhood-level differentiation. While I do not deny that neighborhood organizations may both affect individuals' behaviors and capacities and make contributions to "community," I have tried in this book to understand how neighborhood-based groups contribute to a broader conception of social integration and social order. I believe that an organizational approach to this classic sociological problem has much to offer scholars who approach the contemporary city from other theoretical traditions.

ACKNOWLEDGMENTS

I could never have written this book without the generosity of time and spirit shown me by the community-based organizations and people of Williamsburg and Bushwick. The eight CBOs that allowed me to conduct participant-observation in them were the I.S. 111 Beacon Center (operated in Bushwick by the YMCA of Greater New York), the New Life Child Development Center, the Ridgewood-Bushwick Senior Citizens Council Housing Office, Saint Barbara's Catholic Church (and two of the Saint Barbara's Plaza member organizations, the Maura Clarke–Ita Ford Center and El Puente–Bushwick Center), the Nuestros Niños Child Development Center, the Southside United Housing Development Fund (Los Sures), Transfiguration Catholic Church, and the Williamsburg Beacon Center (operated by the Saint Nicholas Neighborhood Preservation Corporation). Without the dedication of these organizations, whose staffs work extremely hard under difficult conditions, the lives of the residents of Bushwick and Williamsburg surely would be poorer.

Within each of these CBOs I am indebted to a large number of individuals who collectively spent untold hours talking with me, sharing a wealth of information about themselves, their organizations, and their neighborhoods. The kindness with which so many assisted me was remarkable. With apologies in advance to those people whom I inadvertently omit, as well as those whose last names I never learned, I would like to extend my thanks to the following individuals (listed in alphabetical order by organization).

At the I.S. 111 Beacon Center: Cookie Lopez, Elvira Medina, Rory Morlos, Willie Perez, David Rivera, Jose Rivera, Rick Rivera, Daisy, Dennis ("Foots"), Frances, Leslie, and Mr. Waters.

At the New Life Child Development Center: Daisy Alicea, Carmen Camacho, Carol Krueger, Carmen Mendez, Hilda Sanchez, Cecilia, Elba, Lily, and Linda.

At the Ridgewood-Bushwick Senior Citizens Council Housing Office: Ivan Arvelo, Angela Battaglia, Carmen Bonilla, Evelyn Cardona, Maritza Dávila, Mindy Feinberg, Matt Feldman, Donald Manning, Richard Rathbun, Linda Rosario, Richard Velasquez, Sheldon Wheeler, Elizabeth, and Yolanda. Also Chris Fisher, executive director of the Ridgewood-Bushwick parent organization.

At Saint Barbara's Catholic Church: Sister Mary Burns, Sister Mary Dowd, Milagros Hilario, Alberta Williams, and Iris (all of the Maura Clarke–Ita Ford Center at Saint Barbara's Plaza); Asenhat Gomez, Ernesto Malavé, Arnaldo Simo, and Leslie (of the El Puente–Bushwick Center); and Monsignor John Powis.

At the Nuestros Niños Child Development Center: Myriam Cruz, Ana Cruzado, Amantina Duran, Natalio Duran, John Mulhern, Marilyn Pabón, Sonia Raices, Leila Ramos, and Brunilda Bido.

At the Southside United Housing Development Fund (Los Sures): Lydia Bonilla, Cathy Herman, Rosa Lendof, Debbie Medina, David Pagán, Marilyn Rivera, Barbara Schliff, Gladys Torres, and Jerry Urbaez.

At Transfiguration Catholic Church: Amantina Duran, Monsignor Bryan Karvelis (R.I.P.), Heroina Ortega, and all the members of the *fraternidad* led by Heroina.

At the Williamsburg Beacon Center: Frank Alvarado, Eddie Calderón-Melendez, Mary Ann Giordano, Hector Medina, Laurie Rosenfeld, Sarah Tilgman, Delia, and Virginia. At the Saint Nicholas Neighborhood Preservation Corporation, the Williamsburg Beacon's parent organization: Alison Cordero, Michael Rochford, and Zully Rolan.

Because the CBOs where I based my research are part of a broader neighborhood ecology, there were a number of people involved in community work in Williamsburg and Bushwick who were not formally affiliated with any of the study organizations but who also made important contributions to the research. I would like to express my gratitude to them as well. Again, with apologies for unintended omissions, they are Carmen Calderón, Roberto Camacho, Jeanne Hynes, Assemblyman Vito J. Lopez, Foster Maer, Sister Kathy Maire, Anthony Medina, Adela Miranda, Marty Needelman, Diana Reyna (now Councilwoman Reyna), Councilman Victor Robles, Wayne Saitta (now Judge Saitta), Alice Silva, and Pat Williams.

Throughout the years of writing this book, I have been supported by colleagues, friends, and family in innumerable ways. I received generous financial support from the National Community Development Policy Analysis Network, the Nonprofit Sector Research Fund of the Aspen Institute (Grant Number 96-2-NSRF-07), and the United States Department of Housing and Urban Development (Agreement No. H-21140SG). Mitch Duneier provided constant encouragement for the project, which I especially appreciated during my darkest days of writing. Sudhir Venkatesh generously read and commented on nearly every chapter of the book, and always reminded me that the ethnographic road is long. Florencia Torche read not only every word of every chapter, but also, seemingly, every word of everything I have ever written; I am grateful for her friendship and intellectual collaboration. The Hylan F. Lewis Urban Ethnography Workshop at the City University of New York Graduate Center offered much-needed respite and a true commitment to fieldwork in the city; special thanks go to workshop leaders Mitch Duneier, Phil Kasinitz, and Bill Kornblum.

Among my colleagues in the sociology department at Columbia University, I owe thanks to Karen Barkey, Peter Bearman, Priscilla Ferguson, Debra Minkoff, Mignon Moore, Chuck Tilly, and Diane Vaughan. I am especially indebted to Herb Gans, without whose firm yet gentle skepticism I never would have arrived at this book. At Columbia's Center for the Study of Ethnicity and Race, I benefited enormously from many conversations with Nick De Genova about the intellectual project of Latina/o Studies; I also thank Gary Okihiro. Other Columbia colleagues who provided inspiration and support were Heather Haveman, Ira Katznelson, Rudy de la Garza, Ester Fuchs, and Patricia Grieve; thanks also to Erzsébet Fazekas and Paul-Brian McInerney, cofounders of Columbia's Workshop on Nonprofit Organizations in Economy and Society. My work on this book also connected me to a broader community of scholars, many of whom gave generously of their time and insights in ways that improved the book immeasurably. I thank Kelly Moore, Michael McQuarrie, Mario Small, Harvey Molotch, Doug Guthrie, Rob Sampson, and Neil Fligstein. At the University of Chicago Press, I am indebted to Doug Mitchell, Tim McGovern, and Joel Score for their wonderful support throughout the review and publication process.

For keeping me more or less sane during this entire process, I thank Robin Aronson, Lisa Torres, Marlon Portela, Joel Feinleib, Josh Machleder, Cielo Irizarry, and Carlos Vazquez-Firpi; I especially thank Carlos for making possible the most honest conversations about gender and race that I have ever had. My parents, Jerry Marwell and Barbara E. Marwell, and my brother, Evan Marwell, made this book possible in more ways than they will ever know, and I am extraordinarily grateful to them. My most heartfelt thanks go to Luis Burgos, whose love and friendship have sustained me for many years.

Notes on Research Design and Method

Sociologists engaged in participant-observation research increasingly recognize the importance of providing readers with an explicit discussion of the research design and methodology of their studies. While I do not believe that participant-observation will ever be—nor should it strive to be—"scientific," it can—and should—be rigorous and systematic. Information about a study's design and method add to a reader's ability to evaluate the merits of the research on its own terms. It is in that spirit that I offer the following brief remarks.

Design: The Birth and Development of a Research Project

One of the most useful features of the research reported in *Bargaining for Brooklyn* is that the project's design allowed me several comparative dimensions of analysis: across neighborhoods (two neighborhoods); across organizational types (four types); and across organizations (eight organizations). Few studies based on participant-observation data have this potential for comparison, as research sites are often singular: a street corner or block (e.g., E. Anderson 1978; Duneier 2000; Liebow 1964; Susser 1982), a housing project (e.g., Small 2004; Venkatesh 2000), a neighborhood (e.g., Bourgois 1996; Gans 1964; Hannerz 1969; Kornblum 1974), an organization (e.g., Halle 1984; Owen-Smith 2001; Vaughan 1996), and so on (for ethnographies with comparative designs, see, e.g., McRoberts 2003; Newman 1999; Sullivan 1989). While I have discussed some of the interesting differences between neighborhoods, organizational types, and organizations over the course of the preceding chapters, the strength of the comparative design turned out to be the view it afforded me onto a broader sociological process common to all: the structural position of community-based organizations within fields of action, and the opportunities and constraints this position affords and imposes on CBOs as they attempt to strike better resource bargains for the residents of their neighborhoods. The fact that I was able to see this process in operation across multiple organizations, different organizational types, and distinct neighborhoods is a critical evidentiary basis for my conclusions. Since comparative claims are only as good as their basis for comparison, it seems appropriate to discuss how I selected my research sites.

The participant-observation method of research allows for the emergence and exploration of themes beyond those that the researcher originally intended to study. Indeed, participant-observation research is full of such accounts, where the original focus of the project faded into the background as other, more important issues were uncovered. This research was one of those instances. When I designed the initial phase of this project as my doctoral dissertation research, I envisioned a comparative study of poor urban neighborhoods' efforts to promote their own revitalization. At the time, both scholars and policy makers were becoming increasingly interested in the idea of "social capital" as a resource for improving the conditions of poor neighborhoods, and I was particularly interested in the role of resident participation in this process. The design called for one study neighborhood to be "successful" in these efforts, and the other to be "unsuccessful." The object was to determine what contributed to "success" in neighborhood revitalization. Within each neighborhood, I planned to study four organizations, one of each of the following types: a community development corporation, a child care center, a church, and a family support center. On the most basic level, I selected these four organizational types in order to capture a range of neighborhood functions and residents, thereby gaining broad information about usage patterns, key residents, important gathering places, residents' opinions of the neighborhood, and other factors important to understanding revitalization efforts in the local environment. In addition, I had a rationale for choosing each of these specific organizational types, centered around my core interest in resident participation.

I included community development corporations (CDCs) in the study because it is their explicit mission to improve the conditions found in their neighborhoods. CDCs usually focus on the provision and maintenance of affordable housing, but they often pursue other activities as well, including the involvement of local residents in their work (e.g., Saint Nicholas Neighborhood Preservation Corporation 1997; Vidal 1992). I selected child care centers on the assumption that most parents are highly motivated to seek a safe, quality environment for their children, and so would be likely to become involved in these organizations. I chose churches based on a then-growing interest in the importance of religious institutions as centers of neighborhood participation and action, particularly in low-income communities (e.g., Carle and DeCaro 1997; Rooney 1995; Scheie et al. 1994). Within the larger category of churches, I selected Catholic churches, for three reasons. First, as I will discuss shortly, I planned to focus my research on Latino neighborhoods, and most Latinos in the United States, as well as in their countries of origin, are Catholic (Espinosa, Elizondo, and Miranda 2005). Second, the Catholic church has a long history of activism on behalf of the poor, including recent church-based community organizing efforts (Rooney 1995; M. R. Warren 2001). Finally, the Catholic parish's organizational structure ties each church more closely to its geographic setting than is the case in other Christian denominations, and this has significant implications for neighborhood improvement work (McRoberts 2003). Finally, I included school-based family support centers in the study because of recent efforts to make school buildings "one-stop shopping centers" for a range of services to children and families. The logic behind these programs is that school buildings sit empty for much of each day, while youth and families desperately need facilities for activities that can constructively fill nonschool time and assist adults with efforts to upgrade their education and job skills. In addition, school-based service centers are thought to enhance parents' and children's relationships with the educational system. New York City has adopted these principles for its Beacon program, which has grown rapidly over the last ten years (C. Warren, Feist, and Nevarez 2002).

These decisions about the basic structure of the research design then led to the specific question of where—in which two neighborhoods and in which eight organizations—I would actually conduct my participant-observation. One of my dissertation advisers at the University of Chicago, Richard Taub, wisely pointed out that no matter how meticulous my research design, there were no guarantees that I would be able to find real-life research sites that matched the plan I had put down on paper. Of course, he was right. The neighborhoods and organizations where I conducted my research hewed close to my goal of establishing valid comparisons, but the complexity of social life meant making some compromises as well.

Choosing the Study Neighborhoods

Since the year 2000, when Latinos officially became the largest minority in the U.S. population, scholars have produced a rapidly growing number of ethnographic studies about this group.[1] *Bargaining for Brooklyn* is part of a continuing effort to examine the wide range of Latina/o histories, achievements, exclusions, and challenges in the United States. When I began this project, despite the fact that poverty and its related social problems were widespread among U.S. Latinos, most research on these issues focused on African Americans. This was particularly true of urban ethnographies, where a rich tradition of using this method to study African Americans existed alongside a relative dearth of similar studies on Latinos.[2] I had begun to develop an interest in New York City's Latino population at the end of the 1980s, when I worked for several years at a Latino arts organization while I was an undergraduate student. As John and Lyn Lofland remind us, researchers' professional interests often emerge from "where we are" in our personal lives (Lofland and Lofland 1995), and my work experience with Latinos in New York dovetailed with the state of the urban ethnography literature. Thus, I chose to conduct my research in two predominantly Latino neighborhoods.

The next step was to further delimit the characteristics of the study neighborhoods. I decided that they should be low-income—thereby assuring that some kind of neighborhood revitalization efforts would be operating—but not the most devastated areas in the city. Thus, I chose neighborhoods that met the social science standard for "moderate poverty": between 20 percent and 40 percent of residents living below the federal poverty line (Sampson, Morenoff, and Earls 1999; Wilson 1987). Recognizing the effects that immigrant populations have been shown to have in revitalizing distressed areas (Winnick 1990), I sought areas with similar concentrations of immigrants. Finally, I wanted to avoid neighborhoods that were the recipients of unusually high levels of attention to and resources for neighborhood improvement work, such as being the targets of extensive private philanthropy or being designated as federal Empowerment Zones. It seemed unlikely that I would be able to match neighborhoods on more than these four basic characteristics, so they became my baseline for neighborhood selection.

1. See, e.g., Arlene Dávila (2004), De Genova (2005), Dohan (2003), Freidenberg (2000), Hondagneu-Sotelo (2001), Mele (2001), Menjívar (2000), Pérez (2004), Ramos-Zayas (2003), and R. C. Smith (2006).

2. Some classic examples of urban ethnographies focusing on African Americans include Drake and Cayton (1945), Liebow (1964), Hannerz (1969), Rainwater (1970), Stack (1974), E. Anderson (1978), and Duneier (1992). Prior to 2000, only a few ethnographic studies examining (partially or exclusively) the experience of Latinos in U.S. urban settings had been published: Bourgois (1996), Moore (1978), P. C. Sexton (1966), Susser (1982), Suttles (1968), von Hassell (1996).

There are many ways to define a neighborhood (e.g., Hillery 1955; Sampson, Morenoff, and Gannon-Rowley 2002). I decided to use the administrative boundaries of New York City's fifty-nine community districts, which have cultivated a sense of common organization and identity among local residents since they were established in the early 1970s. It is hard to imagine today, but when I started this research in 1997, it was not possible for a researcher to immediately access the vast amounts of data now readily available online. Instead, I learned about the population characteristics of the community districts the old-fashioned way: from the occasional profiles published by the New York City Department of City Planning (New York City Department of City Planning 1992, 1993). A review of these sources, which used data from the 1980 and 1990 U.S. Censuses, revealed thirteen community districts where Latinos outnumbered other racial and ethnic groups.[3] One additional neighborhood had nearly equal percentages of Latino and white residents, so I also considered it as a possible study site.[4]

I eliminated seven of these fourteen neighborhoods because they did not meet the other three basic criteria I had set up for the study (Marwell 2000). With seven neighborhoods remaining, I conducted interviews with fourteen informants knowledgeable about neighborhoods and neighborhood revitalization efforts in New York City including scholars, philanthropic foundation program officers, community activists, and employees of city and nonprofit agencies.[5] The goal of these interviews was to develop

3. Mott Haven (Bronx CD 1, 66.9 percent Latino); Hunts Point (Bronx CD 2, 78.9 percent Latino); Morris Heights/University Heights (Bronx CD 5, 56.8 percent Latino); East Tremont/West Farms (Bronx CD 6, 58.8 percent Latino); Kingsbridge/Bedford Park (Bronx CD 7, 50.6 percent Latino); Soundview/Unionport (Bronx CD 9, 53.5 percent Latino); the Lower East Side (Manhattan CD 3, 32.3 percent Latino); East Harlem (Manhattan CD 11, 51.9 percent Latino); Washington Heights/Inwood (Manhattan CD 12, 67 percent Latino); Jackson Heights/North Corona (Queens CD 3, 43.7 percent Latino); Elmhurst/South Corona (Queens CD 4, 41.8 percent Latino); Bushwick (Brooklyn CD 4, 65 percent Latino); and Sunset Park/Windsor Terrace (Brooklyn CD 7, 51.4 percent Latino).

4. Williamsburg-Greenpoint (Brooklyn CD 1, 43.6 percent Latino).

5. I conducted interviews with Eric Brettschneider (Agenda for Children Tomorrow, New York City Administration for Children's Services), Dena Davis (community development consultant), Mariana Gaston (New York director, Resolving Conflict Creatively Program), Marilyn Gittell (professor of political science, City University of New York Graduate Center), Marc Jahr (New York City director, Local Initiatives Support Corporation), Patricia Jenny (director, Neighborhood Strategies Project, New York Community Trust), Phillip Kasinitz (professor of sociology, Hunter College and the City University of New York Graduate Center), Melvin Oliver (program officer, Asset-Building and Community Development Program, Ford Foundation), Aida Rodriguez (program officer, Equal Opportunity Program, Rockefeller Foundation), Robert Sherman (program officer, Surdna Foundation), Susan Saegert (professor of environmental psychology, Housing Environments Research Group, City University of New York Graduate Center), April Tyler (community activist and former member of New York City In-Rem Task

more in-depth profiles of the seven neighborhoods in order to choose two that showed noticeable differences in the success of their neighborhood revitalization efforts but were similar in terms of other descriptive characteristics.

In the interviews, I briefly described my research project, then asked respondents to name neighborhoods they felt were conducting successful revitalization efforts, as well as areas where work to improve the neighborhood had been unsuccessful.[6] When asked where exciting neighborhood improvement work in Latino areas was taking place, many of my informants immediately named Williamsburg, in Brooklyn. They repeatedly described Williamsburg as an energetic neighborhood with vibrant community-based organizations accomplishing many important tasks. One informant remarked that Williamsburg was widely considered to be the site of the most successful grassroots-oriented neighborhood revitalization work in all of New York City.[7] Another described in detail the housing development history of Williamsburg's two CDCs, which he said together owned and managed some twenty-four hundred units of housing, as many as the neighborhood's largest private landlord.[8] A third informant noted that Williamsburg had recently been selected as one of only three New York City neighborhoods to take part in a new neighborhood preservation project being spearheaded by the New York Community Trust, the city's community foundation.[9] Other expert informants made similar observations about Williamsburg, and no informant disagreed with the evaluation of Williamsburg as a place where highly successful neighborhood revitalization efforts were taking place.

Force), Avis Vidal (director, Community Development Research Center, New School for Social Research), and Louis Winnick (Fund for the City of New York and professor emeritus, New School for Social Research).

6. Although I did not realize it at the time, my "expert" informants' own definitions of what constitutes "success" in community revitalization proved to be extremely important to their characterization of the potential study neighborhoods. As a result, although I began the research with the belief that I was contrasting a "successful" and an "unsuccessful" neighborhood, I abandoned this notion about midway through the project. A reader will note that the "successful" versus "unsuccessful" dichotomy does not appear in this book. For a discussion of this aspect of the research, see Marwell (2000).

7. Field notes on interview with Professor Susan Saegert, Department of Environmental Psychology, City University of New York, February 3, 1997.

8. Field notes on interview with Marc Jahr, New York City Director, Local Initiatives Support Corporation, February 10, 1997.

9. Field notes on interview with Patricia Jenny, Director, Neighborhood Strategies Project, New York Community Trust, February 28, 1997.

Williamsburg is one identifiable section of Brooklyn's Community District 1, which also contains the Greenpoint section. In 1997, the best available data showed that CD 1's overall population was 43 percent Latino and 46 percent white, but that the two sections of the CD had extremely distinct population compositions (New York City Department of City Planning 1992). Williamsburg was majority Latino, though it also contained one of the city's highest concentrations of Hasidic Jews, who are classified as whites in the census. Greenpoint was majority white, home mostly to people of Italian and Polish ancestry (DeSena 1990). By focusing only on the Williamsburg section of CD 1, then, I would have an area that met my criterion of a majority Latino population and continued to meet my other three criteria as well. Furthermore, my expert informants indicated that Williamsburg was extremely active in neighborhood revitalization work. Williamsburg thus became an attractive option for the "successful" study neighborhood.

Using Williamsburg as a likely research site, I explored with my expert informants the characteristics of the other six neighborhoods as possible comparison sites. I eliminated two Manhattan neighborhoods, Washington Heights and the Lower East Side, primarily because their population mixes were quite different from that of Williamsburg (Marwell 2000). The remaining four neighborhood possibilities included one in the Bronx, one in Manhattan, and two in Brooklyn. Given that the community districts are parts of various larger administrative areas in the five boroughs of New York City, it seemed appropriate, all other things being equal, to select my two research sites from the same borough. This would eliminate some of the political and administrative variation that would otherwise obtain: two neighborhoods in Brooklyn necessarily would have more similarities than would one neighborhood in Brooklyn and one in the Bronx. They would deal with the same borough president and might have the same U.S. representative, state assemblyman, state senator, or city council representatives. Also, certain government offices and personnel might be the same for two neighborhoods in the same borough but not for two in different boroughs. For this reason, I decided to eliminate both East Harlem (Manhattan) and Soundview/Parkchester (the Bronx).[10]

10. Coincidentally, I myself lived in the Soundview/Parkchester section of the Bronx during the time I was conducting the participant-observation for this book. I had moved to that area (corner of Castle Hill Avenue and Chatterton Avenue) for several reasons, among them the idea that my research sites might turn out to be in the Bronx, the city's only majority Latino borough. Although I ultimately conducted the research in Brooklyn, the fact that I returned from the

This left me with two neighborhoods from which to choose: Sunset Park/ Windsor Terrace or Bushwick, both in Brooklyn. Both areas were good candidates. They had similar mixes of Puerto Rican and Dominican residents. Both incorporated industrial areas into their largely residential character, although Sunset Park/Windsor Terrace had a healthier industrial sector. There were some major differences in the economic status of the two neighborhoods, however. While Sunset Park/Windsor Terrace had a poverty rate of 23 percent, and a median household income of $25,875, Bushwick's poverty rate was 40 percent, and its median household income only $16,285. Another significant difference was the population breakdown by race. In addition to its 51 percent Latino population, Sunset Park/Windsor Terrace had a significant and growing Asian—largely Chinese—population (10.4 percent). In addition, Sunset Park/Windsor Terrace was 34 percent white and only 4 percent African American. In contrast, Bushwick's 65 percent Latino population was followed in size by the African American population (25 percent). Whites and Asians each comprised less than 5 percent of the Bushwick population.

Comparing the two potential study sites with Williamsburg, Bushwick appeared to be more demographically similar. Williamsburg/Greenpoint's poverty level was 35.7 percent, and its median household income was $18,905. My decision to focus only on the Williamsburg section of the area, removing the somewhat better-off Greenpoint section, pushed the poverty level slightly higher and the median household income slightly lower. Thus, Bushwick appeared more on a par with Williamsburg, in socioeconomic terms, than was Sunset Park/Windsor Terrace. Perhaps most important to my original research design, many of my expert informants indicated that Bushwick's neighborhood revitalization efforts were largely "unsuccessful." Informants described Bushwick as being hopelessly factionalized, mired in political corruption, and generally the type of place where accomplishing anything at all was a monumental struggle. They made various negative statements about Bushwick, including claims that the local school district was by far the worst in the city in terms of both operations and performance; that social service programs sucked in money without producing any positive outcomes; and that very few competent community organizations existed.

---

field each night to a neighborhood quite similar in many respects to the study neighborhoods lessened the sense of fieldworker dislocation that might have occurred had I been living in, for example, an upper middle-class, largely white neighborhood like the one where I live now.

Based on all of the available evidence, then, I selected Williamsburg and Bushwick as my study neighborhoods. At the time, the two areas had the most similar demographic profiles of any of the potential study areas. Both had between 60 percent and 65 percent Latino populations, poverty rates of between 35 percent and 40 percent, and median household incomes between sixteen thousand and eighteen thousand dollars. The most important demographic difference between the neighborhoods was racial: the two areas have approximately inverse proportions (about 30 percent and 10 percent) of whites and African Americans. The two neighborhoods are contiguous, both lie within the borough of Brooklyn, and they have four district-based political representatives in common. And while Williamsburg was widely seen as successful in neighborhood revitalization, Bushwick was not.

Choosing the Study Organizations

I had already selected the four organizational types for the study, so my first step in choosing the specific organizations where I would conduct participant-observation was to enumerate the organizations of each type that existed in Williamsburg and Bushwick. I already had collected the names of several organizations in each area from my initial round of interviews. I contacted these organizations to set up interviews with their executive directors in order to get a more comprehensive, insider's view of the local organizations. Prior fieldwork experience had taught me that getting a response from the overworked staffs of community-based organizations generally is better achieved through a personal visit than a telephone call. This strategy was at least partially confirmed, as I was able to schedule immediate appointments in all of the organizations. Something about being seen as an actual body rather than simply a voice on the telephone seems to make the request for an interview more tangible. Although I had been worried that my identity as a student from a university outside New York might be a liability, in fact it turned out to be something of an advantage. People seemed flattered that I had come "all the way from Chicago" to learn about their organization and their neighborhood.

When I met the executive directors to conduct my interviews, I identified myself as a doctoral student from the University of Chicago and said I was doing a research project on community development and community building in Williamsburg and Bushwick. I asked them to describe the work of their organization, their targeted population, and anything else they felt was relevant about their neighborhoods. I also asked these contacts to name other organizations in the area that were doing "good work in the community." (Williamsburg organization representatives were asked to name other Williamsburg organizations, and Bushwick organization representatives to name other Bushwick organizations.) In addition to allowing interview respondents to generate their own lists of organizations, I specifically asked them to name community development corporations, child care centers, and Catholic churches. I already knew that each neighborhood had only one Beacon, and so did not specifically inquire about this fourth type of organization. I supplemented the information gathered in these interviews with newspaper articles, academic studies, government agency documents, and other archival material.

In Williamsburg, I identified two CDCs, four child care centers,[11] four Catholic churches, and one Beacon. In Bushwick, there were two CDCs, five child care centers, three Catholic churches, and one Beacon. My research design called for selecting the most active organization of each type for my study. This decision was based on the overall direction of the project, to focus on the role of active resident and organizational participation in neighborhood revitalization efforts. Restricted time and resources, as well as limited past research, made it appropriate to seek out information on the most effective improvement work occurring in each study area. I made my final selection of the eight organizations where I would conduct my participant-observation after discussions with the growing number of neighborhood informants whom I was meeting with each successive day in the field. All eight organizations that I approached were generous enough to allow me to conduct my research there. The Williamsburg organizations were the Southside United Housing Development Fund Corporation (Los Sures), Nuestros Niños Child Development Center, Transfiguration Catholic Church, and the Williamsburg Beacon Center. The Bushwick organizations were the Ridgewood-Bushwick Senior Citizens Council Housing Office, New Life Child Development Center, Saint Barbara's Catholic Church, and the I.S. 111 Beacon.

Method: Doing Participant-Observation

The participant-observation data reported in this book come from fieldwork conducted over the course of three years, from May 1997 to September 2000. The first sixteen months of this period were the most intensive.

---

11. In both Williamsburg and Bushwick, I inquired only about child care centers that served low-income families and had significant or majority populations of Latino children.

During this period I performed between six and nine months of weekly volunteer work at each of the eight study organizations. My stints at the various CBOs were staggered over the course of these months, but I maintained ongoing, regular contact with my informants at the organizations where I had worked early in this sixteen-month period as I completed my volunteering in the remaining organizations. In addition to my regular assignment at each organization, I took part in numerous other aspects of community life, attending community meetings, social gatherings, and political rallies, visiting people's homes, and participating in general street life.

I established my role as a volunteer in each organization through the same process. I first visited each group to request a meeting with the executive director.[12] Whenever possible, I used a referral from someone I had already interviewed formally or met casually in the neighborhood. At the first meeting with the executive director, I conducted an open-ended interview about his or her organization's history, programs, and achievements. These interviews lasted from forty-five minutes to three hours. I concluded the interviews by offering my services as a volunteer for half a day each week, for a period of six months. I placed no restrictions on the type of work I was willing to do, except to ask that I be given a volunteer assignment that would put me in contact with neighborhood residents who were involved in the organization's work. Most of the organizations responded enthusiastically to my offer of volunteer work. Only one executive director expressed some reservations about my participation, mostly centered on concerns that with research as my main focus, I would not be a reliable volunteer.[13] After assuring him that this would not be the case, he agreed to locate a volunteer assignment for me within the organization.

The underlying rationale for my volunteer strategy was the notion of reciprocal exchange. On the one hand, I hoped that by offering something of value—my commitment of labor—to the organizations, and particularly to the staff members with whom I worked, I might encourage a favorable perception of me. In turn, I hoped this would facilitate greater access to and candid discussion about the organization and the neighborhood. At the same time, I recognized the value of the organizations' allowing me to

---

12. While "executive director" was not the title of all of the organization heads with whom I met—for example, at the two Catholic churches, this initial meeting was with the pastor—for ease of expression, I apply it to all the organizations.

13. Field notes on interview with Michael Rochford, executive director, Saint Nicholas Neighborhood Preservation Corporation (administering agency of the Williamsburg Beacon), June 13, 1997.

conduct my research there and wanted to give something in return. I was aware of many cases in which CBOs had opened their doors to researchers, then received nothing for their cooperation—not even the courtesy of a report on the research results. I wanted to avoid this situation by contributing something to the organizations immediately. I also gave each organization a copy of my dissertation when it was completed, and I intend to do the same with this book when it is in print.

All of the organizations' executive directors except one referred me to another staff member to set up my volunteer assignment. This staff member usually became my closest informant within each organization.[14] I engaged in a wide variety of tasks, ranging from laying the groundwork for the opening of a new child care facility, to documenting housing code violations in tenants' apartments, to tutoring reading and English, to writing funding proposals. I also made myself generally helpful whenever I was at the organizations, pitching in with ad hoc tasks like making copies, stuffing envelopes, finding materials, cleaning up, or entertaining children whose parents had business at the organization. As I conducted this work, I spent many hours discussing the organizations and the communities with my main informants. Hanging around with them in turn facilitated numerous conversations with other staff members, community residents, staff at other local organizations, and key political and community leaders. My main informants also steered me toward an array of community events, which provided further important observational opportunities.

At each organization, I maintained productive fieldwork relationships with at least four staff members. All of the staff members were aware of my status as a researcher, as well as of my volunteer work. Generally, for the first month or two of the fieldwork period these informants provided me with basic information on organizational and community issues. They hesitated to discuss the deeper meanings of these issues, however, particularly the sensitive ones. They often asked if they were being tape-recorded, if they were going to be quoted, or if what they said would "be in the book." I assured them that they were not being recorded, and that, whenever they requested it, what they said would not be attributed to them. After I had spent some time at the organizations, informants appeared to gain some confidence in me and for the most part stopped asking these kinds of questions. They also became more willing to discuss the sensitive issues and to provide me with their own analyses of the factors underlying events that I observed.

14. One executive director oversaw my volunteer work himself, and he became my main informant at that organization.

The importance of my being a reliable and accommodating volunteer during this process of confidence building cannot be overstated. The simple fact that I consistently showed up for work on time and was willing to do whatever tasks the staff requested of me went a long way toward ensuring that I was seen in a positive light. At numerous times during the course of the participant-observation, and especially in its latter stages, informants mentioned that they had been skeptical of me at the beginning but had come to see that I followed through on my commitments. Several informants explained their early skepticism by contrasting my behavior with past negative experiences they had had with researchers or volunteers. As Mitchell Duneier (2000) reminds us, however, informants' acknowledgment of my reliability as a volunteer should not be confused with some holistic notion of "trust."

My initial fieldwork interactions were largely open-ended, unfocused conversations in which I learned a wide variety of things about each organization's work, as well as about the history, politics, organizations, leaders, and issues in each of the study neighborhoods. As the fieldwork progressed, and important themes relating to my research questions emerged, I tended to ask more focused questions of my informants, guiding the conversations more than I had previously (Duneier 2000). After sixteen months of volunteering and conducting intensive participant-observation, I moved into a second stage of data collection, in which I conducted eighty formal interviews with organization staff members and participants. During the four months that it took to complete these interviews, I maintained regular though unstructured contact with staff members at all of the organizations and continued to attend many organizational and neighborhood events.

In February 1999, I suspended data collection in Williamsburg and Bushwick for about eight months, returning the following September as part of a new research project on second-generation immigrants in New York City (Kasinitz, Mollenkopf, and Waters 2004; Marwell 2004a). I resumed participant-observation for the next eleven months, during which time I did not have any regular volunteer assignments but rather drew on my status as a known person in the two neighborhoods to circulate freely among organizational events, gatherings in people's homes, and the general flow of daily life inside the organizations and on the street. As I continued to pursue my earlier interest in the role of community-based organizations in neighborhood revitalization, I also paid particular attention to the ways in which the organizations were involving the second generation of Dominican immigrants in their work. In addition to my fieldwork in Williamsburg and Bushwick, I conducted participant-observation in three community-based organizations in the Washington Heights neighborhood of Manhattan during this period.

Throughout the entire time I conducted participant-observation, I kept detailed narrative field notes on my experiences, documenting both events and conversations. I wrote these notes as soon as possible following field-work experiences, sometimes drawing on short notes I had been able to take down in the field. I also regularly made entries in a separate ana-lytical file, writing about my own interpretations of the fieldwork, raising questions about the meaning of my experiences, and developing emerging themes of the research. I wrote these analytical notes more sporadically, as ideas and themes emerged over the course of the fieldwork. Throughout the preceding chapters, much of the evidence I present in support of my arguments comes from material recorded in my field notes. I present this material both in the general narrative of the book and in actual excerpts from my field notes. All such instances are cited in the footnotes, which indicate the date on which the events in question took place.

On My Use of Real Names

It has long been standard practice among ethnographers to use pseu-donyms and otherwise mask the real names of research sites and infor-mants, with the stated objective of protecting informants' confidentiality. In recent years, however, this practice has come under discussion, and some ethnographers have provided identifying information in their work (e.g., Duneier 2000; Kasinitz 1992). The most explicit rationale and strategy for identifying places and people by their real names comes from Mitchell Duneier. In his acclaimed book *Sidewalk*, Duneier argues that scholars can-not continue to appeal solely to personal and professional ethics when ask-ing readers to trust their accounts and interpretations of events in the field. In light of recent scandals involving major newspapers' printing stories fab-ricated by journalists (e.g., Barry et al. 2003; Pogrebin 1998), Duneier asks why ethnographers should be viewed any less skeptically. His own answer to this question was to use both real names and photographs of many of the research subjects in *Sidewalk*, as well as to employ an innovative tech-nique for obtaining the "informed consent" required by universities and the federal government when working with human subjects who might be harmed by research activities.

In this book, I have replicated components of Duneier's model, giving the real names of the neighborhoods, organizations, and people featured in its pages. Although in prior publications (Marwell 2004a, 2004b) covering earlier phases in this research I followed the traditional practice of using pseudonyms, it seemed impossible to do so once the research was completed and written in its present form. The historical material on Williamsburg and Bushwick, reported mostly in chapters 2 and 3, constitutes a critical part of my argument. Key details that render the neighborhoods and organizations identifiable could not be left out without undermining the analysis. This state of affairs, however, did not absolve me of the necessity of obtaining informed consent from the people who appear in the book; I engaged in a strategy similar to Duneier's in order to do so.

During my writing process, I sat down with each person who is named in the book and portrayed as either doing something or saying something that I observed. I gave them a printed copy of the passages in which they appear, sat with them as they read through the pages, and gave them the choice of remaining a named actor or being made anonymous. Somewhat to my surprise, only a very few passages prompted actors to request anonymity; I complied with all of these requests. There were two exceptions to this practice: One was for people who spoke at public meetings, such as community board meetings or city council hearings, whose comments are thus on the public record. The other was for individuals considered to be "public figures," who do not have an expectation of anonymity as regards their public duties; these were mainly elected officials. Although I did not review with the public figures the specific passages of the book that describe their actions and utterances, all of these individuals knew who I was and were aware that I was carrying out research. In addition to the protections of informed consent given by the strategy described here, this research was examined and approved by the institutional review boards of the University of Chicago and the City University of New York.[15]

Access and Subjectivity in the Field

Practitioners of participant-observation continually grapple with the fragility of access to their research settings. In part, access turns on a researcher's success at convincing potential research subjects to allow him or her to "hang out" in relevant settings, thereby enabling data collection. Another point of vulnerability lies within the researcher's own "subject position"—

15. The University of Chicago Institutional Review Board approved the first phase of my fieldwork (May 1997 to February 1999), on which my dissertation (Marwell 2000) was based. The fieldwork conducted between September 1999 and August 2000, under the auspices of the Second Generation in Metropolitan New York project, was authorized under that project's examination by the Institutional Review Board of the City University of New York.

that is, in his or her own identity, in the ways that identity informs how the researcher understands events in the field, and in the process by which the putative research subjects themselves construct the researcher as a subject.

Numerous discussions of how to "gain access" to fieldwork settings in the first of these two senses already exist in the literature (e.g., Lofland and Lofland 1995; Schatzman and Strauss 1973). One particular barrier, however, has not received much comment: conflict among research subjects. Gaining and maintaining a researcher role on both sides of a conflict requires fraught judgments about how each side will react to the researcher's spending time on the other side. Will doing so prompt accusations that the researcher is a spy? Will access to one side be cut off once the researcher is known to have access to the other side? In most instances of conflict that arose during this research, I was able to carry out participant-observation on both sides. These instances included the ongoing and flaring tensions between Los Sures and Assemblyman Vito Lopez; the disagreements between staff at Los Sures and the Nuestros Niños Child Development Center over tactics for creating social change; the longstanding antipathy between Saint Barbara's Catholic Church and the Ridgewood-Bushwick Senior Citizens Council; the internal dispute between parents and staff at the Williamsburg Beacon; and the disdain in which certain leaders at the New Life Child Development Center held Ridgewood-Bushwick and Assemblyman Lopez.

In one instance of conflict discussed in this book, I was unable to conduct research on both sides: the battle between Williamsburg's Latinos and Hasidic Jews over affordable housing resources, recounted in chapter 2. When I began fieldwork at the four Williamsburg organizations, all of them (by design) substantially representing the interests of the neighborhood's Latinos, I was unaware of the Latino-Hasidic conflict. As I learned about its content, longevity, and depth from the Latino organizations, I felt it would be impossible to conduct fieldwork with the Hasidim, for two distinct reasons. First, I was pessimistic that the leaders of the Hasidic organizations, all Hasidic men, would allow a female fieldworker into their midst. Prohibitions on cross-gender social interactions are extensive among the Hasidim, and it seemed very unlikely that I would be able to surmount them. Although female staff members of government officials have been able to work with male Hasidic organizational leaders, these women have had the advantage of controlling access to public resources that the Hasidic organizations are seeking. I had no such standing. A second reason for not attempting fieldwork among the Hasidim was rooted in my already existing relationships with the Latino organizations. The tensions between the Latino and Hasidic organizations—especially at Los Sures—were so high that I was convinced I would jeopardize my continuing access to the Latino organizations if I attempted fieldwork in the Hasidic organizations. All of the information on Hasidic organizations and interests that I present in this book, then, comes from others' published accounts or my own observation of Hasidic individuals and organizational leaders in public settings.

In all of the other instances of conflict, I was forthcoming with all parties about the fact that my role was that of a researcher, and that I was spending time "hanging out" on both sides of what I had learned was a conflict. I was extremely vigilant about not repeating to people on one side of a conflict what someone on the other side had told me. Most everyone seemed to respect my position, as evidenced by the fact that almost nobody asked me for information about what was going on on the other side of a conflict. On the very few occasions when I did receive such requests, I reiterated my understanding of my role as a researcher and explained that I did not feel comfortable providing such information. This was usually sufficient to resolve the immediate situation and to preempt future requests of this sort.

In addition to navigating these and other potential barriers to basic access to research settings, my own subject position fundamentally influenced the scope of my observations and the findings to which they led. As George Herbert Mead and Erving Goffman pointed out many years ago, our individual identities are always a social encounter—a "presentation of self" to others (Goffman 1959; Mead 1956). This presentation, or performance, of identity contains both conscious and unconscious dimensions. In addition, our own identity performances elicit responses in others, who simultaneously construct identities for us on the basis of their own characteristics and experiences. Certainly, substantial overlap exists between our own sense of our identity and others' sense of our identity, but there is divergence as well.

While doing fieldwork, I was conscious of performing certain of my personal characteristics differently than I did in my "regular" (that is, non-fieldwork) life. This is not to say that I lied about those characteristics—only that they became more salient to my identity when I was positioned as a researcher in the field. At the time of my research, I had the following key personal characteristics: fourth-generation U.S. American, upper middle class, white, Jewish (nonobservant), Spanish-speaking, student, young, heterosexual, and female. Some of these were easily visible, others discernible during conversation, and others largely hidden from view. Each one affected my research, more so even than I could possibly know. I think that my age, student status, gender, and ability to speak Spanish fluently and without an "American" accent proved most important to the process of my fieldwork.

My relative youth (I was twenty-nine when I began the research) and my identity as a student helped legitimate my usual approach to the organizations where I hoped to conduct fieldwork. When I first introduced myself to organizational leaders and participants, I told them (truthfully) that I was a student interested in finding out as much as possible about the people, organizations, and neighborhoods of Williamsburg and Bushwick. The "student" role proved to be one that most everybody understood, and people often said they were happy to be helping me out with my "school project." My age reinforced my student status, and both characteristics seemed to contribute to a sense that since I had so much to learn about the neighborhoods and organizations, it was appropriate for me to be hanging around a lot. I am acutely interested in how I will establish a role in a new participant-observation project when I no longer have the young student role as an option.

Being female created both opportunities and constraints during the research. As Nancy Naples has argued, female ethnographers can gain a kind of access to the experiences of women that male ethnographers cannot (Naples 1998). Since many of the Williamsburg and Bushwick organizations I studied had largely female staffs, my gender afforded me a certain ease throughout much of my fieldwork. It was not seen as peculiar or threatening for me to spend time alone with other women; to engage in cooking, child care, or other tasks associated with nurturing; or to be interested in helping others through community work. Being female was the usual condition in the settings where I conducted most of my research, although a number of the highest-ranking staff members at the organizations were male. My gender did not pose a barrier to frequent interactions with these men, but our interactions did tend to be of shorter duration and more focused on a particular topic—in contrast to the often unstructured, undirected time I spent in the company of women.

While the gender-based advantages I obtained in my fieldwork in fact seem to me more difficult to identify and enumerate, the gender-based constraints I faced are (and were) very clear. Nothing delimits the possibilities of one's own identity and experience like running up against a barrier. As I have already noted, I presumed that my gender would have proven an insurmountable barrier to an attempt to conduct fieldwork with the Hasidim. One gender-based barrier that was apparent stemmed from my own and others' perceptions about my personal safety while in the field. When I was a beginning graduate student contemplating the undertaking of a participant-observation project in a poor neighborhood, a very senior sociologist expressed to me his concerns about whether I, as a young woman, would be safe in such an environment. He suggested that rather than exposing myself too often to the dangers of the streets, I might be better off doing something that he described as akin to Method acting. From the safety of my own room, with little else but a mirror and my imagination, I could enact some of the experience of doing fieldwork, an approximation of the "feel" of the poor community I hoped to study.

I was very much confused by this odd, if well-intentioned, suggestion. I went ahead and did fieldwork the old-fashioned way despite it. But the encounter itself is food for thought with regard to my gender and its role in my urban ethnographic project. Most of the "classic" works in the still-solidifying urban ethnography canon aimed to investigate the deviance and social problems often associated with city life in the sociological imagination: slums, crime, poverty, unemployment, gangs, "oppositional culture," and so on.[16] Most (though not all) of the authors of these works have been men, a fact that might prompt us to ask why maleness has been so strongly associated with these kinds of questions. Perhaps male researchers, as part of their own subject position, consistently identify these issues as the preferred, somehow most legitimate, province of urban ethnographic inquiry. And perhaps this equation underlay the erstwhile advice that senior sociologist gave me those many years ago.

Of course, there are also works of urban ethnography, some of them "classics," that do not focus explicitly on deviance and social problems. Some have been "community studies" in the Chicago School sense, attempting to gain an understanding of the entire social milieu of a particular urban neighborhood (Drake and Cayton 1945; Kornblum 1974; Molotch 1972; Pattillo 1999; Susser 1982). Others—including my own—have been animated by questions about poverty and poor neighborhoods but have explored different dimensions of the experience of the urban poor, such as family life, community formation, religion, the economic demands of motherhood, and activism (e.g., McRoberts 2003; Naples 1998; Newman 1999; Small 2004; Stack 1974). Urban ethnographies by women have been more likely to examine these latter kinds of issues, rather than choosing deviance as their starting point. My own research interest in neighborhood revitalization thus may have been connected to my gender from the start,

16. See E. Anderson (1978, 1990), Bourgois (1996), Duneier (1992, 2000), Gans (1964), Hannerz (1969), Liebow (1964), Moore (1978), Sanchez-Jankowski (1991), Stack (1974), Suttles (1968), Venkatesh (2000), and Whyte (1943).

while the setting of my fieldwork—inside formal organizations—may have offered some relief for gendered anxieties over how to gain entry into an unfamiliar place where I felt my safety might indeed be an issue.

Ethnography and folk wisdom alike point to the risks of unfamiliarity in settings where social order is shaky (as indicated, for example, by higher-than-average crime rates) or governed by highly parochial rules (as in Gerald Suttles's [1968] concept of the "defended neighborhood"). To be unknown in such settings is to be a potential threat, a status that can easily make one a target.[17] A common strategy among urban ethnographers is to acquire a "sponsor" who can provide an introduction into the field setting: someone who has an accepted place in the social world of interest. At worst, this helps to reduce the ethnographer's unfamiliarity; at best, it conveys legitimacy to him or her. My own fieldwork took place largely (though not entirely) inside formal organizations. This decision derived primarily from my overarching interest in neighborhood revitalization, a process in which community-based organizations are central actors, but it also offered me a shortcut to reducing my unfamiliarity. The organizations I studied provided controlled settings with regular participants and (largely) benign, predictable rules of social order. Ethnographers who choose to conduct fieldwork in more informal settings often need to negotiate a much wider and less predictable range of social situations. While women have done and are continuing to do fieldwork in such settings (e.g., Jones 2004; Maher 1997; Moore 1978), I suspect that gendered forms of risk play an important role in the distribution of men and women over ethnographic research questions, and thus over fieldwork settings.

Finally, the importance of language during my research cannot be understated. The first language of many residents of Williamsburg and Bushwick, including many staff members and participants at the organizations I studied, was Spanish. Some spoke little or no English, while others spoke English well. I spoke exclusively in Spanish with some of the people I met in the field, in a combination of Spanish and English with others, and exclusively in English with others. My Spanish has a not-quite-identifiable Caribbean accent, a sort of mishmash of the clearly distinctive Puerto Rican, Dominican, and Cuban pronunciations. Being able to speak Spanish, and this particular kind of Spanish, not only facilitated communication with organizational staff and neighborhood residents, but also complicated their

---

17. See, e.g., Sudhir Venkatesh's account of being detained and threatened (and subsequently released unharmed) by gang members in Chicago's Robert Taylor Homes (Levitt and Dubner 2005, chapter 3).

assumptions and perceptions regarding my subjectivity in ways that perhaps made me seem less of an outsider. Upon hearing me speak Spanish, many people assumed that I had Latina, probably Caribbean, heritage. Numerous times, some months after an initial casual meeting, a person would be surprised to learn that I did not in fact come from this background.

My language skills thus often took precedence over the visual aspects of my privileged location in the complex arrangements of racial and ethnic identity in the United States. Given the racial diversity and ambiguity of those classified as "Latino" in this country, it was perfectly conceivable that a person of my appearance—light skin, green eyes, reddish hair—could be Cuban, Puerto Rican, Dominican, or of some other Latina ethnicity. The fact that I spoke fluent, Caribbean-accented Spanish enhanced this possibility. This haziness about my ethnicity often remained even for people with whom I spoke mostly or entirely in English, since they had usually heard me speaking to others in Spanish. Language thus offered me a dimension of plasticity in my subject position, which, when combined with my other characteristics, allowed me, *in certain ways*, to "pass" as an insider. At times, a person in the field would ask me directly about my ethnic roots. In the early months of my research, this question left me rather flummoxed, as my ethnic roots were not a salient part of my own identity formation, and I did not have a comfortable response. I usually said something about being "from here"—that is, born in the United States—and that I did not have any Latina heritage. I quickly learned that this was not a satisfactory answer for most of my questioners, and began to offer the only other category I could think of: that my family was of Jewish origin, but not religious. I do not know what response this answer provoked in my questioners, but it usually proved sufficient to bring the conversation on this topic to a close.

These comments only begin to scratch the surface of the complex and thorny issues surrounding subject position, its effects on fieldwork practice, and the ways it conditions the findings of participant-observation research. I offer them here largely to give the reader additional insight into my research process. Participant-observers whose practice includes reflection on their own subjectivity confront a series of important choices at all stages of their work: data collection, data analysis, and data reporting. At one extreme lies the conviction that subjectivity is so decisive that we cannot make claims about anything in a fieldwork project besides ourselves and our own experiences. At the other extreme lurks a vision of the researcher's detached, technical relation to the object of analysis. *Bargaining for Brooklyn* is ultimately my own bargain with my research subjects, my readers, and myself.

WORKS CITED

Abbot, A. 2002. "Los Angeles and the Chicago School: A Comment on Michael Dear." *City and Community* 1:33–38.

Ahlbrandt, R. S. 1984. *Neighborhoods, People, and Community*. New York: Plenum.

Aiken, M., and R. R. Alford. 1970. "Community Structure and Innovation: The Case of Urban Renewal." *American Sociological Review* 35:650–65.

Ainsworth, J. W. 2002. "Why Does It Take a Village? The Mediation of Neighborhood Effects on Educational Achievement." *Social Forces* 81:117–52.

Alba, R. D., and J. R. Logan. 1993. "Minority Proximity to Whites in Suburbs: An Individual-level Analysis of Segregation." *American Journal of Sociology* 98:1388–1427.

Anderson, E. 1978. *A Place on the Corner*. Chicago: University of Chicago Press.

———. 1990. *Streetwise: Race, Class, and Change in an Urban Community*. Chicago: University of Chicago Press.

———. 1999. *Code of the Street: Decency, Violence, and the Moral Life of the Inner City*. New York: W. W. Norton.

Anderson, N. 1923. *The Hobo: The Sociology of the Homeless Man*. Chicago: University of Chicago Press.

Andrews, K. T. 2001. "Social Movements and Policy Implementation: The Mississippi Civil Rights Movement and the War on Poverty, 1965 to 1971." *American Sociological Review* 66:71–95.

Angell, R. C. 1942. "The Social Integration of Selected American Cities." *American Journal of Sociology* 47:575–92.

Auletta, K. 1982. *The Underclass*. New York: Vintage Books.

Barry, D. 1998. "Combative AIDS Group Says City Cut Financing Out of Spite." *New York Times*, April 12, p. 25.

Barry, D., D. Barstow, J. D. Glater, A. Liptak, and J. Steinberg. 2003. "Correcting the Record: Times Reporter Who Resigned Leaves Long Train of Deception." *New York Times*, May 11, p. A1.

Bartelt, D., and N. Brown. 2000. "The Social Reconstruction of the City: Social Capital and Community Building—Introduction." *Journal of Urban Affairs* 22:U5–U7.

Bennett, C. G. 1968. "Lindsay Steps Up City Halls Drive." *New York Times*, July 13, p. 24.

———. 1969. "Mayor Opens 'Little City Hall'; Tells of Gift to Help 5 Libraries." *New York Times*, May 17, p. 17.

Berger, J. 1995. "Court Affirms Public School for Hasidim." *New York Times*, March 9, p. B1.

———. 1996. "School District of Kiryas Joel Is Ruled Illegal." *New York Times*, August 27, p. B1.

———. 1998. "Hasidic Village Loses Again in Schools Ruling." *New York Times*, July 10, p. B7.

———. 1999. "Albany Tries Again to Aid Hasidic Village." *New York Times*, August 5, p. B5.

Beyerlein, K., and J. R. Hipp. 2005. "Social Capital, Too Much of a Good Thing? American Religious Traditions and Community Crime." *Social Forces* 84:995–1013.

Boggs, C. 2001. "Social Capital and Political Fantasy: Robert Putnam's 'Bowling Alone.'" *Theory and Society* 30:281–97.

Borough President of Brooklyn (Marty Markowitz). 2004. Recommendation Report Greenpoint–Williamsburg Rezoning Plan. Brooklyn, NY: Borough President of Brooklyn.

Bourdieu, P. 1984. *Distinction: A Social Critique of the Judgement of Taste*. Cambridge, MA: Harvard University Press.

Bourgois, P. 1996. *In Search of Respect: Selling Crack in El Barrio*. Cambridge: Cambridge University Press.

Breton, R. 1964. "Institutional Completeness of Ethnic Communities and the Personal Relations of Immigrants." *American Journal of Sociology* 70:193–205.

Briggs, X. N. d. S., E. J. Mueller, and M. L. Sullivan. 1997. *From Neighborhood to Community: Evidence on the Social Effects of Community Development*. New York: Community Development Research Center, Graduate School of Management and Urban Policy, New School for Social Research.

Brint, S. 2001. "*Gemeinschaft* Revisited: A Critique and Reconstruction of the Community Concept." *Sociological Theory* 19:1–23.

Brooklyn Community Board One Rezoning Task Force. 2004. Greenpoint–Williamsburg Rezoning Position and Recommendations. Brooklyn, NY: Brooklyn Community Board One.

Brooks-Gunn, J., G. J. Duncan, and J. L. Aber, eds. 1997. *Neighborhood Poverty: Context and Consequences for Children*. Vol. 1. New York: Russell Sage Foundation.

Bursik, R. J. 1988. "Social Disorganization and Theories of Crime and Delinquency: Problems and Prospects." *Criminology* 26:519–52.

Bursik, R. J., and H. Grasmick. 1993. *Neighborhoods and Crime: The Dimensions of Effective Community Control*. Lexington, MA: Lexington Books.

Burstein, P., and A. Linton. 2002. "The Impact of Political Parties, Interest Groups, and Social Movement Organizations on Public Policy: Some Recent Evidence and Theoretical Concerns." *Social Forces* 81:381–408.

Burt, R. S. 1992. *Structural Holes: The Social Structure of Competition*. Cambridge, MA: Harvard University Press.

Carle, R. D., and L. A. DeCaro Jr., eds. 1997. *Signs of Hope in the City: Ministries of Community Renewal*. Valley Forge, PA: Judson Press.

Caro, R. A. 1974. *The Power Broker: Robert Moses and the Fall of New York*. New York: Knopf.

Carr, P. J. 2003. "The New Parochialism: The Implications of the Beltway Case for Arguments concerning Informal Social Control." *American Journal of Sociology* 108:1249–91.

Carroll, M. 1972. "4 District Heads Named by Mayor." *New York Times*, January 5, p. 41.

Castells, M. 1977. *The Urban Question: A Marxist Approach*. Trans. A. Sheridan. Cambridge, MA: MIT Press.

Charles, C. Z. 2003. "The Dynamics of Racial Residential Segregation." *Annual Review of Sociology* 29:167–207.

Chase-Lansdale, P. L., R. A. Moffitt, B. J. Lohman, A. J. Cherlin, R. L. Coley, L. D. Pittman, J. Roff, and E. Votruba-Drzal. 2003. "Mothers' Transitions from Welfare to Work and the Well-being of Preschoolers and Adolescents." *Science* 299:1548–52.

Chaskin, R. J. 2001. *Building Community Capacity*. New York: Aldine de Gruyter.

Chavis, D. M., and A. Wandersman. 1990. "Sense of Community in the Urban Environment: A Catalyst for Participation and Community Development." *American Journal of Community Psychology* 18:55–77.

City of New York. 2003. *Slots for Tots: New York City's Failure to Manage Daycare Enrollment*. New York: Office of the Comptroller, Office of Policy Management.

Clark, A. E. 1966. "At Last, Mayor Gets a Little City Hall." *New York Times*, August 31, p. 35.

Clark, R. F. 2000. *Maximum Feasible Success: A History of the Community Action Program*. Washington, DC: National Association of Community Action Agencies.

Clemens, E. S., and D. C. Minkoff. 2004. "Beyond the Iron Law: Rethinking the Place of Organizations in Social Movement Research." In *The Blackwell Companion to Social Movements*, ed. D. Snow, S. A. Soule, and H. Kriesi, 157–70. London: Blackwell.

Cloward, R. A., and L. Ohlin. 1960. *Delinquency and Opportunity: A Theory of Delinquent Gangs*. Glencoe, IL: Free Press.

Cohen, A. J. 1996. "A Brief History of Federal Financing for Child Care in the United States." *Future of Children* 6:26–40.

Coleman, J. S. 1988. "Social Capital in the Creation of Human Capital." *American Journal of Sociology* 94 (supp.): S95–S120.

———. 1990. *Foundations of Social Theory*. Cambridge, MA: Belknap Press.

Danziger, S., and P. Gottschalk, eds. 1994. *Uneven Tides: Rising Inequality in America*. New York: Russell Sage Foundation.

Dao, J. 1994. "Albany in Accord on School District for Hasidic Group." *New York Times*, July 2, p. 1.

Davila, Albert. 1984. "Dedicate Bushwick II." *Daily News* (New York), August 29.

Dávila, Arlene. 2004. *Barrio Dreams: Puerto Ricans, Latinos, and the Neoliberal City*. Berkeley: University of California Press.

DeFilippis, J. 2001. "The Myth of Social Capital in Community Development." *Housing Policy Debate* 12:781–806.

DeGenova, N. 2005. *Working the Boundaries: Race, Space, and "Illegality" in Mexican Chicago*. Durham, NC: Duke University Press.

DeHoog, R. H. 1984. *Contracting Out for Human Services: Economic, Political, and Organizational Perspectives*. Albany: State University of New York Press.

DeSena, J. N. 1990. *Protecting One's Turf: Social Strategies for Maintaining Urban Neighborhoods*. Lanham, MD: University Press of America.

DiMaggio, P. J., and W. W. Powell. 1983. "The Iron Cage Revisited: Institutional Isomorphism and Collective Rationality in Organizational Fields." *American Sociological Review* 48:147–60.

Dohan, D. 2003. *The Price of Poverty: Money, Work, and Culture in the Mexican American Barrio*. Berkeley: University of California Press.

Domhoff, G. W. 2005. "The Ford Foundation in the Inner City: Forging an Alliance with Neighborhood Activists." http://sociology.ucsc.edu/whorulesamerica/power/ford_foundation.html (accessed December 19, 2005).

Drake, S. C., and H. R. Cayton. 1945. *Black Metropolis: A Study of Negro Life in a Northern City.* New York: Harcourt, Brace.

Duncan, G. J., and P. L. Chase-Lansdale, eds. 2001. *For Better and for Worse: Welfare Reform and the Well-being of Children and Families.* New York: Russell Sage Foundation.

Duneier, M. 1992. *Slim's Table: Race, Respectability, and Masculinity.* Chicago: University of Chicago Press.

———. 2000. *Sidewalk.* New York: Viking.

Durkheim, E. 1893. *The Division of Labor in Society.* Trans. W. D. Halls. New York: Free Press, 1984.

———. 1912. *The Elementary Forms of the Religious Life.* Trans. K. Fields. New York: Free Press, 1995.

Edwards, B., and J. D. McCarthy. 2004. "Resources and Social Movement Mobilization." In *The Blackwell Companion to Social Movements,* ed. D. Snow, S. A. Soule, and H. Kriesi, 116–52. London: Blackwell.

Eisinger, P. K. 1969. "The Anti-poverty Community Action Group as a Political Force in the Ghetto." PhD diss., Yale University, Department of Political Science.

Erie, S. P. 1988. *Rainbow's End: Irish-Americans and the Dilemmas of Urban Machine Politics, 1840–1985.* Berkeley: University of California Press.

Espinosa, G., V. Elizondo, and J. Miranda, eds. 2005. *Latino Religions and Civic Activism in the United States.* New York: Oxford University Press.

Faux, G. 1971. *CDCs: New Hope for the Inner City.* New York: Twentieth Century Fund.

Fender, L., C. T. O'Brien, T. Thompson, K. Snyder, and R. Bess. 2002. "Recent Changes in New York Welfare and Work, Child Care, and Child Welfare Systems." http://www.urban.org/url.cfm?ID=310564 (accessed August 4, 2005).

Fiorina, M. P. 1981. "Some Problems in Studying the Effects of Resource-Allocation in Congressional Elections." *American Journal of Political Science* 25:543–67.

Fischer, C. S. 1975. "The Study of Urban Community and Personality." *Annual Review of Sociology* 1:67–89.

———. 1982. *To Dwell among Friends: Personal Networks in Town and City.* Chicago: University of Chicago Press.

Fishman, R. 1987. *Bourgeois Utopias: The Rise and Fall of Suburbia.* New York: Basic Books.

Fligstein, N. 2001. *The Architecture of Markets: An Economic Sociology of Twenty-first-Century Capitalist Societies.* Princeton, NJ: Princeton University Press.

Fligstein, N., and D. McAdam. 2005. "The Theory of Fields Revisited." Paper presented at the conference "Bourdieuian Theory and Historical Analysis," Yale University.

Foderaro, L. W. 1999. "Hasidic Public School Loses Again before U.S. Supreme Court, but Supporters Persist." *New York Times,* October 13, p. B5.

Foley, D. L. 1950. "The Use of Local Facilities in a Metropolis." *American Journal of Sociology* 56:238–46.

Foucault, M. 1977. *Discipline and Punish.* New York: Pantheon.

Fowler, G. 1973. "Residents Advise City on Housing." *New York Times,* December 9, p. 40.

Freedman, A. E. 1994. *Patronage: An American Tradition.* Chicago: Nelson-Hall Publishers.

Freidenberg, J. 2000. *Growing Old in El Barrio.* New York: New York University Press.

Friedman, N., C. J. Bloom, and D. Marks. 1974. *Neighborhood Variation: An Analysis of an Ethnically Mixed Low-Income Neighborhood.* New York: Bureau of Applied Social Research, Columbia University.

Fuller, B., S. L. Kagan, G. L. Caspary, and C. A. Gauthier. 2002. "Welfare Reform and Child Care Options for Low-Income Families." *Future of Children* 12:97–119.

Gans, H. J. 1964. *The Urban Villagers: Group and Class in the Life of Italian Americans.* Updated and expanded ed. New York: Free Press, 1982.

———. 1967. *The Levittowners: Ways of Life and Politics in a New Suburban Community.* New York: Columbia University Press, 1982.

Gatenio, S. 2002. "A Historical Overview of Early Childhood Education and Care in New York City." Working paper, Foundation for Child Development, New York.

Gecan, M. 2002. *Going Public.* Boston: Beacon Press.

Gillette, J. M. 1926. "Community Concepts." *Social Forces* 4:677–89.

Gillette, M. L. 1996. *Launching the War on Poverty: An Oral History.* New York: Twayne Publishers.

Gittell, R. J., and A. Vidal. 1998. *Community Organizing: Building Social Capital as a Development Strategy.* Thousand Oaks, CA: Sage.

Goffman, E. 1959. *The Presentation of Self in Everyday Life.* Garden City, NY: Doubleday.

Gonzalez, C. 1997. "Latinos Hit Jews on Zoning." *Daily News* (New York), May 15, p. 6.

Gordon, D. N. 1968. "Immigrants and Urban Governmental Form in American Cities, 1933–60." *American Journal of Sociology* 74:158–71.

Gottlieb, M. 1979. "Bushwick Housing OK Near." *Daily News* (New York), May 3.

———. 1993. "Bushwick's Hope Is a Public Project." *New York Times*, August 15, p. 35.

Gottlieb, M., A. Browne, J. Hamill, and G. James. 1977a. "The Bulldozing of Bushwick." *Daily News* (New York), August 5.

———. 1977b. "Bushwick's Trial by Fire." *Daily News* (New York), August 4.

Granovetter, M. S. 1973. "The Strength of Weak Ties." *American Journal of Sociology* 78:1360–80.

Greenhouse, L. 1994. "High Court Bars School District Created to Benefit Hasidic Jews." *New York Times*, June 28, p. A1.

Gregory, S. 1998. *Black Corona: Race and the Politics of Place in an Urban Community.* Princeton, NJ: Princeton University Press.

Grutzner, C. 1958. "City Housing Unit Shelves Project." *New York Times*, September 19, p. 29.

———. 1959. "Slum Plans Stir Area in Brooklyn." *New York Times*, January 17, p. 21.

Guest, A. M., and B. A. Lee. 1983. "The Social Organization of Local Areas." *Urban Affairs Review* 19:217–40.

Guest, A. M., and R. S. Oropesa. 1984. "Problem-solving Strategies of Local Areas in the Metropolis." *American Sociological Review* 49:828–40.

Guterbock, T. M. 1980. *Machine Politics in Transition: Party and Community in Chicago.* Chicago: University of Chicago Press.

Haines, H. 1984. "Black Radicalization and the Funding of Civil Rights." *Social Problems* 32:31–43.

Hall, P. D. 1992. *Inventing the Nonprofit Sector and Other Essays on Philanthropy, Voluntarism, and Nonprofit Organizations.* Baltimore: Johns Hopkins University Press.

Halle, D. 1984. *America's Working Man: Work, Home, and Politics among Blue-collar Property Owners.* Chicago: University of Chicago Press.

Halpern, R. 1995. *Rebuilding the Inner City: A History of Neighborhood Initiatives to Address Poverty in the United States.* New York: Columbia University Press.

Hamilton, C. V. 1979. "Patron-Recipient Relationship and Minority Politics in New York City." *Political Science Quarterly* 94:211–27.

Hannerz, U. 1969. *Soulside: Inquiries into Ghetto Culture.* New York: Columbia University Press.

Harding, D. 2003. "Counterfactual Models of Neighborhood Effects: The Effect of Neighborhood Poverty on Dropping Out and Teenage Pregnancy." *American Journal of Sociology* 93:75–87.

Harvey, D. 1973. *Social Justice and the City.* Baltimore: Johns Hopkins University Press.

Hawley, A. H. 1944. "Ecology and Human Ecology." *Social Forces* 23:398–405.

———. 1950. *Human Ecology: A Theory of Community Structure.* New York: Ronald Press.

Helfgot, J. 1981. *Professional Reforming: Mobilization for Youth and the Failure of Social Science.* Boston: Lexington Books.

Hernandez, R. 1997. "Albany Vote Defies Courts Again to Back a Hasidic School District." *New York Times,* August 5, p. A1.

Hillery, G. A., Jr. 1955. "Definitions of Community: Areas of Agreement." *Rural Sociology* 20:111–23.

Holloway, L. 2000. "Levy Details Plan to Adjust Bilingual Class." *New York Times,* December 20, p. B1.

Hondagneu-Sotelo, P. 2001. *Doméstica: Immigrant Workers Cleaning and Caring in the Shadows of Affluence.* Berkeley: University of California Press.

Honig, M. 1963. "Jews Ask Jersey Court's Aid in Fight on Tract." *New York Times,* September 25, p. 36.

Hunter, A. 1974. *Symbolic Communities: The Persistence and Change of Chicago's Local Communities.* Chicago: University of Chicago Press.

———. 1985. "Private, Parochial and Public Social Orders: The Problem of Crime and Incivility in Urban Communities." In *The Challenge of Social Control: Essays in Honor of Morris Janowitz,* ed. G. D. Suttles and M. N. Zald, 230–42. Norwood, NJ: Ablex Publishing.

Hunter, A., and S. Staggenborg. 1986. "Communities Do Act: Neighborhood Characteristics, Resource Mobilization, and Political Action by Local Community Organizations." *Social Science Journal* 23:169–80.

Institute of Public Administration. 1966. *Developing New York City's Human Resources: Report of a Study Group of the Institute of Public Administration to Mayor John V. Lindsay.* New York: Institute of Public Administration.

Jackson, K. T. 1985. *Crabgrass Frontier: The Suburbanization of the United States.* New York: Oxford University Press.

Janowitz, M. 1952. *The Community Press in an Urban Setting.* Glencoe, IL: Free Press.

———. 1975. "Sociological Theory and Social Control." *American Journal of Sociology* 81:82–108.

———. 1978. *The Last Half-Century: Societal Change and Politics in America.* Chicago: University of Chicago Press.

Jaret, C. 1983. "Recent Neo-Marxist Urban Analysis." *Annual Review of Sociology* 9:499–525.

Jencks, C., and S. E. Mayer. 1990. "The Social Consequences of Growing Up in a Poor Neighborhood." In *Inner-City Poverty in the United States,* ed. L. E. Lynn Jr. and M. G. H. McGeary, 111–86. Washington, DC: National Academy Press.

Jencks, C., and P. E. Peterson, eds. 1991. *The Urban Underclass.* Washington, DC: Brookings Institution Press.

Jenkins, J. C., and C. M. Eckert. 1986. "Channeling Black Insurgency: Elite Patronage and Professional Social Movement Organizations in the Development of the Black Movement." *American Sociological Review* 51:812–29.

Johnson, L. 1965. "To Fulfill These Rights." Howard University commencement speech, June 4. In B.J. Schulman, *Lyndon Johnson and American Liberalism: A Brief Biography with Documents.* Boston: Bedford/St. Martin's, 1995.

Johnson, R. 1971. "'Forgotten' Senior Citizens Uniting to Improve Services in Brooklyn." *New York Times*, November 28, p. A8.

Jones, N. 2004. "'It's Not Where You Live, It's How You Live': How Young Women Negotiate Conflict and Violence in the Inner City." *Annals of the American Academy of Political and Social Sciences* 595:49–62.

Jones-Correa, M. 1998. *Between Two Nations: The Political Predicament of Latinos in New York City*. Ithaca, NY: Cornell University Press.

Kain, J. 1968. "Housing Segregation, Negro Employment, and Metropolitan Decentralization." *Quarterly Journal of Econmics* 82:175–97.

———. 1992. "The Spatial Mismatch Hypothesis: Three Decades Later." *Housing Policy Debate* 3:371–460.

Kasarda, J. D. 1989. "Urban Industrial Transition and the Underclass." *Annals of the American Academy of Political and Social Science* 501:26–47.

Kasarda, J. D., and M. Janowitz. 1974. "Community Attachment in Mass Society." *American Sociological Review* 39:328–39.

Kasinitz, P. 1992. *Caribbean New York: Black Immigrants and the Politics of Race*. Ithaca, NY: Cornell University Press.

Kasinitz, P., J. H. Mollenkopf, and M. Waters, eds. 2004. *Becoming New Yorkers: Ethnographies of the Second Generation*. New York: Russell Sage Foundation.

Katz, M. B. 1996. *In the Shadow of the Poorhouse: A Social History of Welfare in America*. 2nd ed. New York: Basic Books.

Kennedy, R. 1996. "Council to Bar Elimination of Alarm Boxes." *New York Times*, March 7, p. B1.

Kifner, J. 1966. "City Reorganizes Poverty Program to End Confusion." *New York Times*, September 18, p. 1.

Knight, M. 1974. "Brooklyn Hasidim Believed Planning Large Colony at Upstate Resort Site." *New York Times*, September 16, p. 37.

Knowles, Clayton. 1967. "Lindsay Alters 'City Halls' Plan; Bill Would Give Councilmen Voice in Naming Staff." *New York Times*, January 4, p. 25.

Kolbert, E. 1989. "Town Wants a Hasidic Public School District." *New York Times*, July 21, p. A1.

———. 1990. "Suit Contests Hasidic District." *New York Times*, January 21, p. 28.

Kornblum, W. 1974. *Blue-Collar Community*. Chicago: University of Chicago Press.

Kornhauser, R. R. 1978. *Social Sources of Delinquency*. Chicago: University of Chicago Press.

Kramer, R. M. 1982. "From Voluntarism to Vendorism: An Organizational Perspective on Contracting." Working paper, Program on Nonprofit Organizations, Yale University.

Kranzler, G. 1961. *Williamsburg*. New York: Philipp Feldheim.

Kremen, G. R. 1974. "M.D.T.A.: The Origins of the Manpower Development and Training Act of 1962." Washington, DC: Historical Office of the U.S. Department of Labor. http://www.dol.gov/oasam/programs/history/mono-mdtatext.htm (accessed January 18, 2006).

Kretzmann, J. P., and J. L. McKnight. 1997. *Building Communities from the Inside Out: A Path toward Finding and Mobilizing a Community's Assets*. Evanston, IL: Center for Urban Affairs and Policy Research, Northwestern University.

Kriesi, H., R. Koopmans, J. W. Duyvendak, and M. G. Giugni. 1995. *New Social Movements in Western Europe*. Minneapolis: University of Minnesota Press.

La Rosa, P. 1987. "Bushwick: Reviving." *Daily News* (New York), July 12.

Laumann, E. O., and D. Knoke. 1987. *The Organizational State: Social Choice in National Policy Domains.* Madison: University of Wisconsin Press.

Laumann, E. O., and F. U. Pappi. 1976. *Networks of Collective Action: A Perspective on Community Influence Systems.* New York: Academic Press.

Leavitt, J., and S. Saegert. 1990. *From Abandonment to Hope: Community-Households in Harlem.* New York: Columbia University Press.

Lee, B. A., R. S. Oropesa, B. J. Metch, and A. M. Guest. 1984. "Testing the Decline-of-Community Thesis: Neighborhood Organizations in Seattle, 1929 and 1979." *American Journal of Sociology* 89:1161–88.

Levine, A. G., and A. R. McCabe. 1965. *The Public-Voluntary Agency Sponsored Day Care Program for Children in New York City.* New York: Community Service Society.

Levitan, S. A. 1969. "The Community Action Program: A Strategy to Fight Poverty." *Annals of the American Academy of Political and Social Science* 385:63–75.

Levitt, S. D., and S. J. Dubner. 2005. *Freakonomics: A Rogue Economist Explores the Hidden Side of Everything.* New York: William Morrow.

Levy, G. 1988. *Dollars and Dreams: The Changing American Income Distribution.* New York: Norton.

Lichterman, P. 1996. *The Search for Political Community: American Activists Reinventing Commitment.* New York: Cambridge University Press.

Liebow, E. 1964. *Tally's Corner.* Boston: Little, Brown, 1967.

Liff, B. 2001a. "Rezone Sparks Bias Blast: Hasidic Developers' Plan Called Segregated Housing." *Daily News* (New York), March 30, p. 3.

———. 2001b. "A Very Promising Mayor: Rudy Says Last Year Will Bring New Homes and Dodgers Museum." *Daily News* (New York), January 10, p. 3.

Lofland, J., and L. H. Lofland. 1995. *Analyzing Social Settings: A Guide to Qualitative Observation and Analysis.* Belmont, CA: Wadsworth.

Logan, J. R., and H. L. Molotch. 1987. *Urban Fortunes: The Political Economy of Place.* Berkeley: University of California Press.

Logan, J. R., and L. B. Stearns. 1981. "Suburban Racial Segregation as a Nonecological Process." *Social Forces* 60:61–73.

Lyall, S. 1992. "Hasidic Public School District Is Unconstitutional, Judge Rules." *New York Times,* January 23, p. B6.

Maher, L. 1997. *Sexed Work: Gender, Race, and Resistance in a Brooklyn Drug Market.* Oxford: Clarendon Press.

Maire, K. 1997. "A Gospel of Power: The Story of St. Barbara's Church." In *Signs of Hope in the City: Ministries of Community Renewal,* ed. R. D. Carle and L. A. DeCaro Jr., 101–14. Valley Forge, PA: Judson Press.

Mansbridge, J. J. 1980. *Beyond Adversary Democracy.* New York: Basic Books.

Marris, P., and M. Rein. 1969. *Dilemmas of Social Reform: Poverty and Community Action in the United States.* New York: Atherton Press.

Marwell, N. P. 2000. "Social Networks and Social Capital as Resources for Neighborhood Revitalization." PhD diss., University of Chicago.

———. 2004a. "Ethnic and Postethnic Politics: The Dominican Second Generation in New York City." In *Becoming New Yorkers: Ethnographies of the Second Generation,* ed. P. Kasinitz, J. H. Mollenkopf, and M. Waters, 257–84. New York: Russell Sage Foundation.

———. 2004b. "Privatizing the Welfare State: Nonprofit Community-Based Organizations as Political Actors." *American Sociological Review* 69:265–91.

———. 2005. "Beyond Neighborhood Social Control: From Interaction to Institutions." Unpublished manuscript, Columbia University.

Massey, D. S., and N. A. Denton. 1993. *American Apartheid: Segregation and the Making of the Underclass*. Cambridge, MA: Harvard University Press.

Mayor's Task Force on Bilingual Education. 2000. *Recommendations for Reform: Report of the Task Force on Bilingual Education to Mayor Rudolph W. Giuliani*. New York.

McLanahan, S. S., and G. Sandefur. 1994. *Growing Up with a Single Parent: What Helps, What Hurts*. Cambridge, MA: Harvard University Press.

McQuarrie, M. 2007. "From Backyard Revolution to Neoliberalism: Community Development, Civil Society, and the American Third Way." PhD diss., New York University.

McRoberts, O. M. 2003. *Streets of Glory: Church and Community in a Black Urban Neighborhood*. Chicago: University of Chicago Press.

Mead, G. H. 1956. *The Social Psychology of George Herbert Mead*. Ed. Anselm Strauss. Chicago: University of Chicago Press.

Mele, C. 2001. *Selling the Lower East Side: Culture, Real Estate, and Resistance in New York City*. Minneapolis: University of Minnesota Press.

Menjívar, C. 2000. *Fragmented Ties: Salvadoran Immigrant Networks in America*. Berkeley: University of California Press.

Meyer, D. S., and S. Tarrow. 1998. "A Movement Society: Contentious Politics for a New Century." In *The Social Movement Society: Contentious Politics for a New Century*, ed. D. S. Meyer and S. Tarrow, 1–28. Lanham, MD: Rowman and Littlefield.

Meyer, J. W., and B. Rowan. 1977. "Institutionalized Organizations: Formal Structure as Myth and Ceremony." *American Journal of Sociology* 83:340–63.

Meyers, M. K. 1995. "Child Care, Parental Choice, and Consumer Education in JOBS Welfare-to-Work Programs." *Social Service Review* 69:679–702.

Mollenkopf, J. 1983. *The Contested City*. Princeton, NJ: Princeton University Press.

Molotch, H. L. 1972. *Managed Integration: Dilemmas of Doing Good in the City*. Berkeley: University of California Press.

———. 1976. "The City as a Growth Machine: Toward a Political Economy of Place." *American Journal of Sociology* 82:309–32.

Moore, J. W. 1978. *Homeboys: Gangs, Drugs, and Prison in the Barrios of Los Angeles*. Philadelphia: Temple University Press.

Morenoff, J. D., and R. J. Sampson. 1997. "Violent Crime and the Spatial Dynamics of Neighborhood Transition: Chicago, 1970–1990." *Social Forces* 76:31–64.

Morenoff, J. D., R. J. Sampson, and S. W. Raudenbush. 2001. "Neighborhood Inequality, Collective Efficacy, and the Spatial Dynamics of Urban Violence." *Criminology* 39:517–59.

Moynihan, D. P. 1969. *Maximum Feasible Misunderstanding: Community Action in the War on Poverty*. New York: Free Press.

Moynihan, D. P., and J. Q. Wilson. 1964. "Patronage in New York State, 1955–1959." *American Political Science Review* 58:286–301.

Munger, F., ed. 2002. *Laboring below the Line: The New Ethnography of Poverty, Low-Wage Work, and Survival in the Global Economy*. New York: Russell Sage Foundation.

Murray, C. 1984. *Losing Ground: American Social Policy, 1950–1980*. New York: Basic Books.

Musuraca, M. [1991?]. "'It's a Shame': The Decline of a Working Class Neighborhood: Bushwick, Brooklyn, 1945–1985." Unpublished manuscript in the author's possession.

Nagourney, A. 2002. "TV's Tight Grip on Campaigns Is Weakening." *New York Times*, September 4, p. A1.

Naples, N. A. 1998. *Grassroots Warriors: Activist Mothering, Community Work and the War on Poverty.* New York: Routledge.

Neckerman, K. M., and J. Kirschenman. 1991. "Hiring Strategies, Racial Bias, and Inner-City Workers." *Social Problems* 38:433–77.

Nesiba, R. F. 1996. "Racial Discrimination in Residential Lending Markets: Why Empirical Researchers Always See It and Economic Theorists Never Do." *Journal of Economic Issues* 30:51–77.

Newman, K. S. 1999. *No Shame in My Game: The Working Poor in the Inner City.* New York: Russell Sage Foundation.

New York City Administration for Children's Services. 2001. *Counting to 10: New Directions in Child Care and Head Start.* New York.

New York City Department of City Planning. 1992. *Demographic Profiles: A Portrait of New York City's Community Districts from the 1980 and 1990 Censuses of Population and Housing.* New York: Department of City Planning.

———. 1993. *Socioeconomic Profiles: A Portrait of New York City's Community Districts from the 1980 and 1990 Censuses of Population and Housing.* New York: Department of City Planning.

———. 1997. *197-a Plan Technical Guide.* New York: Department of City Planning.

———. 2002. *Williamsburg Waterfront 197-a Plan, as Modified and Adopted by the City Planning Commission and the City Council.* New York: Department of City Planning.

———. 2003. *2003 Annual Report on Social Indicators (DCP #05-08).* New York: Department of City Planning.

———. 2004a. ULURP Application N 050110 ZMK. New York: Department of City Planning. September 30.

———. 2004b. ULURP Application N 050110 ZMK(A). New York: Department of City Planning. December 22.

———. 2005. Adopted Greenpoint-Williamsburg Rezoning Text. New York: Department of City Planning. May 11.

———. No date. *1990–2000 Community District Socioeconomic Profile.* New York: Department of City Planning. http://www.nyc.gov/html/dcp/pdf/census/socionyc.pdf (accessed September 24, 2004).

New York Times. 1946. "$25,000,000 Artery Begun in Brooklyn." August 21, p. 26.

———. 1952. "Expressway Link Will Open Today." December 6, p. 16.

———. 1963. "Housing Project to Aid in Keeping Sect Intact." May 17, p. 50.

———. 1966. "A Neighborhood City Hall." September 6, p. 46.

———. 1986. "Unwise Wall in Williamsburg." September 29, p. A14.

———. 1989a. "Districts at a Glance." April 27, p. B6.

———. 1989b. "Reading Scores for New York City Schools." February 17, p. B4.

———. 1997. "Hasidic School Provision is Challenged 3d Time." September 13, p. 29.

O'Connor, A. 2001. *Poverty Knowledge: Social Science, Social Policy, and the Poor in Twentieth-century U.S. History.* Princeton, NJ: Princeton University Press.

Oliker, S. J. 1994. "Work Commitment and Constraint among Mothers on Workfare." *Journal of Contemporary Ethnography* 24:165–94.

———. 1995. "The Proximate Contexts of Workfare and Work: A Framework for Studying Poor Women's Economic Choices." *Sociological Quarterly* 36:251–72.

Oliver, M. L. 1988. "The Urban Black Community as Network: Toward a Social Network Perspective." *Sociological Quarterly* 29:623–45.

Owen-Smith, J. 2001. "Managing Laboratory Work through Skepticism: Processes of Evaluation and Control." *American Sociological Review* 66:427–53.

Pacenza, M. 2002. "Williamsburg Brewhaha: A Waterfront Development Revives Rifts between Two Communities." *City Limits Monthly*, May.

Park, R. E. 1915. "The City: Suggestions for the Investigation of Human Behavior in the Urban Environment." *American Journal of Sociology* 20:577–612.

———. 1936. "Human Ecology." In *Robert E. Park on Social Control and Collective Behavior: Selected Papers*, ed. R. H. Turner., 69–84. Chicago: University of Chicago Press, 1967.

Park, R. E., and E. W. Burgess. 1921. *Introduction to the Science of Sociology*. Chicago: University of Chicago Press, 1924.

———. 1925. *The City*. Chicago: University of Chicago Press.

Pattillo-McCoy, M. 1999. *Black Picket Fences: Privilege and Peril among the Black Middle Class*. Chicago: University of Chicago Press.

Pearl, A., and F. Riessman. 1965. *New Careers for the Poor: The Nonprofessional in Human Service*. New York: Free Press.

Pérez, G. 2004. *The Near Northwest Side Story: Migration, Displacement, and Puerto Rican Families*. Berkeley: University of California Press.

Perez-Peña, R. 1997. "Court Rules against Hasidic School Plan." *New York Times*, May 7, p. B8.

Perkins, D. D., B. Brown, and R. Taylor. 1996. "The Ecology of Empowerment: Predicting Participation in Community." *Journal of Social Issues* 52:85–111.

Perlez, J. 1986. "Court Bars School Partition for Brooklyn Hasidic Girls." *New York Times*, October 4, p. 25.

Perrow, C. 1992. "A Society of Organizations." *Theory and Society* 20:725–62.

———. 2002. *Organizing America: Wealth, Power, and the Origins of Corporate Capitalism*. Princeton, NJ: Princeton University Press.

Peterson, R. D., L. J. Krivo, and M. A. Harris. 2000. "Disadvantage and Neighborhood Violent Crime: Do Local Institutions Matter?" *Journal of Research on Crime and Delinquency* 37:31–63.

Pettit, B., and B. Western. 2004. "Mass Imprisonment and the Life Course: Race and Class Inequality in U.S. Incarceration." *American Sociological Review* 69:151–69.

Pfeffer, J., and G. R. Salancik. 1978. *The External Control of Organizations: A Resource Dependence Perspective*. New York: Harper & Row.

Piven, F. F., and R. A. Cloward. 1971. *Regulating the Poor: The Functions of Public Welfare*. New York: Pantheon.

Plunz, R. 1990. *The History of Housing in New York City*. New York: Columbia University Press.

Pogrebin, R. 1998. "Magazine Dismisses Writer Accused of Hoax." *New York Times*, May 12, p. A1.

Polletta, F. 2002. *Freedom Is an Endless Meeting: Democracy in American Social Movements*. Chicago: University of Chicago Press.

Pollinger, K. J., and A. C. Pollinger. 1972. *Community Action and the Poor: Influence vs. Social Control in a New York City Community*. New York: Praeger.

Portney, K. E., and J. M. Berry. 1997. "Mobilizing Minority Communities: Social Capital and Participation in Urban Neighborhoods." *American Behavioral Scientist* 40:632–44.

Powell, W. W., and E. S. Clemens, eds. 1998. *Private Action and the Public Good*. New Haven, CT: Yale University Press.

Powell, W. W., and P. J. DiMaggio. 1991. *The New Institutionalism in Organizational Analysis*. Chicago: University of Chicago Press.

Price, S. C. 1979. "The Effect of Federal Anti-poverty Programs and Policies on the Hasidic and Puerto Rican Communities of Williamsburg." PhD diss., Brandeis University, Boston.

Putnam, R. D. 1993a. *Making Democracy Work: Civic Traditions in Modern Italy*. Princeton, NJ: Princeton University Press.

———. 1993b. "The Prosperous Community: Social Capital and Community Life." *American Prospect* 13:35–42.

———. 2000. *Bowling Alone: The Collapse and Revival of American Democracy*. New York: Simon & Schuster.

Quadagno, J. 1994. *The Color of Welfare: How Racism Undermined the War on Poverty*. New York: Oxford University Press.

Rainwater, L. 1970. *Behind Ghetto Walls: Black Families in a Federal Slum*. Chicago: Aldine.

Ramos-Zayas, A. Y. 2003. *National Performances: The Politics of Class, Race, and Space in Puerto Rican Chicago*. Chicago: University of Chicago Press.

Rankin, B. H., and J. M. Quane. 2000. "Neighborhood Poverty and the Social Isolation of Inner-city African American Families." *Social Forces* 79:139–64.

Redfield, R. 1941. *The Folk Culture of Yucatán*. Chicago: University of Chicago Press.

Ridgewood-Bushwick Senior Citizens Council. N.d. Annual Report. New York: Ridgewood-Bushwick Senior Citizens Council.

Rooney, J. 1995. *Organizing the South Bronx*. Albany: State University of New York Press.

Rose, E. 1999. *A Mother's Job: The History of Daycare, 1890–1960*. New York: Oxford University Press.

Rose, N. E. 1995. *Workfare or Fair Work: Women, Welfare, and Government Work Programs*. New Brunswick, NJ: Rutgers University Press.

Ross, E. A. 1896. "Social Control." *American Journal of Sociology* 1:513–35.

Ross, S. L., and J. Yinger. 2002. *The Color of Credit: Mortgage Discrimination, Research Methodology, and Fair-Lending Enforcement*. Cambridge, MA: MIT Press.

Ross, T. A. 1996. "The Impact of Community Organizing on East Brooklyn, 1978–1995." PhD diss., University of Maryland, College Park.

Saegert, S., J. P. Thompson, and M. R. Warren. 2001. *Social Capital and Poor Communities*. New York: Russell Sage Foundation.

Saint Nicholas Neighborhood Preservation Corporation. 1997. "Local Initiative Support Corporation Community Building Initiative: Lessons Learned." New York: Saint Nicholas Neighborhood Preservation Corporation. Internal document; in author's possession.

Salamon, L. M. 1995. *Partners in Public Service: Government-Nonprofit Relations in the Modern Welfare State*. Baltimore, MD: Johns Hopkins University Press.

Sampson, R. J. 1988. "Community Attachment in Mass Society: A Multilevel Systemic Model." *American Sociological Review* 53:766–79.

———. 1999. "What 'Community' Supplies." In *Urban Problems and Community Development*, ed. R. F. Ferguson and W. T. Dickens, 241–79. Washington, DC: Brookings Institution Press.

Sampson, R. J., and W. B. Groves. 1989. "Community Structure and Crime: Testing Social-Disorganization Theory." *American Journal of Sociology* 94:774–802.

Sampson, R. J., and J. D. Morenoff. 1997. "Ecological Perspectives on the Neighborhood Context of Urban Poverty: Past and Present." In *Neighborhood Poverty: Policy Implications in Studying Neighborhoods*, ed. J. Brooks-Gunn, G. J. Duncan, and J. L. Aber, 1:1–22. New York: Russell Sage Foundation.

Sampson, R. J., J. D. Morenoff, and F. Earls. 1999. "Beyond Social Capital: Spatial Dynamics of Collective Efficacy for Children." *American Sociological Review* 64:633–60.

Sampson, R. J., J. D. Morenoff, and T. Gannon-Rowley. 2002. "Assessing 'Neighborhood Effects': Social Processes and New Directions in Research." *Annual Review of Sociology* 28:443–78.

Sampson, R. J., S. W. Raudenbush, and F. Earls. 1997. "Neighborhoods and Violent Crime: A Multilevel Study of Collective Efficacy." *Science* 277:918–24.

Sanchez, T. 1990. *The Bushwick Neighborhood Profile*. Brooklyn, NY: Brooklyn In-Touch Information Center.

Sanchez-Jankowski, M. 1991. *Islands in the Street: Gangs and American Urban Society*. Berkeley: University of California Press.

Sassen, S. 1991. *The Global City*. Princeton, NJ: Princeton University Press.

Saunders, P. E. 1986. *Social Theory and the Urban Question*. 2nd ed. New York: Holmes and Meier.

Schatzman, L., and A. S. Strauss. 1973. *Field Research*. Englewood Cliffs, NJ: Prentice-Hall.

Scheie, D. M., J. Markham, T. Williams, J. Slettom, S. M. A. Ramirez, and S. Mayer. 1994. *Better Together: Religious Institutions as Partners in Community-Based Development*. Minneapolis: Rainbow Research.

Schur, R., and V. Sherry. 1977. *The Neighborhood Housing Movement: A Survey of the Activities and Services Provided by Non-profit Community-based Organizations to Residents of Low- and Moderate-income Communities in New York City*. New York: Association of Neighborhood Housing Developers.

Scott, W. R., and J. W. Meyer. 1991. "The Organization of Societal Sectors: Propositions and Early Evidence." In *The New Institutionalism in Organizational Analysis*, ed. W. W. Powell and P. J. DiMaggio, 108–40. Chicago: University of Chicago Press.

Scully, P. L., and R. C. Harwood. 1997. *Strategies for Civil Investing: Foundations and Community-Building*. Dayton, OH: Kettering Foundation.

Sexton, J. 1997. "New Housing Is Approved for Brooklyn." *New York Times*, June 8, p. 44.

Sexton, P. C. 1966. *Spanish Harlem*. New York: Harper & Row.

Shaw, C. R. 1930. *The Jack-Roller: A Delinquent Boy's Own Story*. Chicago: University of Chicago Press.

Shaw, C. R., and H. D. McKay. 1942. *Juvenile Delinquency and Urban Areas*. 2nd ed. Chicago: University of Chicago Press, 1969.

Shevky, E., and M. Williams. 1949. *The Social Areas of Los Angeles: Analysis and Typology*. Berkeley: University of California Press.

Shin, P. H. B. 1997. "New Housing for W'Burg." *Daily News* (New York), September 17, p. 1.

Silverman, R. M. 2001. "CDCs and Charitable Organizations in the Urban South: Mobilizing Social Capital Based on Race and Religion for Neighborhood Revitalization." *Journal of Contemporary Ethnography* 30:240–68.

———. 2002. "Vying for the Urban Poor: Charitable Organizations, Faith-Based Social Capital, and Racial Reconciliation in a Deep South City." *Sociological Inquiry* 72:151–65.

Simcha-Fagan, O., and J. E. Schwartz. 1986. "Neighborhood and Delinquency: An Assessment of Contextual Effects." *Criminology* 24:667–703.

Skocpol, T., and M. P. Fiorina. 1999. *Civic Engagement in American Democracy*. Washington, DC: Brookings Institution Press.

Slum Clearance Committee. 1951. *Williamsburg Slum Clearance Plan under Title I of the Housing Act of 1949*. New York: Slum Clearance Committee.

Small, M. L. 2002. "Culture, Cohorts, and Social Organization Theory: Understanding Local Participation in a Latino Housing Project." *American Journal of Sociology* 108:1–54.

————. 2004. *Villa Victoria: The Transformation of Social Capital in a Boston Barrio*. Chicago: University of Chicago Press.

Small, M. L., and M. McDermott. 2006. "The Presence of Organizational Resources in Poor Urban Neighborhoods: An Analysis of Average and Contextual Effects." *Social Forces* 84:1697–724.

Small, M. L., and K. Newman. 2001. "Urban Poverty after *The Truly Disadvantaged*: The Rediscovery of the Family, the Neighborhood, and Culture." *Annual Review of Sociology* 27:23–45.

Smith, G. B. 1996. "Renters, Own Up—City." *Daily News* (New York), March 24, p. 7.

Smith, J. R., J. Brooks-Gunn, P. K. Klebanov, and K. Lee. 2000. "Welfare and Work: Complementary Strategies for Low-Income Women?" *Journal of Marriage and the Family* 62:808–21.

Smith, N. 1984. *Uneven Development*. Cambridge, MA: Blackwell.

Smith, N., and P. Williams, eds. 1986. *Gentrification of the City*. Boston: Allen & Unwin.

Smith, R. C. 2006. *Mexican New York: Transnational Lives of New Immigrants*. Berkeley: University of California Press.

Smith, S. R., and M. Lipsky. 1993. *Nonprofits for Hire: The Welfare State in the Age of Contracting*. Cambridge, MA: Harvard University Press.

Smith, S. S. 2005. "'Don't Put My Name on It': Social Capital Activation and Job-Finding Assistance among the Black Urban Poor." *American Journal of Sociology* 111:1–57.

Southside United Housing Development Fund Corporation. 1975. *Housing Recommendations: The Los Sures Moderate Rehabilitation Report*. Brooklyn, NY: Southside United Housing Development Fund Corporation.

————. 1997. *25th Anniversary Commemorative Journal*. Brooklyn, NY: Southside United Housing Development Fund Corporation.

Squires, G. D., ed. 1997. *Insurance Redlining: Disinvestment, Reinvestment, and the Evolving Role of Financial Institutions*. Washington, DC: Urban Institute Press.

Squires, G. D., R. DeWolfe, and A. S. DeWolfe. 1979. "Urban Decline or Disinvestment: Uneven Development, Redlining, and the Insurance Industry." *Social Problems* 27:79–95.

Squires, G. D., and S. Kim. 1995. "Does Anybody Who Works Here Look Like Me? Mortgage Lending, Race, and Lender Employment." *Social Science Quarterly* 76:823–38.

Squires, G. D., and C. E. Kubrin. 2005. "Privileged Places: Race, Uneven Development, and the Geography of Opportunity in Urban America." *Urban Studies* 42:47–68.

Stack, C. 1974. *All Our Kin*. New York: Basic Books.

Stankus, F. B. 1972. "Bushwick Residents Assail Planning." *New York Times*, January 23, p. A3.

Stearns, L. B., and J. R. Logan. 1986. "The Racial Structuring of the Housing Market and Segregation in Suburban Areas." *Social Forces* 65:28–42.

Steinberg, J. 1999. "Rabbi in Plot to Siphon Millions in Public Money to Private School." *New York Times*, April 16, p. A1.

Steinfels, M. O. 1973. *Who's Minding the Children? The History and Politics of Day Care in America*. New York: Simon & Schuster.

Stier, H., and M. Tienda. 2001. *The Color of Opportunity: Pathways to Family, Welfare, and Work*. Chicago: University of Chicago Press.

Stoll, M. A. 2001. "Race, Neighborhood Poverty, and Participation in Voluntary Associations." *Sociological Forum* 16:529–57.

Stone, R., ed. 1996. *Core Issues in Comprehensive Community-Building Initiatives*. Chicago: Chapin Hall Center for Children.

Strawn, J., and K. Martinson. 2000. *Steady Work and Better Jobs: How to Help Low-income Parents Sustain Employment and Advance in the Workforce*. New York: MDRC.

Sugrue, T. J. 1996. *The Origins of the Urban Crisis: Race and Inequality in Postwar Detroit*. Princeton, NJ: Princeton University Press.

Sullivan, M. L. 1989. *Getting Paid: Youth Crime and Work in the Inner City*. Ithaca, NY: Cornell University Press.

Sundquist, J. L. 1969. *On Fighting Poverty: Perspectives from Experience*. New York: Basic Books.

Susser, I. 1982. *Norman Street: Poverty and Politics in an Urban Neighborhood*. New York: Oxford University Press.

Suttles, G. 1968. *The Social Order of the Slum*. Chicago: University of Chicago Press.

Taub, R. P., G. P. Surgeon, S. Lindholm, P. B. Otti, and A. Bridges. 1977. "Urban Voluntary Associations, Locality Based and Externally Induced." *American Journal of Sociology* 83:425–42.

Thomas, W. I., ed. 1923. *The Unadjusted Girl with Cases and Standpoint for Behavior Analysis*. Boston: Little Brown.

Thomas, W. I., and F. Znaniecki. 1918. *The Polish Peasant in Europe and America*. New York: Knopf.

Tilly, C. 1986. *The Contentious French*. Cambridge, MA: Belknap Press.

Tilly, C., and S. Tarrow. 2006. *Contentious Politics*. Boulder: Paradigm Publishers.

Tocqueville, A. 1835, 1840. *Democracy in America*. Trans. H. Reeve and F. Bowen. New York: Vintage Books, 1990.

Toennies, F. 1887. *Community and Society*. Trans. C. P. Loomis. East Lansing: Michigan State University Press, 1957.

U.S. Department of Housing and Urban Development. 2000. *Teaching and Learning for Community Building: New Roles, New Skills, and Stronger Partnerships*. Washington, D.C.

Vanecko, J. 1969. "Community Mobilization and Institutional Change: The Influence of the Community Action Program in Large Cities." *Social Science Quarterly* 50:609–30.

Van Natta, D., Jr. 1995. "Bracing for Furloughs and Locked Offices." *New York Times*, November 14, p. B10.

Vaughan, D. 1996. *The Challenger Launch Decision: Risky Technology, Culture, and Deviance at NASA*. Chicago: University of Chicago Press.

Venkatesh, S. A. 2000. *American Project: The Rise and Fall of a Modern Ghetto*. Cambridge, MA: Harvard University Press.

———. 2003. "Whither the 'Socially Isolated' City?" *Ethnic and Racial Studies* 26:1058–72.

———. 2006. *Off the Books: The Underground Economy of the Urban Poor*. Cambridge, MA: Harvard University Press.

Vidal, A. C. 1992. *Rebuilding Communities: A National Study of Urban Community Development Corporations*. New York: Community Development Research Center.

von Hassell, M. 1996. *Homesteading in New York City, 1978–1993: The Divided Heart of Loisaida*. Westport, CT: Bergin and Garvey.

Wacquant, L. 2002. "Scrutinizing the Street: Poverty, Morality, and the Pitfalls of Urban Ethnography." *American Journal of Sociology* 107:1468–1532.

Waldman, A. 1997. "Hasidic Pioneers Set Forth from Williamsburg to Seek Space across a New Frontier." *New York Times*, August 10, sec. 13, p. 8.

———. 1998. "A Slight Hint of Progress, Maybe, on Needed Housing." *New York Times*, February 22, sec. 14, p. 8.

Wallace, D., and R. Wallace. 1998. *A Plague on All Your Houses: How New York Was Burned Down and National Public Health Crumbled*. London: Verso.

Walsh, J. 1997. *Stories of Renewal: Community Building and the Future of Urban America*. New York: Rockefeller Foundation.

Walton, J. 1993. "Urban Sociology: The Contribution and Limits of Political Economy." *Annual Review of Sociology* 19:301–20.

Ware, A. 1985. *The Breakdown of Democratic Party Organization, 1940–1980*. Oxford: Oxford University Press.

Warner, W. L., and P. S. Lunt. 1941. *The Social Life of a Modern Community*. New Haven, CT: Yale University Press.

Warren, C., M. Feist, and N. Nevarez. 2002. *A Place to Grow: Evaluation of the New York City Beacons, Summary Report*. New York: Academy for Institutional Development.

Warren, M. R. 2001. *Dry Bones Rattling: Community Building to Revitalize American Democracy*. Princeton, NJ: Princeton University Press.

Warren, R. L. 1967. "The Interorganizational Field as a Focus for Investigation." *Administrative Science Quarterly* 12:396–419.

Weber, M. 1905. *The Protestant Ethic and the Spirit of Capitalism*. Trans. T. Parsons. London: Routledge, 2001.

———. 1914. *Economy and Society*. Trans. E. Fischoff. Berkeley: University of California Press, 1978.

Weick, K. E. 1976. "Educational Organizations as Loosely Coupled Systems." *Administrative Science Quarterly* 21:1–19.

Weinraub, B. 1969. "Lindsay Steps Up City Services to Soothe Working Class Anger." *New York Times*, November 30, p. 1.

Wellman, B. 1979. "The Community Question: The Intimate Networks of East Yorkers." *American Journal of Sociology* 84:1201–31.

Wellman, B., R. Y. L. Wong, D. Tindall, and N. Nazer. 1997. "A Decade of Network Change: Turnover, Persistence and Stability in Personal Communities." *Social Networks* 19:27–50.

Western, B. 1998. "Institutions and the Labor Market." In *The New Institutionalism in Sociology*, ed. M. C. Brinton and V. Nee, 224–44. New York: Russell Sage.

Western, B., M. Kleykamp, and J. Rosenfeld. 2006. "Did Falling Wages and Employment Increase U.S. Imprisonment?" *Social Forces* 84:2291–2311.

Whyte, W. F. 1943. *Street Corner Society: The Social Structure of an Italian Slum*. 3rd ed. Chicago: University of Chicago Press, 1981.

Wilson, W. J. 1987. *The Truly Disadvantaged*. Chicago: University of Chicago Press.

———. 1999. *When Work Disappears*. Chicago: University of Chicago Press.

———, ed. 1989. *The Ghetto Underclass: Social Science Perspectives*. Newbury Park: Sage.

Wines, M. 1995. "Federal Agencies Are Planning a Shutdown in the Event of a Budget Deadlock." *New York Times*, August 24, p. B15.

Winnick, L. 1990. *New People in Old Neighborhoods: The Role of New Immigrants in Rejuvenating New York's Communities*. New York: Russell Sage Foundation.

Winship, C., and J. Berrien. 1999. "Boston Cops and Black Churches." *Public Interest* 136:52–68.

Wirth, L. 1928. *The Ghetto*. Chicago: University of Chicago Press.

———. 1938. "Urbanism as a Way of Life." *American Journal of Sociology* 44:1–24.

Wood, R. L. 1997. "Social Capital and Political Culture: God Meets Politics in the Inner City." *American Behavioral Scientist* 40:595–605.

Yen, I. H., and G. A. Kaplan. 1999. "Neighborhood Social Environment and Risk of

Death: Multilevel Evidence from the Alameda County Study." *American Journal of Epidemiology* 149:898–907.

Yinger, J. 1995. *Closed Doors, Opportunities Lost: The Continuing Costs of Housing Discrimination.* New York: Russell Sage Foundation.

Young, A. 2005. *The Minds of Marginalized Black Men.* Princeton, NJ: Princeton University Press.

Zorbaugh, H. W. 1929. *Gold Coast and the Slum: A Sociological Study of Chicago's Near North Side.* Chicago: University of Chicago Press.

INDEX

The letter *f* following a page number denotes a figure; *m* following a page number denotes a map.

President's Committee on Juvenile
   Delinquency and Youth Crime, 26
Price, Stephen C., 50
Progressive era settlement houses, 25
public housing. *See* housing programs
Public School 16, 61–62, 61–62nn16–17
Puerto Rican communities: access to public
   housing in, 50–53; bilingual education
   in, 137–43; competition for CAP funds
   in, 43; competition for housing in,
   56–72; Lindsay's "Little City Halls,"
   100–101; migrations to Southside of,
   40–41; migration to Bushwick of,
   98–99, 129–31; outmigration from,
   190; Southside community
   organizations, 42–43, 45–49;
   Williamsburg Fair Housing lawsuit,
   51–53, 61
Pupa Hasidic sect. *See* Hasidic Jewish
   community
Putnam, Robert, 210, 220

racial/ethnic issues: racial quotas in public
   housing, 49–51; Williamsburg Fair
   Housing lawsuit, 51–53, 61. *See also*
   African American community; Hasidic
   Jewish community; Latino
   communities
Raices, Sonia, 170, 176
Reagan, Ronald, 153, 169
real estate markets, 7, 21–22, 35,
   59n12
redlining, 7, 35
Reiter, Fran, 173–74
rent control/rent stabilization laws,
   59n12
research design and methods, 239–59;
   access, 253–55; analytical notes, 252;
   comparative aspects, 239–40; field
   notes, 251–52; focus on organizations,
   229–34; gender-based considerations,
   256–58, 258n17; informant interviews,
   243–44, 243–44nn5–6, 251; informed
   consent process, 253;
   participant-observation, 5, 194–96,
   196n7, 199–201, 232, 240, 248–52;
   selection of ethnic/racial group,
   241–42; selection of neighborhoods,
   241–47; selection of organizations,

240–41, 247–48; Spanish language
   fluency, 258–59; subjectivity, 253–56;
   use of real names, 252–53
resident participation in community-based
   organizations. *See* participation in
   community-based organizations
Ridgewood, Queens, 99
Ridgewood-Bushwick Senior Citizens
   Council, 97, 101–28, 145–48, 233;
   Brooklyn Unidos retreat, 122–26, 123f,
   125n22; *Bushwick Observer* newspaper,
   121–22; constituent display activities
   of, 122–26, 123f, 219–20; electoral
   politics of, 115, 119–22, 126–28, 146,
   219–20; employment opportunities
   through, 109–10, 119–20, 119–20n16,
   153, 161–62; eradication of drug
   dealers by, 12; funding sources of, 10,
   103, 103n4, 105, 109–14, 127–28, 165,
   220–21; governance of, 220; helping
   people philosophy of, 105–9, 133;
   holiday events at, 105–6, 117–18;
   home health care program, 161–62,
   166; home ownership skills
   development, 204, 206–7; Housing
   Office, 96m, 106–9, 116, 127–28,
   206–7; housing programs, 103–9, 116;
   jobs program, 8–10; map, 96m;
   neighborhood ties of staff, 154–55;
   nursing home project, 166; private
   politics of distribution of, 97, 128, 148,
   233; reciprocity, 115–18; relationship
   with Assemblyman Lopez of, 109–10,
   113–15, 121–22, 147; role of resident
   participants in, 219–21; service area of,
   105n6; social activities of, 117–18;
   social service provision of, 97; as a
   "society of organizations," 146,
   147n52; tenant organizing of, 12,
   106–9; voter education by, 119–22,
   120n17; voter turnout, 126–28
Rijo, Iris, 141–42
Rivera, Marilyn, 67–68, 77
Roberto Clemente Plaza, 51–53
Roberts, Richard, 124
Robles, Victor L., 54f, 109, 122; Southside
   housing struggles, 70–71, 81–83;
   Williamsburg Beacon conflicts, 212–14,
   216